IRISH CONSTABULARIES

Donal J. O'Sullivan

To John,
With sincere good
wishes and I hope you enjoy the read.
Donal J Sullivan.
June 10TH 2000.

THE IRISH CONSTABULARIES

1822–1922

A century of policing in Ireland

Published in 1999 by
Brandon
an imprint of
Mount Eagle Publications Ltd
Dingle, Co. Kerry, Ireland

ISBN 0 86322 257 9

10 9 8 7 6 5 4 3 2 1

This book is published with the assistance of the
Arts Council/An Chomhairle Ealaíonn

Cover design: id design, Tralee
Typesetting: Red Barn Publishing, Skeagh, Skibbereen
Printed by Estudios Gráficos, Zure, Spain

CONTENTS

Chapter One

HISTORICAL BACKGROUND

Outline of Early Peace Preservation Arrangements in Ireland

From the earliest times, Ireland always had some system to preserve the peace. In early Christian times, the native Irish had the Brehon Laws and the *Cain Domn-haigh*, or Sunday observance laws, which together set out a comprehensive set of rules for everyday living and the maintenance of order. Penalties and sanctions were provided for breaches of the laws and regulations, but no specific provisions were made for military or police forces to enforce them. In the case of the *Cain Domn-haigh* laws, which were made at the behest of the Christian religious orders, presumably these religious orders enforced them themselves. Although the Brehon Laws (along with the Irish language, dress and customs) were outlawed at the Parliament of Kilkenny in 1366, to prevent the English settlers becoming "more Irish than the Irish themselves", some aspects of them did survive for at least another two or three centuries.

In early England, where agricultural communities controlled their local affairs, the shire and its administrator, the sheriff, assumed a central position in administering local justice and resolving local disputes. The sheriff had authority to expel lawbreakers from the community and could order wrongdoers to stand trial.

John, son of King Henry II, received the title Lord of Hibernia in 1177. It was during his reign that Dublin Castle – which served as the headquarters for British rule in Ireland until 1922 – was built. He established a system of central government for Ireland, dividing the country up into counties and appointing a sheriff in each. The sheriffs in turn set up courts in their counties. The Magna Carta of 1215 contained a definite statement relating to the enforcement of the law: "We shall not make men justiciaries, constables, sheriffs or bailiffs, unless they understand the law of the land and are well disposed to observing it." At this time it was left to the communities to police themselves and to impose their own sanctions on the offender. John, who became king of England in 1199, had by 1195 extended his authority over England, and a royal edict directed that criminals were to be referred to local knights before whom they could be charged and, if necessary, held for the circuit judges. The knight was the predeccessor of the justice of the peace, who dealt with local disputes and criminals between visits of circuit judges or the quarter sessions.

By 1228 every county in Ireland was obliged to accept English laws, and before the end of the thirteenth century the Statute of Winchester, 1285, was applied to Ireland. After 1285, if a criminal who had murdered or robbed a traveller was not produced by the community within forty days of an inquest held by the local lord, a fine, to be collected by the lord's constable, was imposed on that county for the crime. The holding of the inquest and the imposition of the penalty was designed to force ordinary citizens to fulfil judicial obligations.

The Statute of Winchester delegated authority to the justices of the peace to hear criminal and civil cases, pending to the court of Westminster. It also formalised and provided for the "night-watches" and "wards" in towns and cities, in which all males between fifteen and sixty years of age were to take their turns. Should a stranger or suspicious person flee on being challenged, the nightwatchman had to raise a "hue and cry", which compelled all able-bodied men to join in the chase. If a male refused to serve on the night-watch or join in the chase of a suspect, the local constable reported him to the local justice, who reported to the king; the king fixed the penalty for the individual concerned.

A statute of 1360 provided for the arrest and punishment of offenders by justices. This was followed by a bar on native Irishmen's, becoming mayors, bailiffs or holding any office of the king, but it did not prohibit them from performing their duties as watchmen. There were special laws for those residing within the Pale. In 1598 a curfew came into force in Dublin city and "Civic Regulations for the Defence and Protection of Dublin" were introduced by the Archbishop of Dublin, Adam Loftus. The Dublin watch was increased in number and they were armed with swords, muskets and pikes. While Ireland had its watch and wards system during this period, England had its equivalent, and those who operated it were known as the "Charlies".

Although various enactments relating to law and order of a relatively minor nature were implemented up to the end of the eighteenth century, basically these amended and up-dated the provisions of the Statute of Winchester. For example, in 1715, constables were given responsibility to attend at fires and to assist at extinguishing them. The primary provision of the Winchester act, however, survived for over five centuries and stood the test of time reasonably well, bridging the gap between the thirteenth and eighteenth centuries, when more modern legislation was enacted.

Every town and city was protected by gates which were closed between the hours of sunset and sunrise. Nightwatchmen took up duty in sentry boxes at the town or city gates to challenge all persons wanting to enter or leave the town. Other watchmen were assigned to sentry boxes at strategic locations within the town or city itself, keeping stretches of streets under their observation with a view to preventing robberies, housebreakings or crimes of violence. They were also obliged to provide time-checks for the inhabitants by walking along the streets in their section at two-hourly intervals, on the hour, calling out the time and assuring the inhabitants that all was quiet and peaceful. Up to the 1880s, nightwatchmen still called the time in many towns in Ireland: "Past eleven o'clock. All's well."

Constable

The word "constable" has dominated peacekeeping and policing in Ireland since the thirteenth century. In his book, *The Irish Police* (1974), Seamus Breathnach clarifies its history:

> The word "constable" is multimeaningful and defies definition. This arises from the fact that the office of constable, like that of a marshal, has changed both in time and in territory of usage. The word itself appears in the Domesday Book as *constabularia* and is also mentioned in the Great Charter of Ireland in 1216, and it can be spelled in at least ten different ways and has as many derivative meanings. It comes from the Latin comes-stabuli, meaning keeper or count of the king's stable or horses. The constable also commanded the king's army, particularly under the Frankish kings, when in the thirteenth century, the constable became the king's provincial lieutenant and, in the fourteenth, his commander-in-chief. Unknown in Ireland or England before the Norman invasion, the office came to be synonymous with a high-ranking military post. It then became associated with castles, garrisons and ships, and by the Winchester Statute, the offices of high and petty constable managed to assimilate the military aspects of the Saxon militia and the civil or magisterial aspects of the sheriff (shire-reeve) and tithingman. It was predominantly in this sense that the meaning of the word came to be used in Ireland.

The System of Government and Local Government

The supreme authority representing the Crown in Ireland was the lord lieutenant – otherwise referred to as the viceroy – who received his appointment from the king or queen of England on the recommendation of the British prime minister. The lord lieutenant was advised by the Privy Council, consisting of the Irish lord chancellor, the attorney-general and the solicitor-general. He was assisted in Ireland by the chief secretary and by a civil and a military under-secretary. They effectively ruled the country, and the British home secretary had little more than a passing interest in Irish affairs. The lord lieutenant appointed a lord lieutenant for each county, who in turn appointed a deputy to assist him, with the approval of the lord lieutenant. All these office holders were invariably of the landed gentry or ascendancy class. Up to 1822, the baronial magistrates within a county were appointed by the grand jury, their appointments being honorary in nature and unpaid. They in turn had authority to appoint constables.

From that time onwards, constables could only be appointed by the chief magistrate of the county – otherwise known as the stipendiary or paid magistrates. The county lord lieutenant was in fact the head of the civil and military authorities within his county and he, along with his deputy, high sheriff, grand jurors and magistrates, constituted the system of local government for that county.

Each county maintained its own militia and had one or more central barracks within the county to accommodate them. The militia was formed in 1793 with thirty-seven county or city battalions and regiments, and in the period up to 1816 it was very active. Militia units were raised in particular counties or cities to supplement the regular British army, and they often moved around from county to county as required. The county militia was under the overall control of the county lord lieutenant, who normally delegated his day-to-day authority for the operation of the force through his deputy. The militia – normally mounted and fitted out with the best equipment – was substantial and had several hundred members in most counties, with a total strength in the early years of the nineteenth century of 20,000. Again, its members were of the landed gentry class and its leaders, who were also of the ascendancy, had as a rule served abroad with the British army. While the militia was involved in dealing with serious disorders and was available to be called upon at the behest of the lord or deputy county lieutenants or magistrates, it did not have a policing role as such.

In addition to the militia, the Irish Yeomanry Corps, a semi-military group of some 35,000 men, was available in most areas. Formed in 1796 as a civilian volunteer defence force to augment the regular army and militia, it operated locally and was confined to specific districts. Made up mostly of Protestants, it played a prominent role in the 1798 insurrection and was disbanded in 1834. In addition to the yeomanry and the militia, the British maintained a military force in the country, comprising a total force of about 40,000 men. The numbers varied from time to time, depending on the British involvement in wars. It was headed by a commander of the forces based in Dublin, and he took his orders directly from London.

The Baronial Constables

An act of 1715 (2 Geo. 1, c. 10) authorised the grand jury at quarter sessions to appoint a high constable for a barony. On confirmation of his appointment by the grand jury, he took an oath of office and received his warrant of appointment from the Clerk of the Crown of Peace, who was the senior legal court administrator in the county. There were approximately 300 baronies, defined areas within a county, which were convenient for county rates estimates, in Ireland at that time. Where land was good they were normally small and compact, but where land was poor or mountainous they covered huge areas. In the time of poor communications and transport systems, they were manageable areas for administration within a county. The headings to all official correspondence submitted to Dublin Castle or the lord lieutenant set out the county, the barony and the townland. As time went on, the size of baronies became contentious on a number of issues, and later where small baronies adjoined one another, they were combined.

The baronial high constable was paid a nominal salary. Under the high constable, arrangements were made whereby each parish would have a watch or a ward system. These watchmen were appointed by the local justices in each parish and by the chief magistrate in the cities. The justices and the chief magistrates prepared lists of able-bodied men to perform watch duty during the period from September through to the following March, between the hours of sunset and sunrise. There was no payment, but penalties were provided for to punish those who refused or failed to perform the watch duties. The appointed watchmen were authorised to stop and search persons, and on finding anyone who could not give an account of himself, were empowered to bring him before the local justice to be dealt with. To facilitate the performance of these watch duties, the grand juries provided "watch houses" and, for the protection of the watchmen, watch-bills, halverts and staffs.

In 1719 a further act (6 Geo. 1, c. 10) made some minor amendments to the provisions of the 1715 act. Further legislation in 1733 (7 Geo. 2, c. 12) directed that the high constables in charge of baronies should be appointed at the general assizes rather than at the quarter sessions as heretofore. The high constable was to hold office for one year and was responsible for handing overall rates collected by him to the county treasurer. At that time, the grand jury was really the local authority for the county and the members approved the estimates of expenditure when they met at the local assizes. Despite the one-year term of office laid down, efficient high constables who succeeded in collecting the full rate and performed well were often called upon within a few years to serve again. Eventually they succeeded in getting a seven-year exemption after completing their one-year period of office.

An act of 1743 (17 Geo. 2, c. 6) provided for the payment of 3d. per mile to a constable for conveying a prisoner to the nearest county gaol and a similar payment to each of two men to accompany him and carry arms. Legislation of 1749 (23 Geo. 2, c. 14) tightened up the appointments of petty constables, many of whom were apparently carrying out duties they had not been officially appointed to. Many of these had received their "appointments" from land stewards and sheriffs who had utilised them to their own advantage. A further act in 1789 (23 & 24 Geo. 3, c. 42) made provision to appoint four additional sub-constables to each barony and fixed wages for them at £4 per annum.

Payment for the Watchmen

While the role of the watchmen in the more rural areas went into decline as the century progressed, that of watchmen in the cities took on greater importance. There were many homeless and disruptive people on the streets at night causing disturbances to the residents, who naturally complained, and there was also an increase in petty crime. As a natural sequence to this, from 1750 onwards, the Dublin city watchmen demanded pay for their work. In the interests of providing a better service, the city corporations commenced to pay salaries, financed by a property tax, to the watchmen, and the bigger towns throughout Ireland followed suit shortly afterwards. Still, some cities and towns were not prepared to make any payment to their watchmen and got away without paying them until well into the nineteenth century.

The Belfast Watch Police

Belfast had the benefit of a fairly efficient watch system for almost fifty years –1816 to 1865 – which developed into a police force of its own as time progressed. In August 1816, Belfast Town Council announced the setting up of the new night-watch system. The pay rates fixed were 9s. per week for constables and 10s. 6d. per week for sergeants. The watchmen were armed with pikes and their base was at a barracks in Rosemary Street. One heavy manual duty performed by the watchmen involved manning the fire engines. The fire pumps were operated with four or six men on either side of the pumping machine pulling on a bar which operated a crank powering the pump mechanism. The force in its early days was very efficient and had numerous arrests and convictions to its credit for all types of crime. In 1824, for example, they were able to assist their opposite numbers in Greenock, Scotland, by arresting three men who had absconded by boat to Belfast and handing them over to their Greenock counterparts.

The watchmen worked in two shifts: the day shift from 6am each day to 9pm at night, including meal-breaks, and the night shift from 9pm to 6am on the following morning. In 1861 they got a change of uniform to one which resembled that of the London Metropolitan Police. In the same year, one chief constable, eight inspectors and ninety-four men were employed on night duty, and on day duty there were fifty-four men, four inspectors and one chief constable. The chief constable on night duty got a salary of £125 per annum; his colleague on day duty received £85; the inspectors got £60 per annum and the constables got £40. Two detectives were also employed at the same pay as that of the inspectors. Another member of the force, the "inspector of cars", received £70 per annum.

By 1858, more than twenty regular beats were being operated by the force, and in the year 1859 the force had 2,400 persons committed to prison. In 1860, Captain W. Shaw, a former military officer from Cork, was appointed to the dual role of chief of police and chief fire officer for Belfast at a salary of £300 a year. He introduced military style discipline to the force, including regular drill instruction, and he re-organised the fire service. In 1861 he was appointed as head of the London fire service. During his time in Belfast he succeeded in getting a pay increase for all ranks of the police force there.

The Belfast force in its early years was probably the most successful of all the watch forces. As time went on, flaws in the system became apparent. There was a strong Protestant influence as the force was run by the town council, with its lord mayor, and the local magistrates closely identified with it. The Catholic population regarded it as being sectarian in nature. As the whole policing arrangement was "comfortable" for all those in authority, the legislation of 1787, 1792, 1814, 1822 or 1834 appears to have been irrelevant, and no regular constabulary force was appointed to the city. One reason given for this omission was that Belfast was not regarded as being "a county of a city" nor was it the "county of a town". It should be noted that Cork, Galway and Limerick had constabulary forces from the outset. A section of the County Antrim constabulary was stationed in the Belfast suburbs, while a section of the County Down constabulary was stationed in another suburb of Ballymacgarret.

In 1864 very serious rioting took place in Belfast which resulted in loss of life. A commission of inquiry investigating the circumstances recommended the disbandment of the Belfast City Police force, and this took place in 1865. (See Chapter 3.)

The Dublin Metropolitan Police

The policing of Dublin, as in many other cities, had its origins in the watch system. From early times Dublin city was divided into twenty-one parishes; each parish had fifteen watchmen under the supervision of a constable, who was appointed to that position by the church wardens. As stated earlier, the first watch system had no day patrols and operated only at night for about six months of the year. At the start of the eighteenth century, in 1715, with crime and violence on the increase, the city corporation was authorised to appoint watchmen and constables to keep the night-watches and an annual levy of 3d. in the pound valuation was imposed to pay for the service.

In 1723, an act (10 Geo. 2) authorised the church wardens and parishioners to meet once a year "to choose a sufficient number of fit and able persons inhabiting within the said parish, who shall be housekeepers, to be constables for a period of one year from the first day of June of that year". The persons so chosen were obliged to lodge their names and addresses with the lord mayor, and furthermore it was decreed "that so the intent that the inhabitants may also know his place of residence, every such constable shall nail up in view of their respective doors a short Constable's staff or paint the figure of such staff". By 1729, an act (3 Geo. 2, c. 13) directed "that persons keeping public inns, ale houses or houses of entertainment, or any Papists shall not act in the person of a constable, but if any such should be chosen to serve as a constable, they shall find some fit Protestant to serve in their room". They were obliged to take their constable's oath to enforce the laws without favour or affection, malice or ill will. The constables were obliged to make a daily report to the lord mayor, detailing the activities of the watch, including details of all arrests made, details of absenteeism by the watchmen and whether they had lost any of their staffs or lanterns while on duty.

An act of 1765 (5 Geo. 3) authorised the appointment of three inspectors for each parish at a salary of not more than £10 per annum. The watch hours were extended from 10pm to 5am in summer, 9pm to 6am in spring and autumn, and 8pm to 7am in winter. The lord mayor was to inspect the watch on 1 May and 1 November each year, and he had authority to dismiss members who were unsuitable. Very stiff fines were imposed on watchmen who failed to carry out duties assigned to them. Further amendments to legislation made specific provision for the maintenance of watches at the Liberties and the governors of the Lying-in Hospital received authority to raise the sum of £128 per annum from the residents of Rutland Square (now Parnell Square) to maintain a constable and eight watchmen. By 1785, the pay scales were £16 per annum for constables, £12 for watchmen and an allowance of £12 per annum for provision of candles and fuel. In the 1770s, parishioners elected a "ward mote court" to select constables and watchmen, and those selected had no option but to serve.

The Dublin Metropolitan District was organised in 1786 under an act of parliament (26 Geo. 3, c. 24). Under a high constable, the district was divided into four divisions. Each division had a chief constable and ten petty constables. Three magistrate commissioners were appointed by the lord lieutenant and were given judicial and administrative control of the force, which patrolled the streets by day and night. The watchmen already in existence continued to function under the supervision of their constables, but they were brought under the control of the commissioners. The latter were empowered to fix levies on householders to pay for the new force.

The 1786 act appears to have been the first act of parliament which made provision for "police" in the British Isles. While its provisions were modest and perhaps primitive, they nevertheless did lay a basis for a police force, and Dublin city can rightly lay claim to the first legislation authorising a "police force" in these islands.

In 1808 the number of divisions in the Dublin Metropolitan District were increased to six and the area of jurisdiction was defined. The district covered an area of an eight-mile radius all around Dublin Castle. The divisional justices were under the control of the lord lieutenant, and they were the magistrates in the new police divisions. Horse patrols under the control of the chief magistrate were provided for. In 1825, the number of divisions within the district reverted to four and a police office was established for each under the authority of the lord lieutenant. The latter also appointed the divisional justices. A barrister, a Dublin Corporation alderman and a sheriff's peer (nominee) were also to attach to each of the four police offices.

Finally in 1836, The Dublin Police Act (6 & 7 Wm. 4) brought the entire Dublin police force under the control of the chief secretary. The force came under the direction of two justices of the peace appointed by the lord lieutenant. The force was organised along the same lines as the London Metropolitan Police force, established seven years earlier. The first recruit for the new force was attested in 1837. The majority of its recruits came from the rural areas, particularly from the counties adjacent to Dublin. The minimum height was 5 feet 9 inches, with a mean chest measurement of 36 inches. Recruits were required to be single and under twenty-six years of age. Before joining, they had to satisfy the superintendent that they had at least 30s. in their possession and that they had a respectable suit of clothes, two pair of strong serviceable half boots and four pairs of stockings. They were directed to devote their whole time to the police service. Recruits were paid 10s. 6d. per week for the first six months and the top rate of constable's pay was 15s. 9d. per week in 1838.

Of the first four superintendents appointed to the new force in 1836, three were former inspectors of the London Metropolitan Police and the fourth was a former military sergeant major. Most of the officers during the lifetime of the DMP were promoted from the ranks.

The headquarters for the Dublin Metropolitan District was in Dublin Castle, and its recruit training depot was situated at Kevin Street. As distinct from the Royal Irish Constabulary, the Dublin police was at all times an unarmed police force. It remained intact as a police force and operated independently of the RIC. From 1922 until 1925 its official title was *Póilíní Átha Cliath*, the Gaelic version of "the Dublin police". Under the Garda Síochána Amalgamation Act, 1925, it was combined with the Garda Síochána and came under the direction of the Garda commissioner. A guarantee of tenure to every serving member of the force, with a further guarantee that its members would not be required to serve outside of Dublin, was given by the government prior to amalgamation.

The Dublin Metropolitan Police was generally a very successful force, always tightly controlled and maintaining high standards. It established a reputation for itself in the athletic world, winning the world tug-of-war championships on a number of occasions.

Through no fault of its own, the DMP force got caught up in the big lock-out strike of 1913. It was perceived by the strikers and the general public to have acted totally on the side of the employers, and it took a number of years for the wounds connected with this to heal. It had a difficult period of duty during the 1916 Rising and the six years which followed, but it survived. On amalgamation in 1925 it fitted in very well with the Garda Síochána.

The Appointment of Baronial Constables, 1787

The first act of parliament which had relevance to the policing of Ireland was passed in 1787 (27 Geo. 3, c. 40). It was titled "An Act for the Better Execution of the Law, and the Preservation of Peace within the Counties at Large". This act empowered the lord lieutenant of Ireland to appoint a chief constable to each one or more baronies, while the grand juries had power assigned to them to appoint sixteen sub-constables to each of the same districts. It was a provision of the act that all those appointed should be Protestants and that they should all be already in employment. They were entitled to a sum of 3d. per mile for the conveyance of prisoners to the county gaol. A like sum was also paid to any person who might assist them in performing this duty – provided that they were also Protestants. The chief constables appointed under the act were to receive £150 per annum and the sub-constables £10. The baronial constabulary took their orders from the magistrates.

In many counties which were peaceful the provisions of this act were not implemented. In fact, only four counties were divided into districts without undue delay: Cork, nine districts; Tipperary, seven; and Kilkenny and Kerry, five districts each. The baronial constabulary as a force was inefficient and incapable of tackling policing problems. The constables had no knowledge of law, underwent no training course, and the only brief they appear to have had was that they they had the same powers as the high constable or petty constable had had up to that time. They received their salaries only on certification from the justices at general sessions that they had carried out the functions of their office in a satisfactory manner. While this act did form a rough plan for the general policing of the country, it was not very effective as it was only implemented in the counties which really had problems at that time. Other grand juries obviously felt that their old systems were adequate, and they resisted the payment of what they deemed to be high salaries.

Authorities to Grand Juries to Appoint Additional Constables

In 1792 an act entitled "An Act for Regulating the Office of Constable and for the Better Enforcing of the Process of Criminal Law in Parts of the United Kingdom" (32 Geo. 3, c. 16) came into force. This legislation, in effect, gave a cheaper policing system to these counties than the 1787 act. The 1792 act only provided for eight constables per barony at £4 each per annum. Each constable appointed was required to carry arms, for which he was entitled to an allowance of £2. Further authority was again given to the grand juries in 1796 to appoint more constables.

The men appointed under the 1792 and 1787 acts, officially titled "baronial constables", were more commonly known by the Irish people as "the Barnies". These constables did not wear uniform. Under no supervision, nor subject to any disciplinary code or control, they were incapable of dealing with serious riots or disorder. Their principal duties amounted to carrying out searches for stolen property and looking after the interests of the local magistrates. To carry out searches, they were required to have warrants, a requirement which they greatly abused and which anyway meant very little to illiterate Irish peasants when they were produced by constables who wanted to search their homes or land for stolen property. They occasionally accompanied bailiffs making seizures or carrying out evictions. They provided protection for courthouses for court sittings and served writs on behalf of the courts. In the oath taken by them when assuming office, they undertook the removal of all nuisances from the public highways and the prevention of obstruction and encroachments.

Many of the baronial constables were elderly men retired from other positions and only performed duty where no trouble was anticipated. The collection of rates was probably their primary duty. When trouble or disorder was expected, the magistrates called out the military or yeomanry to provide protection and the baronial constables had no effective role. In 1812 (excluding Dublin and Belfast) there were almost 3,000 petty or sub-constables whose annual wage bill came to £19,750. In Counties Cork, Kilkenny, Tipperary, and in Waterford city, they were paid £20 per annum each; in Kerry, Limerick, Longford, Meath and Westmeath they were in receipt of £12 per annum; in seventeen other counties their salary was only £4 per annum; in County Down and in Cork and Kilkenny cities the petty and sub-constables received no pay.

The baronial constables appear to have outlived their usefulness by the early 1820s. In anticipation of new legislation relating to policing, the views of chief magistrates appointed under the 1814 act were sought by the chief secretary. Samson Carter, who was a chief magistrate at Doneraile, County Cork, wrote a scathing account of the baronial constables:

> They are corrupt, being influenced by motives of personal emoluments.
> It is a well known fact that a baronial constable will not execute a

warrant without a fee accompanying the delivery thereof to him, after which he contrives to inform the delinquent and suspends the execution in consideration of another fee. Their services are inoperative from their feelings of partiality to their local connections and by a dread of becoming abnoxious to the disaffected.

Following the setting up of the provincial constabularies in 1822, the baronial constabulary was phased out, although it dragged on in some counties until the late 1820s. During the lifetime of the baronial constabulary, numerous secret societies existed amongst the Irish in opposition to evictions, payments of tithes to clergy and agrarian problems, as well as religious divides of Orangemen and Ribbonmen and all kinds of divisions on Protestant/Catholic lines.

The Revenue Police

Towards the end of the eighteenth century, illicit distillation was a major problem in Ireland. Besides a huge loss of revenue to the authorities, the effect of the spirits on the persons who drank it gave cause for concern, as it led to bitter fights and even murder. Poteen was being distilled all over rural Ireland, in bogs, mountains, forests, islands and all kinds of desolate places. There was a never-ending demand, and, to cater for this, huge groups of people got together and engaged in its distillation. The army did not get involved in trying to control the problem and there was no proper police service in existence to deal with it.

The loss of revenue from the poteen making in Ireland, and presumably the many other complaints being made about it, resulted in revenue officers being appointed by the British government in the year 1800. Initially they operated with the back-up of the military authorities, but after some time, the military refused to provide this service to the revenue officers on the grounds that it was deleterious to morale and discipline.

Major James Darcy, who was the chief magistrate of the Peace Preservation Force in the Innishowen Peninsula, County Donegal, where poteen making was rampant, had thirty revenue men allocated to him by the Board of Excise around 1820 to attempt to put down the trade. The initial experiment under Major Darcy proved successful but it was not adopted as a practice elsewhere. The revenue officers depended on the military or Peace Preservation Force as back-up, and where it was not available, groups of armed men were enlisted to provide the support for the revenue officers. The leaders of these groups, commissioned as excise men, took on the title of "lieutenant", but by the mid–1830s all involved had become discredited.

In 1836, Colonel William Brereton, formerly a Royal Artillery officer, was placed in charge of the revenue police with instructions to reorganise and revitalise the force. Legislation was also passed to provide more severe penalties for poteen making. Colonel Brereton took his assignment very seriously, quickly dismissing two-thirds of the force. Majella McLoughlin in an article in the *Garda Review* of March 1991 wrote that Colonel Brereton "found an undisciplined and untrained body of men who were 'objectionable in every way'". He started a new recruiting campaign for the force and insisted that candidates be literate, under twenty-five years of age, single and of good character. He had the country divided into four divisions with a revenue lieutenant in charge of each. The revenue police worked from about eighty stations throughout the country, with the greatest concentration along the west coast. The members of the force wore a uniform which consisted of a tight-fitting jacket buttoned at the front, a belt, a shako-style cap, blue trousers in winter and white trousers in summer. The officers wore a more elaborate uniform, as was customary in that period. The members were armed with carbines similiar to those of the Irish Constabulary.

The force had an administrative headquarters at Enniskillen, County Fermanagh, but this was later transferred to the Dublin Custom House. A training school for the members was situated at Clonliffe, Dublin. Under Colonel Brereton's command the force became very efficient in putting down illicit distillation. They proved so effective along the west coast that the illegal distilleries moved to the many islands off the coast. Colonel Brereton managed to persuade the government of the day to purchase a steam-powered vessel – aptly named the *Warrior* – to enable his force to raid on the off-shore islands. In the early 1850s it was evident that the 1,100 revenue police were winning the battle against the poteen makers, and a commission of inquiry was set up in 1854 to assess the entire situation. Due primarily to its own success, and the fact that the Irish Constabulary was becoming increasingly efficient in law enforcement, there was little work for the revenue police to do, and it was disbanded in 1859 when the enforcement of the illicit distillation laws passed to the Irish Contabulary.

Credit must also go, indirectly, to the force for helping to bring organised "faction fighting" to an end. The decline of the faction fighting ran parallel with the vigorous enforcement of the illicit distillation laws from the time Colonel Brereton took over in 1836.

The Role of Robert Peel in Policing, in Ireland and England

It is not possible to review the policing of Ireland or England without reference to the role played by Robert Peel, the pioneer of policing. Through his brilliance, determination and commitment, he convinced the people and his fellow parliamentarians that police work and the maintenance of law and order could not be carried out solely by the military, and conceived and developed the role of the police which has stood the test of time.

He was the single most influential individual involved in establishing constabularies and police forces in Ireland and England during the first half of the nineteenth century. The police forces established by him became role models for the police forces of the British Commonwealth and for other modern police forces around the world.

He arrived in Ireland as chief secretary on 1 September 1812, when he was only twenty-four years of age. He was the Tory member for Cashel. He had a difficult relationship with the lord lieutenant, the Duke of Richmond; but he retained his office when a new lord lieutenant, Viscount Whitworth, took over in 1813. Despite the enormous responsibility of holding such an influential position at his young age, Peel was not deterred by the problems which faced him. There was a general state of lawlessness and disorder in the country. Dublin city was the only place which had an established police force. The watch and ward systems and forces of yeomanry and militia dispersed throughout the country were not sufficient to contain the situation. Due to the Napoleanic Wars, the total military force at the time numbered only about 14,000 members, approximately one-third of the normal strength.

He found that the baronial constabularies had outlived their usefulness and were totally inadequate to deal with the situation. A stronger and better regulated force was essential. He was also very unhappy about the magistrates who had the responsibility for enforcing law and order in their districts. Most of the them were corrupt and they only had the interests of the landlords and ascendancy classes at heart. While the lord chancellor had power to appoint magistrates, he normally selected them on the recommendations of the county lord lieutenant. All those appointed were Protestants and the qualifications which ensured their appointments hinged on their ownership of property, their profession or their business interests. They had become a law unto themselves. When serious issues arose they made themselves unavailable. Many of them resided for the greater part of their time in England. Only a small minority could be regarded as taking their appointments and duties seriously. With a view to getting a better service from the magistrates, Peel decided in 1814 to appoint the first stipendiary (paid) magistrates.

In his book *Rural Disorder and Police Reform in Ireland, 1812–1836*, Galen Broeker summarises the problem facing Peel:

> If Peel can be said to have an Irish policy during his years as Chief Secretary, beyond a desire for good, resolute government, it was founded on the belief that in Ireland the traditional system of local leadership had broken down. The country gentlemen who were expected to provide magistrates and Grand Jurors from their ranks, and thus dominate the machinery of local government, were failing to perform what Peel and others considered the functions of their class. The result of this failure

was the crime, agrarian outrage and near revolution that made government by ordinary processes almost impossible. As Peel saw the situation, the leaders of Irish society had to be persuaded, if neccessary coerced, into the proper performance of their traditional duties, after which much of the Irish problem would solve itself. From this belief, originated Peel's feud with the Irish magistrates, which provided one of the major themes of his period as Chief Secretary and led directly to the first of his police reforms. The struggle between the Castle and the Irish magistracy was to continue in some form for the next twenty-two years, and prove to the Irish Government that the traditional system of maintaining order, centred on the magistrates and their constables and reinforced by the military, could no longer function effectively. In its place there gradually emerged a system based on a new concept of police, which after years of trial and error could in its final shape be characterised as "the most valuable boon conferred by imperial legislation upon Ireland".

Things had changed in the early part of the nineteenth century due to the Industrial Revolution, but the English establishment could not come to terms with the idea of a police force. Even the word "police" was objectionable to them. They had a hang-up about the power and force of the military to solve all their problems and could not be shifted from this entrenched position, Robert Peel, however, belonged to a younger generation with other positive ideas, and he was satisfied that some type of an organised policing system was essential. In spite of his initial failure to get suitable legislation through parliament, where his ideas and proposals met with considerable opposition from his parliamentary peers, he persevered and successfully steered new legislation through parliament in 1814. His success in getting the new Peace Preservation Act (54 Geo. 3, c. 13) on to the statute books in 1814 – through the manipulation of words and their meanings – was a tribute to his outstanding intelligence, determination, astuteness and diplomacy. While he did not get all that he wanted, he nevertheless succeeded in establishing at least a prototype of policing system which could be monitored and improved upon as necessary. Having established the Peace Preservation Force, he monitored its progress and noted its flaws. He was very fortunate in having selected excellent stipendiary magistrates and good officers to lead that new force.

In 1818 Peel resigned his position as chief secretary and moved to the parliamentary backbenches. In 1822 – at the age of thirty-four years – he was appointed home secretary. It was clear that parliament wanted to use his initiative and talent to sort out its law and order problems. The most immediate problem facing him was the state of lawlessness and disorder in London itself, which was policed only at night.

On 14 March 1822 he set up a select sommittee consisting of twenty people, including his brother William, "to examine the possibility of setting up as perfect a system of policing as was consistent with the character of a free country" for London. The committee submitted its report to him in June of the same year. Peel had hoped to get more scope from his select committee of 1822 relating to the policing problem in London and an observation made by the committee was most interesting:

> It is difficult to reconcile an effective system of policing with that perfect freedom of action and exemption from interference which are the great privileges and blessings of society in this country, and your committee think that the forfeiture or curtailment of such advantages would be too great a sacrifice for improvements in police, or facilities in the detection of crime, however desirable in themselves, if abstractedly considered.

The committee did recommend the setting up of a Bow Street foot patrol by day. Within two months this patrol was a reality. Twenty-four men were hand-picked from the night patrol and dressed in the same uniform as the horse patrol. Peel had succeeded in getting a uniformed day patrol on to the streets of London.

Just one week prior to the implementation of the new day patrol in London, Peel had succeeded in getting new legislation through parliament to set up a new police system for Ireland. As home secretary, he was again confronted with the seriously deteriorating state of law and order in Ireland. While the Peace Preservation Force had fulfilled a very important role from its introduction in 1814, it had gradually become unable to cope with the problems of the period. He succeeded in having the Constabulary Act of 1822 (6 Geo. 4, c. 103), another new concept for the policing of Ireland, passed by parliament.

Peel had made a major breakthrough in the policing of Ireland and had lain the foundation stones for the London Metropolitan Police.

By 1828, there was an acceptance that it was necessary to improve the quality of policing in London and Peel believed that real reform of the force was essential. He introduced a bill in parliament titled "Bill for Improving the Police in and near the Metropolis" (10 Geo. 4, c. 44). Again, he had a difficult time in steering the bill through both houses of parliament, but it became law in June 1829 and provided for the establishment of the London Metropolitan Police.

The legislation provided for the appointment of two magistrates, each with equal responsibility to lead the force. They later became known as "commissioners". Peel selected two Irishmen to fill these positions: Charles Rowan and Richard Mayne.

Charles Rowan was a native of County Antrim. At fourteen years of age he joined the army and served under Sir John Moore, who instilled a new concept of self-discipline into his rifle brigade to replace the old British army discipline of "the lash and blind obedience" to orders. Charles Rowan had no formal education but was an excellent soldier who had made rapid progress through the ranks and reached the rank of colonel. He was about forty-six years of age and had retired some years before being called upon by Robert Peel to head up the new force. He was seen as the more influential of the two commissioners appointed. In the edition of *John Bull* of 27 September 1829, it was commented that, "Colonel Rowan, the head of the new establishment, was one of the ablest and best experienced Quarter Master Generals in the army."

In *The Blind Eye of History* (1952), Charles Reith observed: "The unquestionable facts emerge of the dominance of the mind and personality of Charles Rowan and the major role played by him in creating, not only the frame and fabric of the existing British police institutions but the spirit of practical idealism which inspires it." He retired from the force in 1850 and died a few years later.

Richard Mayne (later knighted) was a brilliant young barrister who had graduated from Trinity College, Dublin, and whose father, Edward, was a judge of the King's Bench in Ireland. He was thirty-two years old and was practising in northern England.

Both commissioners met for the first time early in July 1829 and within two weeks they had submitted a blueprint for the new London police force. The force was divided into five divisions, with one headquarters and four territorial divisions. Each division was allotted a letter of the alphabet and was policed by a company consisting of one superintendent; four inspectors; sixteen sergeants (who were allocated numbers one to sixteen) and 144 police constables. The training was of short duration and included basic drill. Each recruit took an oath of office. Towards the end of September 1829, notices signed by Rowan and Mayne disbanding the night-watchmen were posted at prominent locations in London and the new force was on duty on the streets before the end of the month.

The reaction by the public and press was most favourable. One newspaper commented: "The ease and despatch with which the New Police conduct their night charges, forms a striking contrast to the slovenly and unsatisfactory manner in which the defunct night watch performed their duty, and proves the superiority of the new system, even while yet in its infancy." The members of the new police wore top hats and blue-coloured, belted frock coats. The starting pay for a constable was 18s. 6d. per week, increased by 6d. per week a few years later.

Discipline was strict. On the first day after the new force had taken up duty, there were twenty-eight resignations in one company alone. Within a week, several had been dismissed for drunkenness and other disciplinary offences. By the year 1833, only 562 of the original 3,300 members who had enlisted in 1829 remained. Eventually the force settled into being a strictly disciplined organisation. The instructions issued by the commissioners, farsighted for their time, have stood the test of time, and have helped to create a "mission statement" for all police forces in the intervening period. They placed an emphasis on the prevention of crime by the new police rather than on only reacting to crime after it had occurred and defined the pro-active role as a policing model. Details of the instructions for the new force were published in the *Morning Chronicle* of 24 September 1829, before they had been finally ratified and sanctioned by Peel. The following was the introduction to the instructions:

> The following General Instructions for the different ranks of the Police Force are not to be understood as containing rules of conduct applicable to every variety of circumstances that may occur in the performance of their duty; something must necessarily be left to the intelligence and direction of individuals; and according to the degree in which they shew themselves possessed of these qualities, and to their zeal, activity and judgement on all occasions will be their claim to future promotion and reward.
>
> It should be understood at the outset, that the principal object to be attained is "The Prevention of Crime". [It is believed that the word "principal" was inserted by Peel himself who personally amended the original draft.]
>
> To this great end every effort of the Police is to be directed. The security of person and property, the preservation of the public tranquillity, and all the other objects of a police establishment, will thus be better effected, than by the detection and punishment of the offender after he has succeeded in committing the crime. This should constantly be kept in mind by every member of the Police Force as the guide for his own conduct. Officers and Police Constables should endeavour to distinguish themselves by such vigilance and activity, as may render it extremely difficult for any one to commit a crime within that portion of the town under their charge.

In 1842, a crime detection unit was set up, consisting of two inspectors and six sergeants, to investigate crime and bring criminals to justice. In the 1850s a "Special Branch" unit, commonly referred to as the "Special Irish Branch", was established to combat the threat of Irish-American bombers. The head of the unit was Howard Vincent, who, along with the other members of the unit, was Irish.

Peel learned many lessons from his Irish experiences – all of which stood him in good stead in establishing the very successful London Metropolitan Police force. It was extraordinary that he selected two Irishmen to lead it.

In 1835 and 1836, when Thomas Drummond decided that a fresh approach was needed for policing in Ireland, his greatest supporter was Robert Peel. During the passage of the new legislation in parliament in 1836, Peel made a very powerful speech in support of it, arguing that it was far better to have the police appointed by the Crown than by any local authority. His support guaranteed the passage of the bill through parliament and it became law a short while later as the Constabulary (Ireland) Act, 1836.

County constabularies and city police forces were subsequently established in Great Britain and later extended throughout the British Commonwealth, all based on the Irish models. Robert Peel left a legacy to the world through his policing initiatives and reforms, initially in Ireland and later in England, and his name will be forever synonymous with the history of policing.

The Peace Preservation Act

In 1814, Peel's Peace Preservation Act (54 Geo. 3, c. 131) empowered the lord lieutenant to proclaim any county or city in Ireland "to be in a state of disturbance" and at once to appoint a paid chief magistrate, a chief constable and fifty sub-constables to that county or district for the preservation of the peace. The chief magistrate was obliged to live within the county or district for which he was appointed. The local magistrates were to submit all examinations, informations and items of intelligence relating to crimes or outrages committed or likely to be committed within their jurisdictions. The chief magistrate was given absolute power over the local magistrates. He directed all duties of the constables under his command and also appointed the constables who were to work with the local magistrates. As a result, the local magistrates lost much of their control and authority. The chief magistrate had a substantial salary of £700 per annum and he was provided with a house and a clerk. (The chief constable was paid only £150 per annum.) He effectively instructed and controlled the actions of the Peace Preservation Force. All serious outrages were reported to him. He did have authority to remand or discharge persons arrested, but matters of summary jurisdiction were left to the local justices of the peace. The position of chief magistrate carried the title of major.

In the early nineteenth century, policing was essentially a local matter. Criminals had little mobility. The only means of getting from one place to another was either on foot or horseback or by horse-drawn chaise or car, and the principal mode of contact between towns and cities was via the mail coach. Travel was slow, allowing for no rapid escapes.

Problems Experienced Getting Legislation Through Parliament

It was not without some difficulty that Chief Secretary Robert Peel had managed to get the legislation through parliament. He had earlier endeavoured to get the Insurrection Act for Ireland (47 Geo. 3, c. 13), dormant since 1810, back on the statute books and at the same time he wanted to have a proper permanent police system put in place for Ireland. He was supported by the Irish viceroy and by the British home secretary, Viscount Sidmouth, but the prime minister, Lord Liverpool, opposed both proposals very strongly. He considered the Insurrection Act a coercive measure and took very serious objection to the term "police", considering it to imply an abhorrent Continental system for government oppression and the curtailment of freedom.

In 1814 Peel reintroduced his bill before parliament. This time he avoided any reference to "police" and likened his proposed Peace Preservation Force to the Bow Street horse patrol in London, which had been introduced in 1805 while Lord Liverpool had been home secretary. Peel's masterly and diplomatic presentation of the bill gained favour, and it was passed into law. No doubt buoyed by this success, a few weeks later he steered through the reintroduction of the Insurrection Act. He argued that this act was originally passed by the Dublin parliament in 1796 and that the bill was only required as a reserve measure in the event of all other legislation proving inadequate.

The Peace Preservation Force, 1814

The first detachment of the Peace Preservation Force was assigned to the barony of Middlethird in County Tipperary in September 1814 under the command of Major Wilcocks. He set up the headquarters for his unit in Cashel. A state of lawlessness connected with agrarian problems existed in this barony during 1811, 1812 and 1813. Two factions, the "Shanavests" and the "Caravats", as well as a number of criminal groups, had terrorised the district, and this terror had spread into the adjoining counties of Kilkenny and Waterford. In a very short period of time, the force had restored law and order in the barony. The initial success of the force was most encouraging. The new force had authority to operate with much flexibilty; at very short notice they could be drafted into any area under the provisions of the act. In 1815, Major Darcy, with 100 constables and sub-constables, was despatched to County Louth and Major Warburton, also with 100 constables and sub-constables, was sent to County Clare. While operating in any district, they were under the direction of their chief constable, who worked in close co-operation with the local chief magistrate. The districts where the force was employed were responsible for the remuneration of the force. This system had its own drawbacks: the administrators in many counties were loath to admit that they had a problem when it would cost them money to have it rectified.

Within a very short time, the members of the force became known as "Peelers" – a term which has frequently been used in reference to the Irish Constabulary, Royal Irish Constabulary and indeed to the Garda Síochána and the Royal Ulster Constabulary ever since. The catchy term cannot be attributed to any particular individual, nor is there any record of when it was first used. As a synonym for all the police forces in Ireland since 1814, it is now heading for its bicentenary. The term is perceived as being a derisory one and very few policemen – if any – who served their full service in Ireland over the last 180 years have escaped without, at one time or another, being called a Peeler by some disaffected client, usually by one with a particular political or anti-establishment orientation. The use of the word by any person towards the police almost invariably indicates the nationalist personality and character (to put it at its mildest) of the person using it.

Around the year 1830, a poet who was also a farmer and hedge-schoolteacher, Darby Ryan of Bansha, County Tipperary, composed a lengthy ballad with numerous verses titled "The Peeler and the Goat". A very popular ballad, sung in Ireland for well over a hundred years, it apparently relates to the impounding of a goat in the Bansha area by the constabulary. The first two verses and concluding two verses of the very lengthy ballad are as follows:

The Peeler and the Goat

The Bansha Peelers went out one night on duty and patrolling-O,
And they spied a goat upon the road and took him for a strolling-O,
With bayonets fixed they sallied forth and caught him by the wizen-O,
And then swore a mighty Oath, they'd send him off to prison-O.

"Oh Mercy, Sir," the goat replied, "and let me tell my story-O,
I'm no rogue, no Ribbonman, no Croppy, Whig or Tory-O,
I'm guilty not of any crime of petty or high treason-O,
And our tribe is wanted at this time for this is the ranting season-O."

Final two verses:

"The consequences be what they will, a peeler's power I'll let you know,
I'll handcuff you at all events and march you to the Bridewell-O,
And sure, you rogue, you can't deny before the judge or jury-O,
Intimidation with your horns and threatening me with fury-O."

"I make no doubt you are drunk, with whiskey, rum and brandy-O,
Or you wouldn't have such gallant spunk to be so bold or manly-O,
You readily would let me pass if I had money handy-O,
To treat you to a poteen glass -'tis then I'd be the dandy-O."

The members of the Peace Preservation Force were the first paid policemen in Ireland. Their predecessors had acted only on a voluntary basis, being entitled only to expenses in connection with duty performed by them and an annual payment of £4 – not a living wage. Members of the new force were also authorised to pay money to informants, and there were many instances of abuse relating to this.

After their success in County Tipperary, there was a continuous demand for the services of the force over the next few years. It was in fact a flying squad or riot squad, moving from one district in the country to another, quelling disturbances. It had a very high level of success, particularly in Cork, Limerick and Tipperary, where there was serious crime, as well as disturbances arising from faction fights.

In February 1815, a petition was sent to the viceroy by the magistrates attached to the barony of Middlethird in County Tipperary, to have the Peace Preservation Act replaced by the Insurrection Act. This petition was followed by a number of others, all similar in nature, aiming to have the stipendiary or paid magistrates removed from office, thereby handing back power to the local magistrates. With on-going friction between the local magistrates and the stipendiary magistrates, the local magistrates saw their power and influence being whittled away. Furthermore, local taxpayers thought that pay for armed troops would come from central government funds, rather than being an expense on the county as was the case with the Peace Preservation Force.

Peel did not accede to these petitions, but he had an amendment passed to the Peace Preservation Act which resulted in the government's paying two-thirds of the cost of the Peace Preservation Force.

A vivid eyewitness account from Maryborough (now Portlaoise) conveys the appearance of the force:

> I was standing at assize time, in the street of Maryborough, near the hotel, when I heard the sound of horsemen rapidly approaching and suddenly a body of forty men came sweeping round the corner at a sharp trot, scarcely giving me time to get out of their way. They drew up opposite the hotel, under the command of Major Nicholson (then late of the Wicklow militia) who was commandant of so much of the Peace Preservation Force as were then in the province of Leinster. This officer wore a dark blue jacket, closely braided in front with round black silk cord, and small black buttons, red cuffs and collar, red and gold lace girdle, and tall beaver cap and feathers with crescent Turkish-shaped scimitar. Of the men, ten wore scarlet cloaks over their uniforms, reaching down over their horses tails, brass helmets, and plumes and "Waterloo" on the helmets. Ten were in hussar uniforms with loose jackets slung over the shoulders and hussar saddles with sheepskin. Ten others were in uniform, and sitting behind them on pads were "voltigeurs" with short rifles resting on the thigh. These "voltiguers" were made to dismount and remount occasionally by their eccentric commander. This motley force was brought in for duty, attending upon judges and escorting prisoners etc. They were mounted on splendid horses, several of

which were worth from fifty pounds to one hundred pounds, as at that time the finest horses in the world were in this country.

This Major Nicholson was also known to attend at fairs where serious faction fights took place. He and his men dashed in at a charge at the faction fighters and spectators with scarlet cloaks floating in the wind, causing the country folk to scatter in all directions and putting an end to their activities. On other occasions he drove in a light chaise drawn by four horses and postillions, with two outriders in front and two behind carrying their rifles. Occasionally he was accompanied by a bugler who gave notice to all and sundry of their arrival and presence in the locality. The major had much influence with government, which, it was said, had supplied him with the "Waterloo" helmets and cloaks.

After the Napoleanic Wars, thousands of Irishmen who had fought in the wars returned to Ireland. Badly off financially and many in poor health, they were restless, idle and troublesome over the next few years. As well, the harvests of 1816 and 1817 were bad, resulting in a lot of poverty, and disease.

By 1818 there was general disorder throughout the country. While the Peace Preservation Force coped fairly well, it was evident that some changes in policing would have to be made. The force, despite its successes, failed to find favour with the government. The people of Ireland had at all times a hatred for the militias based throughout the country, and in 1814 Robert Peel, addressing parliament, said: "The frequent use of soldiers in that manner, made the people look upon them as their adversaries rather than as their protectors." As time went by, the people equated the Peace Preservation Force with the military, and they were totally opposed to its tactics. Major Going, who was the chief constable in charge of the Peace Preservation Force for County Limerick, was shot dead near Rathkeale in 1821. An inquiry into his death followed, and it transpired that he was the leader of an Orange Lodge within the force.

Despite legislation in 1822 setting up a new policing system, the force remained in existence until it was disbanded under the Irish Constabulary Act, 1836.

It had fulfilled one positive achievement in that it bridged the gap between the old baronial constabulary and watch systems and the establishment of a newer and more modern civil police forces, helping to break down the traditional, but the very inefficient magisterial system.

Chapter Two

1822–1836

THE ORGANISATION OF THE COUNTY CONSTABULARY

Robert Peel, on taking up his position as home secretary, was again confronted with a seriously deteriorating law and order situation in Ireland. To rectify the situation, he steered a bill through parliament (3 Geo. 4, c. 103) on 5 August 1822 – otherwise known as the Constabulary Act. This act empowered the lord lieutenant to appoint a chief constable in each barony and to require, by proclamation, the magistrates of each county to appoint a limited number of constables for the same – sixteen to each barony within the county. The chief, and other constables so appointed, were to be under the supervision of four inspectors general – one for each province. This act superseded the power of the grand juries to appoint constables, and under it constabularies organised on a county basis were inaugurated. The act did not however repeal the Peace Preservation Act already in existence, which was left on the statute books. The new constabulary was a para-military force, commanded by former army officers, and the inspector general in each province had autonomous control over his province as the legislation actually provided for four separate provincial constabularies for Ireland – excluding Dublin, Belfast and Derry cities.

The act authorised, for the whole of Ireland, a combined force of 313 chief constables and 5,008 constables, assigned (see overleaf):

The new force was not organised all at once but according to proclamation as announced in the *Dublin Gazette*. It was organised on a county-by-county basis, with the counties where the Peace Preservation Force was operating being left to last. The first members of the new constabulary made their appearance in County Limerick on 24 October 1822. The next contingents were sent to Counties Cork,

Province	Chief Constables	Constables
Leinster	114	1,824
Ulster	74	1,184
Munster	67	1,072
Connaught	58	928
Total	313	5,008

Offaly, Waterford, Kerry and Tipperary on 31 October of the same year. For periods, both forces continued to work in the same counties as independent forces, each under separate control. While there was little legal basis for the title, the new police force became commonly known as the "county constabulary" because each county was organised independently within its province, rather than on the old baronial system. The force was also referred to occasionally as the "constabulary police".

The majority of the recruits were farmers' sons from all over Ireland, with a small number being from the ascendancy classes. They responded well to the demands made of them. They were well disciplined and restrained in confrontational situations and benefited from good leadership. In instructions issued from Dublin Castle in 1824 the official items of uniform and accoutrements for each member of the force were classified as "clothing" or "necessaries". The clothing for unmounted men was a coat, undress jacket, trousers, duck trousers, flannel drawers, great coat and cap with tuft and oilskin cover. The "necessaries" included a forage cap, stock and clasp, knapsack and straps, haversack, greatcoat straps, belt clasp, set of brushes, picker and brush, and a turn-screw and worm (handcuffs). It took some time before the force became consistent in wearing the standard uniform, specified for the new force as a "rifle-green" frock-coat and trousers and a black shako, cylindrical-shaped cap for dress, with a soft cloth cap and short or slop jacket for undress, with Russian duck trousers for summer. ("Rifle-green" refers to the colour of the uniform worn by the Rifle Brigade at the time.) The members were armed with short flintlock carbines which were subsequently replaced with carbines having percussion locks.

A headquarters for the new force was set up in each province: at Armagh for Ulster, Ballinrobe for Connaught, Ballincollig for Munster and Philipstown (now Daingean, County Offaly), for Leinster. The first four inspector generals were Major Darcy for Ulster, Major Warburton for Connaught, Major Wilcocks for Munster and Major Powell for Leinster. Each of these inspector generals had previously been in charge of sections of the earlier Peace Preservation Force. Each had carved out an excellent reputation for himself in different ways.

Major Darcy was a native of County Westmeath and was appointed a brigade major of the County Longford Yeomanry in 1803. Some years later he was appointed a magistrate. In 1813 he inherited an extremely difficult assignment as a magistrate, when work on the construction of the Royal Canal came to a sudden halt due to a dispute amongst workmen and sub-contractors engaged by the main contractors. It was imperative that the work should proceed, and the government directly took on the construction work which had to be completed under military and constabulary protection with Major Darcy in charge of the security operation. Over a period of three years the next thirty miles was completed against all the odds. In 1816 he was transferred as a special magistrate to the Innishowen Peninsula following the brutal murder of Norton Butler, a landlord at Grouse Hall. A short time afterwards, the Peace Preservation Act was invoked for the peninsula and Major Darcy and his contingent of twenty men were quartered at Grouse Hall. To deal with a serious illicit distillation problem in the district he was given another thirty men as an experiment by the Board of Excise to enforce the revenue laws, and it proved a success. He was a well-qualified man when appointed inspector general for Ulster.

Major Richard Wilcocks was a native of County Dublin and had been a captain of yeomanry in the county for some years up to 1808. He was then appointed a magistrate and served in a number of southern counties until 1814. He was appointed chief magistrate for the barony of Middlethird in County Tipperary in 1814 and commanded the first detachment of the Peace Preservation Force to that barony which was then in a disturbed state. He restored law and order in the barony and a few years later he was given responsibility for the adjoining barony of Clanwilliam. While in County Tipperary he was based at Cashel. Regarded as being extremely efficient in the discharge of his duties, he managed to assert his authority over the local magistreates. In November 1821 he transferred to Rathkeale, County Limerick. In 1823 he took up his appointment as the first inspector general for the province of Munster. Towards the end of 1827 his health broke down and he had to resign his post; he was replaced by Inspector General W. Miller.

Major George Warburton was an extremely able and capable individual who already had a proven record in policing and a reputation for his down-to-earth humanity when dealing with people. He was a native of Garryhinch near Tullamore, County Offaly. In 1815, he was assigned to Clare as chief magistrate, with 100 constables and sub-constables as a unit of the Peace Preservation Force. He set up his headquarters in Kilrush town. He brought the disorder and lawlessness in Clare to an end, apparently in a low-profile way. Rough or tough tactics by those under his command were not permitted, and he persistently encouraged his men to deal with people in a mannerly and mild way and with as little vexation towards people as possible. This is the first record of an attitude such as this being displayed by any peace keeping force or constabulary in the country. It was a new approach and in this regard Major Warburton was ahead of his time.

He also responded to the poverty arising from recurring famines in County Clare in the early 1820s. He arranged to have a survey carried out of poor people in the county and discovered that there were about 75,000 badly off. He endeavoured to get work schemes going so that people could have an opportunity to earn money. In 1822, when County Clare was hit by a very bad famine, the policing of the county ceased to be his priority and he threw himself and the personnel and resources available to him wholeheartedly into providing for the poor and destitute. He was instrumental in having the collection of the county rate in Clare suspended for that year, to relieve the distress of the poor. Not alone that, but he put pressure on the landed gentry and wealthy people of the county to contribute to a fund which he had set up for the relief of the poor. He managed to raise over £3,000 – a big sum in 1822. He also succeeded in getting a grant from government funds of £2,000 and with this he purchased yellow corn meal. He arranged the distribution of five tons of the meal in each of the nine baronies within the county. When fever and dysentry followed the famine, he maintained pressure on the authorities for greater care and medical facilities, and he likewise kept persuading the well-off people in the county to keep up their generosity.

His work with the poor people – particularly during the 1822 famine period – did not go unnoticed by the London authorities and he was later appointed a member of the Irish committee in London for the relief of the poor. The exceptional work done by Major Warburton and those under his command for the people in County Clare was above and beyond the call of police duty. It indicated the type of humane person which he was, and his endeavours in Clare can be recorded as being the first solid and successful effort at "community policing" in Ireland.

On his transfer to Connaught as inspector general for that province in 1823, there was much genuine regret at his departure from County Clare. A large public meeting in Kilrush was presided over by the parish priest, Revd Matthew Corbett. By any standard, this was an extraordinary event for the time. In an address presented to him, by Fr Corbett, Major Warburton was described as being a friend of the poor and an efficient protector of law and order. Again in later years, he displayed his humanity and feelings and consideration for the underprivileged of society when he took an absolute stand against the local magistrates by refusing to allow the constables under his command to execute at night time warrants issued by the magistrates for petty offences and minor matters. His authorities at Dublin Castle supported his view.

A *Garda Review* feature of November 1986 titled "Genesis of the Code; Rules and Regulations", by Garda archivist Gregory Allen observes:

The Garda Síochána Code, based in its first edition (1928) on the Code of the Royal Irish Constabulary, originated in the rules and regulations devised for the Peace Preservation Force (1814) and the County Constabulary (1822). They first appeared in a booklet compiled by George Warburton, printed in Ennis, Co Clare on 2nd March 1820. In a slight publication of eight pages, Warburton stressed the need for sobriety and avoidance of "profane or immoral" conduct. Members of the Peace Preservation Force were required to attend divine service on Sundays. The highest standards of professional and personal deportment were demanded. It was of great importance that the men should be respected by the people.

The foregoing speaks for itself and indicates the high standards which Major Warburton aspired to for his men. It may well have been the first written police code.

The Barrack Regulations

During the same period the "Munster Constabulary Barrack Regulations" were drawn up by Inspector General W. Miller of Munster:

1. The Constable in Charge of the Station, will be careful to instruct the men, under his orders, as to the Duties of their office as Constables and will see that they make themselves acquainted with the contents of the Books provided for that purpose. He will impress upon their minds, that they are not only required to be vigilant in the prevention and detection of Crime, but are to endeavour, by a just, temperate and impartial exercise of their authority, to secure to themselves the confidence of all classes of the Community.

2. He will be responsible that the Rules, Orders and Regulations of the establishment are duly enforced, that the men are regular in their conduct, cleanly in their Persons, neat and uniform in their Dress, civil and conciliating in their demeanour towards their Fellow-Subjects.

3. He will be answerable for the Cleanliness of the Barrack; that the Arms, Appointments, Ammunition and articles of Furniture, are kept in good order. All damages must be immediately reported.

4. There will be a daily Parade, under Arms, at 9 oclock in Summer and at 10 oclock in Winter, when the Constable in charge will inspect the men of the Party and see that they are clean and properly shaved, uniform in their appearance and that their Arms are in order.

5. The Constabulary of Munster are to appear in full marching order, at the morning Parade, on every Sunday throughout the year.

6. An Orderly is to be named daily, for duty for 24 hours. He is charged with the care of the Barracks, which he is not to quit while thus on duty. He is not to undress during the night but is to be in readiness to answer any call and to rouse his comrades in case of alarm. The Constable in charge, is to take his turn of this duty, wherever the Party consists of less than five effective Policemen.

7. The men are not permitted to work at Trades nor to engage in private pursuits. Their time belongs to the public and is to be devoted to its Service.

8. The bedding is to be folded every morning by eight oclock in Summer and nine oclock in Winter. No deviation from this Regulation will be tolerated, excepting in cases of sickness. The rooms must be swept out and set in order, by the above mentioned hours. By the summer season it is to be understood the term comprised between 1st April and 1st October.

9. The men are prohibited from using their bedsteads, as seats when folded up.

10. The Sheets are to be changed on the first Monday of every month. The soiled ones are to be washed, under the directions of the Constable in charge and the cost is to be defrayed by the men.

11. Clean Straw, in the proportion of 24lbs. for each Paillasse, will be granted once in every three months and the amount will be admitted as a charge in the Lodging Allowance.

12. The Officer of the District will minutely inspect the articles of furniture and bedding, at least once a month. If any part of the latter be found unduly dirty, he will order it to be immediately washed, at the expense of the person for whose use it was allotted. The women and children of the Constables are prohibited from using any part of the Bedding belonging to the Establishment.

13. No Dogs, or Pigs, are to be kept in any House, Out-house, or Yard, belonging to any premises used as a Barrack for the Constabulary.

14. The Men, under the direction of the Constable in charge, are to keep every part of the barrack, its Approaches, the Passages and yards. clean and in good order; and are to study to uphold an appearance of regularity and neatness, in every thing connected with their Post.

15. The Constable in charge will be held responsible that this table of orders is hung up in a conspicuous part of the barrack, that it is kept clean and not defaced, and that he will read it aloud, from beginning to end, to the men on Parade on the First Sunday of every month.

Recruiting and Training for the County Constabulary

The members who joined the new force mostly came from rural farming backgrounds and some had military service. They underwent three months training at their provincial headquarters: Ballinrobe, Philipstown, Ballincollig and Armagh. Much of the training consisted of drill and, as it was an armed force, there was much emphasis on firearms training. On completion of the training, they were allocated to a county within that province. Provision was also made under the act for the purchase of horses and accoutrements, and some members were trained to form mounted units within the force. The horses were allocated to the principal barracks in each county.

The force's priority was the protection of life and property and the provision of security for all citizens, and it had a large measure of success. As its protective nature became more understood. its influence with the people – particularly with the ascendancy classes – increased, resulting in a gradual decrease in crime. The Catholic population, however, looked on the force as being partisan. The officers were Protestant, as were the majority of the constables. Orange Lodges were known to exist amongst its members.

As the appointment of the constables in the force was the prerogative of the magistrates, it resulted in the constabulary not having the freedom and independence which it should have had and it remained too closely aligned to the magistrates in the eyes of the poorer classes. On several occasions when the constabulary intervened to quell faction fights, both factions joined forces and fought the police. The Catholic Emancipation campaign of the 1820s, as well as agrarian troubles at that time, caused much tension and unrest amongst the population, with Catholics marching openly and holding protest meetings until Catholic Emancipation was ratified in 1829. The constabulary could regard themselves as being fortunate in containing the situation up to that point.

The Tithes War

Immediately after the ratification of Catholic Emancipation, there followed a fresh campaign to abolish the payment of tithes to the clergymen of the established Protestant Church, which was at all times a source of grievance with the Roman Catholics. The practice was denounced openly by some prominent Catholic clergy, led by Bishop James Doyle of the Kildare and Leighlin diocese. In Waterford, a very well organised "Householders' Club" adopted a practice of permitting their goods to be seized in lieu of payment and later boycotting the sale of the seized goods. The campaign, so intensive that it was often referred to as the Tithes War, was at its worst between 1830 and 1834. A number of attempts were made through legislation to find a solution but they failed.

At Carrickshock near Hugginstown, County Kilkenny, on 14 December 1831, a process server named Butler, with several processes to serve for tithes due to the Revd Mr Hamilton, went to the Hugginstown area under the protection of Chief Constable Gibbons and thirty-six members of the constabulary. Some 2,000 country people assembled, all called together by the ringing of the Catholic chapel bells throughout the entire area, and ambushed the party at a laneway overlooked by high banks. The mob demanded that Butler be handed over to them and, when this was refused, they launched an attack on the entire party, hurling stones and missiles down from the banks. Because of the positions held by the attackers, it was difficult to discharge firearms at them. Eventually as the attackers became more exposed, the police did fire a volley of shots at them and two of the attackers were killed. Before the police had time to reload their weapons, a violent attack was made on them with sticks, stones, pitchforks, scythes, reaping hooks and iron bars. Chief Constable Gibbons and fourteen of his men were killed on the spot. Eight constables were very badly wounded, two of them and and Butler dying on the following morning. It was the biggest loss of life ever inflicted on constabulary or police in any one incident in Ireland.

On 23 May of the same year, a riot occurred between two factions at a fair in Castlepollard, County Westmeath. The police under Chief Constable Blake went to restore order, but to their surprise both factions joined forces against them and attacked the police with sticks, stones and other missiles. The police decided to withdraw to the barracks, but they found themselves cut off and totally surrounded. The police fired at the attackers, killing thirteen of their assailants. A verdict of manslaughter was brought in against Chief Constable Blake at the inquest into the deaths, but no further action was taken by the grand jury when the next assizes met. This incident, which had no connection with the collection of tithes but arose from a faction fight which were commonplace events at fairs all over Ireland during that part of the nineteenth century, shows the attitude of the local population towards the constabulary.

On 18 June of that year, another very serious incident took place at Newtown-barry (now Bunclody), County Wexford. Three heifers belonging to a local man named Doyle had been seized from him after he had refused to pay tithes to the local clergyman, the Revd Mr Erlington. A large number of local men gathered for the purpose of retrieving the animals. The bailiffs and an auctioneer were present under the protection of the constabulary led by Chief Constable King. During a skirmish, Mr Hoare, the justice of the peace, was knocked off his horse and seriously injured and his servant had one of his arms completely severed by a blow of a scythe. Despite the seriousness of the disturbance, Chief Constable King, confident that his force could handle the situation, decided that his party should not use their firearms as the crowd was so dense and so close. A group of about 150 mounted yeomanry who happened to be in the neighbourhood under the command of Captain

Graham entered the town to assist the constabulary. The chief constable begged Captain Graham to withdraw his men from the scene and assured him that the constabulary were capable of containing the situation and providing whatever protection was neccessary for the bailiffs and auctioneer. Captain Graham ignored the chief constable's request and, when a move was made to rescue the cattle, he ordered his troops to open fire. Seventeen people were shot dead and several people were seriously wounded. The constabulary discharged no firearms in this serious incident.

In 1834, a tithe collector at Rathcormac, County Cork, was attacked while collecting tithes. Several people were killed in the ensuing disturbance.

The Contribution Made by County Constabulary

The role of the Peace Preservation Force of 1814, which continued to operate under the direction of the chief magistrates was diminishing during the 1820s, but in the early 1830s it was brought back to full strength to assist the constabulary, and it provided a vital supporting role in quelling disturbances during these critical years.

One of the problems resulting from the 1822 legislation was that while the magistrates had the authority to appoint members to the new force, the management of the force was the responsibility of the inspector general in each province. Although the authorities never wanted the appointment of the constables to be in the hands of the magistrates, parliament had to accede to it to overcome opposition to the bill by Irish members. The magistrates, who were people of influence, did everything possible to assert control over the force, but the inspector generals held firm. This friction between the inspector generals and the magistrates continued until fresh legislation came in to force in 1836.

Each inspector general had his own view of how his province should be administered, and a rule which suited one province might not suit another. The four provinces in effect became four different constabulary forces despite the provisions of the 1822 act, which had provided rules and procedures for all. On 2 May 1825, with the approval of the lord lieutenant, "The Standing Orders and Regulations for the Conduct and Proceedings of the Chief Constables and other Constables in the County of ...." had been published.

After thirteen years' experience, the authorities decided that new legislation was essential to create uniformity in the constabulary and to provide for a general re-organisation. In fairness to the inspector generals who had held office from 1822 to 1836, it must be acknowledged that they were reasonably effective in controlling crime and maintaining peace and stability. Of the four original inspector generals, only Major Warburton remained in office when new changes were implemented in 1836.

Despite its many shortcomings, the constabulary force founded in 1822 was the forerunner of all police forces established in the British Isles or probably anywhere in the world. It was seven years ahead of the London Metropolitan Police force established by Robert Peel in 1829. The force had its share of disciplinary problems: a total of ninety-six members were dismissed over a three-month period early in 1836 because of their involvement with secret societies. While its lifespan was only thirteen years, the force did create basic model for subsequent police forces.

Chapter Three

1836–1864

THE FAMINE AND
THE 1848 UPRISING

Thomas Drummond was a native of Edinburgh and a qualified civil engineer by profession. Following his graduation he carried out work for the Ordnance Survey in Ireland and in the course of this work he travelled through the country. From 1824 to 1830 he made a special study of the character of the Irish people and their way of life and traditions. He spent the years 1828 and 1829 in Ireland, staying in the rural areas during the summer months and in Dublin during winter. It was acknowledged by everybody that Drummond had a great feel and love for Ireland and its people, with a particular interest in the poorer sections of society, and was never appreciated fully by the Irish people until after his untimely death in April 1840. He was under-secretary in Ireland from 1835 to 1840. His affection for the country was demonstrated by his wish to be buried in Ireland, and he is interred at Mount Jerome Cemetery in Dublin.

On his arrival as under-secretary, he immediately identified the need for a re-organisation of the policing system, particularly the neccessity of bringing it under central control. He caused outrage and anger amongst the landowning classes when, in the course of a reply to Lord Donoughmore of south Tipperary, a magistrate and a landowner who sought more protection against attacks, he stated: "Property has its duties as well as its rights, to the the neglect of those duties in times past is mainly to be ascribed to the diseased State of Society in which crimes take their rise and it is not in the enactment or enforcement of statutes of extraordinary severity but in the better and more enlightened and humane exercise of those rights that a permanent remedy for such disorders is to be sought." In 1836, he and Lord Morpeth, the chief secretary, succeeded in pushing a bill through parliament (6 Wm. 4, c. 13), known as the Constabulary (Ireland) Act, 1836. He had previously endeavoured to get the bill through parliament where it was introduced on 10 August 1835, but having passed through the House of Commons (after much debate), it was rejected by the House of Lords, where very strong and impressive arguments were made against it, all on the side of the magistracy and aristocracy. One lord argued that the bill "would take the appointments out of the hands of the Magistrates who were a most excellent and fearless body of men". The objectors won the day and the bill was defeated by fifty-one votes to thirty-nine.

Lord Morpeth and Thomas Drummond strengthened the proposed measure, and it was again presented by Morpeth before the House of Commons. They were better prepared for the opposition on this occasion. In a spirited contribution in support of the bill, Robert Peel stated that it was better to have the police appointed by the Crown than by any local authority. His contribution ensured an easy passage for the bill through the House of Commons. Opposition in the House of Lords was this time based on the extra costs of the new proposed force – more than £200,000 annually in excess of the previous force – rather than the interests of the magistrates. There was stiff opposition to the proposal, which was led by the Duke of Wellington. After some negotiations the proposed number of county inspectors was reduced and the bill passed into law on 20 May 1836.

When Peel had tried to get this type of legislation through parliament twenty-three years earlier, every effort had been frustrated by the magistracy, aristocracy and landholding classes. The delay caused much frustration for the Dublin Castle authorities during the intervening period. Peel and Drummond were discouraged by the fact that the magistrates had so much control and influence over the policing situation that the constabulary force could only be regarded as a partisan force. They had an intimate knowledge of the Irish people and Ireland and they were well aware of all the shortcomings of the previous policing systems.

The Principal Provisions of the 1836 Act

The new act abolished the Peace Preservation Force and incorporated the four provincial forces into one national force – excluding Dublin and Belfast which had their own separate police forces. The entire force was put under the control of one inspector general, who was directly responsible to the lord lieutenant and the chief secretary. The inspector general was – subject to the approval of the lord lieutenant – responsible for introducing a code of regulations for the conduct of the force and for the proper distribution of all the officers and men. Local magistrates lost their powers to appoint constables, who henceforward were to be recruited and trained by the force itself. Provision was made in the act for the retention of all inspectors, chief constables and constables then serving, subject to their subscribing to the prescribed oath within one month.

An order was made that all houses, horses, arms, accoutrements, saddles, bridles, books, papers and appointments, etc. already in possession of magistrates and constables under previous acts were to be handed over to the control of the new force. The uniform of the new force was again rifle green in colour, and this continued to be the official colour of the Royal Irish Constabulary and later the Royal Ulster Constabulary uniforms. The changeover went smoothly, with the existing constabulary manning their barracks and continuing to perform police work as they had been doing.

The legislation of 1836 was the basis for the policing of Ireland while it remained under British rule until 1922.

Administration of the Force

The top administration of the force consisted of one inspector general, two deputy inspector generals and four county inspectors. The latter were later reduced to two and became known as provincial inspectors. Thirty-five sub-inspectors were appointed – two each for Counties Cork, Tipperary and Galway, and one for each of the remaining counties. These sub-inspectors were later redesignated as county inspectors. The number of chief constables was not fixed but left to the discretion of the lord lieutenant, and under later legislation they were redesignated as sub-inspectors. Eighteen paymasters were appointed to attend to the pay and allowances of the new force. The inspector general and both deputy inspector generals were obliged to reside in Dublin. The Constabulary Office was established and took up almost a complete wing in the Lower Castle Yard of Dublin Castle All official correspondence from the thirty-two counties was directed to the inspector general's office.

The salary of the inspector general was £1,500 per annum; the deputies £800 each; the county inspectors £500 each; the sub-inspectors £250; and the chief-constables £150. The salary of head constables was fixed at £70, constables received £35 and sub-constables £25 per annum.

Section 6 of the 1836 act empowered the inspector general:

> To establish such rules, orders and regulations for the general arrangement of the several persons to be appointed under the Act, as well with respect to the places of their residence, their classification, rank and particular services, their distribution and inspection, as to the description of their arms and accoutrements, and other necessaries to be furnished to them, and which of them should be supplied with horses, and all such

other rules, orders and regulations relative to the said force, so as to render it efficient for the discharge of the several duties thereof.

The remodelling of the force proved to be an enormous task. Problems were encountered with the rank structures and particularly with the classes within the ranks and the relative pay structures. It was found necessary to introduce the new ranks of head constable and acting constable. The member in charge of a barracks was a "constable", and the "acting constable" was introduced for the purpose of ensuring responsibility for barrack control in the event of absence or illness of the constable. In 1883, the rank of constable was changed to sergeant, and sub-constables became constables. Constables wore three gold chevrons on their arm, while acting-constables wore two.

Establishment of Barracks and Sub-Districts

The baronial system was found to be impractical, and the sub-districts system was selected for policing by small units. The sub-districts consisted of approximately the same area in size and a similar number of townlands (normally about 100). The barracks for the sub-district was located as near as practical to the centre of the area. Where a town or village was situated close to the centre of the sub-district, the barracks was located there, but in many cases the constabulary barracks was a lone house at a crossroads many miles from a town or village. One-third of all barracks – 567 – were described as rural roadside barracks.

The badge of the force which was made of heavy black metal, fourteen inches deep and ten inches wide, was displayed over the main entrance door. The word "Constabulary" was painted in large, raised, white letters on a half-circle between a shamrock leaf in the centre and a crown on top. This was the official badge of the force until its title was changed to the "Royal Irish Constabulary". The sub-district was distinguished by the name of the town or village, or by the name by which the locality was best known. Within the space of a few years, constabulary barracks existed all over the country, including some of the inhabited islands off the coast, and by the year 1852 there was a total of 1,594 barracks, No place in Ireland was more than walking distance from a constabulary barracks.

In 1840, the barracks occupied by the constabulary at Arklow, Baltinglass, Banagher, Ballaghadereen, Ballinrobe, Bandon, Carrick-on-Shannon, Clogheen, Dunmore, Foxford, Meelick, Mitchelstown, Roscommon, Sligo, Waterford and Wexford were disused military barracks. The constabulary at Athy, County Kildare, had the distinction of being housed in a castle in the centre of that town. Very few barracks in Ireland had been purposely built for the constabulary. Those which were included the Curragh, Ballinacurra, the Heath, Macroom, Mulgrave, Longwood,

Glenbane and Lisclougher. In 1868 the following instruction was given by the inspector general: "When selecting a house to rent as a barracks, officers should choose a building which is dry and has a supply of water on or near the premises. It should be spacious. It should be slated and detached from other buildings but a thatched house could be rented if no slated one is available."

Most of the sub-districts as then constituted under the 1836 act have remained intact for policing purposes in Ireland until the present day. It was remarkable how quickly and efficiently the new constabulary force became established and settled in barracks all over the country.

Mr and Mrs S.C. Hall, in the course of their travels in Ireland in 1840, made the following observations about the new force in their book *Hall's Ireland*:

> During our latest visit to Ireland, we had frequent opportunities of testing the advantages that had accrued to the community at large from the admirable mode in which this force is conducted. Our attention was first attracted by the exceedingly neat and clean-looking houses, fitted up as their barracks, in many instances built expressly for them, and the remarkably soldier-like air and manner of the fine-looking young men who compose the corps. The first police station we visited was at Ballyneen [Ballineen], a village near Dunmanway [County Cork] which we were merely passing through, and of course, as our inspection was quite unlooked for, it was consequently unprepared for. The sergeant, a remarkably fine and intelligent young man, Alex Hewston, readily complied with our request to be permitted to examine the barrack. It contained five men, strong and active fellows; the rooms were all whitewashed; the little garden was well cultivated and free from weeds. The men slept on iron bedsteads, and the palliasses, blankets, pillows etc were neatly rolled up and placed at the head of each. The Fire-arms and bayonets, each as polished as a mirror, were hung up over each bed, and the floors were as clean as a new pin. Each man had his small box at his bed foot. All was in as perfect order as if all had been prepared in this little out-of-the-way place for the accustomed call of an inspector. The sub-inspector we learned visited the station once a month and the county inspector once a quarter. In this barracks, the men were all bachelors but it is not unusual to assign one married man with his wife to each barrack – the wife of course, arranging the rooms, and providing the meals of the men who always mess together. We afterwards examined many other stations and invariably our first impressions were borne out.

At all times up to 1922 there was absolute obsession about the cleanliness of barracks and the general tidiness of gardens and surrounds.

The First Inspector General

Colonel Shaw Kennedy was the first inspector general. He was assisted in his office by two deputies: Major Warburton and Major (later Colonel) Miller. Both deputies had formerly served as provincial inspector generals and Major Warburton had been one of the first officers appointed in 1814 to lead the Peace Preservation Force.

There were four provincial depots for the training of recruits. The Leinster depot was at Phillipstown (later Daingean), under Major Holmes. That for Munster was at Ballincollig under Major Galway, Connaught was served by Ballinrobe under Major Priestly, and Ulster was served by the depot at Armagh under Captain Roberts. The inspector general brought in another six high-ranking military officers and appointed them as sub-inspectors. He had hoped that this intake of military officers would inject new blood into the veins of the police service, but it proved to be a mistake. In the military, everything had been very specific, with orders being promptly responded to and with systems and precedents to meet all contingencies. They found that police work was very much different, with varied problems every day and no ready solutions for many of them. Furthermore, their imposition on police officers with several years service was not welcomed by the latter.

A military captain who had been appointed county inspector for Carlow and who was on duty in Carlow town for an election had an altercation with the resident magistate. He not only refused to take orders from the magistrate about the suppression of a riot, but had to be restrained to prevent him from inflicting personal violence on the magistrate. Colonel Shaw Kennedy had the county inspector transferred to Mayo and recommended his dismissal, but the government refused. The inspector general saw this as interference with his office by government and, on principle, he resigned his position.

Appointment of Colonel Duncan McGregor as Inspector General

The appointment of a successor to Colonel Shaw Kennedy created problems. Major Warburton who was the senior deputy inspector general felt that he should get the position, but Colonel Duncan McGregor, who was serving with a regiment in Canada, was written to and offered the appointment. He did not reply with any degree of urgency but the position was kept open for him. The failure to appoint Major Warburton to the fill the vacancy in the first place defies comprehension. He had been involved in police work in Ireland from 1814 onwards and had acquitted himself with distinction. (See Chapter 1.) As certain legal documents of the day could only be signed by the inspector general, Major Warburton was appointed on a *pro tempore* basis to carry out the duties of inspector general. He held the post for some time, but when Colonel McGregor finally did arrive, Major Warburton refused to step down without compensation. Possession was nine points of the law, and the government had little alternative but to award Major Warburton a substantial pension of £1,500 per annum.

Colonel McGregor was sworn in on 1 July 1838 as the new inspector general. He settled in well and gained the respect of those under his command and the high regard of the general public. In *Hall's Ireland*, Mr and Mrs S.C. Hall commented on their acquaintence with him in 1840:

> The present Inspector General is Colonel McGregor, an officer of great experience, derived from sources in various parts of the world. It is admitted on all hands, that no man is better calculated to occupy so important a position; and he has succeeded – a task by no means easy – in governing the force without incurring the charge of recognising any party. Indeed, the great efficiency of the force arises from the fact that its chief officers have removed all suspicion of its being biased by undue motives, and to the respect and esteem in which the Inspector General is universally held. He is emphatically popular among all the classes. In every instance where we consulted the officers or the men upon this point, we received but one answer given with a feeling akin to personal affection. Colonel McGregor had been known to the world prior to his appointment in Ireland. It was this officer who published an account of the loss of "The Kent" by fire in the Bay of Biscay, and to whose own share of exertion on the melancholy occasion, testimony has been borne by every survivor, except himself.

Strength of the Constabulary Force

When the constabulary force had been reorganised and become operational *circa* 1840, the strengths of the various ranks were as follows:

    1 inspector general
    2 deputy inspector generals
    4 county (later provincial) inspectors
    35 sub-inspectors
    217 chief constables
    260 head constables
    1,350 constables
    8,000 (approx.) sub-constables

A decade later, the strength of the force was 10,500

The Constabulary Oath

The wording of the oath taken by all members of the constabulary on their entrance to the force was approved of by statute (6 Wm. 4, c. 12). It prohibited the members from being members of any secret or political society but made an exemption for the Freemasons, which was regarded as a charitable organisation. It was recommended by their authorities that the members should commit it to memory, so that they might always bear in mind the solemn obligations they were required to fulfil. The words of the oath were as follows:

> I, A..... B...., do swear that I will and truly serve Our Sovereign Lord the King [or Queen], in the office of [Inspector, Constable, Sub-Constable, etc.] without Favour or Affection, Malice or Ill Will; that I will see and cause His Majesty's Peace to be kept and preserved, and that I will prevent, to the best of my power, all Offences against the same; and that while I shall continue to hold the said Office, I will, to the best of my skill and knowledge, discharge all the duties thereof, in the execution of Warrants and otherwise, faithfully according to Law; and that I do not now belong, and that I will not, while I shall, hold the said Office, join, subscribe or belong to any political society whatsoever, or to any secret society whatsoever, except to the Society of Freemasons, So Help Me God.

The oath taken later by the Royal Irish Constabulary followed the same format.

The Constabulary Act, 1836, prohibited members of the force from having seats at parliament and from voting at elections.

The 1837 Code of Regulations

In 1837 the Constabulary Code of Regulations was published. It had 730 sections and was very comprehensive and far reaching. While issued by the inspector general, there can be little doubt but that Thomas Drummond, the under-secretary, had an input in to it. This Code provided the basis for all subsequent codes of the Royal Irish Constabulary, the Royal Ulster Constabulary and the Garda Síochána; many of its provisions were still in force up to the 1950s and a number still exist. The Code really set out a blueprint as to how a police force should be controlled and disciplined and laid down rules and regulations relating to the conduct of its individual members. This guideline for all subsequent police forces in Ireland was incorporated into the police codes of many European and Commonwealth countries.

The provisions of the Code of Regulations were obviously beneficial, because in 1864 Sir Henry Brownrigg (then inspector general) was in a position to report to his authorities:

An undeniable change was now effected in the character of the force. Graduations of rank were instituted; and discipline, before but partial and uncertain, was now established... The men were removed from their local connexions, amongst whom no policeman can in this country, for any length of time, impartially discharge his duty. They could no longer act, as many had known to do, as gatekeepers, gamekeepers, woodrangers and in other private capacities. Partiality, sectarian feeling and other private influences, ceased seriously to affect them; everything in short, calculated to impede them in the discharge of their proper functions was put out of the way.

During the 1830s a practice existed of using members of the constabulary for the private protection of some of the ascendancy classes, an abuse colluded in by the magistrates. In 1837, Shaw Kennedy, the inspector general, saw fit to issue the following circular:

His Excellency has established the rule, that it is only in cases of urgent neccessity that protection is to be afforded to individuals by placing members of the force in their premises. When individuals receive protection, they will in future be obliged to provide the men with lodgings, bedding and fuel; and to pay for each man a sum not exceeding one shilling per night.

When men of the force are thus employed for individual protection or the protection of any private property, it will be the duty of the officers of the force to fully inform me of the whole of the circumstances, in order that the daily allowance for each man employed may be regulated according to the circumstances of the case and the condition of the parties to whom the aid may be offered. The payments so made will be credited by the paymasters to the public in the accounts of the county, by deducting it from the charge of extra allowances, and to enable him to do so, Chief Constables are to account to him monthly in their pay bills – should there be any suspension of payment, the Chief Constable is to report to me, the cause of it and his opinion as to the neccessity for continuing the protection. The authority for granting the protection and fixing the rate of charges, is to be annexed to the pay list, where the deduction for it is made. The constables on such duty, being provided with lodging, bedding and fuel are not entitled to any allowance for being absent from their quarters at night.

It is clearly to be understood by the officers of the force, that these regulations will in no degree, diminish the strictness of the rule by which His Excellency refuses to place, or to leave parties for the protection of individuals, or of private property, except in cases of urgent neccessity, nor will they increase the discretionary power by which the officers of the force may now, in very urgent cases afford such protection without reference to me.

Early Progress of the Irish Constabulary

The new constabulary force showed great promise and made excellent progress in its early years. Galen Broeker, in *Rural Disorder and Police Reform in Ireland, 1812–1836*, observed:

> Testifying before a select committee of the House of Lords in 1839, Justice Arthur Moore, who had been a member of the Irish Judiciary since 1814, stated that he detected in Ireland "a tendency to a state of order and improvement which did not exist in the former periods". Moore was undoubtedly correct, for betwen 1835 and 1841 a "tendency" towards a more peaceful state of affairs could be detected, abetted by the legislative and administrative efforts of the Whig government. In 1835 an Irish municipal reform bill was introduced, based on the British Bill of the same year and designed to remodel the corrupt and exclusively protestant machinery of borough government in Ireland. In 1838, Ireland received the benefits of a Poor Law, and further tithe legislation was enacted during the same year. The tithe was converted to a rent charge based on 70 per cent of the normal value of the tithe, and all arrears were cancelled.
>
> As a further indication of the liberalisation of the Irish government under Russell [the home secretary] and his associates, a certain number of the higher posts in Government were after "caution and selection" given to Catholics. Three of the Irish judges appointed between 1835 and 1841 were Catholics and during this period, either the Attorney General or the Solicitor General was a Catholic. Russell was probably correct when he informed Mulgrave in 1837 that "the Catholic clergy have more confidence in our government than they have had at any time since the revolution of 1688." Of the Irish reforms instituted by the whigs during this period, the reform of the police system, was undoubtedly the most successful.

Policing the Faction Fights

The faction fights, unique to Ireland, were the most frequent occurrences requiring police attention during the first half of the nineteenth century. Long before the nineteenth century, stick fights between combatants were frequent in Ireland, and "stick trainers" instructed "students" in various methods of combat and in the selection and preparation of the most suitable and durable sticks. The practice may have originated purely for entertainment purposes. It did not cost money and was "the sport of the poor", confined exclusively to the lower classes. As it progressed late in the eighteenth century it became more organised and more vicious.

When Major General Thomas Powell, inspector of the Leinster constabulary, gave evidence before a committee of inquiry in June 1834, he described that a faction was a number of men assembled together under a leader, merely for the diversion of fighting, and that they fought sometimes to settle a dispute which had often been handed down from generation to generation. He also said that in England men fought for pleasure or prizes while in Ireland a spirit of pride and vanity moved the faction fighters. He expressed his amazement that large numbers of people in their hundreds and sometimes in their thousands could assemble together and disturb the peace without interference from and sometimes even with the licence of the police.

The fights were fought out between factions led by individuals who had already made a name for themselves at stick fighting. The original confrontation between factions may have been over a division of land, or trespass, or ladyfriends or any other grievance – real or imaginary. The factions continued to fight long after their original grievances were forgotten about, and the fights were carried on by a younger generation forced to uphold family reputations. In different parts of the country factions would sometimes agree on a truce while they jointly supported some other group or cause such as the whiteboys. They would resume their faction fighting when other problems were solved and continue as before. The factions lived in the same or adjoining neighbourhoods throughout the year without interfering with each other.

They travelled far and wide to select the most suitable type of fighting sticks, which were seasoned in manure heaps or lime or up the smoky turf chimneys, or perhaps soaked in whiskey or poteen. The faction fighters had special titles for their fighting sticks and "*Bás Gan Sagart*" (death without a priest) was a favourite one. A good knob on the stick was essential to inflict the maximum damage on the opponent. To retain a secure hold of the stick during fighting, a strong leather strap was sometimes attached to it. The factions met and fought on fair days, race days and on "pattern days". The latter were the local religious feast days when people congregated at holy wells or shrines in their districts and prayed and performed religious "rounds" to honour the patron saint of their parish or diocese. The fairs, races and religious services occupied everybody in the early part of the day. Then there was heavy drinking and a huge build-up of passion amongst the factions in preparedness for the anticipated faction fight. The consumption of poteen prior to the engagement itself was, in many parts of the country, an essential prerequisite.

The faction fights took place on the town or village squares or greens. As a prelude to the actual confrontation, various insults, catcalls and nicknames were traded between the opposing factions, with each faction having its own slogan or war cry. The womenfolk enthusiastically joined in by shouting and screaming and urging on the menfolk from their respective factions and dancing their own warlike dance during the build-up to the fight. Women occasionally participated, and their favourite weapon was a large stone in a stocking. When this was swung around, it had potential to cause serious injury. At the same time, it was considered to be "dishonour to a lady" to retaliate and strike her in reprisal.

The leaders took up positions facing each other in an open area with their sticks at the ready, and on a signal from the leader on either side the vicious fighting commenced. The leaders normally fought each other, to the cheers and urging-on of their supporters who my have numbered a hundred or more. Casualties were many; the fights very frequently ended with one or more deaths and many injured. The womenfolk dragged the wounded away and attended to their wounds. The fights often lasted for hours until both sides could fight no longer. After burying their dead and nursing their wounds, they again settled down to prepare for a repeat performance on the same race day, fair day or pattern day in the following year. The more famous faction fighters fought with a single well-prepared stick having a suitable knob; others fought with two sticks; while the more successful fought with a well-prepared stick in one hand and a suitably sized stone held in the other hand. Details of big faction fights held in towns and villages throughout the country, especially in the Munster counties, have lived on in folklore in their areas.

One of the earliest accounts of a faction fight was given by the travel writer the Revd J. Hall, who witnessed one at Limerick in 1807 and recounted the details in *A Tour Through Ireland in 1807*:

> I chanced to be a spectator of a battle of this description in Limerick which in ferocity surpassed anything I had seen and which indicates that at a distance from towns civilisation is making little progress. The battle took place, in consequence of a misunderstanding a few weeks before between two men at a neighbouring fair. The two, having fought, had to be separated. Each went to his friends and represented that he had been insulted. In consequence, hundreds on each side engaged to resent the quarrel. Having therefore according to agreement, met to fight in Limerick, they began about a half an hour after prayers but were separated by the magistrates. In the evening however, about five o'clock, the whole street again being full of people, I observed one fellow, surrounded by hundreds, without a coat, raise his arm and grasping a thick blackthorn cudgel, about four feet long, swing it around his head pronouncing aloud

(his companions having promised to support him) "Jesus be praised, Jesus, be praised for ever" after which an opening in the crowd was made. He ran down the street with hundreds after him armed with cudgels, to meet the opposite party. In a few minutes, hundreds of cudgels, in all directions were employed, the women as busy as the men. I observed one woman put in a stone at the mouth of a glove which she tied fast, to prevent the stone coming out and then knocked a man on the head, by which he came to the ground. Many of the women, having tied stones in the corners of their cloaks and pocket handkerchiefs, were employed in the same way. To the disgrace of the inhabitants, many of whom shouted and applauded those that were most active, calling them by name from their windows "Bravo. Well Done." while they hissed those disposed to be quiet. In the evening, great numbers of boys, some of them not more than twelve, in imitation of the men were fighting in good earnest, with sticks, scarcely any preventing them, except the magistrates who were going about taking the sticks from them. It was ten at night before the streets could be cleared. In a public house into which I stepped, to see what was doing, a crowd being about the door, I found numbers of both sexes employed in clipping hair, clotted with blood, from the heads of the combatants; and several shirts in the house red and stiff with blood. Man is perhaps, the only animal that bleeds at the nose though in health.

The baronial constabulary displayed very little interest in trying to stop the faction fights, and any serious attempts were made by the military rather than the police. Within a few years, the faction fights had spread all over the Munster area.

The magistrates displayed no great exertions in taking on the problem either. Perhaps they saw it as a natural outlet for the Irish to vent their feelings against each other, and while those being killed or seriously injured were Irish peasants, it did not concern them that much. Another reason put forward for the lack of interest by the magistrates was that many of them were either directly or indirectly connected with the liquor licensing trade, and the events connected with the faction fights were very remunerative for them. It was not unknown either for magistrates to take sides with some of the factions involved. With this lack of commitment by the constabulary and the magistrates to take on the problem, the number of such fights increased dra-·matically and reached a peak possibly during the 1820s. In Tipperary, nine were reported in 1808 and 102 were reported in 1836. Fourteen were reported in County Limerick in 1808 and seventy-five in 1812. Daniel O'Connell and the Catholic clergy at all times opposed and did everything possible to discourage the practice which they saw as evil. Bishops terminated pattern days in many parts of the country to reducing the number of suitable venues for combatants.

The faction fights are recounted in local history records, and the most authoritative book on the subject is that of Patrick O'Donnell, *The Irish Faction Fighters of the 19th Century* (1975).

The first police attempt made to come to grips with the problem was in 1814 when a detachment of the Peace Preservation Force was sent to Middlethird barony, County Tipperary, and took very stern measures in dealing with the problem there. However, there was no unified policing approach to the problem, especially to ensure that those involved were arrested or culprits later charged with murder or manslaughter. At some locations where trouble was expected the force stood by all day and nothing took place. Occasionally a large troop of mounted police would enter a town or village where faction fighting was taking place and charge forwards and backwards with their horses to scatter the assembly. In other cases they made a point of arriving late when the battle was over and taking stock of the casualties and arranging inquests on dead bodies. In a relatively small number of cases where those responsible were arrested, the penalties imposed were derisory, considering the serious nature of the charges preferred.

When the provincial constabularies were established in 1822, faction fighting had taken a firm hold in the rural areas. A report to the under-secretary at Dublin Castle on 13 May 1825 gave details of a faction fight organised for Tipperary town on the previous day, with 600 men on each side. The local magistrate had read the Riot Act, and the constabulary and local militia dispersed the crowd. On 17 July 1826, Mr E. Miller the chief magistrate for south Tipperary reported to Dublin Castle about a very serious riot between two factions at Kilfeacle on the previous day. The fight was between the Hogan and Hickey factions – each with about 300 men – and some of those involved were seen to have firearms. The police had to withdraw and the fight continued for another two hours. Several men on both sides were killed.

On 24 June 1829, a fair day, a big faction fight took place at Tipperary town between two factions who had fought it out against each other for many years. A number of people were killed and several were wounded. The police intervened and had to discharge their carbines in an effort to disperse the crowd. Both factions then joined forces and turned on the police. (This was not the only time this happened, which is probably another reason why the police so often turned a blind eye.) A sworn inquiry was held into the incident.

In June 1829, Borrisokane, a small town in north Tipperary, was the venue for a very vicious faction fight in which a number of of people were killed. One of the dead bodies was left in the local Catholic church until its interment. While the funeral was taking place on the following day, the mourners were fired upon by the faction who had come out worst in the fight, resulting in seven more deaths.

The bloodiest and most tragic of all such incidents took place on the annual race and pattern day at Ballyeagh on the northern bank of the Cashen river near

Ballybunion, County Kerry, on 24 June 1834, adjacent to what is now the world-famous Ballybunion Golf Course. While the exact number of casualties has never been established, at least twenty men were killed and several hundred injured. Two factions who had been fighting sporadically for years decided on one major fight at this location. The supporters on either side numbered between 1,000 and 1,200. The faction from the south side of the Cashen estuary had to cross the river by boats to do battle on the northern bank. The fight, as expected, was furious and bloody. The intervention of the police and military, who were present in large numbers, only worsened the situation, and the whole affair turned into a large scale riot. Eventually the faction from south of the river, which was getting the worst of the battle, started to retreat towards the river and their boats. Many of the casualties, so badly injured that they were unable to get into the boats, fell into the estuary and drowned. Their bodies were washed out to sea without any effort being made to rescue or recover them. There was very definite evidence that a young magistrate was present amongst the fighters and urging on one faction. He eventually got away with a very mild rebuke for his actions from the Dublin Castle authorities. An inquiry into the tragedy was held at Listowel constabulary barracks from 22 to 25 July 1834, but with the influential position of the magistrates of the day, very little resulted from it. Still, it was this faction fight more than anything else which finally influenced the authorities to take faction fighting seriously.

Select committees of inquiry were also set up in 1824, 1825, 1834 and 1837 to look into the problem of faction fighting in Ireland. Although very many people attended and gave evidence at these inquiries, including priests and clergymen, nothing much came of them other than a concensus of opinion that a problem existed for the constabulary.

Thomas Drummond regarded faction fighting as a type of tribal warfare, and a growing evil which he was most determined to stamp out. As soon as the Irish Constabulary was established in 1836 he directed that its main priority would be to put an end to faction fighting. He insisted on the prompt and accurate reporting of every such incident, and chief constables were called upon to account for any held in their districts. He made public appeals, encouraging people to desist from taking part in or supporting faction fights. He directed that the new constabulary were to attend in force at fairs, patterns, race meetings or any other venue where such fights were likely to take place, to act quickly and efficiently in quelling any disturbances and to arrest those taking part. Faction fighters were to be identified, tracked down and charged with any breaches of the law committed by them. Aware that excessive drinking contributed in a big way to faction fights, Drummond arranged for special liquor licensing legislation in 1836, which gave authority to magistrates to close down licensed premises at the request of the constabulary. These measures resulted in the number of faction fights going into decline, and the Great Famine of

1846/1847 brought an end to the activity which had been so much part of the Irish scene for more than a century.

One of the first faction fights to take place after the Irish Constabulary had been established happened at Ballygurteen, a village situated midway between Dunmanway and Clonakilty, County Cork, after a fair being held in the village on 24 June 1836. Two factions, led by Denis Donovan and John Sullivan, had already fought on a number of occasions, and it was no secret that a repeat performance would take place on that date. The constabulary from Dunmanway, under Chief Constable Carpenter, which was on duty at the fair throughout the day, intervened and successfully put an end to the fight between the opposing factions at 7pm. Although both factions continued with their drinking, Chief Constable Carpenter and his men left for Dunmanway at 9pm when they felt that there was little likelihood of the fight's resuming. The factions lined up again immediately after the departure of the police and vicious fighting continued up to 12 midnight. One man named Timothy Sweeney was fatally injured when hit by a stone and about twenty-five to thirty men of each faction were injured. Chief Constable Carpenter was very severely reprimanded by no less an authority than the viceroy himself, who wrote:

> His Excellency desires that the Chief Constable be called on to explain why he left the fair at 9 oclock He cannot be ignorant that such fights may commence after that hour and even much later, and ought to have increased his vigilance. His Excellency desires to know what steps he has taken to make the leaders amicable to justice? His Excellency is surprised that Chief Constable Carpenter's district is so much given to these disgraceful fights.

Chief Constable Carpenter failed to get either of the two local magistrates to be on standby and available to him: one had gone to Clonakilty for the day and the other claimed to be indisposed. There is no record of any censure of them, but the reprimand issued to Chief Constable Carpenter and the tone of the correspondence indicated that faction fights were going to be severely dealt with and that further excuses would not be accepted from the constabulary for not dealing with them according to law.

The following is a report of a faction fight forwarded to the inspector general shortly after an occurrence in Donegal:

> Barony of Banagh, Parish of Killoughter, Townland of Dunkinally.
>   I have to state that on 1st January 1838, about 3 o'clock in the evening when I and a party of 12 men were in attendance at the fair of Dunkinally, Parish of Killoughter, and Barony of Banagh, a serious faction fight took place, many of the rioters cut each other badly with sticks and

I succeeded in arresting nine men in the act of the riot and five men for being intoxicated by liquor. Several others involved in the riot fled on the approach of the Constabulary and this put an end to the affray, I trust with good effect. Some difficulty existed in consequence of no Police Barracks being in the town or any other place of confinement and the Revd Joseph Walsh J. P. presiding within a quarter of a mile of the place, gave a written order to summons the prisoners to Killybegs petty sessions on the 8th inst. This arrangement enabled me to keep up a constant patrol through the town for the night. The inhabitants were very thankful to me and my party for the prompt means taken. Names of Prisoners arrested for the Riot: Edward McCue; Pat Conaghan; John Maguire; John Linehan; William Lyons; John Langan; William Murrin; John O'Neil; John Logan.

In *The Irish Faction Fighters of the Nineteenth Century* (1975), Patrick O'Donnell recounts details of one of the last big faction fights – and the difficulties encountered by the constabulary on the occasion – which took place at Ballinhassig, a village between Cork city and Bandon, on 30 June 1845. Two factions from the neighbourhood who had fought for many years assembled at Ballinhassig where a number of police were on duty under Sub-inspector John Kelly of Kinsale. When the fighting started, the constabulary arrested one of the ringleaders and took him into custody. Set upon by the crowd and totally outnumbered, the police had to retreat from the scene, but held on to their prisoner and took refuge in a house some distance away which was used as a dispensary. Serious attacks were made on the building by the mob and the police, who were then in peril of their lives, opened fire on the crowd. Some of the policemen were seriously injured and at least eleven of the attackers were killed outright by the police bullets. There was an outcry about the manner in which the constabulary had handled the affair and an inquiry was held. *The Nation* newspaper opened a fund for the families of those bereaved and it was generously subscribed to. This faction fight and its tragic consequences appears to have been the final serious incident of this nature before they finally ceased. Some isolated fights in later years after the Famine were of a relatively minor nature and were quickly dealt with by the constabulary.

Reading the Riot Act

The Riot Act (27 Geo. 3, c. 15) was read more frequently at faction fights than at any other incident or event. It was specifically provided for by law that whenever the constabulary was assembled on any occasion for the preservation of the peace, the officer, head constable or constable in charge should have a copy of the following extract from the act in his possession to be read by the magistrate in attendance. The legislation stated that:

> And the Justice, Sheriff, Sub-Sheriffs, Mayors, or head officer of any city or town, or other person authorised by the Act to make the said proclamation shall, amongst the said rioters, or as near to them as he can safely come, with a loud voice command or cause to be commanded, silence to be kept whilst proclamation is making, and after that shall openly and with a loud voice make, or, cause to be made, proclamation in these words or like in effect; Our Sovereign Lady, The Queen chargeth and commandeth all persons being assembled, immediately to disperse themelves and peaceably to depart to their habitations, or to their lawful business, upon the pains contained in the Act made in the twenty-seventh year of King George the Third to prevent riotous and tumultous risings and assemblies; and every such magistrate as aforesaid, within the limits of this jurisdiction, is hereby authorised, empowered and required, on notice or knowledge of any such unlawful, riotous and tumultous rising or assembly as aforesaid, to resort to the place where the same shall be, and there to make, or cause to be made, proclamation in the manner aforesaid.

The Riot Act was read when twelve or more persons were "riotously assembled to the disturbance of the public peace". The officers in charge of parties of constabulary reputedly carried a copy of the document in their helmets.

The Phoenix Park Depot

For the purpose of amalgamating and consolidating the Irish Constabulary, it was decided that there should be one central depot for the force, rather than having one in each of the four provinces. A four-acre site was selected at the city end of the Phoenix Park. By the end of 1839, Jacob Owens of the Office of Public Works had plans ready for the new depot. The building, which was erected by Charles Carolan of Dublin and was ready by 1842, cost £10,000. An extensive gravelled parade ground was provided at the front of the main building, surrounded by a low dyke which was replaced some years later by the existing substantial railings. Houses were provided within the depot for the surgeon to the force and the depot commandant, who with the rank of assistant inspector general was the senior officer in charge of the depot.

In August 1852, Sir Francis Head, former governor of Canada, visited Ireland and paid a visit to the depot. The depot had then been in existence for ten years, and the infirmary and riding school had been added in 1845. In his book, *A Fortnight in*

Ireland in 1852, Sir Francis described the depot, which greatly impressed him, as being "romantically laid out in a retired portion of the Phoenix Park", and added that, "It was a group of barrack-looking buildings, forming three sides of a rectangular, capacious, dark coloured gritty parade ground, and approached by a rutted old fashioned type of roadway." He observed that the main block was occupied by the "infantry section" of the constabulary, with the commandant occupying the residence at the eastern end of the block. The wing at the eastern end was occupied by "infantrymen, while the block at the other end housed the cavalry and transport section". The ground floor of the western wing was laid out in stables with sleeping accommodation overhead. The sergeants' mess was located at the inner end of this wing. The daily mess charge was 11d. per day, including laundry. The main block consisted mostly of "squad rooms, all whitewashed", on the ground and upper floors. The rooms in the upper floor interconnected with each other, the single rooms off the stairways being occupied by the constable-in-charge.

In the building of the depot, precautions were taken against attack, as Sir Francis describes the windows of the main block being protected by iron loop-holed shutters. Very descriptive details are given of the sleeping accommodation: "Round by the walls lay the heavy iron bedsteads, each with its palliasse and pillowcase filled with straw, and underneath the bed, a black box of standard pattern to hold the owner's civilian suit and other articles of personal property. At the head of each bed was a fixture to hold a carbine, and on his portion of the wooden shelf overhead were arranged the man's spare uniform, spare boots, knapsack and other accoutrements." The squad rooms had bare wooden floors. Sir Francis was very impressed with the hospital which had a "luxurious system of hot and cold water". The patients wore "blue bottle-coloured dress to prevent them from flying unseen to their healthy green coated comrades". The fact that all inmates at the hospital, whether Catholic or Protestant, partook of fish on Fridays impressed him.

At the lower end of the depot, Sir Francis watched a number of mounted recruits going through their paces in the riding school. He visited the police duty schoolroom and described it as an "excellent, healthy, well ventilated classroom containing in two divisions, sixteen long desks and benches. In front of them were the teachers' tables with globes and a bookcase." On the square, he watched a drill display of senior men (presumably members of the Reserve force) and admired the various movements of the men – the infantry section being commanded by bugle and the mounted men by trumpet. Tactical exercises were being performed by the men on foot to deal with hostile crowd situations through wedge-shaped formations.

Outside the depot in a grassy area of the Phoenix Park, he found squads of new recruits being put through their paces. Each squad was twenty to thirty strong. The most senior had only three weeks' service and a number had only joined up on the previous day. On the new recruits he commented:

The recruits generally are handsome intelligent lads of 18 to 20 years, the sons of small farmers and the senior of whom had already made such progress at their drill as exemplified the oft-cited aptitude of Irishmen for the military career. They were clasping their thighs and in various stages of strangulation, since they had only that morning been gifted with a hard stiff patent leather stock which gave a protuberance to the eyes.

During his visit to the depot he obviously consulted the regulations, and quotes: "It is in vain for any man to expect promotion who cannot write with facility a good legible hand and spell well." The fact that smoking, card-playing and gambling of every kind was prohibited throughout the barracks did not escape his notice. The most objective observations relating to life at the depot and the functions which it served in the 1850s are those given by Sir Francis who had a long and distinguished career behind him in the military and as governor of Canada.

In 1860 a new officers' mess and cavalry barracks with stabling were added. The inspector generals of the Irish Constabulary and later the Royal Irish Constabulary retained their offices and headquarters at Dublin Castle, but the depot played a strategic role in the policing of Ireland up to 1922. The four provincial depots were closed down when the depot was opened in 1842 and training of the constabulary was centralised. The riding school was converted to a church in the early days of the Garda Síochána and was later adapted for use as a recreation hall and band hall which it still is. On 14 May 1922, the depot was vacated by the RIC and handed over to the care of the Royal Horse Artillery. It was used for the training of the Garda Síochána from early 1923 until 1963 when training was transferred to a new training centre at Templemore, County Tipperary. The depot is now the administrative headquarters of the Garda Síochána.

The Reserve

Under legislation passed in 1839, provision was made for a reserve force within the constabulary. The act decreed that: "they shall be employed as occasion may require, in aid of, and in conjunction with the said constabulary force, established in and for the said several counties and places throughout Ireland". This Reserve was to be ready at a moment's notice, at the order of the inspector general to go to any part of Ireland, help whichever regular force needed it, and consisted of two sub-inspectors, four head constables and 200 constables and sub-constables. The reserve, appointed by the lord lieutenant, had a surgeon appointed exclusively to it at a salary of £300 per annum and included fifty mounted policemen. It comprised of specially selected members of the constabulary, with a minimum service requirement and a minimum height of 5 feet 10 inches. (The members of the Reserve were normally 6 feet or more in height.) Later increased to 400 members, the Reserve force was maintained by the Royal Irish Constabulary at the depot up to its disbandment in 1922.

Recruiting and Training of the Rank-and-File for the Irish Constabulary

The number of recruits from different counties in Ireland varied at different periods of time. Roscommon, Leitrim, Sligo, Monaghan, Cavan, Fermanagh, Longford, Queen's County (Laois) and Tipperary were consistent with their supply of recruits. They came from various backgrounds, but the majority had either farmers' sons or farm labourers. Others had worked as clerks, servants, weavers, gardeners, artisans, grooms or shop assistants. A small number had been employed as teachers or as school monitors. Student priests and Christian Brothers who discovered that they did not have a vocation invariably ended up joining the constabulary. A tiny number came from the once wealthy classes who had fallen on hard times. One such member was Sir Thomas Echlin, a baronet from Kilmeague, County Kildare. He served from 1863 to 1893 and retired with the rank of sergeant. One of his brothers also served in the force from 1862 until 1865. Approximately 10 per cent of the recruits over the years were sons of members or retired members of the constabulary. The preference for farmers' sons was based on the fact that they were regarded as "independent respectable fellows", and even during the Land War of the 1880s there was a steady stream of farmers' sons into the RIC. During the Great Famine when there was a substantial increase in the strength of the constabulary, there was little problem in getting suitable recruits. Six years later the situation was almost totally reversed due to the very bad pay for the force. The minimum height for recruits had to be reduced by one inch in the 1850s to obtain sufficient recruits. There were numerous resignations from the force during the 1850s and 1860s due to the poor pay – leading to an even greater demand for recruits. Many of those who resigned emigrated to Australia and joined the police there. While many others left to join police forces all over the world, some members just emigrated to join up with members of their family who had emigrated during the Famine and who were now doing well abroad.

Recruit training at the depot in Phoenix Park was far longer and more intensive than that of any of the English constabularies or police forces. The emphasis on cleanliness became a kind of religion. Apart from being taught drill, musketry, police duties and physical training, the early recruits were taught arithmetic, orthography, geography, grammar, bookkeeping and first aid. By 1870 the course was of four months' duration and by 1900 it was six months. To correct poor posture, during the early part of their training course recruits were obliged to wear a stiff leather type of harness known as a "stock". A leather belt was worn around the neck, with an extension from the back tied down to another belt around the waist to hold up the recruit's head and improve his posture. It was crude but effective.

A recruit was obliged on entering the depot to have a suit of plain clothes, four linen shirts, a hat, two pairs of half boots and four pairs of woollen socks. He also had to have £2 in his possession to tide him over to his first payday. The latter requirement was suspended for recruits during the Famine period.

Apart from a minimum height requirement (5 feet 9 inches originally), recruits had to be well built with a minimum chest measurement, have good eyesight and health and not be suffering from a specified range of diseases. In 1852 the height distribution of the Irish Constabulary was as follows:

Above	Feet	Inches	Number of Members
	6	3	23
	6	2	161
	6	1	506
	6	0	1,104
	5	11	1,794
	5	10	2,921
	5	9	4,623
	5	8	1,518

Introduction of Cadets

Prior to 1842 all officers of the constabulary were former army officers. In 1842, the government arranged to appoint cadets, the first police force ever to do so. It was a preliminary step to the rank of sub-inspector to which they succeeded as vacancies arose. While they trained as cadets they only received the same pay as a constable, but they wore the uniform of an officer. The government most likely perceived the cadet system as an opportunity to break the mould and counter widespread objections about the military influence on the constabulary. At first, the number of cadet appointments was limited to, at any one time, three more than the number of sub-inspectors in the force but due to above-average wastage in that rank, the number of cadets was increased to six per sub-inspector. The cadets underwent an intensive training course in the depot at the Phoenix Park. The course included arithmetic, the geography of Ireland, orthography, geometry, algebra, bookkeeping, grammar, drill, musketry and, of course, horse riding. The standard of education required for entry was higher than average for the time. They also studied police duties and procedures. Despite their youthfulness when they went to take up postings in the country, they were theoretically better prepared than their predecessors had been in police work.

Salaries of the Constabulary

On 28 August 1846, legislation was passed which regularised the salaries of the Irish Constabulary. It directed that all expenses relating to the force should henceforward be paid from the "Consolidated Fund" (or central fund), relieving the counties from paying the expenses of the constabulary, as they had been doing up to this time. Provision was made that charges could be made on a county or city for any extra police employed in curbing disorders, as declared by the lord lieutenant. The strength of the reserve force was increased to 400 constables and sub-constables, with an appropriate number of head constables and sub-inspectors. The act also empowered the lord lieutenant to appoint additional constables and officers in counties where disturbances were taking place, who were to be removed when the disturbances ceased.

The salaries payable to the different ranks at this time were as follows:

Sub-constable: £2. 6s. 2d. per month
Constable: £3. 0s. 0d. per month

Mounted constables got an extra £2 0s. 0d. per annum and mounted sub-constables received an extra £1 14s. 0d. per annum of an allowance
Sub-inspectors (three grades): £100, £120 and £150 per annum
County inspectors (three grades): £220, £250 and £280 per annum

Daniel O'Connell

The Risings of 1798 and 1803 were a disaster and did not further the Irish nationalist cause. Galen Broeker, in *Rural Disorder and Police Reform in Ireland 1812–1836*, vividly describes the situation during the first decades of the nineteenth century:

> The small but growing Irish Catholic middle class was still seeking its place in society and was widely separated from the masses by income, education and interest. Leadership of a sort was provided by the Catholic clergy in their efforts to check the growing tendency towards rural violence, but with very limited success. Thus during the early decades of the nineteenth century, until Daniel O'Connell gained prominence, the Irish peasant was left alone to work out his own economic and social salvation. The result was the rise in agrarian secret societies and the spread of terrorism, designed to enforce peasant-made law over the law of the state. The activities of the peasant organisations presented the Irish

government with a problem that demanded a major portion of its time and kept the authorities in a state of nervous apprehension for many years. All too frequently the arrival of autumn brought a fresh series of outbreaks of rural violence which Dublin Castle anxiously investigated for signs of "insurrectionary activity of a political nature" or evidence of "leadership by respectable people, which indicate, not the usual agrarian disturbances, but the beginning of a revolution".

It is difficult, probably impossible, to separate and identify the many peasant organisations – Whiteboys, Carders, Rockites, Caravats and others – which helped to create the rural chaos of this period. Different local officials in the same area might designate a single organisation by several names. A degree of order can be introduced by ignoring problems of regional distribution and identification by name and attempting to classify the groups by organisation and purpose. So classified, they fall into three categories; agrarian secret societies, religious societies and local factions. The categories however tend to overlap.

There was a marked absence of leadership amongst the Irish people during these decades. Secret societies of all descriptions and with different objectives abounded throughout the country but there was no cohesiveness or overall unity. The Orange Order, which was both political and religious, was founded in 1795, rapidly grew in strength and was militantly Protestant and extremely conservative in opposing any measure which it saw as a threat to Protestantism. The Ribbon Society was the Catholic reply to Orangeism. A secret society with its membership concentrated mainly in Ulster, it was mainly a Catholic protection organisation, set up as a counter-force against the ultra-Protestant Orange Order.

Daniel O'Connell, "The Liberator", came to prominence during this period with his fight for Catholic Emancipation. He, more than any other person of the period, saw the utter folly of any further insurrection, and the message consistently preached by him was that the liberation of Ireland must be attained without the shedding of blood. Most of the Penal Laws in Ireland had been abolished by the 1770s, and in the 1790s Pitt promised full emancipation for Catholics. He was unable to keep his promise as the king did not agree, with the result that the Catholics became more frustrated about their situation as time went on. They did not have a vote, thereby giving total and absolute control to the landlords of the day for whom the Protestants naturally voted. They were not entitled to a seat in the British parliament and thereby had no voice in the democratic process nor any say in their future welfare.

In Daniel O'Connell, a very able and flambuoyant barrister from County Kerry whose name was a household word throughout Ireland from his success in the courts defending persons from all walks of life charged with serious crimes, the Catholics found a natural leader to fight their cause. O'Connell succeeded in obtaining Catholic emancipation in 1829. The campaign, which started out without funds of any kind and without influence from any quarters on its side, demonstrated to the Irish and the English what could be achieved by peaceful means. O'Connell proved that it was possible for the Irish Catholic middle class and the peasantry to unite and peacefully achieve their goal. An exceptionally brilliant speaker and a charismatic leader, Daniel O'Connell drew huge crowds wherever he went. The Irish people loved him. He was a sincere, warm-hearted individual and his honesty was above reproach. Neither he nor his followers ever caused serious trouble to the constabulary, and the constabulary regarded him with some respect. As early as 1825, O'Connell stated, "the situation of a policeman is an extremely valuable one to the Irish peasant and he would not lightly forfeit it". He was of course meeting members of the constabulary on a very regular basis in the cut-and-thrust of criminal court trials, where he was deemed capable of driving a coach and four through acts of parliament.

When Catholic Emancipation had been granted, O'Connell embarked on another campaign to repeal the Act of Union. He did not violently oppose the existence of the Union as such and would have accepted it if a proper constitutional policy had been in place to adequately deal with the Irish question. He was unlucky in his efforts during the 1830s. Parliamentary affairs in the House of Commons were unstable and the House of Lords seemed determined to give no quarter whatsoever to Ireland. During his campaign for repeal of the Union, hundreds of thousands of people turned out to his meetings. Meetings the size of O'Connell's had never been witnessed in the British Isles previously, but they were orderly and well conducted and created no problems for the constabulary. Three expressions often repeated by him were listened intently to by his followers: "He who commits a crime gives strength to his enemy"; "that civil and religious liberty would be too dearly bought if purchased by the loss of one drop of human blood"; and that their objectives should be achieved "through legal, peaceful and constitutional means".

For many reasons, O'Connell's long, democratic campaign for repeal did not attain the results which it should have. In 1842, Thomas Davis, John Blake Dillon and Charles Gavan Duffy, who had been prominent members of the Young Ireland party since its foundation about two years previously, established *The Nation* newspaper and supported O'Connell with his Repeal Association. From this point, the government appeared to have changed its views about O'Connell and proscribed a large rally organised by him for Clontarf in Dublin. This action was followed up by the arrest of O'Connell and Gavan Duffy in October 1842, followed by their subsequent trial in February 1843. O'Connell was sentenced to imprisonment, but fought his case through appeal to the House of Lords, where his conviction was quashed. When he was released from prison in September 1843, his health had deteriorated – he was then in his sixties.

There is no evidence available that the Irish Constabulary had any wish to have O'Connell arrested, as the force did not see him as a threat to peace; nor did they have any incriminating material to justify charges against him. The constabulary, knowing the esteem in which he was held, anticipated serious repercussions by the Irish people following his trial, but O'Connell's doctrine and plea for calm to his followers were clearly an influence.

The Young Ireland movement had become very militant during O'Connell's absence. He did everything possible to encourage them to pursue their objectives through peaceful means, but his pleas fell on deaf ears. The Young Ireland party separated from the official Repeal Association and set up one of its own. From O'Connell's policy "that civil or religious liberty would be too dearly bought if purchased by the shedding of one drop of human blood", the Young Ireland party adopted a policy that the demand for their rights should "be heard from amidst the roar of musketry and the clash of swords". O'Connell died at Genoa on 15 May 1847 on his way to Rome. With his death, the Repeal Association died for want of leadership and the Young Ireland party then became the dominant anti-government force in Ireland. O'Connell's influence in Irish affairs during the quarter of a century prior to his death had created stability in the political scene and his voice was the voice of moderation. Were it not for his able and respected leadership. the County Constabulary and later the Irish Constabulary might very well have had more serious situations to deal with over the period.

The Young Ireland Movement

During the Great Famine, the Young Ireland movement became far more aggressive. It spoke of civil and religious liberty being obtained for Ireland on the green hills of Ireland at the point of the bayonet or the pike through a deluge of their enemies' blood which should redden the mountain streams. This was a far cry from the policy of Daniel O'Connell a few years earlier. The Young Irelanders took advantage of the terrible conditions of the Famine to whip up support, and never in the history of Ireland was the Irish peasant more vulnerable than at this particular time. All the indicators were there for another insurrection or at least a huge demonstration of physical force against the government. Charles Gavan Duffy of *The Nation* was arrested and imprisoned. His newspaper was suppressed and the printing machinery was destroyed. John Mitchel, proprietor of *The United Irishman* newspaper, was arrested and imprisoned and his newspaper was suppressed. This newspaper, along with *The Nation*, and *The Felon* published much seditious material and inflammatory statements over the period, as well as urging the people "to be ready at a moment's notice". In May 1848, John Mitchel was charged with "treason felony" and was convicted and sentenced to transportation for fourteen years. The constabulary anticipated an attempt to rescue John Mitchel following his conviction, but with military reinforcements they ensured that it did not happen.

William Smith O'Brien was for a number of years one of the most influential leaders of the Young Irelanders. He was a member of a prominent Protestant family from County Limerick, and in his early years he was elected as a conservative member of parliament for his native county. He developed a sympathy for the poorer and destitute classes of society and concluded that the problems of Ireland were due to misgovernment and mismanagement by the British authorities, resulting in serious injustices being perpetrated on the Irish people. He was described as being obstinate, warm-hearted and generous. He renounced parliament, family and friends and joined the rebellious Young Ireland movement.

In July 1848 Dublin city was proclaimed under the Crime and Outrage (Ireland) Act, 1847, and habeus corpus suspended. Warrants were issued by the lord lieutenant for the arrest of the leaders of the Young Irelanders, who were then in the southern counties. On 28 July, a proclamation was issued, offering a reward of £500 for the arrest of Smith O'Brien, who was to be charged with high treason, and the sum of £300 each for the arrest of Thomas Francis Meagher, John Blake Dillon and Michael Doheny. Smith O'Brien would certainly have known that if he were convicted of high treason the only penalty which could be imposed was death. In Wexford town he told his friends: "Better die the death of a soldier than that of a felon, and the hour has come." He believed that Tipperary and Kilkenny were the strongholds of the Young Ireland movement and he settled on these counties for his first demonstration of strength, which he was sure would be successful.

He proceeded from Wexford to Kilkenny city where he stopped for a time. On the same evening he moved on to Callan, where he was welcomed by a huge crowd of the peasantry, to the alarm of the local ascendancy classes. On the following day, Sunday, news spread all over the locality of his presence. A large meeting was addressed that evening outside Callan town by one of his associates, who told the crowd that all they needed for success was arms and men. He moved from there to Mullinahone, County Tipperary, where a large crowd of people again assembled to meet him, but in size it did not measure up to what he had expected. Those who turned up had very few arms and had brought no provisions. It was a very wet day and the crowd had been there for hours. He had sympathy for them and gave them money to buy up all the bread available in the town, which he then distributed amongst them. He told them, however, that he had no more money to buy food and that they would have to purchase any further provisions themselves. This seemed to be a setback to the crowd, who had high expectations of food and provisions. He warned them that he would not permit any provisions to be obtained at the expense of violence to any man's property. At Mullinahone, he wore a green cap with a gold band and a peak. The new Irish Tricolour of green, white and orange was also carried on display for the first time.

Smith O'Brien had convinced himself that if he could have one successful demonstration, all the people would rally to his cause. On 26 July he marched to Ballingarry village (south Tipperary) about six miles away. As he travelled, he was accompanied by a crowd of people, mostly women and boys. An estimated 100 able-bodied men were in the group. There was a lot of shouting and hurrahing as they travelled to Ballingarry, where he met the local leaders of the movement. The group increased in numbers, due in no small measure to the fact that the chapel bell in Ballingarry was rung all through the night. Less than one quarter of the menfolk accompanying him were armed; and of those fifty or sixty had some type of firearms and ammunition and a similiar number had pikes.

Thursday, 27 July, saw him on his way to Killenaule, a small town about six miles distant. On his way there, he was met by the local parish priest and curate who begged him to abandon his demonstration before it was too late. He refused to halt his mission and told the priests that it was already too late, that he was at the head of his army and that he was obliged to see things through. There was a huge reception for him and his followers at Killenaule and bouquets of flowers were thrown at the party from upstairs windows. There was, however, no increase of his able-bodied followers and those who were with him had no food.

On Friday, 28 July, he moved to an area known as the Commons, which was a predominantly coal-mining area about four miles from Ballingarry and Killenaule villages. At the Commons he met up with the other leaders: Thomas Francis Meagher, John Blake Dillon, Michael Doheny, James Stephens and others. Speech-making took place there, and the organisers had hoped for a very good response from the colliery workers who were all able-bodied men and who might like some distraction for a day. This did not materialise. Smith O'Brien sent for the foreman of the collieries and gave him a letter addressed to the mining board of the colliery which he asked him to deliver. This letter was later produced at his trial and played no small part in his subsequent conviction.

All the leaders met to assess their situation and agreed that they had failed to attract the assistance which they had hoped for and required. The majority were in favour of abandoning everything at that point, but Smith O'Brien refused to change course or change his mind, although the others did everything possible to prevail on him to abandon the mission. They eventually left him and went their separate ways with a promise that they would return to him with aid – which would appear to be merely an excuse to leave him to his own devices. On the following day, Saturday, 29 July, Smith O'Brien was at the Commons alone in charge of an "army" which had no previous experience in military affairs or engagements. Nor had he any experience which qualified him for leadership of the group. He was determined to press on and encouraged those around him as best he could.

Many versions have been given of "the Battle of Ballingarry", or what has frequently been referred to as "the Widow McCormick's Cabbage Patch Rebellion", which was the main event of the Young Ireland Rising of 1848. The most accurate account is probably that taken from official records of the Irish Constabulary and published in *The History of the Irish Constabulary* in 1869:

The Battle of Farrinrory – Defeat of the Rebel Army by the Constabulary

It was now known by the authorities that O'Brien was encamped on The Commons in the County of Tipperary, bordering the County of Kilkenny and it was time to adopt hostile measures. There were no telegrams in those days, at least not in these parts and the trains upon the railway had not commenced to run the whole way through from Dublin to Kilkenny. The line however had been finished. The Royal Agricultural Cattle Show had been held in Kilkenny, on the Wednesday, Thursday and Friday of the week which was destined to terminate with so much excitement and alarm. As usual, the Show was concluded by a "grand ball" which was held on this occasion at the Railway Terminus which had just been completed and had been boarded in and fitted up for the purpose in a most tasteful manner. The whole aristocracy of the County Kilkenny and the surrounding counties had assembled. There could not have been less than five hundred people present. Amongst them were the Duke of Leinster, Lords Bessborough, Ashbrook and Desart; in fact all the nobility of the province and many more distant parts of Ireland together with about fifty military officers, then quartered in Kilkenny. But not in one head was there a thought of Smith O'Brien or a "rising". To compare small things with great we might, at this point bring our reader's memory back to the night before the Battle of Waterloo.

The County Inspector of Constabulary, disengaged himself from the arm of his partner, and retired to a corner to receive a despatch. In spite of his discretion and assumed self-possession, the rumour soon ran through the rooms, that rebellion was around them – almost at the doors. The despatch had been brought direct from the Castle of Dublin by Head Constable John Crowley of the city of Cork Constabulary, who travelled express. It contained the proclamation offering five hundred pounds for the apprehension of Smith O'Brien and further stated, that

it was supposed the said Smith O'Brien was then encamped with the
rebel army somewhere upon the borders of the counties Tipperary and
Kilkenny. The County Inspector [Mr Blake] cast a glance over it's contents and turning to one of the county authorities he handed it to him.
It was no secret. It was not marked "private and confidential" and the
fact, for it was now more than rumour of open rebellion became known.
Confusion and disorder ensued, and of course the military disappeared
unceremoniously and at once. Carriages had been ordered in all directions, forthwith, and in less than half an hour the rooms did not contain
a single noble lord, or sprig of nobility of any sort or title, those who
remained consisted chiefly of persons belonging to the town and vicinity, wondering and alarmed and waiting for carriages.

Mr Blake left Kilkenny on that morning the 29th about four o clock
and proceeded to Killenaule where he ascertained the exact whereabouts
of Smith O'Brien and his army. He at once wrote a despatch to Callan
to Sub-Inspector Trant with the men then at his command to march for
The Commons so as to arrive at three o'clock p.m. and he sent the same
order to Mr Joseph Cox [sub-inspector] at Cashel as he expected to
arrive there himself with the military from Thurles at that hour. Mr
Blake then pushed on to Thurles where General McDonald was quartered in command of the troops. Mr Trant received the despatch, he got
his men ready and started at once without calculating the time of arrival
and found himself approaching the intended place of his destination
between twelve and one o clock instead of three as directed in the
despatch. On his approach to The Commons he found himself surrounded on all sides by the rebels, shouting and hurrahing and firing
shots. Crowds poured down the hills before, behind and on both sides
of him to the number of about three thousand men, many of whom were
armed with guns, pikes, scythes and pitchforks. Smith O'Brien was in
their midst, organising or endeavouring to organise them. Sub-Inspector Trant saw or thought he saw, that in open conflict, with such tremendous odds against him, it would be a mere sacrifice of life to give battle.
But he may have been wrong. He had forty-six men of all ranks with
him, well armed and disciplined. However a large slated house appear-
ing not far off, he ordered his men to break and rush forward to take
possession of it. In this they succeeded, Mr Trant however leaving his
horse and accoutrements in possession of the enemy. They had scarcely
got inside, shut the door and commenced to fortify the house, when the
crowd of rebels surrounded it on all sides firing into it whenever a
chance of injury to the inmates presented itself. There were five young

children in the house, orphans, belonging to the widow McCormick when the police entered and they were kept by Mr Trant as hostages.

An interesting incident here occurred, which as it is indicative of his manly feelings and warm-heartedness, may be recorded of the poor mad enthusiast Smith O'Brien.

The widow McCormick in whose house the constabulary party had taken refuge, had gone from home for a short time that morning, leaving her children in the house in the care of the eldest, a boy not more than ten years of age. A messenger soon followed who told her the state of affairs, viz. that there were about forty police shut up in her house, that they had her children shut up along with them and that the house had been riddled with bullets for volley after volley of shots were firing into it and out of it. Of course the messenger was not below the mark. The poor woman ran home in a state of distraction, but dared not venture up to the house, the windows of which she saw bristling with carbines and fixed bayonets. She then rushed through the crowd until at last Smith O'Brien was pointed out to her when casting herself down before him she poured forth a volume of abuse and entreaty calling on him "to deliver her five poor orphans from the murderous peelers who would ate her lambs. Was she to be robbed of her home and her children the same day, the same hour. Oh, wirra, wirra, wirrastru, that I should ever live to see this day. If you be a man," she added suddenly, "come up to the house this minute and get me my childer." O'Brien was a man, and could not resist this appeal to either his courage or humanity, and said that he would go to the house and demand her children but he would not permit her to risk her life by going near it. This she sternly refused, and broke from those who had held her back, and they approached the house together. They went to the rear where there was most cover from the command of the windows and having gained the gable, they crept around to the parlour window where they were actually in conversation with one of the police respecting the children, when unfortunately some fool in the crowd threw a stone at one of the upper windows and smashed a couple panes of glass. This was a signal for a fresh volley from within by which two men were killed and several wounded. It was no use remaining longer in such an exposed place and Smith O'Brien and the widow McCormick made the best of their way to the road again. The siege may be said to have now commenced in good earnest. A brisk fire was kept up on both sides, some of the assailants were shot and some wounded while the police being under cover escaped completely uninjured.

About this time a mounted policeman in plain clothes – Constable Carroll from Kilkenny – was making his way to Mr Trant with a message from Mr Greene, the resident magistrate, when he was met by Father Fitzgerald P.P. Ballingarry and his curate Father Maher both of whom undertook to go up to the widow McCormick's house along with him. It is right however to point out that neither of these gentlemen, were in any way connected with the movement, they were diametrically opposed to it on every grounds and their object was peace. On their way to the house they met Smith O'Brien who took Constable Carroll's horse from him and rode it for the rest of the day. Carroll was at once looked upon as a rebel by the enemy, and what was worse, a spy, and he would have been shot on the moment were it not that Smith O'Brien himself ordered and guaranteed his safety. Father Fitzgerald had then some conversation with Smith O'Brien after which Constable Carroll and he approached the house. At first Constable Carroll was not known and was in much danger as carbines were pointed at him from several of the windows but some of Mr Trant's men soon recognised him and they covered their arms. Father Fitzgerald advanced to the window under the same immunity which had been afforded their comrade. A conversation then took place between them, on the part of the priest as to making peace and preventing any further bloodshed. The opposite party would be satisfied by their giving up their arms and they would be permitted to depart uninjured etc., and on Mr Trant's part as to the strength of their position and their firm determination never to surrender or deliver up their arms but with their lives. The conversation embraced a great deal more than the above. On the one part, some suggestion as to the impossibility of holding out from the want of provisions and the possibility of the opposite party setting fire to the house.; and on the other part as to a certain amount of provisions which they had found in the house, sufficient to sustain them until relief should arrive, and the hostages which they had in the widow McCormick's children against the burning project. Father Fitzgerald's arguments having failed to stagger Mr Trant's loyalty or courage, he then retired with Constable Carroll who had been committed to his care and protection at Mr Trant's earnest request and which it was faithfully promised he should receive. The result proves that the promise was sincere for Constable Carroll arrived safely in Kilkenny, late on the same evening on his own horse which Smith O'Brien had returned to him with many thanks.

Father Fitzgerald finding his mediation of no avail had returned home and left matters to take their course. The insurgents finding that they could not succeed in making an entry into the house, and that they had altogether the worst of the firing, were about to attempt to set it on fire, notwithstanding the hostages who were within. To effect this, a load of hay had been procured and driven up close to the back door. It may here be remarked that the rere of the house was by no means so much exposed to the fire of the police as was the front. Here, McManus who was the only leader then with O'Brien, endeavoured to ignite the hay by snapping a pistol several times close to it but he could not succeed as it had got wet from the heavy rain on the previous night. This project was then abandoned and a more systematic and determined attack by all the armed men determined on; and some sledges and heavy pieces of timber were procured with which to smash in the door. Just then the cry arose that "here are the Cashel Police" and almost at the same moment, Sub-Inspector Cox with about six-and-thirty men were seen coming up the hill to the rescue. Then indeed the dispersion of the rebels began to take place in earnest. After some faint and timid attempts to make a stand, the first volley from Mr Cox's party – which makes us believe that open air fighting would all through have been the best – sent them flying in all directions and Mr Trant and his brave forty were set at liberty and they arrived home in Callan on that same evening without a scratch.

Thus was the miserable attempt at Insurrection scattered to the winds by a few of the constabulary without even the appearance of the military to support them. Upon this subject it may be added, that when Mr Blake had sent off the despatches to Cashel and Callan directing the constabulary to march to The Commons so as to arrive there at 3 p.m. he had made his calculations that he should himself have arrived in Thurles where General McDonald was in command of the troops, explain to him the precise state of affairs and reach The Commons with the military by that hour. But he did not reach the Commons at all and his absence may be accounted for, by the fact, that the general in command of the military at Thurles was so matter-of-fact an old gentleman, that he would take nothing for granted and when at last he was obliged to admit himself satisfied of the abstract facts, he would not stir until he first consulted maps, roads and distances in order that he might make no mistake – and he certainly did make none – at least he thought so. But the constabulary, whose map of the country was under their feet, not rolled up against the Grand Jury room wall, and whose knowledge of roads and distances were in their heads and not in memorandum books, had rendered the study of both by the general a work of supererogation, for they had already repulsed the rebels and dispersed the leaders without the presence of a single soldier. Virtually and indeed actually this abortive attempt at "freeing the country from a tyrant's yoke" was at an end; the leaders who had left Smith O'Brien on the previous day to "rise the country" found it too heavy for them and had not fulfilled their mission, if such indeed it were, and Smith O'Brien had fled, none knew whither. But he soon turned up. Upon Saturday, the 5th August, just one short week from the day of his discomfiture and humiliation, he walked into the Railway Station at Thurles and took a ticket for Limerick. He was buttoned up to the chin in a brown frock coat and his trousers which did not appear to have felt a brush for many days were turned up at the insteps. Hulme a railway porter thought he cut a very shady figure, and at the same time he thought of the five hundred pounds. He kept his eye on him for a few moments when seeing Head Constable Haniver coming up the road towards the station-house, he considered no further time should be lost, if he hoped to receive the undivided reward; so walking up to him he laid hold of him by the arm saying "you are Smith O'Brien and I arrest you in the name of the Queen". He was unarmed and made no resistance, but remained silent. Head Constable Haniver then came up, just in time to be late, and Hulme told him that he had arrested Smith O'Brien "and here he is". The Head Constable then took charge of him and the train being about to start, Hulme was obliged to resume his more legitimate duties but turning to the Head Constable he said "recollect that Smith O'Brien is my prisoner but not being able to remain I hand him up to the civil authorities". Haniver laughed and replied "you are the lucky man". O'Brien was as docile as a lamb and sat in the ante-room of the station-house with the Head Constable until a re-inforcement of the constabulary which he had sent for arrived. He was then conveyed to gaol. Some of the other conspirators were soon after taken and they were all transmitted to Dublin where they lay in Kilmainham Gaol until the Special Commission was issued in the month of October following. It was necessary to describe so much of the history of this mad rebellion, in order to connect the constabulary with its suppression but it will not be necessary to follow the prisoners through the tedious detail of their trials and convictions. Suffice it is to say that they were convicted, upon the most overwhelming evidence of high treason and sentenced to the awful and soul-harrowing penalty attached to that highest of crimes. The extreme penalty, however was subsequently remitted, through the clemency of the Queen, but they were all transported for life.

Lord Chief Justice Blackbourne declared in his charge to the jury on Smith O'Brien's trial that the Irish Constabulary had saved their country and deserved its lasting gratitude.

The Aftermath of the 1848 Rebellion

The Young Ireland rebellion was put down by the Irish Constabulary without the assistance of the military. They were entitled to take the credits and kudos for it, but there was an element of luck in their success. The arrival of Sub-inspector Thomas Trant from Kilkenny at the Commons about three hours earlier than arranged, dictated the whole course of events. Although they were all armed, their weapons were muzzle loaded and required an interval to reload after each volley. Police in this situation were always at a disadvantage when confronting a large mob.

Sub-inspector Trant was fortunate in being able to take refuge in what was a substantially built stone and slated dwelling house with Widow McCormick's children inside to prevent the attackers setting fire to it. The visit of the parish priest must have had an influence on the situation also, and the arrival of the Cashel constabulary under Sub-inspector Joseph Cox was timely, even though Sub-inspector Trant and his party might have managed to hold out for several more hours. (Sub-inspector Cox was later awarded the Constabulary Medal, while Sub-inspector Trant does not appear to have received the honour.) It is surprising that Mr Blake had not arranged a central rendezvous point for all the constabulary parties to meet, such as Killenaule or Ballingarry, before then marching to the Commons.

The biggest question of all relates to the apparent lack of basic intelligence in the lead-up to the confrontation. The offer of high rewards for the leaders indicates that everybody, including the constabulary, had sensed for weeks before that, that a rebellion of some kind was in the offing. The sight of Smith O'Brien's parading through the countryside with a large noisy mob of people could not have gone unnoticed, especially when some of them carried firearms and pikes. His advance was through open and thickly populated country, but the parish priest and curate from Ballingarry were the only people who confronted him along the way. It is difficult to comprehend why the constabulary or military did not challenge him long before he arrived at the Commons since a warrant had been issued by the lord lieutenant for his arrest. The roundabout way in which County Inspector Blake was informed about the situation by Head Constable Crowley, who had presumably travelled to Kilkenny by the mail coach, was also unusual. Obviously, Dublin Castle had its sources of information well established. The accuracy of the information transmitted to County Inspector Blake enabled him, when informed, to waste no time in putting arrangements in train.

If the constabulary learned one important lesson from the events at the Commons, that was the neccessity for intelligence gathering. From this rebellion onwards, the gathering of information by the constabulary became a priority and a preoccupation. This was continued right through by the Royal Irish Constabulary – to whom it almost became an obsession – up to 1922. The situation was far different in later years. When the Fenian Rising and other serious events occurred, the constabulary and the RIC were in possession of good quality advance intelligence.

Smith O'Brien was a poor military leader and could probably have made a far greater contribution to the cause of the Young Irelanders in parliament or elsewhere. He was deserted in his greatest hour of need by the other leaders of the movement, who at least had the ability to see the hopelessness of their situation and did everything possible to get him to abandon it. While his patriotic ideals could not be questioned, he was certainly not the type of individual capable of leading a rebellion with a group of untrained and poorly armed men, nor even a single skirmish against a small group of trained and armed constabulary. He lacked the ability to get ordinary men to rally to his cause, even at a time when many appeared to want some action. He did not have what it took to turn a mob of simple country peasants into an efficient fighting force, and there may have been some lingering doubt in the minds of the people about his sincerety of purpose because of the priviliged upper class background from which he came. He sacrificed a lot and lost everything. Were it not for his background he might very well have paid the supreme penalty, rather than being transported for life.

The rising at the Commons created much amusement in the British press, who seized on the more ridiculous aspects of the events. The long-awaited outbreak which had come at last in Ireland was very derisively referred to as the "the Widow McCormick's Cabbage Patch Rebellion". They stated that a small body of police driving off a huge body of the insurgents showed that the Irish were stupid and cowardly and dangerous only when it was quite safe to do so. The Widow McCormick's cabbage patch became a symbol of national failure and ridicule.

James Stephens and the Fenian Flame

The rebellion at the Commons in 1848 indirectly kindled the flame which resulted in the Fenian Rising of 1867 – nineteen years later. Ineffective as it had been, its miserable failure drove men like James Stephens, Michael Doheny, McManus and O'Mahony to reorganise and try again when they were better prepared. Thereby the Fenian movement and the Fenian Rising had their roots in the failure at Ballingarry. Smith O'Brien's aide-de-camp at Ballingarry and during the events that led up to it was James Stephens. He was born in Kilkenny in 1824, where he was educated in St Kieran's College. He came from a well-to-do family, trained as a civil engineer and was employed in the construction of the new railway system in Ireland. He was very much influenced by the Young Ireland movement and became actively involved with the Confederate Clubs in his native Kilkenny. In 1848 he joined up with Smith O'Brien and received a gunshot wound to his chest from the weapons discharged by the constabulary at the Commons. Although he received medical attention and made a full recovery, it was rumoured that he had been fatally injured by the gunshot. For some time the constabulary believed that he had died and been buried with a very big funeral. With Michael Doheny he left for France, disguised as a maid, and arrived in Paris around September 1848.

In Paris, Stephens and Doheny joined up with John O'Mahony, another Young Irelander who had escaped to France a short while earlier. Little is known about Stephen's lifestyle while in Paris other than that he spent much time studying the organisation of the secret societies there. The bond between himself and O'Mahony was strong. They both lamented the outcome of the 1848 Rising and vowed that any further attempt at rebellion would be more succesful.

In 1854, O'Mahony left Paris for America where he made contact with the Irish sympathisers there. Stephens returned to Ireland in 1856 and took up a post teaching French to senior classes at a girl's boarding school run by the Miss Norrises at High Street in Killarney, where he was free to come and go as he pleased. About 1857 he moved to Dublin where he took up a position as a private tutor with a family.

He travelled extensively throughout Ireland – reputedly a total of 3,000 miles – and concluded that a fresh start would have to be made. With encouragement from O'Mahony and Doheny, he set out to enlist 10,000 men, making a demand for a guarantee of £100 per month from the other leaders to meet expenses. On St Patrick's Day 1858 he launched a new secret society with the avowed aim of making Ireland an independent democratic republic. He chose some French or European organisation as a model for his new society. Basing it on a complicated series of "circles" or cells, each of which was to operate independently of the others, he hoped to eliminate informers and spies. The organisation was known in its early existence as "the Society" or "the Organisation" but later it became known as "the Brotherhood". This laid the foundations for the Fenian movement and Rising of 1867, and through it James Stephens, who was injured at the Commons in 1848, kept the embers of rebellion alive.

One of James Stephens' staunchest supporters in America was Colonel Michael Corcoran. Born in Ballymote, County Sligo, on 21 September 1827, he joined the Irish Constabulary at the age of nineteen and resigned in 1848 due to his sympathy for the Young Ireland movement. He joined the 69th New York State Militia of the U.S. army in 1851 and attained the rank of colonel by 1859. In 1860 the Prince of Wales visited New York, but Corcoran refused to parade his regiment in his honour. He was arrested for his refusal, and while awaiting court martial his services were again required by the U.S. army following the attack made on Fort Sumter. He proved to be a very loyal friend to "the Brotherhood" and was decorated prior to his death by the San Francisco Fenians for the stand he had taken in not parading his regiment for the Prince of Wales.

Thomas Francis Meagher

The trials of Thomas Francis Meagher, Patrick O'Donoghue and Terence Bellew McManus took place at Clonmel Courthouse in October 1848 and were made famous by the utter defiance of the prisoners for the duration of the trial and by Meagher's impassioned speech from the dock. Thomas F. Meagher was born in County Waterford about 1825 and received a good education. He joined the Young Ireland movement and was one of its leaders in 1848. He was arrested prior to the rising, convicted and sentenced to death. This was later commuted to deportation to Tasmania, from which he escaped and made his way to America in 1852. On arrival there he practised law in New York, joined the 69th New York State Militia and was badly injured in the First Battle of Bull Run. He recovered and fought in the subsequent battles with his regiment. He rose to the rank of brigadier general and resigned his commission in July 1863 when refused permission to take his troops out of battle while he organised reinforcements. He remained loyal to the Irish cause and gave succour and help to Irish leaders when they went to America seeking funds or help.

The Irish Constabulary and the Great Famine

Prior to the Great Famine, a considerable amount of constabulary time was taken up with the protection of sheriffs, bailiffs and land agents enforcing payment of rents to landlords and collecting the Poor Law rate. In the worst-off parts of the country this was a major problem.

In March 1844, fifty members of the constabulary under two sub-inspectors were engaged in enforcing Poor Law rate in Mayo, accompanied by two stipendiary magistrates and supported by two companies of the 69th Regiment and a troop of the 10th Hussars. In addition, a British warship, the *Stromboli*, and two revenue vessels, the *Dee* and the *Comet*, stood by in Clew Bay. In the House of Commons, it was admitted that one or two warships were used for "moral effect". In Ireland around the same period, a large number of the constabulary and about 700 troops were engaged on the same duties in County Galway.

On 13 March 1846, when a mass eviction took place on the Gerrard estate at Ballinglass, County Galway, the sheriff and bailiffs were protected by fifty members of the constabulary under the direction of Sub-inspector Cummins and supported by ninety members of the 49th Infantry. The village of Ballinglass consisted of sixty houses with about 300 inhabitants. The tenants had most industriously reclaimed about 400 acres of a nearby bog, and the landlord wanted the land. A demand was first made of the tenants to give up their homes, the roofs were then systematically torn off and the houses were demolished. The scenes which followed were frightening and distressing, with women and children endeavouring to retain possession until they were forcibly removed and then leaving with the few worldly possessions they had. To prevent their building any kind of temporary shelter on the site, the walls were levelled to the ground. The sub-inspector's report condemned these evictions, and he was strongly supported by his superior, County Inspector Lewis. There was an outcry about the eviction, and the circumstances surrounding it were investigated by Lord Londonderry, a landlord and a member of the Tory party. In the House of Lords on 30 March, he stated that he was deeply grieved by the events at Ballinglass and said that not alone had seventy-six families totalling 300 persons been evicted from their homes, but that the unfortunate wretches were driven from the ditches where they had attempted to take shelter. He concluded his address by stating, "If scenes like this occurred, was it to be wondered at, that deeds of outrage and violence should occasionally be attempted?"

When the potato crops failed, the constabulary were initially more concerned about it than any other government agency. The monthly reports made by sub-inspectors to their county inspectors and by the latter to the inspector general commented on how bad the situation was in the rural parts of Ireland at that time. The constabulary gave ample notice of the impending disaster, but the reports made by them were ignored. In the autumn of 1845 the constabulary delivered government leaflets relating to potato crops to every household in Ireland.

In August 1846, a sub-inspector from County Cork wrote: "A stranger would wonder how these wretched beings find food. Clothes being in the pawn and there is nothing to change. They sleep in their rags and have pawned their bedding." The hunger gave rise to many demonstrations in towns all over the country, and when these took place, the force was always in the front line endeavouring to control the situation. It is very doubtful if any government agency worked as hard at the coalface during the Great Famine as did the Irish Constabulary. In one particular case, over 700 hungry men marched from the rural parish of Caheragh into Skibbereen town in County Cork armed with spades and shovels. A personal appeal by the local sub-inspector and head of the local military, who made arrangements for the distribution of food, calmed an explosive situation and the marchers dispersed.

The monthly report submitted by the county inspector for Roscommon in October 1846 stated that 7,500 people were existing on boiled cabbage leaves.

Due to a heavy snowfall early in the month, December of 1846 was one of the worst months of the Great Famine. Members of the constabulary at Skibbereen, assisted Richard Inglis, a government inspector, to remove and bury a number of bodies found on the street. Sub-inspector Pinchen earned the admiration of everybody in that district for the efforts made by him and the constabulary under his control to alleviate the hunger, poverty and suffering which was more acute in that part than anywhere else. In the following year he contracted the "yellow fever" which developed from the Famine and became seriously ill.

When the government eventually decided to make some money available through work in relief schemes, "presentment sessions" were held in the towns to give people an opportunity to make a case for essential works to be carried out in that locality, so that able-bodied men could work and earn some money to buy food. In a number of cases when angry people felt that they were not getting sufficient opportunity to earn money, there were violent scenes and the constabulary had a problem in coping. Board of Works officers involved in these schemes were intimidated and a number resigned; at least one was shot at and seriously injured. The pay clerks were considered to be especially at risk and had armed escorts during the course of their duties. In January 1847 a sub-constable was shot dead at Dundrum, County Tipperary, while escorting a pay clerk. In March of the same year, a sub-constable and pay clerk were shot dead on the Chapelizod estate in County Kilkenny. Another sub-constable was shot dead in November 1847 while protecting bailiffs in the seizure of cattle at Moneygall, County Offaly.

In September 1846 a serious riot took place at Dungarvan, County Waterford. About 700 unemployed and starving people entered the town. They threatened shopkeepers and merchants, warning them not to export their grain, and forcibly stole food from some of the shops. The magistrates had the leaders placed in custody, but this made things worse. In spite of efforts by the constabulary to bring the situation under control, a full-scale riot developed, with stone-throwing and damage to property. When a company of the Royal Dragoons, called in to assist the constabulary, failed to clear the streets, their commanding officer gave the order to fire. Several people were injured and two shot dead. Fearing the total breakdown of law and order, the government dispatched extra troops to the most distressed areas of the country.

The soup kitchens introduced as a relief measure in late 1846 and early 1847 provided an additional duty burden for the constabulary. At many centres where soup was being dispensed stampedes occurred, and a number were wrecked by riotous starving people when members of the constabulary were not present. Strong recommendations were made to government to have the soup kitchens set up at the constabulary barracks throughout the country. After some consideration it was decided that the constabulary were already overburdened with duties connected with the Famine and could not provide the service. However, a soup kitchen was set up in the constabulary barracks at Castletown, Queen's County, and members of the force at Ballinasloe delivered soup and provisions to starving people in that area.

Where no relief committees existed, the constabulary had to protect and distribute the Indian meal (maize meal) and oaten meal which had been provided as a relief measure. The force also had the responsibility of assessing the level of destitution of families and individuals throughout the country and reporting to the relieving officers. The constabulary were also frequently needed to restore order at the workhouses. People fled to the already packed workhouses and refused to leave until they got shelter. Those who failed to gain entry roamed the roads of Ireland, starving and dressed in rags, or simply waited outside the workhouse, where many of them died. As the Famine progressed, the same problems in keeping order cropped up at the overcrowded Fever hospitals, where big numbers tried to gain admission.

Early in 1847, starving and destitute people arrived daily at the Liverpool docks, over 300,000 in all. The then chief constable at Liverpool, who took an extraordinary interest in the Famine and the suffering of the poor in Ireland, sent two detectives to Ireland to enquire into the situation and consult with the Irish constabulary. The detectives travelled through a number of counties and gathered what information they could on the tragedy. In a report submitted by the chief constable to his authorities in England, he was scathing in his remarks about some of the landlords in Ireland and their eviction policies.

There were a small number of reasonable and generous landlords who looked after their tenants very well and supported them, but the majority of the landlords contributed in a big way to the worsening situation. The harsh landlords, who were singled out for attack by the disaffected, caused additional problems for the constabulary who had to provide protection for them. Seven landlords were shot during the winter of 1847. The death of Major Denis Mahon, Strokestown, County Roscommon, who had only a short while previously inherited his estate when he was fatally shot on 2 November 1847, caused controversy as there existed two very different views as to how he treated his tenants. (A museum now exists at Strokestown House commemmorating the Great Famine.)

The shootings gave rise to much apprehension and fear amongst the landlords, and they appealed to the lord lieutenant and British government for more protection for themselves and their land agents. Late in 1847 the Crime and Outrage (Ireland) Bill (11 & 12 Vic, c. 2) was passed, authorising the lord lieutenant to move the constabulary from one area to another as he saw fit. The area into which the constabulary were drafted, however, would be responsible for paying the additional costs. Only named classes of persons were permitted to carry firearms, while householders could have them in their houses for their own protection. Should a murder occur in a district, the constabulary were authorised to call upon all able-bodied men between sixteen years and sixty years to assist them in tracing the culprit. A considerable number of additional troops were drafted into Ireland and distributed to different towns in key areas as a back-up to the constabulary.

In addition to all the other duties relating to the Famine, the constabulary also had ordinary policing duties to carry out. They had the task of making arrangements for coroner's inquests on the many dead bodies found. They frequently had to force an entry into houses and cabins where entire families had been dead for days. They had to identify dead bodies and make arrangements for burial, in many cases carrying out the interments themselves.

Raids were made by starving people on flour mills, grain stores and meal stores in different parts of the country. While the number of serious agrarian-related crimes during the Famine was small, there was a substantial increase in petty crimes – most of which were attempts by starving people to obtain food for themselves or their families. In 1847 there was an increase of 60 per cent in crime over 1846, with 10,000 reports of cattle and sheep stealing, 1,000 reports of firearms thefts and 1,200 robberies of provisions, and the force was expected to bring those responsible to justice. They also had to keep an eye on the activities of the Young Irelanders who were planning an insurrection and recruiting members at this time.

During the Great Famine the members of the Irish constabularies dealt with the problems facing them with humanity and patience. There were many instances of their generosity to destitute people during the crisis. It could not have been an easy task, especially in parts of the country which were badly affected by famine and disease. They were all Irishmen and mostly from rural backgrounds, and it would have been very difficult for many of them not to have been affected by this terrible event, either through family connections or through experience of tragedies encountered by them in the course of their duties. They were devastated by the sufferings of the people in the rural areas, coupled with the on-going evictions by many landlords.

In 1847, the members were required to collect agricultural and livestock statistics throughout the country, a duty which must have seemed very ironic at that time.

There was a considerable increase in the strength of the force. From 9,500 members in 1845, the number had increased to 12,500 by 1850. The members were working very long hours, seven days a week, in stressful conditions during the Famine period. The *Tipperary Vindicator* of January 1847 reported: "Thefts of sheep and cows are carried on in this neighbourhood to an alarming extent. Scarce a night goes by that some farmer is not minus a sheep or something else, and the police and the military, between escorts and patrols are harassed off their feet." In 1848 the inspector general expressed his concern about the large number of resignations from the force when he said that "many of our respectable men have sought refuge from such excessive work by withdrawing altogether from the force.... young men of character having begun within the last 12 to 18 months to refuse entering the Constabulary service, notwithstanding he general want of employment".

The Great Famine took a terrible toll on members of the force. In contact with people stricken with fever and dysentery and frequently having to handle dead bodies, it was impossible for many of them to avoid contacting the deadly fever rampant at the time. At one stage, the inspector general issued an instruction to the force to cease providing coffins for dead people or placing bodies in coffins as the risk was then obvious. Long hours and stressful conditions inevitably lowered some members' resistance to the disease, and they too became victims of the tragedy. The highest death rate ever from sickness amongst the Irish and Royal Irish Constabularies occurred during 1847–1849. With the Land War of the 1880s and the Anglo–Irish War 1919–1922, the period of the Great Famine was the most traumatic and demanding period in the history of the constabularies in Ireland.

The following miscellaneous entries from the journal of the sub-inspector at Moate during the year 1848 indicate the varied duties being performed by the constabulary in 1848:

> 18/1/1848. Patrolled to Streamstown, Lissard, Congrove and Donore. Returned at 12 mn. Entered the houses of one Gaffney, of Congrove, John Kelly of Streamstown John Burney, and made enquiry after one Davis said to have the fever and made off raving.
>
> 10/2/1848. At 2 a.m. Constable Barr and Sub-constables McGrath, Grace and Dowdall posted Govt papers in the sub-district cautioning people against harbouring persons accused of felonious crimes.
>
> 20/2/1848. At 7 p.m. Martin McLoughlin reported to Constable Barr, that a carbine was feloniously stolen out of his house at Dunmore at 7 p.m. on the night of the 15th January by some person or persons unknown.
>
> 10/3/1848. Distributing books of good advice, Constable Barr distributed a admonitions to one Cunniffe of Congrove, one to Patrick Ward, one to Patrick Dillane, one to Peter Carroll, one to Patrick Potts and another to James Carbury.
>
> 3/4/1848. At 10.30 a.m. Constable Barr, Sub-constables Carroll and Dowdall went with the Sheriff to the lands of Whitewood where he dispossessed some tenants. Returned at 6 p.m. There were six houses thrown there on this date.
>
> 12/4/1848. Received Proclamation of the French Government to the Irish Deputation.
>
> At 10 p.m. Constable Barr and Sub-constable McGrath went to the lands of Creeve and posted one of the above notices on a tree near Thomas Martin.
>
> 15/4/1848. Sub-constable McGrath brought the following circular; "The Officers of the Force will give immediate directions to the police

to tear down all inflammatory placards that may be posted within their respective districts. Signed: D. McGregor, Inspector General."

27/4/1848. The following letter is promulgated for the information and guidance of the Force: "Various reports have been received by the Government of meetings and assemblies of persons for the purpose of drilling and training themselves, or of being trained or drilled in the use of arms, or of practising military movements or evolutions. I am directed by the Lord Lieutenant to draw your attention to the Act 60 of George 3rd and the 1st of George 4th, by which all such meetings and assemblies, unless under such authority as is herein mentioned, are prohibited, and persons training or drilling others are liable to be sentenced to transportation. Signed: T. N. Reddington, Dublin Castle, 19/4/48."

5/5/1848. Received 20 fresh rounds of ball cartridges and 25 caps for each of the party making 100 rounds and 125 caps at this issue.

15/6/1848. Murder. Constable Barr went to Horseleap to see and visit a man that was found murdered near the Church last night, and on searching him found a document of character stating his name to be John Cook, and the gentleman who gave the character was named John Evans, Crosshouse, 5th February. At 6p.m. Sub-Constable Grace went to Ballintubber, to what reward Mr Fetherston would suggest for the murder of Mr Cook. He said 50 pounds.

17/6/1848. At 7p.m. Const Barr went to Horseleap to attend Inquest and secured 13 persons with Coroner's summonses and Sub-constable McGrath went on the same duty and served summonses on witnesses.

18/6/1848. At 8a.m. Sub-constable McGrath went to Kilbeggan with a report of a man of the name Patk Cleary being found dead at Ballingale on the night of the 17th inst and Sub-constable Dowdall went with a letter to the coroner. At 4p.m. Sub-constable Grace went to Ballingale to give direction to the Moyaulty Police not to let Patk Cleary be interred until the Coroner would arrive to hold the inquest.

20/6/1848. At 9p.m. Sub-constable Connors went to Templemacleer to the Coroner, Mark Kelly, to know would he hold another inquest on the remains of a woman that there was an inquest held on before, on some fresh information.

Connors proceeded from thence to Kilbeggan with the Coroner's answer.

23/7/1848. Information received from .... that on the night of the 20th inst 2 shots were fired through a small window of the house of Patrick Connors.

27/7/1848. Confidential at 7.30 p.m. Received the following letter from

Sub-constable Gamble, Moyoughly; it is the direction of the Government that all persons selling the Nation and Felon newspapers of the 22nd inst should be brought before the magistrate and held on bail for selling and publishing seditious papers. The Constabulary of the district will act accordingly.

30/7/1848. The accompanying circulars are forwarded for the information of the Constabulary who will report to me any infraction of the results anticipated; the documents to be kept clean and the orders to be issued by private dispatch, to be sealed, from station to station by line of route; (1) You will forthwith instruct the constables of your district to watch closely the proceedings of all immigrants from America, so to report the arrival of any such person in their sub-districts, (2) You will immediately give information to the Resident Magistrate on your discovering that any pikes are making or made in your District, or brought into, or any apprehension of disturbance or the formation of clubs (3) The Officers of the force are informed that the Directors of the Railway to have given instructions to the guards of the trains to convey constabulary dispatches in case of urgency along the line of railway, of which you will give instructions to the men of your station. Application should be made insuch instance to the Supt. or other chief officer of the station from whence the dispatch is being conveyed. Sgd. H.J.W. Walsh D. I.

With the Great Famine and the rebellion behind them, the constabulary settled down to the performance of more ordinary and mundane police work. It was said of them that all they needed at this time were their two-foot batons, having no necessity to carry their carbines.

The Royal Visit of Queen Victoria, 1849

In August 1849, Queen Victoria came on a visit to Ireland accompanied by her husband Prince Albert and four children. She had planned to come in 1848 but was persuaded to postpone it. There was mixed reaction towards her visit as many people felt that she and her government could have done much more to alleviate the hunger and distress of the Irish people. The donation made by her of £2,000 towards the famine relief was considered derisory.

The constabulary were not prepared to take any chances regarding the security of the queen during her visit. In May 1848 a man from Adare in County Limerick had fired a pistol at the queen as she was driven in her carriage down Constitution Hill in London. Her life was probably saved by the fact that the pistol was improperly loaded. Information to hand indicated that a group of people intended to kidnap the queen in Dublin and take her into the Wicklow mountains. (News of the latter plan was conveyed to Charles Gavan Duffy, who may have been instrumental in having those plans scrapped, even though it was alleged later that such a group had in fact met at the Royal Canal in Dublin to carry out the kidnap but abandoned their plans as the group was too small.) None of this was very reassuring for the constabulary, and consequently they took all neccessary precautions. There was a total muster of all the constabulary and the military turned out in force to provide honour guards and outriders for the queen and her entourage.

On 2 August the queen arrived at Cove, County Cork, to a huge welcome and officially named the town "Queenstown". The only diversion which took place for the constabulary was when over-exuberant well-wishers, tending a bonfire in her honour, accidentally set fire to fourteen acres of mature fir plantation close to the town centre. The queen reembarked on her steam-powered yacht, the *Victoria and Albert*, and steamed into Cork city where she received a tumultous welcome from a huge gathering of people. There were no incidents in Cork and the welcome received by her there semed to have set the scene for the remainder of her visit. She continued on the yacht to Kingstown (Dun Laoghaire), with a brief stop at Waterford, where Prince Albert came ashore. She continued by open carriage from Kingstown into Dublin city with Prince Albert and her children and then to the Viceregal Lodge where she would remain during her stay. While officially her visit was classed as a "private" one, she attended numerous functions and met many dignatories. She travelled by carriage as far as Carton in County Kildare to visit the Duke of Leinster. At the end of her stay she went by train from Westland Row to Kingstown, where the royal yacht awaited her. Everywhere she went she received a royal welcome and despite the memories of the previous three years of famine, fever and death, the people of Ireland took her her to their hearts. The royal visit passed off without incident and was regarded as a complete success.

The streets of the towns and cities were crowded with beggars, Famine victims or evicted peasants who could not be accommodated in the workhouses. The priority of the constabulary for the queen's visit was to get the beggars off the streets and to hide them anywhere they could out of the view of the queen. In this, the constabulary were fairly effective, and during the royal visit all the streets were free of these most unfortunate people. While Queen Victoria commented on the beauty of the women in Cork city, the London *Times* correspondent who accompanied the royal entourage described the welcome there as being most enthusiastic, though many of the people who crowded the streets looked poor and haggard. In Dublin, the queen again commented on the beauty of the women seen there, but also said, "I see more ragged and wretched people here than I ever saw anywhere else."

The queen again visited Ireland in 1861 and, availing of the new railway system, travelled much more throughout the country. She visited the Killarney area of

County Kerry, where she stayed at Muckross House for some days. At least 200 members were drafted into Killarney during her stay there. The queen also visited the Curragh Camp in County Kildare to see her son, Bertie, Prince of Wales, who had joined the Guards Regiment there a short while previously. This royal visit also passed off without incident.

Introduction of a Reward Scheme for the Constabulary

A reward scheme for the constabulary was provided for in the Constabulary Act, 1836, to provide monetary rewards for head constables, constables and sub-constables who had displayed exceptional zeal, courage or intelligence in the course of their duties. The scheme did not apply to officers. Early abuses of the system became evident, and in April 1842 the inspector general changed the system to awards of chevrons and medals instead of money. When a man distinguished himself under any of the headings mentioned, be became entitled to wear a particular type of chevron on the left forearm. Further distinctions brought him further chevrons, up to a maximum of four. A fifth distinction earned a silver medal as a replacement for the chevrons. Additional distinctions were added by way of chevrons with the medal. Irrespective of his period of service, the member who held a silver medal took precedence in his rank over all who did not hold such medals. Should the holder of chevrons or medal be found guilty of any misconduct, he was penalised by the loss of one chevron. On retirement, the member holding distinctions received an award from the reward fund: £6 per chevron and £35 for a medal for head constables, and £4 and £25 for lower ranks.

Monetary rewards were later made for detections of offences under the fishery acts and similar rewards for the discovery of stills and breaches of the iIllicit distillation acts. There was an acknowledged abuse of claims for rewards made under the illicit distillation laws, and as early as 1860 Inspector General Brownrigg directed that reports relating to these detections should be "perfectly truthful". In July 1902 an Irish MP claimed that in one particular county in Ireland, a still was regularly "planted" by members of the RIC and had earned over 200 rewards.

The Mounted Constabulary

In 1848, 300 mounted constables were trained and stationed throughout the country in the proportion of one mounted man for each sub-inspector and two to each county inspector. A reserve of young horses was maintained at the depot in the Phoenix Park. By 1872, the number of mounted constables had increased to 382; in 1882 there were 261; by 1897 the number was reduced considerably to 138, including head constables and sergeants. Candidates for this section of the force had to be less than twenty-four years of age, between 5 feet 8 inches and 5 feet 10 inches in height, and not more than 12 stone in weight. Training for the mounted constabulary took place at the depot in the Phoenix Park.

Constabulary Strengths

Prior to specific legislation in 1846, the constabulary strengths were fixed as:

County	County Inspectors	Sub-inspectors	Head Constables & Constables	Sub-constables
Antrim	1	4	11	224
Armagh	1	5	8	145
Carlow	1	5	6	151
Cavan	1	8	12	400
Clare	1	11	12	400
Cork	2	20	28	612
Donegal	1	8	14	176
Down	1	7	9	224
Dublin	1	5	7	231
Fermanagh	1	6	8	182
Galway	2	15	24	704
Kerry	1	7	9	168
Kildare	1	6	8	250
Kilkenny	1	9	12	400
King's County (Offaly)	1	7	9	389
Leitrim	1	6	10	312
Limerick	1	10	18	569
Londonderry	1	4	6	96
Longford	1	5	7	191
Louth	1	5	8	224
Mayo	1	9	14	274
Meath	1	8	11	321
Monaghan	1	5	7	145
Queen's County (Laois)	1	8	12	336
Roscommon	1	8	12	447
Sligo	1	6	9	191
Tipperary	2	20	22	1,030

County	County Inspectors	Sub-inspectors	Head Constables & Constables	Sub-constables
Tyrone	1	6	8	150
Waterford	1	6	8	149
Westmeath	1	8	11	282
Wexford	1	8	20	280
Wicklow	1	6	8	189
Cities and towns:				
Carrickfergus	0	0	1	10
Cork	0	1	3	100
Drogheda	0	1	2	70
Galway	0	1	2	65
Kilkenny	0	1	2	50
Limerick	0	1	3	80
Waterford	0	1	2	70

The imbalance in these fixed strengths, referred to as the "parliamentary strengths", very soon become a bone of contention. County Donegal, which is one of the biggest counties in Ireland, was allocated only 176 constables and sub-constables, whereas County Louth, the smallest, was allocated 224. Legislation to rectify these situations was enacted (20 & 21 Vic., c. 17), and the schedule attached thereto allocated 326 to Donegal and 189 to Louth. As the legislators anticipated further calls for changes as time went on, the act authorised the lord lieutenant, acting on the advice of the Privy Council of Ireland, to review the situation at five-yearly intervals and to make whatever adjustments were needed. A condition attached, however, directed that the overall "official strengths" of officers and men fixed by law would not be exceeded. The lord lieutenant did not in fact have occasion to implement this authority. These figures refer solely to the Irish Constabulary and does not include Dublin city, Belfast and Londonderry, which all had separate police forces. (The latter two police forces were eventually incorporated into the Royal Irish Constabulary in 1865 and 1870 respectively.) The strength of the force had increased from 9,000 in 1845 to 12,500 by the year 1850. The constabulary were then paid from government central funds.

Literary Ability of Constabulary Members

While they may have lacked a high level of education, members of the force were very intelligent, good report writers and generally had excellent handwriting. Some displayed a natural gift for rhymes and poems, which were written about many of the unusual aspects of their duties. One of the most unusual, entertaining and longer examples was penned in 1854 by Sub-constable Henry Waters, Regd No. 1161, while stationed at Vicarstown in Queen's County (Laois), who was in severe disciplinary trouble. Through the medium of the poem, he put his best case forward to his authorities for another chance. He recalled all the highlights and incidents of his career and ended with his plea for mercy. It is gratifying to see that Deputy Inspector General E. G. Priestley, restored the rank, pay and status to Sub-constable Waters. The document was found in the attic of a garda station in County Westmeath 100 years later, and the original was in possession of Sergeant F. H. Maguire of Drumlish Station, County Longford, many years ago. In the poem he described the incident which had got him into trouble:

> To Timoleague the two with me went down
> To petty sessions in that little town.
> Unceasing rain poured on us all the way
> Which drenched our clothes and caused us much dismay.
> After the Court we could not leave the town
> For rain in torrents poured in fury down.
> We ordered dinner at O'Leary's Inn
> And after dinner took a glass of gin.
> One of the party Sir, named Michael Harte –
> A comely lad intelligent and smart –
> Soon left the Inn and rambled through the street
> When he some idle strollers chanced to meet.
> An argument they quickly did begin
> At his expense which they believed no sin
> Nor did they stop until his feelings they hurt
> Then knocked him down and kicked him in the dirt.
> They did insult him and assault him too
> Without a cause which everybody knew
> But why they did so I will here explain
> We fined them all which caused them mental pain.

Having outlined all his experiences in the force he then went on to plead for mercy:

> And this great truth the Sacred Scriptures say
> The just man falleth seven times a day.
> And as it is the sacred will of Heaven
> That restitution makes a sin forgiven.
> Six months reduction, pounds shillings and pence

I humbly hope makes ample recompense.
Now in conclusion one request I crave
Emancipation for a wretched slave;
I humbly ask the rank I held before
Which I will keep unstained for evermore.
Onward haste make no delay;
To Major Priestly get away
Whose answer from the Castle gate
I here in silence humbly wait.

Locations of Constabulary Barracks and Allocation of Personnel

By 1852 the Irish Constabulary was distributed amongst 1,594 barracks – an average of fifty barracks to a county and eight personnel to each barracks. The number of barracks per county was as follows:

Leinster		*Ulster*	
Carlow	21	Antrim	35
Dublin	37	Armagh	30
Kildare	45	Cavan	39
Kilkenny	62	Donegal	47
Queen's County (Laois)	42	Down	44
Longford	29	Fermanagh	26
Louth	26	Londonderry	16
Meath	53	Monaghan	24
King's County (Offaly)	54	Tyrone	29
Westmeath	48		
Wexford	41		
Wicklow	35		
Munster		*Connaught*	
Clare	56	Galway	92
Cork	143	Leitrim	40
Kerry	39	Mayo	52
Limerick	99	Roscommon	63
Tipperary	153	Sligo	31
Waterford	43		

The high number of barracks in some counties, particularly Tipperary, Kilkenny, Limerick, Leitrim, Roscommon and Offaly, reflects the unrest in these counties during the previous decades. Barracks are shown in maps of the period within a few miles of each other in some areas. When deciding on the locations for barracks, consideration was given to the "common reputation" of the county, as well as to the amount of influence which various landlords, who all wanted a barracks at their own door could exert. Barracks were very scarce on the ground all along the west coast of Ireland from Kerry to Donegal. Where no suitable building was immediately available to accommodate the constabulary in rural areas, landlords would erect purpose-built barracks to accommodate them, with adjoining accommodation for the sergeant and his family. The barracks were leased at a nominal rent to the constabulary and it qualified for exemption from rates, even though rateable valuations were fixed on the buildings by the *Griffith's Valuation*. In this way, the landlord was guaranteed a full-time police service, as he controlled the accommodation which housed the local constabulary.

A feature of a small number of such barracks is that they were built with one or more circular or square-shaped "towers" to provide an elevated look-out post or to be used for defence purposes if neccessary. The present garda station at Ballon, County Carlow, built within the former Lecky estate, is a classic example of such barracks. In some places, towers were erected to watch for poachers. A classic example of this type (closed down in 1919 and now in ruins) is in County Kerry on the main Killarney-Kenmare road, at Ladies View. Officially titled Mulgrave Barracks, it was built for the new Irish Constabulary by the Earl of Kenmare, not primarily for the protection of the local inhabitants, who were few, but to protect his game, especially the deer. (Rumour persists that the constabulary there got into serious trouble when it was discovered that they had dug a large pit at the rear of the barracks and covered it over with branches and foliage. The pit was an ingenious trap to catch deer, and the constabulary members were reputed to be regularly dining on venison.)

The German travel writer Johann Georg Kohl, who visited Ireland in 1836, wrote of the latter barracks:

> We visited the police station which has been built on the fine new road between Killarney and Kenmare and found it a new, handsome, spacious building, that at a distance looked like a little castle. Far around, the country had an air of romantic desolation that reminded me of the military stations on the Austrian frontier, which are frequently placed on most picturesque spots in the wilderness. The house contained eight policemen of the constabulary force – an armed force now distributed over all Ireland for the prevention of crime, the discovery and seizure of criminals, the protection of property and the preservation of the public peace. It consists of eight thousand men, disciplined like soldiers and distributed over all the country in small parties of from five to eight

men. Their uniform is much plainer and darker than that of the military, but they are armed with muskets and sabres and are allowed to make use of the bayonet as a dagger. The sergeant who commanded at this post informed me that his district embraced an immense extent of naked mountains, and did not contain more than 200 inhabitants, for whom eight armed policemen seemed a large proportion. And yet the county of Kerry is reckoned one of the least disturbed parts of Ireland. The poor mountaineers are not quarrelsome or refractory, and although they have the most violent party man of their country, Daniel O'Connell, in the midst of them, they have fewer party fights than the people of almost any other county in Ireland.

In towns and villages, practically all the barrack buildings were owned by the ascendancy classes who were pleased to rent them at very nominal rents to the constabulary. In the depressed 1840s, many of the owners were only too willing to be guaranteed a rent and proper maintenance for their buildings. On the part of many large property holders, providing accommodation for Her Majesty's Constabulary was a very patriotic display of their loyalty. Only in a very small number of cases was it necessary for the authorities to construct barracks for occupation by the force.

The provisions of the leases for the buildings in some cases had unusual clauses, the constabulary barracks at Tullow Street, Carlow, being a case in point. It was a fine substantial building in a prime location, and it was leased to the constabulary at a very nominal rent on condition that a mounted policeman would be maintained in Carlow town at all times. This condition was fulfilled by the Irish Constabulary and later by the Royal Irish Constabulary. It served as the principal garda station for Carlow town and as headquarters for most of the county from September 1922 up to the early 1990s, but no "mounted policeman" was maintained there by the Garda Síochána during its period of tenure.

The barracks were very well maintained and, while furnished sparsely, were immaculately clean. The majority of these barracks continued in use during the lifetime of the Royal Irish Constabulary and many continue to be used at the present time by the Royal Ulster Constabulary and by the Garda Síochána. Some larger and more fortified structures were built during the lifetime of the Royal Irish Constabulary.

The quality of accommodation provided at the larger centres, where a big number of men were attached to a barracks, was good. The kitchens were fitted with very large ranges fuelled with turf or coal and which had double ovens and a number of hot plates. The ranges also provided hot water for domestic needs. There was an external ablution room with several low stoneware washbasins fitted around the walls. A cold-water tap was fitted over each washbasin, supplied from a tank on the roof which was filled by a hand-operated pump from a well in the yard (and in later years from the mains supply). In some instances, a cone-shaped copper container, about 12 inches in diameter, with a flat surface in which were drilled several holes, was attached to a cold water pipe about 8 feet over ground level. This extremely primitive device was capable of dispensing a very heavy, cold-water shower.

Toilet facilities consisted in most cases of an open-air urinal with a small number of nearby closets. One of the latter was reserved for the officers. An enamel plate was affixed to some of the closet doors with the notice: "Paper only to be used in this Closet. By Order of the Inspector General."

At the district headquarters and county headquarters barracks, stabling was provided for the horses used by the district or county inspectors or by the mounted constabulary. These stables were of excellent lofted construction, with a separate stall for each horse. The floors were paved with small, smooth stones, and a drainage system was provided. A hayrack was fitted at one side of the manger and a metal oats trough at the other side. Hay was fed into the manger through a trap door in the loft overhead. A ventilation shaft extended from each stall, vertically through the loft and the roof overhead, and on top of which a slatted fixture was fixed on the rooftop. There were wooden partitions dividing the stalls and the top section of the stable doors opened separately to enable the horses to extend their heads out through the openings. The care of horses was of paramount importance at all barracks.

The main problem that all the barracks had was the lack of communication. The fitting of telephones was a very long, drawn-out process and depended on the extension of the telephone system throughout the country. The constabulary directories each year up to 1921 listed the names of barracks which had had telephones installed during the previous year. A telegram facility was available from towns from the 1840s onwards. In the case of some remote barracks, carrier pigeons were used in the event of an emergency to despatch messages. As time went on, barracks in vulnerable locations had Very lights, capable of sending rocket flares several hundred feet into the air, to summon assistance in the event of an attack on the barracks. In almost every town and village in Ireland, the constabulary were the first after the local post office to have the telephone installed, hence the predominance of the final digit "2" in the telephone numbers of all the constabulary barracks (continued under the Garda Síochána and RUC).

By the middle of the nineteenth century there were constabulary barracks in all cities, towns and villages outside of Dublin city. Following the Fenian Rising of 1867 the Dublin Castle authorities again carried out a review of all their police barracks and, as a result, a number of substantial barracks were built as district headquarters. The majority of these had married accommodation for the district inspector and head constable attached to the barracks. They were very substantial buildings, normally three or four storeys high. Depending on their locations, some were fitted with watchtowers. They were designed to accommodate a big number of constabulary, and many were strategically located in isolated areas where military or other assistance was not readily available in the event of an attack. Fine examples of these barracks exist at Naas, County Kildare; Pallasgreen, and Bruff, County Limerick; Dungannon, County Tyrone; Connemara, County Galway; and at Cahirciveen, County Kerry. The last of these was built between 1870 and 1875, and when vacated by the RIC in 1922 it was burned down by the IRA to prevent its takeover by the Free State army or new Civic Guards. It was fitted with two watchtowers: one to observe Valentia Island and its trans-Atlantic wireless station and the sea, and the other to keep watch on the approach roads to Cahirciveen. It was beautifully restored in the early 1990s and is now a local heritage centre. Most appropriately it incorporates a museum dedicated to its original occuppants, the Royal Irish Constabulary.

Duties of the Constabulary from 1850 to 1867

The primary duty of the Irish Constabulary was always to protect life and property, to bring criminals and offenders to justice and to maintain peace and good order. In the mid-nineteenth century, attendance at fairs, race meetings and pattern days continued to be a priority. There was an absolute determination to put down faction fighting at all costs, and slowly but surely it faded out completely. Commenting on the period following the 1848 insurrection, Robert Curtis wrote, in *The History of the Royal Irish Constabulary*, that, "Tranquility prevailed from the Giant's Causeway to Cape Clear and from Achill Head to Ireland's Eye." Many were of the view that the force did not have sufficient work to do at this time. What may have been overlooked was that "the absence of crime proved the vigilance and efficiency of the police". At this period, the force was very much settling down to routine police work and doing all the things expected of it.

The most unpalpable and detestable duty for the force continued to be their involvement at evictions. It was totally alien and objectionable to the members of the constabulary and later the RIC. They did not in fact take an active part in the evictions but were obliged by law to provide protection for the sheriff and the bailiffs carrying out this work. In the majority of cases there was no resistance by the unfortunate families being evicted and the constabulary had nothing to do but stand by as observers. Where resistance was met, the sheriff and bailiffs were equipped with a "battering ram", a long heavy pole transported from place to place on a horse-drawn cart. Slung from a tripod by a rope, it was capable of breaking open doors or knocking down walls.

There was no let-up in evictions when the Great Famine ended. In some areas, evictions were not a problem. In many others, however, where ruthless and merciless landlords and land agents held sway, it was an everyday occurrence. The general situation was exasacerbated where estates had changed ownership under the

Encumbered Estates Act (11 & 12 Vic., c. 48). In 1849, approximately 17,000 families were evicted from their homes. In 1850, there were about 20,000 families (around 100,000 persons) evicted. As most members in the lower ranks of the force were sons of small or medium-sized farmers, their distaste for eviction duty is understandable. There were instances of members organising collections amongst themselves and paying over rent or rates to prevent unfortunate families' being thrown out of their homes.

In 1850, the Tenant League was founded by Charles Gavan Duffy to bring together all the groups which then existed to try to provide some protection for tenants. The Tenant League made three simple, basic demands that: tenants should be assured of a fair rent, fixed by an impartial valuation and not by the landlord; they should have security from eviction as long as they paid their rents; and they should be able to sell the interest in their holdings for the best price they could get. These demands became known as the "Three Fs": fair rent, fixity of tenure and freedom of sale.

The aims of the Tenant League were reasonable and Gavan Duffy insisted on the movement's being constitutional, but it failed to attract the peasant farmers. It was also opposed by the Catholic Archbishop Cullen, who considered its doctrine as being socialist. This dispute between Dr Cullen and Gavan Duffy was detrimental to the movement. Frederick Lucas, one of the leaders of the Tenant League, died, and a very dispirited Gavan Duffy emigrated to Australia in 1855. With his departure the Tenant League faded into oblivion. It was generally a well-conducted constitutional movement which created no problems for the constabulary during its existence.

Transport and Mobility

Up to the mid–1840s the only transport available to the constabulary was the horse. Mounted constabulary were maintained at all the district and county headquarters barracks, but they were limited in number. The sub-inspector in charge of a district had a horse for his private use, and county inspectors had a horse-drawn trap or carriage at their disposal. All patrolling and duties in a sub-district were performed on foot, although mounted members conveyed despatches in times of urgency. Members exchanged routine despatches and official correspondence when they met in the course of the "conference patrols". Members from two, three or more barracks met daily at a pre-arranged crossroads, at a pre-arranged time, to exchanged information relating to happenings in their respective areas and pass on details regarding criminals, crimes and suspects and all information of police interest. Horses or horse-and-traps could be hired for the conveyance of prisoners or for duty where it was absolutely essential. For travel between towns, the mail coach was the principal mode of travel and where areas were served by canals, passengers were taken on the canal barges. The Bianconi carriages also operated.

The construction of railways commenced in the 1840s. The arrival of the railways brought a high level of mobility to the constabulary for attending courts, assembling at locations of disturbances and for other duties. The Reserve constabulary force at the depot in Phoenix Park, who were frequently despatched with their horses and accoutrements by rail to different parts of Ireland, could now reach Cork in about six hours. On the other hand, trains also provided rapid transport and getaway facilities for the criminal. Up to this point all crime had tended to be localised, but now the "travelling criminal" also arrived.

Extra Duties allocated to the Constabulary

Dublin Castle and the British government had in the Irish Constabulary a body of dependable, disciplined, dedicated men, of above average intelligence. Whether it was because the authorities felt that the constabulary had things rather easy at this time or whether it was because they felt that there was no other established agency available to the government, very many extraneous duties were added to those already being performed by the constabulary from 1850 onwards.

The agricultural statistics taken in 1845 by the constabulary, coincidentally just prior to the Great Famine, indicated the huge area under wheat and corn at that time. When the Famine struck, these statistics were used and abused to suit relevant arguments. Beginning in the 1850s, this duty was carried out on an annual basis. Like some of the other duties which were allocated to the constabulary at this time, it was inherited by the RIC, the Garda Síochána and Royal Ulster Constabulary. It took over 120 years to have this aspect of non-police work taken over by another government department from the Garda Síochána.

Following the Famine, as a result of claim and counter-claim about the numbers who died and were forced to emigrate as a result of the Famine, the first authentic census was taken in 1851. (They were taken at ten-year intervals after that and subsequently increased to five-year intervals.) The constabulary completed the census returns for the whole of Ireland except Dublin and did an excellent job. The majority of the people were illiterate, so that it fell to the individual constables to complete the census forms for a great many households. In a few parts of the country only Gaelic was spoken, and the constables coped with that problem too. It was not until the 1970s that the Garda Síochána ceased to collect the census.

The constabulary issued voting papers for the election of poor law guardians and again collected the completed papers. They also had to carry the responsibility of enforcing fishery laws during the close season. Most of this duty was on private property where fishing rights were preserved by the landed gentry and was not an appropriate duty for police to be involved in. When the enforcement of laws relating to weights and measures came into existence in 1878, it fell to some members of the constabulary to enforce them. The enforcement of these laws was again inherited by the forces which succeeded it. Countless attempts to hive off this aspect of non-police work to the department to which it rightly belongs having failed, the Garda Síochána are still enforcing these acts.

The registration and licensing of dogs, which came into force in 1865, was another duty which has continued as a police function since then. The vagrancy acts and the Towns Improvements Act depended on the constabulary for their enforcement. Before the 1850s were out, the force got responsibility for enforcement of the illicit distillation laws, when the Revenue Police were disbanded in 1859, posing ongoing problems. The constabulary took on many tasks during this period which were outside the realm of real police work. The fact that the duties were performed so well and at very little cost to the exchequer resulted in these extraneous duties becoming accepted as part of the norm of police work. It took well over a century before any of them were shed, and only then after much deliberation taking place.

Changes in Higher Administration of the Force

In August 1859, an act of parliament (22 & 23 Vic., c. 22) provided for changes at the head of the Irish Constabulary. It authorised the lapse of the office of one deputy inspector general on the retirement or pensioning off of either of the existing ones. From then onwards there would only be one deputy, who would perform the duties already carried out by both. The constabulary depot in the Phoenix Park was placed under the command of a third assistant inspector general, to be known as "the Commandant of the Depot". The rank survived until 1963 when garda training was transferred to Templemore, County Tipperary. A section of the act empowered the lord lieutenant to add the sum of £100 annually to the salary of one of the two remaining assistant inspector generals or, should he think fit, to divide it equally between them.

Sir Duncan McGregor, who had taken over the post in controversial circumstances, completed twenty years' service as inspector general in May 1858 and decided to retire. His pension amounted to £1,500 per annum. He was regarded by the rank and file as a good inspector general and had the ability to get on well with everybody from the most junior to the most senior within the force. He was reasonably lucky during his term of two decades in office, in that there was general stability in the country during the period, except for the Young Ireland Rising of 1848 and the Great Famine.

Sir Duncan McGregor was replaced as inspector general by Henry John Brownrigg, who was later knighted. He was sworn in as inspector general on 9 October 1858. He was an experienced police officer and an extremely able individual and came to head the force with an exceptional track record. As far back as 1828 he had shown the kind of mettle he was made of while serving as chief constable at Skibbereen, County Cork, when he had a major confrontation with a local magistrate named O'Driscoll, who issued a warrant to arrest a man named Collins against whom a charge of rape had been made. Brownrigg, on receipt of the warrant, had it executed without delay and brought the prisoner before O'Driscoll, who was sitting with three other magistrates. The magistrates did not accept the complainant's story and Collins was discharged. O'Driscoll demanded the return of the relevant arrest warrant from Brownrigg, but he protested and refused to hand it over. O'Driscoll threatened to report him but it made no difference. Brownrigg himself reported the matter, and the authorities at the highest level held that he was quite correct in holding on to the warrant. Brownrigg may not have realised it then, but he established a most important principle in law for the protection of a policeman in similar circumstances, which has stood the test of time for almost 170 years. The possession of a warrant legally issued gives a policeman authority for his actions and safeguards him against civil action.

Later at Doneraile, County Cork, he again took issue with local magistrates relating to the execution of warrants and again he was proved to be right. Mr Brownrigg's term in office was to prove a difficult period for the force.

Criticism of the Constabulary

Towards the end of the 1850s, the official firearms on issue to the constabulary changed from the carbine to the long Enfield rifle. The force was also issued with long sword-bayonets. While the practicality of the rifle was obvious as a replacement for the muzzle-loading carbine, the neccessity for the large sword-bayonet was difficult to explain. Given the fact that the country was relatively peaceful at this time and that the constabulary had settled in as a police force and was not a military force, the wisdom of issuing the long sword-bayonet was, to say the least, questionable. While it may have had a place as an accoutrement with full dress uniform for guard-of-honour duty at assizes or visits of VIPs, it was an imposition and hindrance to members in the course of ordinary police work.

Allegations of a very serious nature about the lack of efficiency by the constabulary became widespread in 1859, chiefly relating to the force's having become too military in character, too much under the control of the local magistracy and inefficient with regard to the detection and punishment of crime. Prior to this, charges had been made that the force was too much taken up with drill and field exercises. Very erroneous impressions were formed in the minds of the public as to the amount of time spent by the force on military exercises, which they claimed rendered it ineffective for "more proper police duties".

The public by now had very high expectations from the force and expected it to be everywhere in anticipation of crime. The new long sword-bayonet became the central butt for jokes about the constabulary, with people wondering how they could chase active criminals or jump over walls and fences while carrying them without causing injury to themselves or at least tripping themselves up.

The first attack from the bench on the efficiency of the costabulary came during the summer assizes of 1859 in County Offaly when the judge addressed the grand jury:

> Gentlemen of the Grand Jury, if I had merely to look to the calendar before me, I would have great reason to congratulate you upon the state of your county. There appear on the calendar six cases only. But I am sorry to tell you gentlemen that this circumstance is one of the very worst symptoms of the state of your county, for, upon enquiry I have found that the quantity of unrepressed crime and outrage which has occurred in your county since the last assizes is sixfold in comparison with the numbers that appear to have been made amenable. I need not say what an index that is to the state of your county. Now gentlemen, you have I presume, magistrates, and police too I presume, that know their duty. I do not know the purpose for which a police force is organised if it be not to prevent crime and outrage. I am willing to believe that the persons to whom this duty has been delegated have attempted to perform it, but with respect to the results, I regret to say that they have been just such as if the duty had not been performed at all. I hope that the purpose for which constables have been organised, and the usefulness of the office, have not been merged in the eclat and renown to which for some purpose or other, they may very laudably aspire – namely the character of a military body; but unquestionably, the primary duty of the police constable is that of an officer for preserving the peace of the country, and where he cannot preserve, of discovering, hunting out, tracing and bringing to justice the offenders. I hope gentlemen that the increased diligence by the police in the discharge of their duties, and the consciousness that it will be for their own advantage to detect crime, will induce them to leave no stone unturned to get at the root of the evil and repress the crime which undoubtedly exists.

This was the first public rebuke of the period for the constabulary.

The judge's charge was most serious in nature and to have remained silent would have indicated acceptance of the allegations made. The inspector general felt obliged to submit a report to government on the issue and went into the matter in great detail:

I must confess myself unable, from any reports in my possession to understand upon what data the statement was founded, that the unrepressed serious crime of the county bears so large a proportion to the amount made amenable, as ten or even six to one. But having called upon the County Inspector for a return of all the outrages reported to have been committed within the period in question, I proceed to examine it in connection with the comments of the judge, so far as they relate to an implied want of zeal on the part of the constabulary. It is true – but this is not peculiar to any particular county – that the cases on the calendar do not afford a complete picture of the state of the county in reference to crime, since the calendar comprises only custody cases and omits cases in which bail is taken, so neither does it afford a fair measure of the exertions or even the successful exertions of the police. The number of cases actually brought forward at the assizes in question was twelve as will be shown in the annexed returns. No 2 is a statement which I think will show that the efforts of the police (who it is important to observe) were engaged either as prosecutors or witnesses in each of the cases tried have not been waning, both in the detection and punishment of offenders, and that their efforts have been attended with a fair share of success.

There was no later censure of a similar nature in County Offaly.

February 1862 was marked with three separate murders in County Tipperary. The three victims – Messrs Fitzgerald, Thibault and Michael Maguire – were all murdered during daylight hours following problems relating to agrarian trouble, and all the murders happened within a few days of each other. Seven people were arrested by the constabulary and a special commission was set up to try them. The man who murdered Fitzgerald was convicted and executed. His accomplice gave himself up because, as he said himself, "his life wasn't worth living" because of the large-scale searches for him by the constabulary. He was convicted and executed. Two other conspirators to the same murder and the man who harboured them after the event were convicted and executed.

The man charged with the murder of Mr Thibault was acquitted and a man charged with the murder of Michael Maguire was discharged on recognisance, as the Crown deemed the evidence insufficient to proceed to trial.

There was general alarm at these three murders, in County Tipperary and elsewhere, not so much that the murders had been perpetrated, but at the fact that they happened in broad daylight. The constabulary fell in for much criticism. Typically, the higher echelons of society complained that they should have been aware that these murders might happen and that they should have prevented them. Their "military character" was again adverted to, and it was alleged that since they had been issued with the long rifle, they were spending too much time drilling. The magistrates also availed of the opportunity to air their grievances, grumbling that the police weren't what they used to be since they ceased to be under the control of the magistrates. The grand jury assembled at the special commission for the trial of those accused forwarded a resolution to government stating that:

> They considered it their imperative duty to call the attention of the government, to the constitution and discipline of the constabulary force, with an earnest hope that they would take into their serious consideration how far that body fulfilled their mission as a preventive or detective police. That for some years past, the constabulary had become more and more a military force, and in exact proportion as that system had been established, their usefulness and efficiency as a domestic force had been weakened and impaired. The Grand Jury wished particularly to call the attention of the executive to three points: First, That the members of the force are taught, not alone to look to their chief in Dublin, as their only source for promotion or reward, but that any expression of approval or recommendation from the local magistrates, no matter how well deserved, is a positive injury and actual bar to professional preferment. Second, That the counties being divided into districts, no properly organised system of communicating intelligence of the commission of crime had been established between one district and another. [As an example, they instanced the fact that the murderous attack on Colonel Knox near Templemore was not reported to Borrisoleigh barracks, only five miles distant, for 24 hours after the occurrence and they added that they had no doubt that a similiar remissness had taken place in regard to other barracks in the vicinity.] Third. That as the principal use of the police is to watch, and protect life and property in the rural districts, their recent equipment with a heavy and delicate weapon, such as the rifle and sword bayonet, rendered it impossible for them to pursue a delinquent over a close or hilly country and did not leave them the unencumbered use of their limbs in close contact. The Grand Jury, however were most anxious to record their opinion that the failure of the system was owing not to the individuals, but to the military organisation established at headquarters.

This very strong censure was sent by the lord lieutenant to the inspector general, who submitted an eight page, typed report in which he made a very able and elaborate defence against all the allegations. In relation to the three murders mentioned, he highlighted the speed and efficiency of the constabulary in bringing those responsible to justice and pointed out that it was not the fault of the constabulary that sufficient evidence was not available to convict all those charged. It was 1864 before judges, in three different counties, again openly criticised the constabulary.

In Roscommon, the judge, enumerating the number of crimes which had been committed since the previous assizes, commented:

> These, gentlemen, are startling facts and to my mind there are only two causes to be assigned for it; either the injured persons were unwilling to have recourse to justice from fear or sympathy; or else another case might be, that the constabulary of the country, however efficient in other respects may be deficient in that delicate part of their functions – the detection of crime. I greatly fear that there is more attention paid by the higher grades of the constabulary in making them a military force than in rendering them efficient in the discharge of their duties.

In County Cavan, the judge at assizes commented very sharply about the amount of crime in the county in which the perpetrators had not been brought to justice. Although he did not mention by name the constabulary as being to blame for this, his remarks could bear no other interpretation.

The judge in Limerick was next to follow and was more stinging in his attack:

> I have been furnished by your County Inspector with his report of crime committed since the last assizes and I am struck with surprise at the numbers set down, for which no person has been made amenable, and others where the prosecution has been altogether abandoned. This gives rise to the question, who is looked to on that head? That question is one easily answered; in fact the answer at once presents itself – the constabulary. This I say is not at all creditable to them and such a state of things should not be. In other places a similiar want of efficiency has been complained of, as I read observations made by one of my brother judges now in circuit in another place, complaining that parties who committed crime had not been made amenable. I am not one of those to join in an unneccessary and unreasonable outcry against the constabulary. I know them to be an excellent body of men and I should like to uphold their position for usefullness and efficiency; but it should not lie at their doors, that to their want of energy is attributable, the non-punishment of offenders, who in many instances are known to be the perpetrators of crime.

Sir Henry Brownrigg was again forced to respond to these criticisms, in the course of which he commented:

It would seem that the revival of this complaint, at the present period of tranquility, is owing to certain observations of some of the judges at the recent assizes, chiefly those of the counties, Cavan, Limerick and Roscommon.. In considering this question I will leave out of view the numerous collateral duties performed by the constabulary, because those who pronounce the force inefficient in the respect adverted to, frankly admit that it renders useful service to the public in other respects. I will not even now claim credit for its preventive efficiency – for the benefits resulting directly from its presence in the country – in preserving the peace at markets, fairs and elections – in averting angry collisions between parties and factions and otherwise. Passing by valuable services rendered and beneficial influence exercised, I am willing to bring the present question within the narrow limits and to inquire simply – though this is the position least advantageous to the force – can it be fairly said of the constabulary as a body, that it is inefficient in making offenders amenable and that the failure of justice in so far as it does fail, is to be laid to its charge either as regards its inactivity or its peculiar constitution. It appears to me that the use which has been made of these observations was not that for which they were uttered. With the exception of a single reference at Roscommon to the military character of the force, and a passing allusion to it in Limerick, the design of the judges it may be fairly presumed was not to condemn the organisation of the constabulary but to give a public solemn expression of detestation of a certain class of offences and by calling upon the officers of justice to use increased exertions for the detection of offenders to warn and deter others from similiar practices. But I must still observe, that it is not fair to reason from three counties in the whole of Ireland nor from the impunity of certain offenders to a sweeping charge of general police inefficiency. It is but reasonable to take the whole case into consideration, and to regard it in all its bearings, before judgement is pronounced. If one of these statements be admitted, the whole should be and as the matter is of importance, I take leave to complete the case, by collecting the testimony of the judges, as respect the remaining twenty-nine counties.

As if the inspector general had some other information then at his disposal, the criticisms of the judges at Roscommon, Limerick and Cavan were followed by public tributes to the constabulary by at least ten other judges and the comments made by them were generous. One county judge commented:

Now in reference to those cases in which punishment did not follow, I think I may exculpate the constabulary from any blame or neglect.

I ought, before passing by the constabulary gentlemen, possibly to make one further observation upon it, more especially as at the present time, serious charges have been made against that force and when it has been alleged generally that they were inefficient. I must say that that is an opinion in which I do not agree. I have had very large experience of that body both during five years when I had the honour of being one of the law advisers of the Crown and after a judicial experience of eight successive assizes I confess that the impression left on my mind and the opinion I formed upon the constabulary (whether I regard them as endeavouring to preserve the public peace or in bringing offenders to justice) was, that it could not, and that it cannot be fairly said that the force is inefficient. On the contrary, I should describe it as zealous and efficient, especially when you take into account that there are parts of this country in which impediments are thrown in the way of administering justice and in the way of discovering criminals.

Another judge made comments on the issue with an excellent observation relating to witnesses which has proved to be so true so often since then:

With respect to the several crimes committed, the perpetrators of which have not been made amenable, the reasons for non-detection appear to be, that the injured parties do not wish to bring those who have committed the crimes against them to justice and accordingly are not willing to give information, although they may be perfectly aware who the offenders are. Now, it is not at all fair to blame the constabulary for not bringing those parties to justice. So though in other counties judges had thought it right to find fault with the constabulary for not doing their duty, I really do not see anything before me that would call upon me to join in such censure.

The inspector general replied to the charges that the constabulary was too military in character as a separate issue:

With respect to this allegation, it is not however easy to deal with a mere general statement. When a definite proposition is advanced, it can be considered and approved or rejected. But when as is most unfrequently the case, it is said that the constabulary are "too military", the exact amount of meaning intended to be conveyed is not very apparent. If for example, it were alleged that the Irish Constabulary should cease to be grouped together in barracks, and live indiscriminately amongst the people – that they should cease to be under authority and control, and go where and do what should seem good to themselves – that they should cease to wear a uniform and dress as they pleased – or that they should cease to carry arms and be served out with walking sticks – such proposals made would at least have the merit of being intelligible. But what is meant by the force being "too military" – too military for what and in what respects "too military"?

If it means that they are not civilians – that the duties they are employed upon are not of a purely civil nature; that those duties have any resemblance to those of the military; or that the existing organisation is not adapted to the state of things in this country, then I am persuaded that everyone really conversant with the subject will be prepared with me to deny the allegation. There is no reason to fear, that the constabulary force as at present constituted and at present governed will ever merge into a mere military body. Everything is against such a contingency – true, they live in barracks, they wear a uniform, they are armed and equipped and they are taught the field exercise, but there the resemblance ends. And is this military appearance which some complain of an unmitigated evil? Has it no tendency to deter breaches of the peace or to impart confidence to the well disposed? Is it nothing to have visible proof that the constabulary can upon occasion, assemble in strength and oppose the concentrated force of a disciplined armed body, to the movements of an ill-organised rabble. The force has indeed been remarkably free from a military mania. The men composing it are of a different stamp from those of the army. They are attached to their own corps and accustomed to its peculiar duties, for which they required a predilection. No attempt to recruit for the army from the constabulary (even for crack regiments) has ever been successful. The effort made during the Crimean war to obtain from the constabulary volunteers for the Guards, even with the advantage of carrying with them their constabulary service, was a failure, and was received by the men with a feeling nearly approaching to merriment.

This fighting reply from the inspector general put an end to allegations that the force was "too military". Ironically it would only be a few years until the constabulary came face to face with the "ill-organised rabble" in the Fenian Rising of 1867.

The Constabulary Band

In 1861 the inspector general, Sir Henry Brownrigg, made arrangements for the establishment of a constabulary band. A former army bandmaster, Harry Hardy, was selected to form the band with twenty-five volunteers with some knowledge of music. The band, established on 21 November 1861, trained very hard over the next number of months. In April 1862 it made its first official appearance in the depot square at Phoenix Park for the official parade of the depot Reserve. The inspector general was so impressed by the performance of the band that he later increased its official strength to fifty members. The band's greatest moment was at the depot on 6 September 1867, the day it performed for the ceremonies connected the the presentation of Constabulary Medals for valour to members of the constabulary and on which the force was granted its "Royal" title. The band performed in the depot square on Friday evenings during the summer period for the entertainment of the public, who came to hear it in great numbers. Under the direction of Mr Hardy, who retired as bandmaster in 1872, the band earned an excellent reputation for the quality of its music.

The *Police Gazette* or *Hue and Cry*

The most important document circulated to the constabulary relating to police work was the *Police Gazette*, better known as the *Hue and Cry*, which had commenced as a one-page document in the 1820s. It was published on behalf of the inspector general on Tuesday and Friday of each week without fail. The document, usually consisting of four pages in tabloid size, was printed by Alexander Thom, 87 Abbey Street, Dublin. It was circulated to all the constabulary and to the Dublin Metropolitan Police. It set out in bold print, on the front page, details of proclamations issued from time to time. Descriptions of persons wanted for criminal activities or persons who had escaped from custody or mental asylums were given in detail. Ticket-of-leave convicts whose licences had been revoked were also included. Individual, alphabetical spaces were allocated to each county, so that it could issue bulletins about wanted criminals. Where details had already been published of persons wanted for serious crime, reminders were inserted from time to time if a suspect had not been arrested. The *Hue and Cry* also published descriptive particulars of escaped or wanted criminals for the Dublin Metropolitan District and on behalf of the British Constabulary where there were Irish connections to a crime there. Those wanted for the shooting of Sergeant Brett in the Manchester Martyrs case of 1867 is a case in point.

A beggar charged with larceny remanded to the Bridewell at Urlingford, County Kilkenny, shortly after the Famine, escaped by climbing over a wall. He was wanted by the constabulary at Johnstown, County Kilkenny, and it was stated that he was twenty-one years of age and collected old rags. His clothing was described as follows: "dressed in an old straw hat; old green broad plaid frock coat; old cord trousers. From travelling without footwear he has very broad feet." Descriptions given of the persons and the clothing worn by them are most extraordinary, but typical of the period.

It was obligatory on all members to study the *Hue and Cry*, and they were expected to memorise details of the persons wanted for crime and their wearing apparel – but most especially any marks or peculiarities which they had. As an incentive to the constabulary, there was a reward of £1 (almost one week's pay) for the arrest of a suspect where the arrest was made solely from the description given in the *Hue and Cry*. On the occasion of inspections by the county or sub-inspector members of the force were always examined on their knowledge of items included in the publication.

The *Hue and Cry* was the primary document of police intelligence in the hands of the constabulary and later the Royal Irish Constabulary. It was meticulously filed and kept up to date. Before the description of any person could be entered in the *Hue and Cry*, an "information" had to be sworn on the subject before a magistrate. Descriptions of persons were normally only inserted where felonies or misdemeanours were committed, or where the crime was of an aggravated nature.

The Liquor Licensing Laws

Police work and enforcement of the liquor licensing laws have always been entwined and have run parrallel with one another. Up to 1735, there was no law governing the sale of intoxicating liquor and trade was left to the conscience and morals of the innkeeper. The first intervention by the law makers, in 1735, merely prohibited the sale of drink to servants. Fifty years after that, legislation decreed that pawnbroking and public-house keeping did not mix. In 1815, the public sense of wrong manifest itself through a law which prohibited the payment of wages by means of drink, or in a tavern or inn. This was the first intervention made into a publican's life by the constabulary and the relationship has continued ever since. Very shortly afterwards, the excise man took an interest in publican's affairs and this relationship has also survived.

The next piece of legislation was more of an assistance to the publican than a hindrance. It came in 1831 and set out to control illicit distillation or poteen making which was very rife at that time. In 1833, the constabulary obtained statutory power to enter licensed premises and eject gluttons and gamblers. Two years later, drinking in the theatre became regularised, and the patron could enjoy a drink while frequenting his local playhouse. Legislation of 1836 prohibited illegal and secret societies from meeting in the public houses and it also prohibited the displaying of flags or symbols of illegal or secret societies on the premises. The civil bill officer and members of the Irish Constabulary joined the list of those who were not eligible to be publicans. Further legislation in 1852 and 1854 gave further authority to the constabulary in relation to enforcement of the licensing laws.

The year 1860 brought a radical change with the introduction of "prohibited hours". Just two years later, further legislation brought restrictions relating to the consumption of alcohol on Christmas Day, Good Friday and certain other days of fast and thanksgiving. Very comprehensive legislation in 1872 exerted many tight controls on licensed premises and their conduct and even compelled the publican to paint his name and business over his door. Many of the provisions of the nineteenth century statutes are still enforceable and relevant. After 1872 there was a break of thirty years without new legislation relating to the sale of intoxicating liquor, and this came with the 1902 act which made provision for "hotels" and the conditions under which drink might be sold and consumed in them.

Legislation (44 & 45 Vic., c. 58) gave far-reaching powers to the constabulary relating to the billeting of the military in licensed premises. Section 104 provided that:

> Soldiers may be billeted in inns, hotels, livery stables or ale houses, also houses of sellers of wine by retail to be drunk on the premises and all houses of persons selling brandy, spirits, strong waters, cider or methylene by retail. Provided that an officer or soldier shall not be billeted in any private house, nor in the house of a distiller, nor in the house of any shopkeeper whose principal dealing is more in other goods than in brandy or strong waters, where no tippling is permitted, nor in a house licensed for sale of beer or cider, not to be consumed on the premises.

Section 105 specified that: "All officers and soldiers of her Majesty's regular forces, all horses belonging to such forces and all horses belonging to the officers of such forces, for which forage is allowed, are entitled to be billeted." The officer commanding the military could order any member of the constabulary to arrange the billetting of officers, soldiers and horses. These were wide-ranging powers and not welcomed by people in the licensed trade.

The Erection of Courthouses

Early in the nineteenth century, the standard of courthouse buildings was very bad. Most towns had bridewells where magistrates and justices of the peace sat and dealt with prisoners brought before them in custody, or persons charged with summary offences. The bridewell was fitted with one or two cells where prisoners could be detained for short periods. The quality of the bridewell depended on the generosity of the local landlord who normally funded it. There were gaols in all the county towns and cities for holding convicted prisoners or prisoners remanded in custody. The gaols were under the control of the military and were in close proximity to large military barracks. Demands were made for the erection of new courthouses from 1800 onwards, and by the 1850s several were in place. Those erected in the county towns where assizes were held were grandiose in their style of architecture and cost in the region of £15,000 to erect. Architecturally many of the courthouses – including those at Naas, Clonmel, Port Laois, Cork city, Waterford, Wexford, Trim, Ennis and Galway, are similar because they were all designed by the same architect – Sir Richard Morrison. He also designed several of the great houses for wealthy landlords, as well as designing or redesigning some of the old Church of Ireland churches. The courthouse at Tralee, County Kerry, was designed by a fifteen-year-old apprentice architect – William Morrison. It was completed in 1835 and cost £14,000. The new courthouses were erected in the most important and central locations in the towns, with imposing porticoes of ionic columns, and were symbols of the power and authority of the British Empire. They still dominate the streetscapes of Irish towns.

Chapter Four

1864–1867

THE BELFAST RIOTS AND
THE FENIAN RISING

From 1800 to the 1860s, parts of Ulster had unique policing problems which sprang from animosity between Roman Catholics and Protestants and blatant sectarianism. There was relative peace in the province during the eighteenth century, when the Catholics, in a minority in many areas and powerless to challenge the Protestant supremacy of the period, humbly accepted their lot. The nineteenth century brought new thinking in Europe towards political democracy and religious freedom. Britain introduced legislation in line with the advances made throughout Europe, and the Catholic Emancipation Act of 1829 (10 Geo. 4, c. 7) brought immense freedom to the Irish Catholics. This act gave Catholics the right to sit in Westminister parliament and to hold certain official positions – which up to then were confined to Protestants. Another act extended the voting rights by reducing the property qualifications. Catholics were now able to vote and elect members of parliament. The Tithes War of the 1830s occasionally resulted in clashes between Catholics and Protestants, and the latter very much resented the measures taken by the British government to alleviate the problem by enacting the Church Temporalities Act of 1833 (3 & 4 Wm. 4, c. 37) and the Tithe Rent Charge Act of 1838 (1 & 2 Vic., c. 109).

The Protestants became concerned at the freedom which Catholics appeared to be enjoying and they were determined to protect their Protestant heritage at all costs. The organisation through which they manifested their displeasure and resentment was the the Orange Order, founded in 1795, which rapidly grew in strength from the mid-1820s onwards. Orange demonstrations and parades were frequently held in north-east Ulster. These demonstrations were most provocative displays of Protestant supremacy, and many of the Orange parades were deliberately directed through predominantly Catholic areas, leading to many disturbances, with the constabulary trying to maintain peace and control. A vicious clash between Protestants and Catholics took place in the course of an Orange parade at Magheramayo, County Down, on 12 July 1849. The Orange parade, accompanied by a large contingent of constabulary supported by military, forced its way through a thickly populated, predominantly Catholic townland. The Catholics endeavoured to halt the parade, and in a vicious confrontation a number of people were killed; very many people, including members of the constabulary who were trying to separate the factions, were seriously injured.

The Catholic Church was very militant and progressive and seemed to have got a new lease of life subsequent to the 1840s, generating fears amongst the Protestants. Less than one third of the population of Belfast were Catholics. They lived in the same area of the city, which gradually became an established ghetto, and did not socialise or mix with their Protestant neighbours. Poverty was rampant and only a small number were lucky enough to find employment in the linen mills and other Belfast industries. Clashes between the religious groupings were frequent, with occasional riots. Neither the mayor, city council, the magistracy, nor the local Belfast police were competent to deal with sectrarian violence which erupted frequently there, and the Irish Constabulary were frequently called upon to assist in Belfast city, normally only after trouble had taken place. The Belfast police were drawn from the Protestant population and they performed their duties in a most sectarian manner, resulting in very bad relations between them and the Catholic community. Matters came to a head in August 1864, when a major riot took place lasting for several days.

Following the death of Daniel O'Connell in 1847, the Catholic Irish people wished to commemorate his memory by erecting a substantial monument. For this purpose, money was collected at home and abroad, and the erection of the monument was undertaken at the lower end of Sackville Street (now O'Connell Street), Dublin. Although the Irish authorities had a policy of not permitting the erection of such monuments in public streets or public places, and this policy was supported by law, this monument was allowed. This infuriated the Ulster Protestants, who claimed that the authorities had "gone soft" and were too timid to enforce the law. About 4,000 displeased Belfast Protestants and Orangement assembled in Belfast and burned an effigy of Daniel O'Connell in protest. Thus started one of the most serious of all Belfast riots.

Four hundred members of the constabulary, 300 infantry and two troops of hussars were drafted into the city. A Catholic chapel and a Catholic female remand home were burned down by a Protestant mob. The local Belfast police were unable to control the situation. Arson, looting and street fighting between opposing mobs continued almost non-stop. The constabulary frequently discharged their firearms to quell disturbances. Several people – believed to total twenty-nine – were killed and very many were injured and mutilated. After eleven days and nights of violence, the situation was got under control, but due to the strong possibility of a recurrence should the forces leave, the constabulary and some of the military remained on and maintained patrols in the city until total peace ensued.

The British and Irish authorities were very disturbed by this serious riot, and a commission of inquiry was set up to investigate it, with specific directions:

> ... to inquire into the existing local arrangements for the preservation of
> the peace of the borough; the magisterial jurisdiction exercised within
> it; the amount and constitution, and efficiency of the local police force
> usually available there; the proceedings taken by magistrates and other
> local authorities towards the prevention, or suppression of the said riots
> and disturbances; and whether those authorities and the existing police
> force were adequate to the future maintenance of order and tranquility
> within the borough; or whether any, and what changes ought to be made
> in the local, magisterial and police jurisdiction and arrangements with
> a view to the better preservation of the public peace and the prevention,
> or prompt suppression of riot and disorder.

The commissioners appointed immediately got down to business. They sat for twenty-one days and examined 128 witnesses, including the mayor, several of the ex-mayors, the local magistrates, a number of the aldermen and councillors and the chairman of the police committee. They took evidence from the clergymen of all denominations, the wealthy mill owners and business people, traders and owners of house property. A number of the constabulary officers and military officers engaged in supressing the riots also gave evidence. On 8 March 1865 the commissioners presented their report to the lord lieutenant and recommended sweeping changes. Due to the inefficiency and other objectionable points in the constitution of the local Belfast police, the report recommended that the whole of the existing system should be done away with and that the preservation of the peace in Belfast city should be handed over to the Irish Constabulary.

Under legislation passed on the 29 June of that year (28 & 29 Vic., c. 70), a complete sweep was made of the entire Belfast police force. From that date onwards, it was deemed unlawful for the Belfast town council to appoint or maintain any police force whatever. All chief constables, inspectors, constables and other officers of the local police were to cease to hold office and all the powers and duties of the local police force handed over to the Irish Constabulary. The total authorised number of constabulary was fixed by law, so a redistribution of the constabulary forces was necessary to replace the 106 Belfast police. The act also directed that the town council of the borough of Belfast would be responsible for paying a substantial amount of the costs of the 130 members of the constabulary allocated to Belfast. The head of the force in Belfast was to be known as the "inspector of constabulary for the town of Belfast", and two sub-inspectors were appointed to assist him. The inspector's salary was fixed at £400 per annum, to be defrayed by the town council. The inspector's title was later changed to "commissioner". A further provision enabled the inspector general to admit into the Belfast constabulary any member of the old Belfast police under forty years old, provided he was in other respects eligible for appointment. The town council was to pay superannuation to any member of the old force not being appointed to the constabulary.

The Irish Constabulary mastered the situation in Belfast and provided a much more professional and efficient police service to the community there. For many years afterwards there was no riots or major disturbances in the city. Throughout the province the force also exercised its authority to a greater degree with the Orange Order and the sectarian problems and contained the violence connected with it.

Belfast proved to be a difficult location for policing by the Irish and Royal Irish Constabularies. Even though there were a number of Catholics in the force after 1865, the force was never trusted by the Catholic minority. On the takeover by the Irish Constabulary, the *Belfast Newsletter* described the constabulary as "a green badge of disgrace imposed on the city", and it claimed that the new police were "by no means civil". In April 1876 the same newspaper had changed its views when it stated that "respectable persons have the fullest confidence in the RIC armed or unarmed, but it is otherwise with the roughs who are often in their hands". Because of their confrontations with the RIC during the "marching seasons", the Protestants had no love for the force either. The Belfast working classes, irrespective of their religion, created the most serious on-going problem for the force. (The situation was almost identical in Dublin city.) There were numerous serious assaults on members and they had to patrol in numbers. Seventy-three RIC men were wounded in the city in 1872. Members received special truncheon training in five-man teams. They were advised to avoid arrests as far as possible as arrests led to organised rescue attempts which frequently ended up in riots. The very serious riots of the 1880s resulted in much animosity towards the police. Tension was always high in Belfast around Twelfth of July celebrations and marches. Many RIC were drafted in from all over the country on an annual basis to preserve the peace and control the marches in July; 2,000 members of the RIC were deployed in getting the 1886 riots under control. Subsequent to 1922, the relations between the Belfast working classes and the new Royal Ulster Constabulary continued to be strained.

The Retirement of Inspector General Sir Henry Brownrigg

Sir Henry Brownrigg, who retired as inspector general on 1 May 1865, after almost seven years in that position, was regarded as one of the most able and efficient inspector generals of the constabulary. While his stay in office was relatively short, it proved to be during a most difficult period for the force. He persistently defended the constabulary against all the charges made against them during these years, and there were many, but he did not disregard genuine complaints and took firm action when the occasion demanded. He placed more emphasis on the study of police duties by the members of the force and despite their long rifle and unwieldy sword-bayonet, he did not want it to be a "military style" police force.

Reports and explanations to the lord lieutenant about allegations made by judges took up a sizeable amount of his time. An eighty-four-page pamphlet incorporating all the defences made by him to the charges which had been levelled against the constabulary was printed before he retired from the force. His reports were brilliant, clear, definitive and most convincing and always included facts and data in support of his arguments. He had the total confidence and support of the lord lieutenant. From his early days in the force, he took an independent stand with the magistrates and endeavoured to assert the independent role of the constabulary. Some of the principles for which he fought are still relevant at the present day. While the magistrates made life difficult for him at the start of his career, the judges and grand juries created some problems for him in the latter years. His son, Thomas Marcus Brownrigg, was appointed assistant inspector general of the constabulary on the same day on which Sir Henry retired, a position which he served with some distinction until 1877. Sir Henry Brownrigg was replaced as inspector general by Colonel Stewart Woods, who had served as deputy inspector general for the previous five years. He was sworn into office in May 1865.

Dissatisfaction with Constabulary Pay

In the late 1850s and early 1860s there was an improvement in the economy, with wages doubling in the space of a short number of years. Tradesmen were earning around 4s. per day and there was a big demand for their services. At the same time, the prices of all provisions also went up nearly double compared with a few years previously. The constabulary, whose pay rates had remained static for thirty years, found that tradesmen and general workers' pay had overtaken theirs, and dissatisfaction sprung up in the force. A considerable number of young, able-bodied single men left the force after only five or six years service to go to America, Australia and elsewhere where other members of their families were earning big money.

At the same time, the number of recruits to the force dropped to almost zero and the force was under its official fixed strength. Calls to the depot in Dublin for trained recruits met with a response: "Get us some candidates down there." Potential candidates found that they could earn as much money elsewhere without risk to their lives.

Just one month after Colonel Stewart Woods took over as inspector general, in June 1865, he submitted a report to government with some very firm recommendations for an increase in pay. When his submissions did not have the desired effect and as the situation deteriorated further, he submitted another report in November of the same year, setting out the existing circumstances and the consequent difficulties which faced him with greater emphasis and urgency. He reccommended a considerable increase in the long-service pay of the men in each rank, while he strongly recommended that a certain number of the older county and sub-inspectors who had over thirty-eight years service should be permitted to retire, carrying their long-service pay with them as part of their pension. The lord lieutenant strongly backed the reccommendations. The government's response was to set up a commission "to inquire into the state of the constabulary force of Ireland, with respect to their pay and allowances, strength and organisation, classification, conditions of service, and system of superannuation, and with reference to the causes which led to the large number of vacancies in the body". Dismayed and disappointed, the members of the force – including the inspector general, supported by the lord lieutenant felt – that there could be no doubt about the merits of their claim. The commission of inquiry went ahead with its work and thirty-six witnesses gave evidence and answered a total of 4,411 questions. The inspector general himself answered 827 questions.

The commission submitted its findings to the lords of the treasury and the recommendations were later incorporated in an act of parliament. To entice recruits into the force a considerable increase in pay was given to those entering the force, all long service pay was done away with and an equivalent addition made to the regular salary. A recommendation was included that the promotion from the ordinary ranks to the position of sub-inspector should be doubled.

The higher ranks received an increase of £12 per annum, while the middle ranks benefitted much less than that. An allowance of £100 per annum was made to the inspector general to forage his horse. The middle and higher ranks were displeased with the findings of the commission, which fell far short of what the inspector general had initially recommended. Officers with long service of up to forty years were demanding a pension equal to their full pay, which they claimed they were guaranteed by the act under which they had been appointed. In an act of parliament in August 1866 (29 & 30 Vic., c. 103), the long-service pay element was done away with, while a proportionate addition was made to the regular salary, but a clause was inserted with the intention of cutting off that increase from the officers who had been appointed prior to the act, when retiring on pension. The senior officers due to retire had a justifiable grievance about the manner in which they were treated and went into retirement feeling very angry and aggrieved.

The Rise of the Fenian Movement

Following the Young Ireland Rising of 1848, James Stephens and John O'Mahony lived in Paris for a number of years and studied the organisation of militant revolutionary groups there. On returning to Ireland James Stephens travelled throughout the country to make contact with former Young Irelanders but found that all of its clubs had ceased to exist. O'Mahony left Paris and went to America to gather support for the Irish cause among more than one million Irish emigrants there as a result of the Famine. Very influential people such as Colonel Corcoran of the 69th Regiment and Michael Doheny, who was by now a lieutenant colonel in the same regiment, supported him. In Ireland, Stephens had enlisted the support of Charles J. Kickham, Thomas Clarke Luby and Jeremiah O'Donovan Rossa, all of whom had become prominent in nationalist affairs in one way or another. He gave an undertaking to his American counterparts to raise an army of 10,000 men, including 1,500 with arms, if he got financial support from America. The amount of finance from America disappointed him, but he went ahead on St Patrick's day 1858 and founded what was to become known as the Irish Republican Brotherhood. On the same day, O'Mahony founded a supporting group in America known as the Fenian Brotherhood. Fenianism sought to establish an independent Irish Republic in the immediate future through the use of military force. Its motto was "It's Now or Never". It took its ideology from the French Revolution and the ideals and doctrine of Wolfe Tone and the United Irishmen.

The Catholic Church strongly opposed the Fenian movement, principally on the grounds that it was an oath-bound secret society and that it encouraged violence. The oath approved by Stephens was as follows:

> I................ in the presence of Almighty God do solemnly swear allegiance to the Irish Republic, now virtually established; that I will do my utmost at every risk, while life lasts, to defend its independence and integrity, and finally that I will yield implicit obedience in all things not contrary to the law of God to the commands of my superior officer. So help me God, Amen.

A supreme council consisting of eleven members controlled the society and declared itself to be in fact and by right the sole government of Ireland. It claimed power to enact laws for the Irish Republic until the country secured its national independence.

The society was divided up by Stephens into a complicated series of "circles" or cells, with 820 men in each (and sub-divided into smaller circles) under the command of an officer or "centre", with Stephens himself being the "head centre". This structure – modelled on a French revolutionary organisation – was to prevent information about its activities being known to too many people and to keep spies from infiltrating the society. Despite his efforts and intentions, the society was infiltrated from its foundation and a steady supply of information and intelligence relating to its activities was communicated to the constabulary and Dublin Castle. Stephens and his associates published a newspaper, the *Irish People*, in which threats and promises of armed insurrection were made. It was difficult to reconcile this with the lengths to which Stephens had gone in setting up an oath-bound secret society. The British government was alarmed at the rapid growth of the Fenian organisation, and in September 1865 the *Irish People* newspaper was seized and most of the Fenian leaders in Ireland arrested in the newspaper office. James Stephens was not there and escaped the net.

In the following November, he was arrested and lodged in the Richmond Bridewell (now Griffith Barracks), Dublin. Within a few days, Stephens' escape from prison was organised by the other Fenian leaders. It was a dramatic escape which got much publicity and caused much embarassment to the authorities. Colonel Kelly, the brains behind it, did not even tell the men he picked to be bodyguards to protect Stephens after his escape what he required them for. (Some of the Irish-American Fenians were very displeased that he had not involved them in the escape.) He was lucky that the escape plan succeeded. A Fenian leaving Dublin by train for County Cork heard a rumour that the escape plans had been made. In his enthusiasm to recruit a soldier attached to Ballincollig military barracks into the Fenian movement, he confided what he had heard to the soldier. The soldier refused to join the Fenians and reported what he had been told to his officer, who communicated the information to his headquarters in Dublin. By the time the message was received in Dublin, it was too late. A prison warder named John Breslin, who was a member of the IRB, had helped Stephens to escape and he had been spirited away by the crowd who had assembled outside the prison under pretence of a protest demonstration against Stephens' imprisonment. Following his escape from prison he was believed to have gone to America for a period.

The American organisation had grown in leaps and bounds and included many former high-ranking officers of the Civil War, but there were serious divisions between the leaders. Planned actions by the organisation in America were published in a feature on the front page of *The Weekly News* (Dublin) of 17 March 1866. Despite the big numbers who had joined and all the dollars collected, the state of the Fenian movement at this time was not good. O'Mahony's policy was for the American Fenians to devote themselves to supplying money, arms and picked officers for an insurrection in

Ireland. The officers were sent, but no arms, and the money was very badly handled. There was misappropriation of some of the funds. Colonel John O'Neill demanded more action in America, and two futile attempts were made to invade Canada in 1866 and 1870. The American organisation was infiltrated by British spies.

In 1866 the Fenian membership in Ireland numbered about 60,000. About 15,000 of these were members of British army regiments – all of whom had taken the Fenian oath. "Disaffected" members were transferred overseas or far away from their bases. So many memberss of the army at the military barracks in Templemore, County Tipperary, were found to be Fenian sympathisers that they were quickly transferred to Newry and Enniskillen, areas in which they were unlikely to cause any problems. The *Nenagh Guardian* in September 1865, reported: "A correspondent informs us that he has strong grounds for stating that not only are the majority of Catholic troops of the Templemore Garrison, Fenians at heart, but that they are actually sworn members of that society." It was not surprising to find the same newspaper reporting in the following December:

> The 11th Depot Battalion now in Templemore under the command of Col. W. Irion, will replace the 1st Battalion 60th Rifles at Newry and Enniskillen. A large portion of the Depot Battalion left Templemore on Thursday last. The 59th Regiment, now in Glasgow, will embark on Saturday for Dublin en route to Headquarters at Templemore, detaching to Birr and relieving the 11th Battalion.

The main problem facing the Fenians was that they did not have firearms. A lot of crude weapons were manufactured such as pikes, but in raids carried out by the constabulary and the Dublin Metropolitan Police, many of these weapons were seized during 1866. Plans to send arms from America were aborted. The American Fenians, restless and despairing, called a conference in New York towards the end on 1866. After Stephens was compelled to fix an insurrection for early 1867, he was deposed and his place was taken by Colonel Kelly. The date fixed for the rising was 11 February 1867.

The securing of arms for the proposed insurrection became the priority. There was a good Fenian organisation in the English cities. A plan was drawn up by Captain John McCafferty, an Irish veteran of the American Civil War and very involved with the Fenian movement, to raid Chester Castle, where it was known that 2,000 rifles were stored, in February 1867. The rifles were to be brought to Holyhead, where the steamer to Ireland was to be commandeered to convey the arms. The British authorities got word of the proposed raid, thousands of British trooops were brought to Chester by train, and the planned raid had to be abandoned. Amongst the Fenians in Chester on that day was Michael Davitt, later to become prominent with the Land League. The Habeas Corpus Act was suspended in 1866. Throughout that year, the constabulary and authorities were on a state of alert. Several prominent persons connected with the Fenian movement were arrested and imprisoned.

The Fenian Rising, which had been fixed for 11 February 1867, was at the last moment – perhaps due to the scarcity of arms – postponed to 5 March 1867. Word of the postponement got to all units of the organisation throughout Ireland, except to that in Cahirciveen in south-west Kerry. On 12 February, a telegram was sent by Sub-inspector Columb of Killarney constabulary to the inspector general at Dublin Castle, stating: "Circumstances show that an immediate outbreak is expected here and elsewhere. I have written." The telegram was forwarded to the under-secretary. On the same date, an anonymous letter was received by the inspector general, which stated: "Warning of general rising of Fenians throughout Ireland tonight. Stephens is in the country and a lot of American officers as well." A report from the commissioner of Dublin Metropolitan Police, dated 15 February 1867, stated: "Fenianism more active than ever, Stephens, Colonel Kelly determined to have a Rising. John Norris, Doctor Lyddy and others in Ireland." A further report received from the commissioner gave brief details of the arrest of thirty-three men on a boat at the North Wall – all supposed to be Fenians.

The Fenian Rising at Caherciveen

Early in 1865, a respectable gentleman named John J. O'Connor arrived in Cahirciveen from America and took lodgings. His parents had emigrated from nearby Valentia Island many years earlier, and the reason given by O'Connor for returning was that he had been advised to do so on medical grounds. He became very popular with the local people; but the local constabulary became very suspicious about his military gait and the fact that there appeared to be very little the matter with his health, and they kept him under close observation. After some time they were convinced that he was recruiting for the Fenian movement and they searched his lodgings but found no incriminating evidence. He was indignant about the interest paid to him by the constabulary. Immediately on the Habeas Corpus Act being suspended, he removed himself from the scene and could not be located. On 12 February 1867, O'Connor's first target was the constabulary barracks in the centre of Cahirciveen town, but the constabulary sought reinforcements from the British naval vessel the *Gladiator*, moored off Valentia Island.

The Killorglin constabulary searched the mail car from Cahirciveen and arrested a man named Mortimer Moriarty, whom they considered suspect. On searching him, they found a note from J. J. O'Connor, which read:

> February 12th 1867. Morning. My Dear Sheehan, I have the honour to introduce to you Captain Mortimer Moriarty. He will be of great

assistance to you, and I have told him all that is to be done until I get to your place. The private spys [sic] are very active this morning. Unless they smell a rat all will be done without any trouble. Success to you. Hoping to meet soon. Yours as ever, John J. O'Connor.

The letter was addressed to "Daniel L Sheehan, Esq, H.C.", who was a draper's assistant and head centre for Killorglin district. The telegraph line to Cahirciveen had been cut, so the sub-inspector at Killorglin, knowing that O'Connor was back in the neighbourhood and believing that an attack by the Fenians was imminent, sent Sub-constable Duggan to Cahirciveen on horseback with the despatch – a distance of about thirty miles.

A detachment of armed marines from the *Gladiator* went to Cahirciveen in response to the call and, with the local constabulary, fortified the barracks. O'Connor and his Fenian insurgents abandoned the idea of attacking the building and moved off inland along the Iveragh peninsula. On that night, they continued to Kells, where they attacked the coastguard station and took away all the arms and ammunition. They called to many private houses in the area and took away guns, ammunition and food. The size of the group numbered somewhere between 100 and 200 men armed with a miscellaneous collection of weapons and a small number of firearms. They then headed along the main road towards Glenbeigh going towards Killarney.

At a bridge along the road, they met mounted Sub-constable William Duggan of Killorglin constabulary who had set out about an hour before for Cahirciveen with a despatch. They called upon him "to surrender to the Irish Republic". He drew his sword, spurred his horse and gallantly attempted to cut his way through. The group of Fenians got out of his way but as he made his way through they discharged their guns at him and badly injured him. He continued on for some short distance, then half fell and half dismounted from his horse. Bleeding heavily, he made for the lights of a dwelling house some distance in from the road. He was followed by O'Connor and his men and shot at again as he tried to cross a fence. The owner, a man named Moriarty, let him in.

O'Connor and others followed him into the house. O'Connor looked at the sub-constable's wounds and made little of them – saying that he himself had received more serious ones in the American Civil War. O'Connor took out a brandy flask and gave a drink from it to Duggan. He searched through the latter's clothes and found the despatch which Duggan had concealed under his shirt. When O'Connor was leaving the house, Duggan, who was conscious, asked him to get a priest. O'Connor promised to do so and added, "and a doctor too", to which the injured Duggan replied, "You need not mind the doctor; you have doctored me yourself."

The Fenians took Duggan's horse, saddle and sword. It was then about 4am. They continued on, entering the valley around Caragh Lake, continuing through the Glencar valley along the foot of the McGillycuddy Reeks and southwards through the Gap of Dunloe.

Extra members of the constabulary were drafted into Killarney from adjoining barracks, and a search of the south Kerry area was commenced for the insurgents. The resident magistrate, Mr Cruice, requested the assistance of the military to support the constabulary in the follow-up operation, and this was given without delay. A detachment of 159 troops from Cork city was despatched to Killarney by train and arrived there at 4.30am on 14 February. The commander of the military forces in Dublin directed that an additional 159 rifles be sent from Cork. Another 150 men of the 6th Regiment followed under the command of Brigadier General Alfred Beresford, who travelled by special train and picked up another 550 men and essential cavalry, artillery and infantry forces at Mallow. A massive search went on for days in the mountains and forests in the south Kerry area. The searchers located stolen firearms and the horse saddle belonging to Sub-constable Duggan, but the Fenians, knowing that they were being followed, scattered and took to the hills. A warrant was issued for the arrest of O'Connor.

On 16 February the following proclamation was issued by the Privy Council: "By Order of the Council made on the 15th inst. directing that the Peace Preservation Act (Ireland) 1856 is now in force and will apply to County Kerry." A copy of the proclamation was sent to Thomas Balfour. A further order was made by the lord lieutenant that: "Whereas the County of Kerry is at present in a state of disturbance, it is therefore expedient to appoint an additional Magistrate for the County." On that date – 14 February – a warrant was signed appointing John B. Greene, Esq., as an extra magistrate for Kerry.

John J. O'Connor had put a lot of work and organisation into preparation for the insurrection, but he was never informed that it was being postponed until 5 March. He had hoped to get all the firearms in possession of the constabulary in Cahirciveen barracks, but he was forced to set out without them. Taking the arms from Kells coastguard station was easy with only one man being on duty there. The fact that he and his followers raided private houses for food and arms – terrifying women and children in the process – indicated that things had gone wrong for him from an early stage.

All the telegraph wires between Killorglin and Cahirciveen were cut in advance by the Fenians. Linesmen going to repair them were threatened and they were out of action for several days. The telegraph wires serving Killarney town were also cut. Cahirciveen was totally isolated, and communications between Europe and America were also severed, as these telegraph wires serviced the trans–Atlantic cable service on Valentia Island which had come into operation a few years before. A notice of intended claim for malicious damage to the telegraph cable submitted by the British and Irish Magnetic Telegraph Company, Dublin, on 16 February 1867, against the lord lieutenant, set out:

Wires and poles cut down at Headford, arms and insulators smashed. Linesmen stopped by about 120 armed men and had great difficulty in persuading them to allow them repair the lines. Wire cut in two places at Deelish bridge. Staff again cautioned by armed men not to repair the breaks. This was on 14th.

On 15th, communications with Valentia still stopped.

On 16th at 1 p.m. Still no communications with Valentia.

In the *Hue and Cry* of 30 April 1867, the following notice appeared in relation to John J. O'Connor:

> Whereas it has been represented to the Lord Lieutenant, that on the 12th, 13th and 14th days of February instant, armed persons have assembled in the districts near and between Killarney, Killorglin and Cahirciveen in the county of Kerry, under the orders of a person calling himself J. J. O'Connor and have committed divers illegal and violent acts. His Excellency is pleased hereby to offer an award of two hundred and fifty pounds to any person or persons, who shall within six months from the date hereof, give such information as shall lead to the arrest of the said J. J. O'Connor.
>
> The above reward will be paid by Daniel J. Cruice, the resident Magistrate at Killarney. Description of the above-named J.J. O'Connor, a native of Valentia Island:
>
> J.J. O'Connor is about 25 or 26 years of age; 5 feet 11 inches in height; stout make; fair complexion; round face; hazel eyes; regular nose; dark brown hair; light moustache; no whiskers; has a very military gait; served in the American army; was since his infancy in America; supposed to have a running wound in his back.

Condemnation by Bishop Moriarty of Kerry

Following the premature insurrection in Kerry, Dr David Moriarty, Bishop of Kerry, in whose diocese the event occurred, delivered a sermon – one of the hardest-hitting sermons ever preached by a bishop – at Killarney Cathedral. In the course of the sermon he described the Fenian leaders as criminals and swindlers and called down upon them "God's heaviest curse, His withering, blasting, blighting curse". In conclusion he said "that for their punishment, eternity is not long enough nor hell hot enough" – a phrase which has been much quoted since.

The Bravery of Sub-constable William Duggan

Sub-constable William Duggan, a native of County Cork, was attached to the constabulary barracks at Killorglin. He was described as a fine, stalwart young man. After the Fenians had left him in their house, the Moriartys tended to Duggan's wounds and did everything possible to ease his pain and stop the bleeding. They sent for the local priest, Fr Maguire, early next morning and he arrived shortly after eleven oclock. The priest had met the insurgents on the road earlier and pleaded with them to stop and disperse but they did not heed him. Dr Spotteswood, a local doctor, arrived shortly after the priest and attended to Duggan. He removed the ball, which had passed almost completely through the sub-constable's body. Although he did what he could for the injured man, he did not think Duggan would recover as his injuries were too serious. The injured sub-constable was moved to a more accessible and confortable location near Glenbeigh. A surgeon who was despatched from Dublin Castle to assist Dr Spotteswood in caring for the injured man remained in attendance for three days but held out no hope for Duggan's recovery and returned to Dublin. For several days Duggan hovered between life and death, suffering terribly from his wounds. The days of agony extended into weeks and months. Although eventually Sub-constable Duggan survived his terrible injuries and was the first member to be awarded the RIC Constabulary Medal for valour, he was still too ill to travel to Dublin to receive it in the following September.

Through the *Hue and Cry* a reward of £500 was offered for months after for any information relating to the shooting of Sub-constable Duggan, but the reward was not claimed. In appreciation for the extraordinary attention given to Sub-constable Duggan, a collection was taken up from the constabulary force in County Kerry, and a presentation of £29 was made to Mrs Moriarty as a token of their gratitude. The services of the Moriartys was also recognised by the general public and by the government which sent a cheque for £10.

In a ballad of eight verses, titled "The Fenians of Cahirciveen", the shooting of Sub-constable Duggan is referred to in one of the verses:

> *We marched all along and our guns we did load,*
> *We then met a policeman, on horseback he rode,*
> *We asked him to surrender but the answer was "No";*
> *And a ball from young Conway soon levelled him low;*
> *Away we marched on and our guns did reload,*
> *We met Father Meegan and for him low we bowed,*
> *He gave us his blessing, saying, "God be your friend,*
> *In the battle of Freedom on which you are bent."*

THE GENERAL RISING OF 5 MARCH 1867

Preparations by the Constabulary

Early on 5 March 1867, the troops in Dublin city and the Dublin Metropolitan Police were put under orders for active service that evening. After twelve noon the Dublin county constabulary was put on a state of alert. The county inspector was called to a briefing by the inspector general. He was instructed to strengthen certain points in the county around Dublin city and to proceed himself to Rathfarnham barracks and to remain there. He was told that everything rested upon his own responsibility and judgement. By 8pm every barracks in County Dublin was alerted and on standby for attack. Strengthening parties were despatched to Tallaght, Rathfarnham and Clondalkin barracks immediately after darkness fell, so as not to attract notice. The county inspector set up his headquarters at Rathfarnham and deployed members of the force for duty as scouts, in plain clothes, on all the adjoining roads to observe and report on anything unusual seen by them. Dominick F. Burke, the sub-inspector for the district, had also taken up duty at Rathfarnham. At 10pm a report came in from one of the scouts that numbers of men on foot and some on horse-drawn vehicles were heading for Tallaght. At the subsequent trial of prisoners before the special commission, it emerged in the address by the attorney-general to the jury what the real plans of the Fenians were:

> One rendezvous was in Palmerstown fields, and there one large body of Fenians were directed to mass themselves together, and when fully assembled to proceed by the Crumlin road to Tallaght Hill, an open unfenced mountain, about two miles behind the village of Tallaght. Another large body were to proceed by another road through Tallaght at the same point. Here, when all had assembled in great force, the different bodies were to form themselves into one strong compact body of many thousands, to whom arms, ammunition, and commands were to be served out, and then the grand plan of attack upon the city of Dublin was to be carried out.

Tallaght, County Dublin

The constabulary barracks at Tallaght, a single-storey building and structurally not very secure, was situated opposite the Crumlin and Roundtown roads and was manned by ten members under a head constable. Acting on information available to them, the county and sub-inspectors decided to reinforce Tallaght barracks. Sub-inspector Burke went to Tallaght taking Constables McCormick and Kenny with him. All were armed. The county inspector was not satisfied with the small number of men accompanying the sub-inspector and discreetly sent two more to Tallaght immediately after the them.

On their way to Tallaght Sub-inspector Burke and his two sub-constables caught up with a party of Fenians with a cart loaded with ammunition. One of the constables seized the bridle of the horse pulling the cart and was attacked by one of the Fenians armed with a sword. In the fight which took place between the constable and the Fenian, the Fenian was wounded with the thrust of a sword-bayonet and later died. The two additional sub-constables sent by the county inspector then arrived on the scene. The night was very dark and with the element of the surprise attack, the Fenians presumed that they were being attacked by large numbers of the constabulary and took flight. The sub-inspector and the sub-constables took the cart and load of ammunition to Tallaght barracks, where they secured the horse and cart in the back yard of the barracks. The ammunition, which was in a large barrel and a number of bags, was stored in the dayroom of the barracks.

Immediately afterwards, the constabulary learned that a large body of Fenians was coming up the Crumlin road towards the barracks. The sub-inspector directed the constabulary party to fall in and told them, "They must not pass, boys." The party of fourteen men of all ranks drew up across the road, blocking the approach of the insurgents. When the insurgents were about forty yards away, the sub-inspector stepped forward and called upon their leaders to surrender or disperse in the name of the queen. He announced to them that he had a large armed party ready. To the amazement of Sub-inspector Burke and the constabulary with him, the party of insurgents turned right about on the road and went back in the direction from which they had come. When some distance away they fired two shots, but the constabulary believed that these were not directed at themselves and they did not return fire.

Soon afterwards another large body of insurgents were heard approaching by the Roundtown road. Mr Burke and his party again formed a line across this road and, when they were about forty or fifty yards away, the sub-inspector again went forward and challenged the advancing insurgents. This time there was a different response when their leader shouted out, "Now's your time, boys. Fire." A volley of about thirty shots rang out – all aimed at the constabulary. On hearing the command to the insurgents, the constabulary instantly dropped to their knees, which probably accounted for the fact that none of them was hit by the volley. Mr Burke then ordered the constabulary to fire and this they did, killing one or two insurgents and injuring a number of others. The insurgents fled in all directions. The constabulary later picked up seventeen rifles and several thousand rounds of ammunition and percussion caps at the scene of this confrontation. Fifty prisoners were later captured from the fleeing insurgents. Through their action in cutting off the insurgents' advance via the Crumlin road and Roundtown road, Sub-inspector

Burke and his party of constabulary effectively prevented the mass gathering of Fenians as prearranged for Tallaght Hill.

Rathfarnham, County Dublin

The county inspector in charge at Rathfarnham utilised his men to patrol all the roads in the vicinity of the barracks, and a total of nineteen prisoners were picked up – all were either wearing military belts or armed with clasp knives or daggers. Some of these prisoners were later convicted before the special commission. Rathfarnham barracks, which was a substantial structure, was not attacked.

Stepaside, County Dublin

The constabulary barracks at Stepaside was manned by one constable and four sub-constables. At about 1am that morning, the Fenians surrounded the barracks and called on the constabulary to surrender to the Irish Republic. At first the constabulary refused and discharged some shots at the attackers, but when the attackers, equipped with straw and matches, set fire to the barracks, they surrendered with all their arms, ammunition and belongings. The same group of Fenians took prisoner four unarmed members of the Dublin Metropolitan Police who were on duty at Milltown. They now had a total of nine members of the constabulary and DMP as hostages under the control of a special armed group of the Fenians.

Glencullen, County Dublin

The same group of Fenians then proceeded to Glencullen barracks on the Dublin mountains. They surrounded the barracks and called upon Constable O'Brien who was in charge to surrender to the Irish Republic. He absolutely and resolutely refused to do so. He had four sub-constables with him in the barracks, and when the Fenians opened fire on the barracks O'Brien and his party returned the fire, wounding some of the attackers. Members of the attacking party got in behind a four-foot high stone wall in front of the barracks and kept up consistent gunfire on the building. The constabulary kept returning the fire, with O'Brien shouting that he would surrender to no man. The attack continued into the daylight hours, but the constabulary held out.

The leader of the Fenian group then arranged to have the nine police hostages brought to the scene and placed them midway between the barracks and the attackers. O'Brien was given five minutes to surrender, otherwise the prisoners would be shot. Then Constable McElwaine, who had been the member in charge at Stepaside and who was known to Constable O'Brien, was sent forward to speak to O'Brien, accompanied by the insurgent leader. McElwain told O'Brien that they had only five minutes to live; that there were a thousand Fenians out there and that many of them were armed and that they were collecting straw and other combustible material with the intention of burning down the barracks. He pleaded with O'Brien not to sacrifice his own life or the lives of the hostages. O'Brien, placed in a most difficult situation, decided to surrender the barracks. He did not do so until certain arrangements were made and guarantees given: no injury was to be done on either side to life or limb; the nine prisoners were to be handed over to him; and he would deliver up all arms and ammunition and bedding in the barracks to the insurgents. The Fenian leader insisted on a stipulation that the constabulary would not leave the barracks for a period of two hours after the Fenians had left, and O'Brien undertook to do this. The barrack door was then thrown open. The terms of the surrender were observed on both sides, but the Fenian leader left a guard of about fifty armed men to ensure that the constabulary did not leave the barracks during the following two hours. The five rifles and other accoutrements belonging to the constabulary in the barracks were taken by the insurgents.

Palmerstown, County Dublin

At approximately 11pm on the 5th, a number of Fenians called to the constabulary barracks at Palmerstown, County Dublin. Only one member – Sub-constable John Blair – manned the barracks at the time, as the remainder of the party had been drafted in to Clondalkin barracks to fortify that barracks against a possible attack. One of the Fenian party went to the door of the barracks pretending to have a report about a missing cow, telling the sub-constable that the letter was from a neighbouring magistrate. Sub-constable Blair partially opened the door, which was secured with a safety chain. The caller put his shoulder to the door and called on the remainder of his followers. The sub-constable managed to squeeze the door shut again and secure it, but before he managed to do so a shot from a revolver grazed his temple. The usual demand was made for surrender, but the sub-constable refused. Some shots were then fired at the barracks before the attackers dispersed and went on to join up with a larger body of Fenians assembling at the Palmerstown fields.

Drogheda, County Louth

On the night of 5 March, about 1,000 Fenians assembled in the Market Square at Drogheda between 10 and 11 o'clock. Most of them were armed with weapons of one kind or another. Sub-inspector Robert Gardiner, who was in charge of Drogheda district, assembled about twenty members of the constabulary and marched to the Market Square. It was dark at the time. As the constabulary approached, the insurgents fired a number of shots at them. The constabulary returned the fire and the insurgents retreated. The constabulary continued to fire until they were totally dispersed. A number were taken prisoner and two or three wounded men were located and taken for medical attention. A number of others were also believed to have been wounded and taken away by their colleagues. The constabulary found some rifles, a large quantity of ammunition, percussion caps and bottles of "Greek Fire" – a highly conbustible mixture of asphalt, nitrate and sulphur – left behind by the insurgents as they fled. This ended the attempted insurrection at Drogheda.

Kilmallock, County Limerick

On the night of the 5/6 March, a large number of Fenians surrounded the constabulary barracks at Kilmallock, County Limerick. They demanded the surrender of the barracks but this was refused. The constabulary party consisted of fourteen men under the command of Head Constable Richard Adams. The attacking party, believed to have been more than 500, were under the command of a man called "General Dunne", who was dressed in a green uniform and wore a cocked hat with feathers. The insurgents first tried to set fire to the barracks but were repelled with a burst of gunfire from the constabulary. A long, drawn-out gunfight ensued between the constabulary and the attackers.

Sub-inspector Oliver Milling, who was in charge of the Kilmallock district, resided in the nearby town of Kilfinane. Not knowing that Kilmallock barracks was under attack, he set out for there in a horse-drawn car with three other constables. About midway along the journey they were brought to a halt by a large group of unarmed people on the road. While held up, the sub-inspector and his party heard gunfire from the direction of Kilmallock. He drove back to Kilfinnane, where he selected another eight constables, and again set out at speed for Kilmallock in three separate cars.

When they arrived the attack on the barracks was still in progress. There were large groups of the insurgents at the front and rear of the building, and about thirty men armed with pikes out of the line of fire at the gable end of the barracks. The sub-inspector and his party spread out and took up positions and he gave the orders to fire. Two of the insurgents were killed and a number were wounded. Most of the insurgents threw down their weapons, the pikemen took to the fields and the remainder of the insurgents fled into the town. The constabulary found two dead bodies and a number of rifles and pikes at the scene. The arrival of the sub-inspector and his party saved the situation for the embattled constabulary within the barracks. When he arrived around 8am the siege had been in progress for about four hours. After the insurgents had retreated from the barracks, a small group of them took up position some distance away and continued with occasional sniper fire at the barracks. Sub-inspector Milling organised all the constabulary men available and marched into the town centre in pursuit of the insurgents who scattered on the approach of the constabulary. There were no more incidents in Kilmallock on that day, and the constabulary regretted that "General Dunne" had not been captured.

Ardagh, County Limerick

Shortly after midnight on the night of the 5/6 March, a large body of well-armed Fenians attacked the constabulary barracks at Ardagh, County Limerick, which was manned by Constable George Forsythe and four sub-constables. Constable Forsythe refused the attackers' demand to surrender to the Irish Republic. The insurgents fired volley after volley through the windows and doors of the barracks and the constabulary vigorously defended the building. Even when the rear door of the barracks was forced in, the constabulary continued to fire, forcing the attackers to retreat. The insurgents finally gave up the attack and left the scene, leaving a number of pikes and other weapons behind. It was believed that some of the insurgents were killed in the course of the attack, but no bodies were left behind. The constabulary suffered no fatalities.

Ballyknockane, County Cork

Sometime during the hours of darkness on the same night, a body of armed insurgents attacked the constabulary barracks at Ballyknockane, County Cork. The constabulary party consisting of four sub-constables under Constable Brown were, as usual, asked to surrender to the Irish Republic and they refused. The insurgents opened fire on the building, the constabulary returned the fire and a gun battle continued for some time. The attackers managed to smash in the insecure rear door, bring in straw and set it on fire. Some of the constable's family were in the married section of the building. The insurgents, from downstairs, again called on the barrack party to surrender, but they fired at the attackers through the dense smoke. What happened after that was recounted by Constable Brown when he was giving evidence later at the special commission:

> One of my family, a daughter, was with me inside, she was nearly insensible from terror and the smoke. I asked them to allow her go out; they refused except I gave up our arms. I told them I would not. After some time, the danger still increasing, I asked them again and they let her out. The smoke soon after became suffocating, and the flames began to burst through it. The lower part of the barrack was impassable. Some of the insurgents then procured a ladder and placed it to one of the upper windows, calling on us to come down and give up our arms, if we did not wish to be roasted alive. There was an armed band of Fenians at the foot of the ladder, about one hundred and fifty. We had no alternative but to descend or to perish in the flames. While we were descending, two shots were fired, but whether at us or not I cannot tell. As each man descended, his arms were forcibly taken from him. One of the insurgents said "This is the day of the general rising, Cork has not been attacked yet but it will

be taken before a week." Our arms ammunition and accoutrements having been taken from us, we were permitted to depart.

Castlemartyr, County Cork

On the same night, a large body of insurgents laid siege on the constabulary barracks at Castlemartryr, County Cork. In this case, the Fenians had set fire to a rick of straw a short distance from the barracks just before the attack occurred, obviously in the hope that the constabulary would leave the barracks to extinguish it, but the constabulary did not fall for the trap. The constabulary party of seven under the command of Constable James O'Connell refused to surrender when the demand was made. Although the attacking party maintained steady fire, the building was of sound construction and substantial from a defensive point of view. One of the attacking party was shot dead by the constabulary. As the attackers could not get in close to the building because of the constant fire from the constabulary, the insurgents eventually aborted the attempt to take the building and retreated. It was possibly the same group of Fenians who disarmed the local coastguard station on the same night and took the arms from there.

Emly, County Tipperary

The constabulary barracks at Emly, County Tipperary, was attacked by a number of Fenians. Constable Patrick Derwan, in charge of the small party in the barracks, refused to surrender when requested to do so. The order "riflemen to the front" was then given by the leader of the Fenian group and a determined attack with rifle fire was made on the building. The constabulary party defended the barracks with continuous rifle fire from the windows. A threat was made to burn down the barracks, but the constabulary kept up their defence and after about one hour the attackers dispersed.

Gurtavoher, County Tipperary

At about midnight on that night, a large body of armed insurgents attacked the constabulary barracks at Gurtavoher, County Tipperary. When Constable Martin Scurry and four sub-constables refused to surrender, there was a long exchange of gunfire. Eventually the insurgents gave up and retreated from the scene. Some of the attackers were injured and they left several pikes behind but no rifles.

Mountmellick, County Laois

On the morning of 6 March, Sub-inspector Myles Blake Burke and his party at Mountmellick were on the alert for Fenian activities. An attack was not made on the barracks there, but when the sub-inspector and his men carried out searches for arms, he did find a number of well-sharpened pikes and several rounds of rifle and revolver ammunition. With his men he succeeded in dispersing a large group of Fenians, arresting several, two of whom had revolvers and were later convicted under the Whiteboys Acts at the following assizes.

Two days later, Sub-constable Hugh Kerr of Maryborough (now Portlaoise) called with a despatch to Mountmellick barracks. He was in plain clothes. While he was there, a man named Dillon fired shots into the building. Sub-constable Kerr left the barracks by the back door and got around to a position behind Dillon. He caught hold of Dillon around the body, arrested him, took his revolver from him and, with the assistance of the other constables, brought him into the barracks. Kerr then left the barracks to return to Maryborough on horseback. Some distance along the road he saw two men acting suspiciously and questioned them about their business. Not satisfied with their answers, he produced his revolver, arrested both and took them to Maryborough barracks. They were carrying incriminating Fenian documents, and it was believed that they had taken part in the Tallaght incidents.

These were the main incidents of the Fenian Rising which had been expected for approximately two years. Some other incidents throughout the country were relatively minor.

The Fenian leaders in Ireland, America and England had put a lot into the organisation and planning of the uprising. From every aspect it was much better organised than the previous attempt made in 1848, and its failure was a grievous disappointment for all concerned. There was no shortage of able-bodied men – several thousand of them – led by seasoned veteran officers of the American Civil War, and it was only natural that expectations were very high. While there were plenty of other weapons, rifles were scarce due to the failure of the raid on Chester Castle and the failure of a proposed shipment of rifles from America to materialise. Apart from attacking the constabulary barracks, because they were perceived as being part of the British establishment, the Fenians had of course hoped to capture rifles and ammunition. In all attacks, the constabulary were totally outnumbered by the insurgents, and it was a tribute to the determination and resoluteness of the constabulary that they held out in every case and were only forced to eventually surrender in three small constabulary barracks after making a spirited defence. None of the constabulary were killed and only Sub-constable Duggan (Killorglin), caught outside alone, was very seriously injured, while there were many casualties amongst the Fenians.

The failure of the Fenian Rising was primarily due to the constabulary, who merited the praise and rewards which they later received. Searches were carried out all over the country for Fenians who were known to have been involved in the insurrection – and more particularly for the leaders. The issues of *Hue and Cry* for months afterwards carried notice of a proclamation relating to James Stephens, in bold print on its front page:

Whereas James Stephens has been an active member of a Treasonable Conspiracy against the Queen's authority in Ireland, and escaped from Richmond Prison on the Twenty-fourth day of November last. Now We, being determined to bring the said James Stephens to justice, do hereby offer a Reward of One Thousand Pounds to any person or persons who shall give such information as shall lead to the arrest of the said James Stephens; and a further Reward of One Thousand Pounds to any person or persons who shall arrest the said James Stephens. And We, do hereby offer a further Reward of Three Hundred pounds to any person or persons who shall give such information as shall lead to the arrest of any one whomsoever who has knowingly harboured or received, or concealed, or assisted or aided in any way whatsoever in his escape from Arrest, the said James Stephens. And We, do also hereby offer a Free Pardon, in addition to the abovementioned Reward, to any person or persons concerned in the escape of the said James Stephens who shall give such Information as shall lead to his Arrest as aforesaid.

The constabulary circulated a description:

> . . . 42 years of age; 5 feet 7 inches high; stout made; broad high shoulders; very tight active appearance; fair hair; bald all round top of head; wore all his beard which is sandy, slightly tinged with grey, rather long under the chin but light around the jaw approaching the ears; broad forehead; tender eyes, which defect seems to be constitutional, and has a peculiar habit of closing the left eye when speaking; high cheek bones, and rather good looking countenance; hands and feet remarkably small and well-formed and he generally dresses in black clothes.

The rewards were the highest ever offered by the authorities up to this time. Few of the leaders involved in the insurrection were arrested.

For a number of months after the event, the trials of those arrested in connection with the insurrection went on before a special commission sitting at Green Street Courthouse, and consisting of the Lord Chief Justice Whiteside, Judge Fitzgerald and Baron Deasy. One hundred and sixty-nine persons were charged arising from it and of these 110 pleaded guilty; 52 were found guilty and the remainder (seven) were acquitted. One notable factor relating to the Fenian insurrection is that it was almost entirely confined to the southern half of Ireland. A total of twelve people lost their lives in the course of the insurrection.

Recognition of the Services Rendered by the Constabulary

During the six months following the Fenian Rising numerous tributes were paid to the Irish Constabulary for putting down the insurrection and for the gallantry displayed by so many of its members. On 14 March 1867, the chief secretary, at the command of the lord lieutenant, wrote to the inspector general, expressing the lord lieutenant's high sense of the gallantry and fidelity displayed by the constabulary, and asking the inspector general to recommend how those members who had particularly distinguished themselves should be rewarded. His Excellency was anxious that rewards should be of a substantial nature and given in a manner which would be most gratifying to the feelings of the force. The fact that such recognition for the force came from the highest level particularly pleased the higher officers of the constabulary.

The inspector general replied expressing the great gratification he felt at the government's attitude. The terms of the chief secretary's letter rendered it unneccessary for him to enlarge upon the merits of the constabulary, the more so as they were so highly appreciated by the public at large. He then came to the point, and recommended that parliament vote him £2,000 to distribute amongst those who had distinguished themselves in the conflict with the Fenians; and that Her Majesty should be moved to recognise their services by graciously directing a letter to be written conveying her thanks and commanding that the designation of the force should hereafter be "the Royal" or the "Queen's Constabulary". The letter of the chief secretary, together with the reply from the inspector general, were then transmitted, by direction of the lord lieutenant, to the secretary of the treasury. The chief secretary recapitulated His Excellency's anxiety, "to take the earliest opportunity of marking in a substantial manner, the high sense he entertained of the gallantry, fidelity and courage which had been so signally displayed by the Irish Constabulary". The chief secretary went on to say:

> The well known and often tried qualities of this splendid force, have never been exhibited in brighter colours than within the last few days. Eleven thousand men, placed by small detachments in one thousand six hundred stations, have for years, discharged with success many and varied duties of an important character. Their conduct has been excellent; the highest state of discipline has been invariably maintained, and while many efforts have been made to corrupt their fidelity, they have never wavered in their allegiance, and not even a suspicion of disloyalty has ever attached itself to the body. The sudden appearance of bodies of armed men connected with the Fenian conspiracy, in various parts of the country on the night of the 5th, and morning of the 6th March, severely tested their courage and faithfulness. The constabulary stations

appear to have been specially marked out as the first object of attack, and in fact, the offensive operations of the insurgents were almost wholly directed against them.

The chief secretary then enumerated some of the most prominent cases of attack and defence which occurred on the night in question. He concluded his letter expressing the earnest desire of the lord lieutenant that a vote of £2,000, as suggested by the inspector general, should be placed in the estimates.

Towards the end of March, the vote was passed without a dissenting voice authorising the payment of £2,000 to the inspector general. The members of both houses of parliament spoke in terms of the most unqualified praise of the Irish Constabulary. The debates and discussions in parliament generated a huge amount of media interest and much publicity in the newspapers of the period. The following are extracts from speeches made in the House of Lords on the subject. Lord Lifford in the course of his address said:

> During the late insurrection, the Irish Constabulary had exhibited such unbending loyalty, as had crowned them with honour, and which could not be surpassed. The men were stationed at outposts, scattered here and there, few in numbers, often without command of any kind, and how did they behave? Why, the blow they struck, which was for the United Kingdon as well as for Ireland itself, they struck in such a manner as to cover themselves in glory and to do honour to the country they protected.

Lord Derby observed:

> This body of police are sprung from that class of the people, amongst whom, if amongst any, there are likely to be found the seeds of discontent; and yet in no case was there the slightest disloyalty amongst them; and their determined and successful efforts to suppress this insurrection have been nothing short of actual heroism.

The Earl of Cork remarked:

> Where all had behaved so well it is difficult to make any distinction; but cannot help referring to the gallant stand made at a place not far from my property by fourteen policemen who bravely resisted some three hundred insurgents for more than three hours. The actions of the constrabulary bore testimony to the great courage shown by the Irish Constabulary, whenever they had been brought into contact with the misguided men who had vainly endeavoured to destroy the British Government.

The Duke of Cambridge said:

> I am glad of this occasion to bear my testimony to the admirable conduct of the Irish Constabulary. I have had opportunities of seeing the reports from various detachments of troops employed in the disturbed districts, and on every occasion, the conduct of the Irish Constabulary was marked with the greatest possible loyalty and bravery.

The Earl of Kimberley said:

> I should be sorry to let the opportunity pass without adding my testimony to the admirable manner in which the Irish Constabulary behaved during the late unfortunate outbreak. Having had full opportunity of observing the conduct of the constabulary during the time I was Lord Lieutenant, I can say most positively that in no instance was there the smallest sympathy with disaffection amongst them. The behaviour of the Irish Constabulary upon the recent occasion is such, as the noble Earl opposite has said, that it is entirely beyond my words to express the honour due to them, and there is no reasonable request of theirs which should not be granted.

In the House of Commons, many tributes were also paid to the constabulary. Mr Monsell said that he wished to call the attention of the house to the courage and self-reliance exhibited, he believed, in every place in Ireland where the constabulary came into collision with the insurgents.

Mr C. Fortescue heartily concurred in all that had been said as to the gallant and patriotic conduct of the Irish Constabulary, and expressed his feeling that the most consoling thing about those unhappy events was the admirable, faithful conduct of that force. It was, however, only what his experience had led him to expect from them, for his acquaintence with the force during the previous year had led him to the conclusion that if their services should be required, they would not be found wanting, and he had not been mistaken.

Mr Herbert (with his County Kerry interests at heart) called attention to the case of Sub-constable William Duggan, saying:

> No compensation in money could reward that man (shouts of hear, hear) and if the Victoria Cross was not to be confined to the army, I could not conceive a more fitting reward for those men.

Mr Bagwell said:

> The bravery of the Irish Constabulary was the theme of admiration over the whole country. There could be no doubt that this unfortunate insurrection had been put down entirely by them.

Finally, Lord Naas, chief secretary of Ireland, observed:

> I entirely agree with my honourable friend as to the impossibility of overrating the services rendered by the Irish Constabulary during the recent outbreak. Every attack upon a police barracks had resulted in such utter failure that the attempt appeared ridiculous. But it should be recollected that at the time these attacks were made, the constabulary were ignorant as to the actual state of affairs. In almost every instance, when called upon to surrender and give up their arms, they were informed that the whole country was up in arms, and that the "Irish Republic" had been established and that resistance would be useless. It therefore appears to me, that the country was placed under a lasting debt of gratitude to the Irish Constabulary, who had defeated the conspirators, wherever they had been brought into contact with them and who had proved to the country and to the world, the utter futility of the movement.

It was said that the praises of the force, "rang from one end of the Houses of Parliament to the other".

The Birth of the Royal Irish Constabulary

Following the inspector general's recommendations, it was decided to strike new medals, the Constabulary Medals for Valour, to honour the members of the constabulary who distinguished themselves during the Fenian insurrection, and to present them at a public ceremony. They would be presented by the Marchioness of Abercorn, the wife of the lord lieutenant. The ceremony was fixed for 3pm on Friday, 6 September 1867, at the constabulary depot in the Phoenix Park. The entire depot constabulary force was drawn up in hollow-square formation. The inspector general was absent on leave and his place was taken by Colonel Hillier, the deputy inspector general, who was in overall command. The full-strength constabulary band under Mr Harry Hardy took up position at the left front, while the medal recipients took up their positions alongside each other in the centre of the square.

Just after 3 o'clock, the chief secretary arrived in his carriage, accompanied by Lords Frederick and Ernest Hamilton. A short while later the lord lieutenant and the Marchioness of Abercorn arrived in their carriage drawn by four horses, accompanied by outriders, and were welcomed at the depot entrance by the constabulary band playing the British national anthem. They were accompanied by Lady Maude Hamilton and by Captain Woodhouse and Mr Gregory, aide-de-camps. The party was officially welcomed and received by the chief secretary and Colonel Hillier. Colonel Hillier then introduced the officers and men who were to be decorated. He read a short citation of the particular service which each man had rendered and for which he was about to be honoured. Each man stepped forward and bowed before the Marchioness, who "gracefully pinned a beautiful silver medal attached to a broad green ribbon, on the left breast of his tunic". The following were the officers and men who were decorated:

1. Sub-inspector Robert Gardiner, in command at Drogheda, who on the night of 5 March dispersed a large body of armed insurgents, taking many prisoners and a large quantity of arms and ammunition. He was presented with a medal.

2. Sub-inspector Dominic F. Burke, in command at Tallaght on the same night when the Fenian insurgents were defeated, many taken prisoners and a large quantity of arms and ammunition captured. He was presented with a medal.

3. Sub-inspector Oliver Milling, who on the morning of 6 March went from Kilfinane to Kilmallock, County Limerick, with a small body of constabulary, to the relief of the police barracks at Kilmallock. He was presented with a medal.

4. Head Constable Richard Adams, in command of the party surrounded by the Fenians in the barracks at Kilmallock who held out for several hours until relieved by Sub-inspector Milling. He received £70 from the government and £50 in private subscriptions..

5. Constable James O'Connell, in command of the party who bravely defended their barrack at Castlemartyr, County Cork, against a large body of armed Fenians, shooting their leader and putting their assailants to flight. He also received £20 from the government and £15 in private subscriptions.

6. Constable George Forsythe, in command of Ardagh barrack when an armed body of Fenians attacked, fired into the barracks and broke open a door; the constabulary from within returned the fire, wounded one of the assailants and compelled the whole to flee. He was also presented with a chevron.

7. Constable Patrick Derwan, in command of Emly barracks, County Tipperary, when the constabulary resisted the attack of a large body of armed insurgents who fired into the barracks and threatened to burn it if not surrendered. He also received a chevron.

8. Constable Martin Scurry, in command at Gurtavoher, County Tipperary, when the constabulary repulsed a large body of armed insurgents who had surrounded the barracks, fired into it and demanded its surrender. He also received a chevron.

9. Mounted Sub-constable William Duggan, Killorglin, County Kerry, still ill, was unable to travel to Dublin for the ceremonies and presentation. He was awarded the new Constabulary Medal and was the first member of the force to have merited it, as his encounter with the Cahirciveen Fenians took place on 12 February 1867. (See p. 120.)

In total, nine members were awarded the new Constabulary Medal, three of whom were awarded chevrons and two were presented with cheques.

After Colonel Hillier had thanked the Marchioness of Abercorn, the lord lieutenant then addressed the assembled gathering:

Colonel Hillier, officers and men of the Irish Constabulary, it has given me great pleasure to be a witness on this occasion with you all, of the distribution of those rewards of merit, so gallantly earned, and so worthily bestowed. I felt that given by the hand of Lady Abercorn, they will be more gratifying to those who so well deserve them than if they were officially conferred by me. I regret to say, that one of the men named in the list – I mean police-constable Duggan – is still suffering so much that he is unable to attend upon this occasion, in consequence of the injuries he received in the very gallant discharge of his duties. And let me assure you, that I consider the rewards have been given for no common service; you the brave men who have received them, have each in your several degrees, whether as officers or constables, rendered no ordinary service to the state. Shut out as you were from any assistance; depending as you were upon your own courage and determination alone, in numbers infinitesimally less than your opponents, you have shown what an effective triumph loyalty and discipline can accomplish. I do not exaggerate when I say, that to your courage and determination is owing the successful resistance in the first instance of the Fenian insurrection, and the instantaneous collapse which it had subsequently under the irresistable and admirably organised military power brought against it. You have had the satisfaction of knowing that your services have been specially recognised by both Houses of Parliament, and that even her gracious Majesty herself has not been unmindful of you. You have also the additional gratitude of knowing, that while your own individual conduct has thus been appreciated, you have been able to reflect honour on the force to which you belong. I believe that gallant and loyal as was the conduct of those who received rewards, it was but the reflex of what would have been the conduct of the whole of the Irish Constabulary, if a like occasion had called for a display of their devotion. This is not my opinion alone. It is the opinion of a just and gracious Sovereign, and I will now proceed to inform you, that as proof of her Majesty's satisfaction of the conduct of the Irish Constabulary, she has been graciously pleased to command that the force shall be hereafter called "THE ROYAL IRISH CONSTABU-LARY" [applause] and that they shall be entitled to have the harp and crown as badges of the force [applause]. Colonel Hillier, in making this announcement, I congratulate most sincerely the Royal Irish Constabulary, both officers and men, on the distinction they have earned, and on the appreciation which they have met with universally throughout the country in the discharge of the very difficult and dangerous duties which devolved upon them. [Cheers.]

Colonel Hillier, then addressing His Excellency, said:

I am directed by the Inspector-General, Colonel Wood, to express his regret at being unavoidably absent on this occasion – certainly the most interesting in the Royal Irish Constabulary force. Were he present, I am sure he would inform your Excellency that no reward could be more acceptable, to any member of the force – from himself as Inspector- General, to the youngest recruit on this parade – than that which your Excellency has just announced to us. And further, that the reward itself has been enhanced in value to us, if such were possible, by being comunicated by your Excellency, who as her Majesty's representative, is cognisant of the extent and nature of the services lately rendered. I beg to assure you that your Excellency's words have been listened to by the officers and men on this parade with the greatest interest and will, I hope, be read in a few hours in every constabulary barrack throughout the land, with feelings of deep loyalty, pride and gratification. [Applause.]

After the Earl of Mayo had addressed the assembly at great length the viceregal party mounted their carriages and left, the constabulary band again playing the national anthem and "the Royal Irish Constabulary cheering to the echoes". A large assembly had collected in the depot square for the ceremonies, amongst them friends and relatives of those who were decorated for their valour. All were "hospitably entertained" at a splendid function in the depot that evening, followed by a dance. This was the "birth" of the Royal Irish Constabulary, a police force which would serve Ireland well over the next fifty-five years, through good times and bad times, and which would be forced to endure the three most difficult and controversial years ever experienced by any police force before its final demise in 1922. The sum of two thousand pounds received by the inspector general was distributed by him in varying amounts to all members of the force (excluding officers) who were engaged in confrontations with the Fenians.

The Constabulary Medal

The Constabulary Medal was first instituted in 1842 and was awarded by command of the lord lieutenant. It was frequently referred to as the "Constabulary VC". The silver medal, when first struck, had a "St Patrick's Blue" ribbon attached. For the 1867 presentations the form of the medal was changed to incorporate the new badge and title of the Royal Irish Constabulary, and in keeping with the new title, the ribbon was changed from St Patrick's blue to green. The medal continued to be struck in silver, and it was awarded only in instances where the greatest courage, gallantry and bravery was displayed by a member of the constabulary. Consequently, the number awarded during the lifetime of the Irish Constabulary and the first fifty years of the RIC was limited, but a large proportion of the medals were awarded during the 1918 to 1922 period.

Chapter Five

1867–1882

THE ROYAL IRISH CONSTABULARY AND THE LAND WAR

Following the ceremonies and announcement of 6 September, the Royal Irish Constabulary was the subject of numerous tributes paid to it by the Irish, British and European press, and it celebrated the acquisition of its new title in different ways for weeks afterwards. Robert Curtis in *The History of the Royal Irish Constabulary* commented on the tributes paid to the force: "From one end of the kingdom to the other, even beyond the confines of the kingdom, far away and over the seas, their well-earned renown has been wafted to the shores of all our colonies, and over all the Continent." It was understandable that the constabulary should have relished and gloried in the tributes, praise and recognition given to them for their succes in effectively putting down the Fenian insurrection.

Although the name was changed, there was no change in the organisation or administration of the force. All existing documents, records, books and stationary were amended with the new title. Arrangements were put in place for the replacement of all the old "Constabulary" metal badges fitted over the entrance doors to barracks with the larger badge of the "Royal Irish Constabulary", incorporating the harp with a spray of shamrock in the centre and surmounted on top with the "Queen's Crown". The new badge was extremely artistic in design and the fitting of these took some years to complete. Likewise, the change of uniform buttons and insignia took some time also, but the basic uniform and accoutrements remained the same. There was no change in the rank structure of the force. There was little change in police work, and it was carried on by the force as it always had been.

Fenian Incidents

Before 1867 was out, there were two serious incidents connected with the Fenian rebellion earlier in the year. The first was at Manchester on 18 September. Two Fenian leaders, Colonel Thomas Kelly and Captain Timothy Deasy, had been arrested in Manchester a week earlier in connection with their Fenian activities. While being transported in a prison van from Manchester police court to Salford Prison, a rescue was mounted by fellow Fenians. Sergeant Brett, who was in charge of the escort, refused to hand over the keys of the van when ordered to do so by the rescuers. A gunshot from outside, through the keyhole of the van, hit Sergeant Brett and fatally injured him. Three men – Allen, Larkin and O'Brien – were later arrested for the murder of Sergeant Brett, convicted, sentenced to death and hanged. There was considerable anger and outrage in Ireland at the execution of the men, whom many believed innocent of the crime for which they had been convicted. They were honoured and remembered all over Ireland through a ballad written about their execution, and monuments were erected throughout the country in their memory. They became known as "the Manchester Martyrs".

The second incident happened at Clerkenwell Prison in London in December of 1867. Two men named Burke and Casey, who had been arrested for their Fenian activities, were detained in custody there. Detectives of the Dublin Metropolitan Police learned of a plot to rescue them from the prison. The detectives transmitted details of the plan to Scotland Yard, but officers from the latter failed to find the barrel of gunpowder which lay adjacent to the external prison wall. Due to a wet fuse, the barrel of gunpowder failed to ignite at the first attempt by the Fenians. When they went back the following day and succeeded in setting it off, the resultant explosion was massive, killing a total of twelve persons and demolishing a large section of the prison wall and a number of nearby tenement houses. The explosion and its consequences created an outcry and panic in England. The London police, who had got advance notice of the plot – down to the minutest detail – from the Dublin police, obviously had not treated the matter with the urgency and attention that it deserved. Consequently, there was much criticism of them and their handling of the matter.

The greatest reputation to suffer was that of the commissioner, Sir Richard Mayne, who with Colonel Charles Rowan had founded the London Metropolitan Police in 1829. While the authorities accepted that he was blameworthy, he was not dismissed nor requested to resign as a result, due to the exceptional leadership and service which he had given to the force up to that point. It was ironic that the worst and most humiliating experience he encountered while in office was caused by his fellow countrymen in the twilight of his career. Sir Richard Mayne died in office in the following year, 1868. The concern caused by the Clerkenwell explosion resulted in the formation of a Special Detective Unit in the DMP, better known as the "Special Branch".

On 14 August 1868, Sub-constable Samuel Morrow and a man named Jeremiah Gorman were shot dead on lands at Ballycahy, County Tipperary, and Sub-constables Patrick Culleton, Richard Cahill and William Kelly were seriously wounded. The members were providing protection for bailiffs when the shooting occurred, and the sum of £500 was offered for information relating to the crime. Four months later, on 31 December 1868, a justice of the peace, George Cole Baker, was shot dead near his home at Ballydavid Wood, Bansha, County Tipperary, by unknown persons. On 11 October 1871, Head Constable Talbot of the RIC was shot dead at Hardwicke Street, Dublin. A Protestant who had successfully infiltrated the Irish Republican Brotherhood, he became a marked man from the time his involvement became known. A carpenter named Robert Kelly was later convicted of his murder.

The RIC Connections with the Royal Canadian Mounted Police

The only other police force in the British Empire to be conferred with the "Royal" prefix was the Northwest Mounted Police of Canada, which later became known as the Royal Canadian Mounted Police (more commonly called the Mounties). The Northwest Mounted Police force was established to maintain order and keep the peace in Rupert's Land (in northern Canada) and later in the northern territories. It policed the prairies territory and preceded the settlements. It occupied land and maintained order until communities settled down. Its priority was to assert Canadian sovereignty over the territory, and when settlements had been completed it withdrew from these territories and the policing was left to provincial forces. As a federal police force it combined law enforcement and judicial functions. The force was modelled and structured along the same lines as the Royal Irish Constabulary. An unusual feature of the force was that it contracted out its services to other districts and municipalities requiring them. The first inspector general of the RCMP was George Arthur French, from Frenchpark, County Roscommon.

Up to 1871, the St John's district of Newfoundland had a watch system, supplemented by navy patrols, and a full-time garrison. With its large harbour and fishing facilities it was a very busy location. In 1871 the garrison left and the governor of the colony decided that a police force modelled on the Royal Irish Constabulary would be the most appropriate for the policing of the area. The newly established Newfoundland Constabulary under former RIC Head Constable Thomas Foley (a native of Cork) concentrated its attention on the St John's district, but over the years it established barracks in other populated centres at Cornerbrook, the Grand Falls and in the Avolon peninsula. In 1950, it amalgamated with the Royal Canadian Mounted Police.

In British Columbia, on the other coast of Canada, the area became invaded by prospectors in search of gold in the Caribou region. The governor of that province also concluded that the RIC model was ideal for the needs of the territory. With the approval of the then colonial secretary, he established a police force on similar structural and operational lines as the RIC and had Sub-inspector Charles Brew (a native of County Clare) of the RIC transferred over to British Columbia to assist him. The new British Columbia Provincial Police first became operational in the gold districts at the south of the province, enforcing the law and providing emergency services to the community there, and the force gradually extended its services northwards. Former military officers were recruited to take charge of the stations set up by the new force. It provided a combination of law enforcement and judicial functions and gave very good service until it too was integrated with the Royal Canadian Mounted Police in 1950.

The three police forces provided an impartial police service, but they were not integrated with the communities they policed due to the isolated situations in which they found themselves. On the amalgamation of the three forces in 1950, the Royal Canadian Mounted Police force became responsible for the policing of all provinces in Canada with the exception of Quebec and Ontario. During the lifetime of the Royal Irish Constabulary, there were continuous links with these three Canadian forces. Canadian officers regularly underwent officer and cadet courses at the RIC depot in Dublin. Ireland and Canada, as member countries of the British Commonwealth, had very close relations and much in common relating to policing.

Claims for Allowances by the RIC

The claims for allowances made by the RIC for December 1868 for the constabulary district of Glasson, Athlone, County Westmeath, were typical of the period. The district of Glasson had six barracks: Glasson with nine members; Ballylin with five; Creggan with five; Littleton with five; Walderstown five; and Ballykeenan six. The strengths included a sub-inspector and two head constables. The following is a summary of the claims made, which were supported by vouchers. All claims were neatly prepared in longhand script. As an indication of the tight control by the RIC over the expenditure of public monies at the time, over ninety signatures were made in the certification of claims (excluding Sub-inspector Milling's), which amounted to about £28.

Sub-inspector's Milling's pay (3rd class ranking) for December was £10 8s. 4d. He received a medical allowance of 1s. A forage allowance, for keeping his horse, amounted to £5 11s. His stationery came to 3s. 4d. and his postage for the month amounted to 8s. 11d. He had submitted an additional claim for 6s. for three nights "for the livery of one public horse" (keeping his horse in a stable overnight while he was away from his district on duty).

Head Constable John Maher claimed expenses of £1 1s. 4d. for travelling to and from the depot at Phoenix Park "for special service by order of the Inspector General". His hackney fare from Broadstone rail station to his hotel was 8d. and the balance was for travelling expense and overnight allowance. This claim was certified for payment by the sub-inspector, the county inspector and by the deputy inspector general.

Postage expenditure claimed for the district for the month amounted to 1s. 2d., Cleggan barracks being responsible for 10d. expenditure and Baylin for 4d. The fuel and light allowance paid came to 8s. 4d. for each barracks in the district. The monthly allowance for medical attendance and medicine amounted to £1 15s. for the thirty-five members of the district force. Glasson barracks received a straw allowance of 1s. 6d., while three of the other barracks received the sum of 10d. under the same heading. This 2d. per man was for fresh straw to refill their mattresses. Each barracks received a monthly "stationary allowance" of 6d.

Marching allowance was paid to a few members. Sub-constable Lynch, who marched for twenty-four miles and was absent from his barracks for thirty-one hours, received an allowance of 1s. Sub-constable McCarthy, who marched ten and a half miles and was absent from barracks for eleven and a half hours, received 6d. Sub-constable Ward, who marched four miles and was absent for ten and a half hours, received 4d. The main conditions which attached to the payment of this allowance was that the minimum distance marched was four miles and that the minimum period of absence was ten hours. Sub-constable Ward just managed to qualify on both counts. Claims for marching allowance were supported by a declaration made by the sub-inspector that, on his honour and to the best of his knowledge and belief, the members included in the return were neccessarily and actually detained from their quarters on the duties and for the purpose specified, that the distances given were actually marched by them and that no marching money was claimed for any distance where public transport was availed of.

A claim of £1 9s. 5d was paid for the carriage and escort of one Sneider carbine, one Lee Enfield rifle and ammunition from Mullingar to Glasson.

On Christmas Eve 1868, two prisoners charged with sheep stealing in the townland of Fairdrum were conveyed by horse and carriage from Ferbane to Moate; the car hire was 6s.

Claims for Pay Increase by the RIC

The Irish Constabulary made a very strong case in 1866 for a structured pay policy for the force but met with limited success. Pay for sub-constables ranged from

£31 4s., rising with long service to £42 18s. per annum. This still left the sub-constable with twenty years service earning less than £1 per week. While no specific claim was lodged in 1867, there was a feeling throughout the force that a modest pay increase might be given to all ranks for the exceptional work done by it in quelling the Fenian insurrection. This did not happen, and when the publicity and celebrations following the conferring of the "Royal" title subsided, the question of a pay increase again came to the forefront. The number of resignations from the force rose and the number of recruits dropped. Recruiting for the English police forces, where the pay rates and conditions of service were much more attractive, was going on over this period. Many would-be RIC recruits went to England instead, as did many of those who resigned. Emigration further afield to America, Canada and Australia was also very attractive, and young men followed older members of their family to those countries. While the political situation in Ireland had settled down somewhat subsequent to 1867, there was still an element of danger for members of the RIC.

A Civil Service commission appointed to look into the pay and remuneration of the force in 1872 examined all the problems relating to recruiting and resignations and related factors. It recommended a substantial pay increase for sub-constables – starting at £39 per annum and rising to £62 per annum over a twenty year period. This was the first time that magic figure of £1 per week in pay was achieved by sub-constables. Pro rata increases were given to the middle ranks and a number of new allowances were introduced. This commission also examined the existing disciplinary procedures, which were the subject of much complaint by the lower ranks, but decided that no change in them was necessary.

Discipline and Control

The Irish Constabulary and the Royal Irish Constabulary had the toughest and most uncompromising code of regulations of any police force in the world. This was partly accounted for by the military background of many officers appointed to the earlier forces and from the fact that the force was constituted on para-military lines. The strictness of the code was understandable. Recruits coming into the forces with only the minimum of education and from free-and-easy backgrounds were expected to become members of a highly organised, disciplined, armed force, charged with enforcement of the law and the preservation of the peace. They had to adapt to a new lifestyle where they were expected to live together in barracks – many in isolated, remote areas – and face danger on a regular basis. To perform their duties efficiently and independently, their freedom to mix freely with the general public was curtailed. The major triumphs of the Irish Constabulary and RIC were based on the loyalty of its members to each other in times of crisis. A tough disciplinary code and the strict enforcement of its regulations was essential to mould, control and maintain the constabularies. The majority of members never had a problem in conforming to it, and its provisions moulded others into compliance. Those who could not conform were severely punished and frequently dismissed from the service.

The first printed *Police Code of Regulations* was compiled by Major George Warburton at Ennis, County Clare, in 1820. In 1837, following the establishment of the Irish Constabulary a very detailed code with 730 sections was produced. It was updated and amended frequently; in 1872 it had 1,387 sections and by 1911 it had just short of 2,000 sections. A copy of the code was on issue to each barracks and all members were obliged to be familiar with its provisions. It had regulations to cover every eventuality. Police codes have frequently been referred to as "being a history of cock-ups". Regularly, when some problem cropped up which was not provided for, a further amendment was made to the code.

The Constabulary Act of 1836 provided for disciplinary inquiries – similar to courts martial in the army – to investigate the most serious breaches of discipline by members. These inquiries, conducted by sub-inspectors when members of the rank and file were investigated and by county inspectors when sub-inspectors were involved, had power to summons witnesses. The vast majority of breaches were dealt with by reporting the facts to the county inspector who imposed what he considered to be an appropriate fine or penalty for the breach.

More than one third of all disciplinary breaches were drink related and varied from members' being found drinking on duty to serious assaults made on supervisors, fellow constables or on civilians. In 1860 a drunken mounted constable in Limerick city lost his horse. He was missing from duty for almost a day and several of his colleagues got into serious disciplinary trouble for covering up for him.

In 1853, thirty-two members of Castleblayney constabulary marched to Carrickmacross for duty at the races. It rained heavily all day. The members pleaded with their district inspector for an opportunity to get some refreshments before leaving for home, but he lined them all up and marched them back through rain and mud the several miles to Castleblayney. The members complained about the treatment they had received but later disputed the compilation of the inquiry board and refused to give evidence. All thirty-two members were dismissed.

A wide-ranging inquiry in the 1850s investigated County Inspector Reed of King's County (Offaly), who was involved in farming on a large scale and engaged several members of his county force to work his land. He was also alleged to have received bribes from members in return for suitable allocations and other favours. A large number of other members who were also engaged in agriculture were drawn into the net, and there were many dismissals arising from the inquiry.

There were very specific regulations relating to the conduct of men in barracks. Discussions and arguments relating to religion were prohibited, and there were very few problems in this regard despite the religious differences of members. There were restrictions prohibiting strangers' being kept in the barracks, smoking, playing cards for stakes, drinking or keeping dogs in the barracks. The latter restriction was eased in 1891, subject to certain conditions.

With members living in confined circumstances day after day and week after week, there was inevitable friction from time to time. In 1862, Thomas Clarke Luby, the prominent Fenian who escaped from custody at Tralee RIC barracks, claimed that his escape was due to friction between a "bright Head Constable and a cunning Sergeant who was jealous about the authority of the former". One of the most serious incidents to occur in a barracks happened in December 1859 at Dungannon, County Tyrone, when a Constable Holden suspected that a Constable McClelland, stationed there with him, had informed his authorities that he (Holden) had married secretly. Holden shot McClelland dead and tried to shoot a senior officer as well. Holden was convicted of murder and was hanged for his crime in August 1860.

Dismissals of members were commonplace – many for what appeared to be the most trivial of reasons, such as that of a constable found playing ball in Limerick on a Sunday. The strict disciplinary code remained in existence until the force was disbanded in 1922. It was generally acknowledged that there was some easing of the situation from 1900 onwards, and this was attributed to the reasonable attitude of an increased number of district inspectors who had been promoted from head constable rank and who, having served in the lower ranks, had a better understanding and feeling for the rank and file.

The RIC Revolver

In 1867 Messrs P. Webley and Sons, Birmingham, introduced a revolver which was to gain recognition for its efficiency and reliability throughout the world and which would remain in production for almost seventy years. It was adopted by the Royal Irish Constabulary in January 1868 and became known thereafter as the "RIC Model". It was later adopted by the governments of Queensland, New South Wales and Victoria, and by the Cape Mounted Riflemen of South Africa. In September 1869 Lord Berkeley, C.S. Paget, presented a pair of RIC revolvers to Major General George A. Custer, the lieutenant colonel of the United States Seventh Cavalry Regiment, who later became famous for his "Last Stand" battle with Indians in 1876.

The RIC Model No. 1 was nine inches in length; weighed thirty ounces; had six chambers; a barrel length of 4.5 inches; and calibre of .442 inches; with the barrel having five right-hand twist grooves. From 1880 to 1885 it was produced with a choice of three calibres: .320, .380 and .450. The price of the weapon was 34s. 6d. A "blued patent model" cost £1. The revolvers which were later on general issue to the RIC were .435 calibre and they carried the stamp of the crown above the initials of the RIC. Most of the weapons issued to the RIC were also fitted with ejectors to expel the spent cartridges.

Many variants of the RIC Model revolver were manufactured by Messrs Webley or by other companies under licence. They were made to take different bullet sizes and they had longer and shorter barrels, along with several other technical refinements. They continued to be the official issue to the RIC until its disbandment. The revolvers gained a reputation which resulted in their being on official issue to several police forces all over the world, but they continued to be known as the "RIC Model".

Policing Problems in the 1870s

In the 1870s the force was fully occupied in coping with political and agrarian problems throughout the country. Almost one complete page of the *Weekly News* of Saturday, 5 March 1870, was devoted to the election at Tipperary on the previous Saturday and its aftermath. The election was to elect a representative to parliament to replace the Fenian, O'Donovan Rossa, who had been elected during the previous year and subsequently disqualified as a parliamentary representative by Gladstone and the House of Commons. Charles J. Kickham was defeated by Mr Caulkfield Heron, QC, by a very small number of votes. The election campaign was a bitter one, involving the constabulary in quelling many disturbances. On election day, over 200 constabulary were drafted into the town of Tipperary alone. They were supported by a large force of military quartered in the Market House. The entire situation was so explosive that "wherever a Heronite met a Kickhamite, a fight was the result". The constabulary was fully stretched dealing with the fights and skirmishes and they lost a number of their rifles.

The *Citizen* of the same week carried details of vicious rioting which took place in Waterford city following the election in which the local nationalist candidate lost out. It erupted suddenly. The report continues:

> ... all this time not a policeman was to be seen but when the damage was done they came up and charged on the crowd and Mr Pallis, high constable, got several bayonet stabs from a strange policeman. Mr Redmond R.M. arrived in George's Street and read the Riot Act. When Mr Smyth's meeting was over last night, the crowd in a mass of several thousands marched along the Quay to Cummin's Hotel and showered stones at it for half an hour. Not a magistrate was to be seen at this time. There were but two local magistrates in the town the whole night – the Mayor and Mr C. Rogers, Tramore – but they might as well have been in bed like the rest. The mob burst open Mr Whitty's tobacco-shop, dragged

out and kicked about rolls of tobacco and boxes of cigars. This morning little girls are going about selling pieces of cavendish and cigars. There was a meeting of the magistrates this morning, at which the police and military officers and the commanders of the gunboats were present.

A correspondent for the *Express* wrote from Newry, County Down:

On Thursday evening, about eight o'clock, five men of the 18th were proceeding through Hill Street on their way to the barracks. Two of them who are supposed to have been drunk, shouted "Hurrah for the Green", "We are Irishmen", "To hell with the bobbies" and used other expressions of a similiar nature. Sub-constables Moriarty and McGroarty, who were on duty at the time interfered and put a stop to the objectionable language. The soldiers then returned to barracks, but a report of their conduct having been made on the following morning to Major Wallace, commander of the detachment stationed in Newry, four of them were identified and arrested by the police but the fifth could not be discovered.

The Conviction of an RIC Sub-inspector for Murder

On 29 June 1871, the savagely wounded body of Mr Glasse, a bank cashier at Newtown Stewart, County Fermanagh, was found lying in a pool of blood in the inner office at the bank. The sum of £1,506 had been stolen. (The bank manager, Mr Strahan, was absent at nearby Drumquin fair.) An investigation revealed that school children and local stall holders had heard moans coming from the bank that afternoon. Local RIC Sub-inspector Montgomery was seen emerging from the bank later that evening, which made him a suspect for the crime. The sub-inspector was excluded from the investigation of the murder and was detailed instead to protect a section of railway line adjacent to Grange Wood. While on that duty on the following day, he was missing for a period after telling one of his subordinates that he was not feeling well and was returning to his home. A search was later carried out in a sandpit in the area and some of the stolen money was located, along with a billhook which might have caused the fatal injuries to the bank cashier. The handle of the billhook was weighted with lead. It was discovered that Montgomery had purchased lead some time previously, saying that he wanted to make bullets. (He would have been officially supplied with bullets.)

The RIC authorities went to extraordinary lenghts in the investigation of the murder. Constable O'Neill dressed up in the same clothes worn by Montgomery when he was seen leaving the bank, to show how the billhook and money could have been concealed underneath them. This evidence was later given at the trial. The apparent motive for the murder was that Sub-inspector Montgomery was in very bad financial circumstances. Besides being pressed very hard for money by ordinary creditors, he had also taken moneyfrom two constables on the pretext that he would invest it for them. The exposure of his financial affairs would automatically have serious repercussions for his position. Sub-inspector Montgomery had been a bank clerk before joining the constabulary. He had been on very friendly terms with the deceased and with Mr Strahan, the bank manager; they often met socially and the sub-inspector frequently visited the bank.

The sub-inspector was arrested and charged with the murder of Mr Glasse. He was tried three times before being convicted; the first two juries could not agree. He at all times denied the charge and pleaded innocence. At his second trial, his defence counsel, Mr MacDonagh, addressed the jury for a total of nine hours. The main plank of the defence was that no blood stains were ever found on his clothing. He was convicted at the third trial on 28 July 1873 – more than two years after the murder had been committed – and sentenced to be executed on 26 August of the same year. All three trials were widely publicised and ranked as a cause celebre. After the conviction, Montgomery made an extra ordinary confession, long and detailed, to the crime, saying that he had been a drunken man for twelve months before he committed the murder. Controversy later followed when members of the press succeeded in getting admission to the gaol in which he was held pending execution and had interviews with him. This was raised later in the House of Commons.

The Campaign for Home Rule

In May 1870, Isaac Butt founded the Home Government Association in Dublin, "to mobilise opinion behind the demand for an Irish Parliament, with full control over our domestic affairs". It became known as the Home Rule movement.

Isaac Butt was born in 1813. The son of a County Donegal Church of Ireland clergyman, he was a distinguished barrister. He had defended Gavan Duffy in 1848 and later defended members of the Fenian movement. He served as a Conservative member of parliament representing an English constituency from 1852 to 1865 and for Youghal from 1865 until his death in 1879.

There was considerable support for Home Rule from Catholics and Protestants alike. It reflected all shades of political and religious opinion and included members of the Orange and Fenian traditions. In the 1874 general elections, fifty-nine members of the Home Rule party were elected to parliament. The movement was a powerful one and managed to unite people with very differing views under the leadership of Isaac Butt, who was an able and respected leader. All activities of the Home Rule movement were constitutional in nature and no problems were caused for the constabulary or authorities in Ireland.

The Royal Irish Constabulary Band

The constabulary band, founded in 1861, was retained by the Royal Irish Constabulary. Subscriptions were made by all the rank and file members of the force for its upkeep. Membership of the band was a full-time occupation; it practised daily and made regular appearances at the morning parades on the depot square. Its normal strength was fifty musicians.

Harry Hardy, the first bandmaster, who had made an enormous contribution to the initial success of the band, retired in 1872 and was replaced by a former military bandsman, J.P. Clarke. In 1875, Mr Clarke retired and was replaced by J.C. Van Maanen, from Gueldesland in Holland, who had previously been a bandmaster with the Scots Guards. He was a gifted musical director and brought the performance of the band up to a very high professional standard, earning much praise for both its performances and the quality of its music. In the 1870s and 1880s the Royal Irish Constabulary Band travelled to England on a number of occasions and gave performances in the principal cities there. Mr Van Maanen conducted the band until the turn of the century, and the band remained an integral part of the RIC until the force's disbandment.

The Murder of Lord Leitrim

During the 1870s agrarian problems and disputes between landlords and tenants kept the RIC busy. The number of evictions each year averaged over 1,000, leaving thousands of people, homeless and in poverty, very angry and embittered against the landlord and his agent who had evicted them. Some of the landlords were reasonable in their dealings with tenants while other landlords could only be described as inhumane tyrants. Lord Leitrim was one of the most infamous. William Sydney Clements, the third Earl of Leitrim, who succeeded to his title in 1854, owned estates in Counties Leitrim, Kildare and Donegal. He treated his tenants ruthlessly through the 1860s and 1870s, evicting tenants not only for non-payment of rent, but because he wanted to clear the land for grazing. He was obsessed with wielding power and at all times carried two pistols. Plans were made on numerous occasions for his assassination. In one incident near Manorhamilton, County Leitrim, he captured one of his assailants single-handedly and handed him over to the constabulary, following which there was a successful trial and transportation for the assailant. His protection created a major problem for the Irish Constabulary and later for the RIC. He was accompanied by a posse of police when carrying out evictions and travelling in the more disturbed parts of the country.

He resided for part of the time on his estate at Manor Vaughan, near Mulroy Bay, County Donegal. On the morning of 2 April 1878 he was travelling by horse-drawn carriage along the Milford/Carrigart road accompanied by his estate agent, William Meekham, and his driver, John Buchanan of Milford. A second horse-drawn carriage followed, driven by Michael Logue, Carrigart, conveying a lot of luggage belonging to the earl and his Scottish valet named Kincaed. As Lord Leitrim's horse and carriage slowed down to negotiate an incline passing through Cratloe Wood, there was a burst of gunfire directed at them by a number of men concealed inside the roadside fence along the wood. Buchanan, the driver, was killed instantly and Meekham received fatal injuries. Lord Leitrim was injured but not killed in the first volley and went to draw his pistols. The attackers jumped over the fence and a hand-to-hand fight ensued between the injured Lord Leitrim and his attackers. He fought valiantly for some time, but was knocked unconscious and killed by several blows to the head from a rifle or gun butt. The assailants did not attack the occupants of the second car, which had come to a halt some distance away, and they immediately made good their escape.

The shooting was reported at Milford barracks at 10am. When Constable Wilson, who was in charge of the barracks, went to the scene accompanied by a number of sub-constables, they found Lord Leitrim, his estate agent and driver dead. At the scene they found an old pistol, a shotgun made by J. Hollis & Sons, London, and a homemade butt for another gun with a piece of a broken gimlet stuck in it. This figured prominently in the subsequent investigations.

The body of Lord Leitrim was conveyed to Dublin by train for burial. His tyranny had generated so much hatred during his lifetime that the Dublin Metropolitan Police had to protect his body until it was later interred at Mount Jerome cemetery. An angry mob gathered for the arrival of the body in Amiens Street swore and spat at the coffin.

The lord lieutenant offered a reward of £500 for information relating to his death. There was considerable pressure on the RIC to bring those responsible to justice and several people were detained in the course of the huge, intensive investigation which was mounted. It was discovered that on the night preceding the attack, a small boat had been taken from its mooring a number of miles away, and three men had rowed in it up the Mulroy near to where the attack took place. They waited all night for Lord Leitrim to arrive early in the morning. After the shooting, they again rowed across the Mulroy to the Hawk's Nest on the opposite shore and went their different ways. When Sub-constable O'Rourke of Kerrykeel barracks found the boat a short time after the murder, it had the barrel of a gun in it. The shotgun found at the scene of the shooting was believed to have been purchased in Scotland, probably by one of the Donegal potato pickers working there. All tradesmen in north County Donegal were interviewed in relation to the gimlet found at the scene. Some information obviously came into possession of the RIC that a gimlet had been broken while carrying out repairs to the butt of a shotgun. As a result, a man named Michael Herrity was arrested for the murder and remanded in custody to Lifford Gaol. There was an outbreak of typhus fever in the prison at the time, and he contracted it and died there on 12 October 1878. All other persons detained were released from custody as there was no evidence against them.

Despite the extensive enquiries and investigations made by the RIC, the murder of Lord Leitrim, his estate agent and driver "officially" remained unsolved. The shooting generated much fear amongst the landlord classes, causing them to seek more protection from the authorities and creating more demands on the RIC relating to their security. There was natural jubilation amongst the native Irish – particularly amongst those who had suffered at the hands of Lord Leitrim – at his death. There was a general belief that the identity of his assailants was well known in that part of County Donegal, but apart from some information being given about the broken gimlet, no other information as to their identity was forthcoming.

The Land League

In 1877 Michael Davitt was released from prison, having served six years of a fifteen-year sentence for his part in the failed Fenian attempt on Chester Castle in 1867. He was a native of Straide, County Mayo, where his father, who was a small farmer, had been evicted in 1852. Young Davitt was six years of age at that time and the entire family emigrated to Lancashire in England. When eleven years of age, he went to work in a Lancashire cotton mill and as a result of an industrial accident there he lost the use of his right arm. He had been in the Fenian movement and was embittered by the eviction of his family and the hardships it subsequently had to endure. He joined the IRB. on his release from prison, and in 1878 he went to America where he met John Devoy and other leaders of the Irish-American organisations. He then travelled to France and met Charles J Kickham and other leaders of the IRB there. Charles Stewart Parnell supported the views held by him relating to the plight of tenant farmers. Early in 1879, Davitt visited Mayo and he was overcome by what he saw there: evictions, emigration, poverty and starvation. He concluded that a national movement representing small farmers was neccessary. He organised a public demonstration attended by about 15,000 people on 20 April 1879 at Irishtown, County Mayo. A further meeting held at Westport on 8 June attracted several thousand people, many of whom were carrying banners. Following the success of these meetings, Davitt founded the Irish Land League in Dublin on 21 October 1879. Parnell was elected president of the new organisation whose main objectives were to prevent tenants from being rack-rented and unjustly evicted and to press for legislation which would enable tenant farmers to become owners of their lands.

While some of its founders had a history of violence, the policy of the organisation was that it would essentially be a moral-force movement and would not resort to violent means to attain its objectives. It rapidly grew in popularity and provided the leadership for the Irish tenant farmers which was decades overdue. A unified movement also provided protection for its members. With its success came substantial funds from America, England and othere countries. It encouraged the tenant farmers to have a measure of independence and to assert their rights in a democratic way. The success of the Land League movement inspired a number of women to establish the Ladies' Land League, which was set up at Clonmel, County Tipperary, on 21 February 1881. The stated objective of this organisation was "to lighten the lot of those who may fall victim to the Coercion Act". This was the first entry by Irish women into politics in modern times and they maintained their influence for a generation.

Policing the Land War of 1879–1882

Captain Boycott, a County Mayo land agent, who was ostracised and isolated by the movement in 1880, was one of the first victims of a then non-violent strategy. So successful were the tactics employed against him that the word "boycott" came into common usage immediately, and for many Irish people it became the most dreaded word in the English language.

Special Land League courts were set up by the organisation to decide land disputes and settle agrarian problems. While the Land League leaders publicly denounced violence of any kind and sought to achieve their objectives through democratic means, some members of the organisation used physical force in furtherance of their aims. The old Whiteboy tactics were reintroduced by the militant activists in the Land League, who encouraged tenants to resist eviction. Where they physically resisted the land agents and bailiffs, they became entitled to compensation from Land League funds. There was considerable physical violence: the killing of landlords and their agents and the destruction of their homes; murder of people who took over occupation of lands from which tenants had been evicted; burning of corn and hay stacks; maiming of cattle by cutting their tails off; driving of cattle off lands from which people had earlier been evicted; and attacks against individuals who were not considered to be assisting the movement in its aims and objectives. The campaign extended to the fishing of privately owned rivers and lakes and hunting over ground which was privately owned or preserved.

The "boycott" became one of the more sinister elements. People were threatened and ordered not to work for particular landlords, land agents or persons who occupied lands which had earlier been seized, or to pay rents to them, or to deal with them in the purchase or sale of animals or any other produce or to assist or serve them in any way whatsoever. These people and the people with whom they would normally have had contact were subjected to threats, intimidation and violence by gangs of men who were known as Moonlighters. They had some firearms under their control and other assorted weapons. Amongst their items of destruction were matches and the inflammable liquid known as "Greek fire". They operated only during the hours of darkness and either wore masks made from pieces of cloth with two slits cut for the eyes, tied at the back with a piece of string, or blackened their faces with lampblack. Ordinary people were so terrified of these groups and their activities that they would not inform the constabulary of their identities under any circumstance – even if they did recognise them. The Moonlighters made contact with each other in advance and arranged to meet on a particular night at a particular time and place. They would then go in a body to the victim's house and carry out the arson, murder or other outrage planned by them. Having left the scene, they quickly dispersed again, with the leaders hiding their firearms and weapons at secret locations until they were required again. There was evidence that they were often drunk.

There were three categories of Moonlighters:

1. The regularly sworn-in men, either farmers' sons or labourers, under the command of a "captain". Known only by numbers – Number 1, Number 2, etc. – these individuals were daring and desperate characters, utterly unscrupulous, vicious and dangerous.

2. The second group were "amateur" Moonlighters, young men who went about for the excitement and "devilment" of the activities and with the object of getting some money for themselves to buy drink.

3. The third group were described as "innocent" Moonlighters, men who kept watch for the constabulary in the countryside and on RIC barracks, monitoring the movement of the constabulary and calculating the numbers of members on duty at a particular time.

Firearms for use by the Moonlighters came into the country through every known smuggling device, principally from America. The rifles imported from America, which had a shamrock emblem stamped into the stock, were commonly referred to as the "shamrock rifles". Numerous firearms were stolen from the gentry and from farmers, and raids made on houses solely to obtain firearms was one of the more common types of crime over the period.

The crime statistics during the years 1879–1882 indicate the extraordinary increase of serious agrarian crime. In 1879 there were 863 cases of agrarian crime reported and registered. In 1880 there were 2,589 cases. In 1881 the number of cases was 4,439, of which 272 were shooting incidents. In 1882 the number was 3,432, including 256 shooting offences. In that year the Crimes Act was passed following the Phoenix Park Murders, and in 1883 this category of crime had dropped to 870 reported cases, including 56 shooting incidents. To add to the serious disorder and criminal activities by the Moonlighters during this period, the farmer's situation was worsened by poor harvests, with the winter of 1880/1881 being one of the harshest winters on record.

With the exception of the Great Famine and the period 1919 to 1922, the worst and most difficult period of policing experienced by the Royal Irish Constabulary was the period from 1879 to 1882. The force was, within the space of a few months, catapulted into what was in fact a "crisis policing situation". The activities of the Moonlighters and the barbarous crimes committed by them struck fear and terror into the hearts of the majority of Irish people. A new Coercion Bill was introduced in parliament by the chief secretary, W.E. Forster. After delays and obstruction, it finally became law on 2 March 1881 as the Protection of Person and Property in Ireland Act, 1881 (44 & 45 Vic., c. 4).

One of the first actions taken by the Irish authorities after its introduction was to arrest Michael Davitt and commit him to prison, which added fuel to the flame. The Land League retaliated stronger than ever following Davitt's arrest, and instead of the act's curtailing the activities of the criminal elements associated with the Land League, they actually thrived under the new legislation. The act gave power to the RIC to arrest persons on suspicion, under a special warrant issued by the lord lieutenant. The warrant remained in force for three months. In reality it was a suspension of the Habeus Corpus Act. Persons arrested under this provision were regarded as heroes in the community and obtained overnight notoriety. (Some of them in later years inserted "ex-suspect" after their name as their title and claim to fame.)

People arrested and charged were in the majority of cases released, after a number of remand hearings, when witnesses failed to testify against them. Where cases did reach trial stage, witnesses again would not testify and juries failed to convict. Fear and terror reigned. Threatening letters were sent to persons singled out for attention by the Moonlighters. Drawings of guns or bullets accompanying the script which conveyed the threat made people who received them aware that they were under notice and in danger of an attack by the Moonlighters. Occasionally, threatening notices in large print were affixed to church gates or wherever people congregated. There was little the constabulary could do to identify the writers.

The British government sent gunboats with full armed complements to Ireland early in 1881. Berthed at strategic harbours and inlets around the coast, they were capable of providing a back-up to the constabulary or the military supporting the RIC at short notice. The Royal Irish Constabulary became commonly known as "the Buckshot Warriors" as a result of receiving a supply of buckshot cartridges for their firearms, with the chief secretary being referred to as "Buckshot Forster". Sheriffs and bailiffs received full-time protection from the constabulary, and a large number of RIC members were deployed during evictions. Farmers who paid their rents to landlords had their hay burned or farm animals maimed. Where the physical safety of these families was endangered, the RIC were obliged to establish a "protection post" at their homes consisting of two members of the force. This put a big drain on personnel.

On 1 June 1881, a serious incident occurred at Bodyke, County Clare, when a party of constabulary under Sub-inspector Hubert Crane, engaged in escorting a sheriff and bailiffs, came under sustained rifle fire from a number of nearby hill-tops. In an exchange of gunfire one civilian was shot dead. Evidently the RIC were now considered a legitimate target for attack in an extension of the disturbances and disorder of the period. The RIC saw the situation as a struggle between landlords and tenants about rents, and that outrages resulted from this struggle, leaving them (the RIC) having to stand in the gap. Observers within the force also noticed a significant change in the attitude of the people, who had become uncivil and occasionally insolent.

To suppress a "Land League hunt" where hundreds of people had turned out to kill game on a particular property near Ballyduff in north Kerry, Sub-inspector C.P. Crane of Listowel had the services of fifty marines, fifty members of the Royal Irish Brigade, carloads of constabulary, some members of the local military and an ambulance crew under his command. The Land Leaguers assembled in their hundreds and brought their own fife-and-drum band, which continued to play nationalist tunes throughout the confrontation. On seeing the military strengths accompanying the sub-inspector, many of the would-be hunters took flight, and those who did stand their ground quickly made a run for it when charged by the constabulary and soldiers. These events and the resultant court proceedings against those arrested wasted much time.

The situation became so serious in December 1881 that the government appointed an Auxiliary Force drawn mainly from the army Reserve to assist the RIC. A total of 440 men joined the Auxiliary Force and approximately half of them came from Britain. They were engaged primarily on protection duties and they released members of the RIC for ordinary and more important duties. The auxiliary force wore a rifle-green uniform similar to the RIC but it had a white band around the collar. In addition to the Auxiliary Force, the Rifle Brigade and Guardsmen were enlisted for protection duties, and they provided very valuable assistance. It proved a curious sight to see two neat, well-turned-out Guardsmen, in white jackets, deep in the mountains of Kerry, protecting a herdsman on an evicted farm, while the civil power was represented by a lone RIC member.

Several requests were made to the government – many by resident magistrates – for the protection of landlords and their agents in the areas worst affected by disturbances. Where no suitable accommodation was available to the RIC men on protection duties, a "constabulary hut" was erected by the authorities. They were constructed of wood, with an outer layer of bricks, loopholed for defence, and contained two rooms: a sleeping room where stretcher beds were arranged in rows and a little kitchen cum sitting room, fitted with a stove, forms and table. Outside the main building a cooking house was built entirely of wood. The huts were warm and cosy in the winter. Many constabulary huts, at numerous locations, were in use up to a few years before the disbandment of the RIC, officially designated as "protection posts".

The RIC concentrated on patrolling the disturbed areas at night to prevent the gangs of Moonlighters committing their serious crimes. There were long arduous tours of duty, many up to fifteen hours' duration, performed in remote country areas, several miles from their barracks in all kinds of weather, without extra allowances or leave.

Legislation early in 1881 made a slight improvement in the situation, but the general disorder of the period had gained momentum and was impossible to halt. Following the murders in the Phoenix Park in May 1882 (see below), the curfew clause of the Crimes Act was very effective when enforced by the constabulary; from that point onwards the troubles connected with the Land League and the Moonlighters was in decline.

Throughout this entire period, the Royal Irish Constabulary were under sustained pressure and on their own were unable to cope with the situation. They worked long unsocial hours in terrible weather conditions and frequently in the remotest of locations. Three members of the force were killed. Constable Armstrong and two other constables protecting a process server near Clogher in County Sligo on 2 April 1881 were attacked by a number of people. The constables fired shots at the crowd killing two civilians. The crowd then set upon Constable Armstrong and beat him to death. In July 1881, Constable Lenton was shot dead at Loughrea, County Galway. On 15 February 1882, Sergeant James Kavanagh, a married man with a young family, was murdered at Letterfrack, County Galway, while engaged on duty relating to an agrarian dispute. Many others were injured in the course of their duties, and many fell into bad health as a result of the arduous duties performed.

Several hundred RIC men died in the years that followed the Land War from tubercolosis, bronchitis, pleurisy and other bronchial diseases. (It was not until 1907 that a fund was set up to provide medical treatment for RIC men suffering from tubercolosis.) Medical experts claimed that members had aged prematurely from the hardships sustained over the period which took a terrible toll on the health of its members.

A number resigned and went abroad to join other police forces. There was discontent on the part of some, but the solidarity, loyalty and *espirit de corps* of the force remained intact, and the force survived. Representations made to government for some compensation for the members were favourably met and parliament voted the sum of £180,000 to compensate them for their efforts during 1880 and 1881. The money was payable to the men alone, not the officers. This payment averaged about three months' salary to each member of the force. The grant was very much appreciated by the members, although the red tape that delayed the payment of it for many months tried their patience. Tributes were paid to the RIC by C.P. Crane, who served as a sub-inspector through this difficult period, in *Memories of a Resident Magistrate 1880–1920* (1928). (Mr Crane was a district inspector from 1883 until 1897 when he was appointed a resident magistrate.)

> And amidst all this trouble and turmoil, the Royal Irish Constabulary stood alone. Boycotted, reviled, insulted, their magnificent discipline and devotion to their Queen stood out in bold relief against the dark cloud of revolution. and not for a short time only, but for year after year. Only one who served with them and had the pleasure of commanding them can tell the hardships they suffered. The long, weary, anxious days and nights of constant watchfulness, protecting the homes of the boycotted and the fearful; the disheartening feeling of ill success when fighting the battle of law and order; the abuse and insult heaped upon them; the cold appreciation of those who ought to have appreciated them more; the sickness and sometimes the wounds, endured through hard duty – all these things were borne by the men of the Royal Irish Constabulary. There was no glory to be gained, no grand display or pageant to thrill them occasionally or incite them to deeds of heroism or valour. The work of the constabulary during the winter of 1882 was very severe.
>
> Night after night and day after day, the men were on duty watching the houses of persons who had paid their rent and who were likely to suffer for it; patrolling here and there to prevent illegal drilling or "moonlighting"; in ambush for hours at a time in torrents of rain to try and detect marauding parties week after week, the dreary unsatisfactory warfare was carried on. But these were fine fellows, these men of the Royal Irish Constabulary, and I never heard a murmur, though many of them went to hospital with lung disease and other illnesses brought on by exposure and hardships of all kinds. They never failed in their duties, they never grumbled and they did their "bit" as long as they could stand up. As it was impossible to get evidence of "moonlight raids" the only thing to do was to persistently patrol on the chance of catching them at work. Sometimes when the names of a "moonlight" commando were known and a raid took place, the police went out the following night and arrested as many of the gang as they could get hold of and marched them in to be bound over to keep the peace and good behaviour towards

all Her Majesty's subjects. It would have been a crowning triumph had the Nationalist party been able to seduce them from their allegiance. But this could not be done, though it was tried. They just did their duty – these men who were drawn from the people of Ireland. But they saved Ireland in so doing.

Due to the long tours of duty being performed by the constabulary and the hostile attitude of a large section of the population towards them, recreation was virtually non-existent. The same district inspector, C.P. Crane, an enterprising officer stationed at Killarney, County Kerry, who was acutely aware of the situation, collected some funds, purchased a six-oar rowing boat and taught the constabulary to row competitively. For several years afterwards the constabulary crew of this boat were unbeaten in competitions which they entered. He organised and trained a tug-of-war team. He obtained a billiard table from a friend for the use of the constabulary under his command. Through some influential contacts he organised a large collection of books and set up a library for the use of the members attached to all the adjoining barracks with a fully organised lending service. Unfortunately, this was an exceptional case, and at most centres throughout the country the constabulary were virtually confined to barracks during their off-duty and recreation periods.

Despite the disheartening nature of their duties and the sheer drudgery connected with it, there are glimpses of a sense of humour throughout it all. One of the amusing facts of life was that the only matches available at the time were "Land League matches". District Inspector Crane observed:

> Even the forces of law and order were constrained to make use of the Land League matches. They were the best and I think the only ones obtainable. It shocked me I know at the time, when I found myself after a fruitless night spent searching for "moonlighters", lighting my candle with the matches which bore openly the name of an illegal association. But it could not be helped. I feel sure that this sense of humour helped to keep spirit in oneself and the men.

Chapter Six

1882–1900
SETTLING DOWN TO ROUTINE POLICE WORK

One of the most notorious crimes of the nineteenth century was committed on 6 May 1882, when the newly appointed chief secretary for Ireland, Lord Frederick Cavendish, and his under-secretary, Thomas Burke, were stabbed to death in Dublin's Phoenix Park. Lord Cavendish had only arrived in Dublin that day and it was his first day in office. The group responsible for the murders was a small terrorist group known as the Invincibles, which was believed to have been a Fenian splinter group but not under Fenian control. The investigation was carried out by the Dublin Metropolitan Police under Detective Superintendent John Mallon. Within a few months of the occurrence, the Crimes Bill became law and conferred extensive powers on the lord lieutenant to assist the constabulary in dealing with outrages in the disturbed areas of the country. A Dublin magistrate, John A. Curran, was appointed to oversee the investigation. The investigation continued into 1883, during which time arrests and detentions were numerous. While the investigation was conducted by the DMP, the RIC renderered assistance, and for years afterwards they were carrying out searches for those known to be involved.

The Maamtrasna Murders

John Joyce and his wife Breege, his aged mother Margaret and his daughter Peggy were brutally murdered in their home at Maamtrasna, County Mayo, on 18 August 1882. The crime was a particularly shocking one. Constable Johnson and Sub-constable Linehan, who were manning a nearby protection hut, were called to the scene by neighbours. The members found two young sons of John Joyce also badly injured in the house, one of whom later succumbed to his injuries. Among the rumours in circulation was that Peggy Joyce – an attractive young girl – was friendly with young members of the constabulary at the nearby protection hut. Another rumour was that John Joyce had not paid his "dues" to the Land League and that he was a sheep stealer. The most likely motive is related to the earlier murders of an elderly land agent on the nearby Guinness estate named Joseph Huddy and his young grandson. In January 1882, they were both killed by local people and their bodies weighted and taken to the middle of Lough Mask. An old woman witnessed the bodies being disposed of and they were recovered shortly afterwards by the constabulary. It was believed that the old woman who witnessed the disposal of the bodies in the lake was John Joyce's mother and that she had informed the constabulary about what she had seen. The perpetrators of the double murder, fearing that the elderly Mrs Joyce might have recognised them, decided to kill her. In doing so, they also murdered her son, his wife and their two children.

A number of men were suspected, but there was little evidence to connect them with the murders until two brothers and one of their sons gave evidence that they had seen eight men, whom they knew, in the vicinity of the murder scene on the night in question, and that they had walked behind them along the road for some distance. Eight men were tried for the murders and all were found guilty. Three were hanged and the rest had their sentences commuted to life imprisonment. Myles Joyce, one of the men hanged for the crime, at all times protested his innocence – even in the Gaelic language on the scaffold.

Some time later, one of the men in prison claimed that he had seen the ghost of Myles Joyce and, along with another sentenced, told the authorities that Myles Joyce was not present when the murders were committed but they fully admitted their own guilt. One of the witnesses who had given vital evidence at the trial stood up in a Catholic church during a church mission and, while holding a lighted blessed candle in his hand, told the congregation that he had been told to give false evidence against Myles Joyce but that Myles Joyce was an innocent man. These incidents resulted in a number of appeals being made – including one from the Archbishop of Tuam – to the government for an investigation into the whole affair.

The government appointed Andrew Reed, who later became inspector general of the RIC and W.H. Joyce, magistrate in charge of criminal investigations in the western region, to conduct an inquiry into the allegations made. Very little came from that inquiry. There was continuing unease about the trial and the fact that Myles Joyce may have been hanged in the wrong. An allegation that the Crown prosecutors had witheld the evidence of a very critical witness in the case was based on the chance finding of documents in Green Street Courthouse following the trial.

The RIC properly investigated the murder, taking numerous statements, several from some witnesses. There was greater criticism of the manner in which the subsequent inquiry was carried out than of the RIC investigation. The trial and its consequences generated controversy for many years afterwards.

After the Land War

In 1882, to decentralise administration, special resident magistrates were appointed. The country was divided into five divisions, each controlled by a highly qualified and experienced individual whose brief was to maintain law and order and bring the criminality of the period under control. They were in charge of all matters connected with criminal administration and were subordinate to the government in Dublin. At local level, they personally supervised all the arrangements made for suppression of crime and disorder and liaised very closely with the officers in the force.

By 1884 the RIC believed that Land League related crime was on the decrease. When the government left office in 1885, the Crimes Act, which had been of considerable assistance, was allowed to lapse and there was an upsurge of agrarian crime. Raids by Moonlighters for money and arms, murder, arson, the sending of threatening letters and boycotting started all over again. Although there was a general deterioration in the overall situation, it did not reach the low levels of 1879 to 1882, but there were many cruel and barbaric murders and very serious outrages during the latter years of the 1880s. The following four incidents over the period merited international publicity when they occurred.

The Dynamiting of a Land Agent's Residence

One of the most hated land agents in Ireland over the period was Samuel Hussey, who lived in a large mansion at Edenburn, midway between Tralee and Castleisland, County Kerry. As he was a noted opponent of the Land League and its activities his life had been repeatedly threatened, and he was receiving full-time protection from the constabulary, who were billetted in a part of the residence. Between 4 and 4.30am on 20 November 1884, a dynamite bomb exploded against the rear wall of the house. All windows were smashed, door frames and window frames were broken, furniture was dislodged, slates were loosened and displaced and there were a number of cracks in the back wall of the house. Despite the violence of the explosion and the extensive damage caused to the mansion, all sixteen people who were in the house at the time escaped injury.

The Tragedy of the Curtin Family of Castle Farm

A murder which received much media attention in Ireland and Great Britain was that of Mr John Curtin, a middle-aged Catholic farmer of Castle Farm, between Killarney and Killorglin, County Kerry, which took place in November 1885. John Curtin, who was married with two sons and two daughters, farmed about 100 acres, and was one of the most respected men in the locality. He did not oppose the Land League and contributed to its funds. His "crime" in the eyes of the Land League was that he paid his rent punctually and was on good terms with his estate agent.

The Moonlighters entered the kitchen of his home with their faces disguised by masks. John Curtin appeared at the top of the stairs and asked the intruders what they wanted. A shot fired at him missed and lodged in the staircase. He fired a shot from a double-barrelled gun which he had and shot dead one of the Moonlighters in the kitchen. All lights in the house were put out by the raiders and a vicious hand-to-hand fight ensued between them and the members of the Curtin family. One of John Curtin's sons pinned one of the raiders armed with a rifle up against the wall and one of the Curtin girls tore the mask from his face – revealing the face of one of their own farm servants. He said to the Curtin girl, "Ah let me go, miss." He was also identified by John Curtin's sons. The Curtins got the better of the fight with the raiders, one of whom ran up the stairs and jumped from an upstairs window. Others got out safely through the back door. The body of the dead Moonlighter remained on the kitchen floor. When John Curtin went to the door and advised the raiders who were still there to leave, he was shot from close range and died before the doctor or priest arrived.

The RIC were at the scene in a short time and tried to intercept the fleeing raiders by manning nearby bridges. In a search of the vicinity near the farmhouse a mask was found which had been made from the right pocket of a trousers, and on this clue one of the Moonlighters was brought to justice. It was known to the police that one of the raiders had been shot in the neck, but despite many searches for him in the following months he was not located. Two of the Moonlighters were subsequently convicted at the Cork assizes and sentenced by Judge O'Brien to penal servitude for fourteen years.

There was considerable praise and sympathy for the Curtin family and a sum of money was collected and presented to the two girls. A constabulary protection post was set up at their house and the members of the family were followed everywhere they went by armed constabulary. Mrs Curtin and her family were cruelly boycotted and people refused to buy from them or sell to them. The lives of the family were made miserable by the boycotting and eventually they broke down and had to sell the farm. The family attended Firies chapel on Sundays, which was about one mile from their home, and they were escorted to and from mass by armed constabulary.

When the RIC learned of a planned attack on the Curtin family when they were to attend mass on a particular Sunday early in 1886, forty members of the constabulary under the district inspector attended at the church in anticipation of trouble. As the Curtin family left the church they and the RIC were pelted with stones and abused. After the constabulary succeeded in getting the family through the assembled mob, the district inspector regrouped his men and charged, scattering the mob in all directions in a violent confrontation. A number of the constabulary and members of the mob were injured in the affray. After the RIC had left, some of the mob regrouped and returned to the chapel, tore out the seats used by the Curtin family and smashed them to pieces in the chapel yard in the presence of the parish priest and a local member of parliament. The parish was put under an interdict by the Bishop of Kerry when he became aware of the riot and no mass was celebrated in the chapel for many weeks afterwards. Mrs Curtin and one of her daughters had to leave the locality after the sale of their farm. The second daughter obtained a position with the post office in England. One son emigrated to Australia. The second son failed to get employment anywhere locally and went to Dublin. In an extraordinary twist of fate he met up with leaders of the National League there, and a few years later he was deeply involved with their activists against the constabulary in the south Tipperary area.

Gun Battle Between RIC and Moonlighters at Lisdoonvarna, County Clare

On the night of 11 September 1887, a large party of Moonlighters attacked the home of Mr Saxton at Lisdoonvarna, County Clare. Since, as a result of agrarian disputes, Mr Saxton had been threatened on a number of occasions and his life was in danger, he had constabulary billetted at his home. The constabulary resisted gallantly and the gunfight went on for several hours. In the course of the gun battle, Head Constable A. Whelehan was fatally injured and Constable A.J. O'Connell was badly wounded. The RIC succeeded in capturing all the Moonlighters involved and they were all brought to justice. On 9 January 1888 eleven members of the Royal Irish Constabulary were decorated with the RIC Constabulary Medal for bravery in a ceremony held at the Phoenix Park depot, Dublin. Constable O'Connell was unable to attend the ceremony due to his serious wounds.

The Arrest of Fr McFadden at Bunbeg, County Donegal

Following a bad harvest in 1886, many tenants again found it difficult to pay their rents, which had bee fixed in 1881. The landlords persisted in enforcement of the rest collection and continued to evict tenants who could not pay. As the situation worsened, the National League evolved a system known as the "Plan of Campaign" to encourage tenants to pay no rent to the landlords. The tenants of particular land-lords were organised into groups and an arrangement made whereby their rents were paid into a fund which was used to help tenants who were likely to be evicted for non-payment of their rents.

The Plan of Campaign was enforced by the Land League in respect of the Hill and Olphert estates in Gweedore, County Donegal, during the early part of 1889. Fr McFadden was the parish priest of Bunbeg, and he was one of the prime lead-ers. He made inflammatory speeches and urged his flock to resist the law. A warrant issued for his arrest could not be executed as he had gone into hiding. (He had refused to obey summonses issued against him.) The local magistrates, Messrs Bourke and Hamilton, sat and adjourned again and again, but Fr McFadden was not brought before them. The government directed that an all-out effort should be made to execute the warrant and arrest Fr McFadden. In February 1889, the RIC learned that Fr McFadden was to celebrate mass either at Bunbeg church or at his second chapel some miles away on Sunday, 10 February. Reinforcements of RIC and military were brought into Gweedore in expectation of trouble should the parish priest be arrested. The county inspector, Mr Lennon, travelled to Bunbeg by sea with a number of constabulary, and District Inspector William Martin who had been given the warrant by Mr Lennon, travelled by road from his base at Gweedore with another party of constabulary.

It transpired that Fr McFadden was celebrating mass at Bunbeg. A large crowd attended. When it was over, as the parish priest emerged from the chapel wearing his soutane and biretta and walked from the chapel to his parochial house, District Inspector Martin followed him and told him that he was arresting him on foot of a warrant held by him. Some people who had left mass shouted, "He struck the priest! He struck the priest!" They tore fencing stakes out of the ground and attacked District Inspector Martin and his small group of constabulary, while oth-ers threw stones at them. The constabulary fought them off as best they could. Dis-trict Inspector Martin, a powerful, athletic man, held on to Fr McFadden with one hand and drew his sword with the other. With Fr McFadden he walked backwards towards the parochial house until he reached the doorway. Fr McFadden wrenched himself free and, as he did so, District Inspector Martin received a blow to the head which knocked him to the ground. Within seconds he was battered to death on the doorstep before members of the RIC, who were only a short distance away, were able to get to him. No shots were fired at the crowd. When the constabulary entered the parochial house, Fr McFadden surrendered to them and was taken into custody. The body of District Inspector Martin was removed to Gweedore Hotel and Fr McFadden was taken to the RIC barracks. After darkness had fallen that evening, the priest was escorted to Letterkenny by constabulary supported by a detachment of military. Where the road ran through a mountain pass, the escort found the road blocked with boulders and, when they stopped, they were ambushed by a number of people. A military officer discharged some shots, and after the road was cleared the escort continued without further incident to Letterkenny.

On the following morning Fr McFadden was taken to Derry Gaol and lodged there. The constabulary had much difficulty in obtaining a coffin for the district inspector in the locality and, when they succeeded, they set out in a large party to Letterkenny, as further attacks were feared. The remains were later conveyed to his final resting place in County Galway. He belonged to the long-established Martin family of that county and he was a relative of Miss Violet Martin, who under the pen name of Ross was co-authoress (with Edith Somerville) of *Some Experiences of an Irish R.M.* and other famous literary works.

Religion and Relationships between the Clergy and RIC

Prior to 1836, the vast majority of members of the County Constabularies were Protestants. In 1830 there wasn't a single Catholic amongst the 136 members of the force in County Down. Drummond strongly encouraged Catholics to join the constabulary between 1836 and 1840. In Ulster, the constabulary continued to be predominantly Protestant but in the rest of the country Catholics over a short period of time became the majority. Inspector General McGregor initiated a scheme to have two Catholics in each barracks for every Protestant member, but this met with little success. By 1840, 51 per cent of the rank and file of the constabulary were Catholics; in 1851 the figure was 64 per cent; in 1871 it was 70 per cent; in 1891 it was 73 per cent and by 1911 it was 77 per cent. Irrespective of what religious beliefs members held, district inspectors were obliged to certify that all members under their command attended divine service each Sunday.

The majority of the constabulary officers were non-Catholics, and of the thirty-five county inspectors in the country, only three to five on average at any time were Catholics. The number of Catholics amongst the district inspector rank varied between 15 per cent and 25 per cent on average. Only one Catholic officer – Sir Joseph A. Byrne, KBE – reached the highest rank of inspector general. Promotion opportunities for Catholics to higher ranks was always limited, and there was a perception that promotion was influenced by Freemason and sectarian influences. About one quarter of promotions to district inspector rank were open to head constables who had come up through the ranks. Many of these were Catholics, resulting in the small number of that religion being always present amongst the officer corps.

An excellent relationship existed between the Royal Irish Constabulary and the Catholic clergy through the 1880s and 1890s. District inspectors and members of the Catholic clergy occasionally dined together. Some members of the Catholic clergy spoke out very strongly against boycotting and the related activities of the

Land League and denounced them at every opportunity. Others adopted an ambivalent attitude towards them, while a small minority openly supported them. A priest was convicted at Athenry petty sessions in April 1882 for "reviling the RIC from the altar" and encouraging potential recruits not to join the force.

The papal envoy, Monsignor Persico, accompanied by his secretary, visited various parts of Ireland during 1887. His mission was to enquire into the state of the country from the religious point of view, and to see whether boycotting was compatible with the teaching of the Catholic religion. In the course of his enquiries he made a point of consulting with RIC officers at different locations. The people suffering under the burden of boycotting and related activities looked forward to a denouncement of the practice from Rome. The papal envoy's mission was followed by the promulgation of a papal declaration which condemned the plan of campaign and the boycotting as being contrary to Catholic morals and teachings. The declaration did not have the force of a "papal bull", and this was used as an excuse by a minority of clergy for not condemning the violence and outrages.

In the *West Cork Eagle* of 1 July 1882, a feature relating to the state of peace in Drimoleague, County Cork, declared: "This district, once a hot and lively spot for blackthorn law, has for some time past been remarkable for the peace and quiet prevailing there. The change is ascribable to the efforts of the much loved Parish Priest and the tact and efficiency with which Constable Oates discharges his duty."

Of the Franciscan Friars in Killarney in the 1880s, C.P. Crane, the local RIC district inspector, who was an English Protestant, an Oxford graduate and whose father was the bursar and canon of Manchester Cathedral, wrote in *Memories of a Resident Magistrate*:

> I always felt great reverence and respect for the Franciscan monks at Killarney. Through a period of turmoil, these devoted men attended simply to their holy work. They had no politics and no hand in the troubles. Morning after morning, Mass was said, and day after day, these good men visited the poor and friendless, showing an example of piety which was remarkable. Their brown-clad figures and sandalled feet were a familiar sight in the town as they went about collecting alms or ministering to the wants of the poor. Many of these men were friends of mine and I frequently paid a visit to their monastery. Sometimes when the crowd of penitents thronged the chapel before Christmas or Easter Day, the Confessor would go out of his way to hear the confessions of the men of the Royal Irish Constabulary first. "These men have their duty to do," said one Father when he saw the waiting constables.

Of the clergy in Dingle, County Kerry, the same author, who was stationed there in the early 1880s observed:

In referring to the peaceful state of Dingle district at this time, I must not forget the factors which accounted for this desirable state of things, the presence of a good resident landlord [Lord Ventry] and a good Parish Priest and clergyman of the Church of Ireland. We were particularly fortunate in those days in having excellent clergy of the Roman Catholic church in the town and district. They were still able and willing to call – right, "right" and wrong, "wrong" – and they were mindful of their high calling, leaving politics to others. The clergyman of the Church of Ireland was Mr Anderson. He was a man of varied accomplishments – a good musician, a good preacher and enthusiastic naturalist. His sympathies extended far beyond the bounds of his own little flock. Of bigotry on the part of Protestants or Roman Catholics there was little or none.

The P.P. at Dingle was Canon O'Sullivan, commonly known as "Father Dan", a man who commanded the respect not only of his own congregation, but of members of the other Church also. His tall figure, handsome refined face and snow-white hair, could not fail to attract attention as he walked through the town in his biretta and old worn soutane, or rode through the wild mountain passes of his large and populous parish. There were two curates, Fr Lalor, a kind gentlemanly man and Fr Eugene O'Sullivan, known far and wide and loved wherever known as "Father Eugene". He was a keen sportsman, equally fond of a day at the snipe or a day with the hounds. His young grey mare for which he had paid five pounds was the pride of his life and he longed to try her mettle across country.

In the Land War there was little or no sectarianism in the south of Ireland. The Roman Catholic landlord suffered as much as the Protestant; in fact, it was perceived by the constabulary that the Catholic landlord was likely to suffer more. In some places, bishops and priests were blamed for leading the agitation, and violent speeches inciting people could not be ignored. At the same time the constabulary understood that the priests were essentially of the people and "sons of the soil", but with a narrow outlook on the affairs of the world. The Land War was a war of class against class and of tenant against landlord. The sympathies of the Catholic Church were on the side of the tenant, while in the Church of Ireland the sympathy was on the side of the landlords. There were very many priests who did everything possible to direct their flocks away from violence and who denounced boycotting, violence and the outrages being committed, while having sympathy with their fellow countrymen in their desire to obtaining justice. Despite all the problems encountered, a bond existed at all times between the Royal Irish Constabulary and the Catholic and Church of Ireland Churches.

Members of the RIC were obliged by their regulations to attend divine service on Sundays and church holy days, but apart from the regulation they were conscientious about attending to their religious duties and subscribing to their church funds. In the Catholic Church of the Sacred Heart in Roscommon, a brass plaque attached to the pulpit indicates that the pulpit was donated by the the local RIC. Gestures such as this were frequently made. An exceptionally big number of sons and daughters of RIC members went on to join the priesthood and religious orders.

St Joseph's Young Priests' Society

In 1899 a remarkable development took place. A fund was set up by the RIC officers to provide financial assistance to young men who wished to study for the priesthood but who might otherwise have found it financially impossible to do so. The St Joseph's Young Priests' Society, which had been founded some years previously by Miss Olivia Mary Taffe of Annagh, County Galway, received the full support of the then inspector general, Sir Andrew Reed, who was a Protestant. The fund was administered by representatives of the higher ranks and rank-and-file, and the sum of 1s. per annum was subscribed by every member of the force. While the contribution was small, it was sufficient to maintain six students at any one time. The members contributed to the fund until their disbandment in 1922. In 1926 the fund was revitalised by senior officers of the Garda Síochána and has flourished since then through contributions from all members of the force.

Detectives in the Constabularies

There was no official detective section in the Irish or County Constabularies. In 1847 the county inspector in charge of each county was given authority to appoint up to six men of his force to prevent and investigate serious crime. Normally they wore uniform but were given permission to wear plain clothes when the occasion demanded. These men were officially referred to as "disposable men". When serious outrages occurred, the county inspector despatched two disposable men in plain clothes to investigate. The inspector general was very cautious about the activities of these members, and he issued a strong warning against bringing criminals to justice through any unjust or improper means. No reference was made to "detectives" as there appears to have been some contempt for that particular term (as there had been some years earlier with the term "police"). The "disposables" continued to be appointed through the lifetime of the Irish Constabulary, but their productivity was poor and their activities were frequently tainted with controversy. Following the Belfast riots of 1886 the number of disposable men in Belfast was increased to twenty.

In 1872, a special detective unit was formed at RIC headquarters under the control of a district inspector titled "detective director". This unit became known as the RIC Special Branch. The unit specialised in crimes and outrages of a political and treasonable nature and in any activity which posed a threat to the security of the country. The appointment of disposable men continued in the RIC and, over a period of years, they became known as detectives. One of their principal duties in the latter part of the nineteenth century and early part of the twentieth century was to keep an eye on returned or visiting "Yanks" and to monitor their activities or contacts. District inspectors and county inspectors had authority to direct uniformed members to wear "coloured clothes". These members performed duties such as detecting offences under the illicit distillation laws, breaches of the licensing laws, in the control of shebeens and bowl-playing on the roads in Counties Cork and Armagh.

Selection and Training of Officers for the Royal Irish Constabulary

Prior to 1842, all officers in the constabularies were former military officers. The cadet system to train officers was introduced in 1842, shortly after the establishment of the Irish Constabulary, and it was retained throughout the lifetime of the RIC, but the standards required and quality of training was upgraded as the force progressed. Amongst the requirements laid down were:

> Each candidate must be at least 5 feet 8 inches in height with adequate chest measurement. He will be required to pass a medical examination by the Surgeon to the force. He must be in good health and free from varicose veins; varicocele; spine curvature; impediment of speech; defects of sight and hearing; or other physical defect or disposition to constitutional or hereditary disease or weakness of any kind; he must in all respects be developed, and should possess sufficient strength to enable him to undergo the fatigues to which officers of the Royal Irish Constabulary are liable. He will have to satisfy the Civil Service Commisioners as they may deem neccessary, that his moral character is such as to qualify him in all respects for appointment.

Suitable candidates sat a stiff open competitive examination conducted by the Civil Service. Half of the applicants sitting for the examination had to be nominated by the lord lieutenant and the remaining half by the inspector general. From 1866 onwards the inspector general had authority to nominate only one third of the candidates. He normally nominated sons of serving officers. It was known that "influence" – political and otherwise – was used to have candidates nominated. The examinations were difficult and candidates – irrespective of their educational qualification – found it necessary to attend cramming colleges in Dublin. The prospective candidates also attended selected lectures at Trinity College. Although the majority came from Ireland, a number from Great Britain spent months in Dublin attending private academies and Trinity College preparing for the examination. Six were normally selected for each course. They received their appointments from the lord lieutenant and reported to the depot at Phoenix Park for training. The average age for cadets was 21/22 years. The minimum height requirement up to the 1880s was 5 feet 5 inches, but that was increased to 5 feet 8 inches. Over one quarter of the candidates had university degrees.

The entrance examination included the following subjects: arithmetic, orthography, handwriting, digest of returns, English composition, geography of the British Isles, British history, Latin or French, elementary principles of law and law of evidence. The maximum marks allocated were 1,850.

The cadet training course was intensive. It included a large element of drill, general constabulary work and horse riding. The latter provided much amusement, as the cadets frequently fell from their mounts. A former district inspector of the RIC – George Garrow Green – described the cadet training as follows:

> We learned what discipline meant and what that esprit de corps in the RIC meant. An officer of the RIC was expected to be a "jack of all trades". He had to know infantry drill, sword exercise and musketry; to understand how to choose forage for his horse and how to "shoe" his horse. He had to go through a short veterinary class and be a good rider. He had to be well up in criminal law and the law of evidence and be capable of instructing his men in all their duties. Moreover, he had to keep accounts and learn the code of Regulations of the force, a formidable work, which nearly drove him distracted by the multiplicity of its instructions. It was a good training for young men. The discipline was strict, stricter than I ever experienced during my army service, even though we were not under military law.
>
> I could draw a map of Chinese Tartary, but had a profound contempt for "Taylor on Evidence". I could form a hollow square but of the necessary steps to be taken in a murder case my head was about equally empty. With these advantages I started to assume command of a lawless station [Killorglin] in the wilds of Kerry and to instruct the fifty peelers therein in all that pertained to crime and outrage.

After six weeks' training, the cadets – if deemed suitable – were given the rank of third-class sub-inspectors, which was equivalent to the rank of lieutenant in the army. They were sworn in, the oath administered being the same as that administered to the lower ranks, with the exception of the rank being specified. A further five months' cadet training followed at the depot, during which examinations had to be passed in drill, musketry, horse riding and general constabulary duties. There was much theoretical and practical musketry drill with blank firing in the Phoenix Park and real target practice at Sandymount. Cavalry drill was practised in the "nine acres" at the Phoenix Park.

The young officers did not escape the witticisms of the drill instructors, who were ex-members of the British regiments. A common comment was, "The men can't hear you whispering, Sir. Shout out so as to make 'em hear you across that square." The youthfulness of the cadets made for boyish pranks and high jinks being very much part of the experience. On commencing their training, they were told by those already in training it was the custom for a new cadet to treat his fellow officers to six bottles of champagne. On promotion to sub-inspector he was required to purchase a further supply of champagne. "Guest nights" were a weekly feature in the officers' mess to which the cadet/officer could pay for and invite a friend. The pay for cadets was £4 per month in the 1880s, and on promotion to sub-inspector it rose to £10 8s. 4d. The cost of keep in the officers' mess was 4s. per day. A valet (orderly) was allocated to three or four cadets.

The cadet's dress consisted of a shell jacket, hooked up, but which was opened for mess, a regulation trousers without the lace stripe and a forage cap minus badge. The uniform and sword were supplied by the military tailor and the sword was worn only for church parade, in the riding school and in the orderly room.

On promotion to sub-inspector/district inspector the cadets were permitted to wear the appropriate uniform for the rank. When promoted, the young officers were given certain responsibilities within the depot when they were obliged to perform orderly duty in their turn. This duty required the orderly to visit the mess at 7.30am and inspect the meat being prepared for dinner for the depot staff and recruits, and at 8am he checked on the breakfast preparation. He had to regularly check that sentries were posted and that they were familiar with their duties. He ensured that lights were out at 10pm and inspected the horses and accoutrements. The most disagreeable duty to the orderlies was visiting sick members of the force in the fever wards at Dr Steevens Hospital, as they dreaded contracting some infectious disease during their visit.

On finishing his training course, the sub-inspector had to undergo a drill test. Fifty men were brought on to the square and, in the presence of the depot commandant, he had to "size", "tell off" and put the squad through every drill movement. He had to examine a party of men on the various duties of the force. He was examined at Dublin Castle on the keeping of force accounts and pay claims and on the framing of official reports. There were also final tests on musketry and horse riding.

On completion of training, the new sub-inspector was assigned to take charge of a district somewhere in the thirty-two counties. The purchase of a horse and saddlery was a neccessary prerequisite to joining a district. A private servant was employed to look after the horse. (Former soldiers were normally employed.)

The young officer was first sent to the county headquarters of his new district for six weeks to familiarise himself with the day-to-day operation of the force. It was essential that he should get some practical experience before taking up command of a district. On arrival at his new district he either took lodgings in a hotel or in rented accommodation. The latter was the most popular choice but it neccessiated the employment of a housekeeper.

On taking up their first assignments, the sub-inspectors were usually the youngest members of the district force. While they were well grounded in theory, they lacked the essential experience which for a policeman can only be obtained in the rough and tumble of police work in the operational field. Very many of these officers openly and frankly acknowledged that they would not have survived in their first districts without the experience and assistance of their immediate subordinate, the head constable, more commonly referred to in the force as "the head".

A head constable was attached to each county and district headquarters and to other selected important barracks. He performed the duties of the sub-inspector whenever the latter was absent on duty or leave. He had joined the force as a recruit constable and had progressed through the ranks over twenty to thirty-five years. Because of his wealth of experience, he was always in a position to advise and influence the young sub-inspector. Heads prevented many young, intelligent, eager officers, who lacked the "feel" of policing, from making unsurmountable errors. One young sub-inspector, who consulted his head constable when making arrangements to police a faction fight, described the consultation as follows:

> My Head Constable, that grand vizier to an Irish Police officer, endeavoured to re-assure me, saying, "As soon as you arrive there, report yourself to a Magistrate, act under his orders and throw all the responsibility on him. They're rale devils to fight over there. The last time, Constable Cox lost an eye from a blow of a stone and another had his leg mostly cut off with a scythe."

The well-quoted reply made by head constables to propositions made by their young sub-inspectors was, "Wait now, Sir."

The Irish-born officer at least had the advantage of understanding the Irish way of life. His English-born counterparts lacked this advantage, and to be successful they were obliged to acquire a grasp of Irish history and to educate themselves in the customs, culture, psyche and mannerisms of the native Irish.

Social life for the young officers was excellent. They were readily welcomed into the social clubs and homes of the wealthy. They rode with the local hunts, sailed with their wealthy friends and had unlimited access to shooting and fishing rights.

One young officer who did not have a hunt in his locality frequently travelled fifty miles each way by train with his horse to join the Mallow Hunt Club for a one-day hunt and get back to his barracks on the same day. The majority of the officers were Protestant, which brought them into contact with the wealthy and professional classes in their district and, in general, they became identified with these classes.

From 1866 onwards, one quarter of all vacancies for the rank of sub/district inspectors were reserved for head constables who had risen from the rank of constable. (This proportion was increased in 1895.) With normally twenty to twenty-five years of service when promoted, they made very good and efficient district inspectors and created much stability in the force. Furthermore, as it was possible for many Catholics to reach the rank of head constable, their promotion to district inspector rank increased the number of Catholics in the senior ranks.

A small number of district inspectors stepped out of line from time to time. One was convicted of murder in 1882, and at different times the district inspectors at Omagh, Headford and Granard absconded with the monthly pay for their district forces.

From the 1850s onwards, one third of all vacancies for resident magistrates were reserved for district inspectors. They earned a reputation for their independence and fairness on the bench, and their decisions were accepted by all those who had recourse to the petty sessions.

Recruiting and Training for the Rank-and-File Members of the RIC

For most periods during the lifetime of the RIC, there were always many candidates willing to join the force, particularly in peaceful times. Like their predeccessors, the vast majority of recruits were farmers' sons with a small number coming from the crafts and from service. They required a nomination from a person of standing in the community; in many cases references from parish priests or school principals were accepted. Their character and background, which had to be exceptional, were always checked out methodically by the local constabulary. A good primary education was necessary. They had to pass a written examination at a local centre in dictation, arithmetic and handwriting, and there were teachers throughout the country who specialised in preparing candidates for it.

Candidates had to be a minimum of 5 feet 9 inches in height, have a mean chest measurement of 36 inches, and be well built and in excellent health. The age limit was nineteen to twenty-seven years, but if they were the son of an RIC member they could join at eighteen years and be 5 feet 8 inches in height.

If successful at the local examination, they were referred to the depot for a full medical examination and interview. If successful they were called for training to the depot at Phoenix Park. When a sufficient supply of candidates was available, the authorities could afford to pick and choose. Those selected were considered as being the cream of Irish manhood in their appearance, physique, temperament and character.

The training lasted for six months. It was tough and discipline was strict. It was difficult to obtain a pass to leave the depot while in training, and the recruits were compelled to wear their uniform whenever they went into Dublin city. Three hours were spent each day learning police duties; one hour at physical training; two hours at drill; and two hours at musketry.

There was much emphasis on drill. The drill instructors had served in British army regiments and brought with them military slang and expressions which survived through the lifetime of the RIC and into the forces which replaced it. One officer, commenting on the quality of the drill instructors, wrote: "There were not even in the army smarter drill sergeants than ours and the ability which they show in turning the country louts [sic] into smart infantry men in a short time is surprising."

Musketry training also received high priority, and one aspect of this was known as the "project arms exercise". With sword-bayonet fixed, the butt of the rifle was brought up to the shoulder and clasped firmly. The company then advanced in line at a slow march. The exercise was supposed to be most useful in dispersing a crowd, but there is no record of its ever having been used in practical circumstances. They also learned elementary first aid and fire-fighting and how to stop bolting horses, which at that time resulted in many fatalities. The recruits had to pass three examinations on all subjects at the different stages of training. Those who failed to pass their examinations left the depot, and many joined the British army at one of the adjoining military barracks, instead of returning home.

The food was plentiful but rough, and each recruit was supplied with an enamel plate and mug. Their mattresses, palliasses and pillows were filled with straw, which had to be replaced regularly, and the bedding was generally uncomfortable.

Disciplinary breaches were dealt with by the depot commandant in the orderly room each morning. Those in breach were paraded by the head constable before the commandant and details of the breach read over. Most were of a very minor nature and usually, after appropriate advice being given, the penalty amounted to performing "fatigues duty" on a Saturday or after tea on weekdays.

On successfully completing their training course, the recruits were allocated to a district headquarters barracks outside their native county and, after a period there, reallocated to another barracks within that district. As a general rule, constables who were well conducted remained in the same district for most or all of their service unless they were promoted or married a local girl. In these case they were transferred a considerable distance from where they had served in the lower rank or their wife's native place.

Changes in Rank Titles

In 1883 there was a redesignation of rank titles involving all ranks other than county inspector and head constable. The sub-inspector became known as a district inspector, the constable became known as sergeant, and the sub-constable became known as constable. The duties and responsibilities of the ranks remained unchanged, with the county inspector being in charge of a county, the district inspector in charge of a district, and the sergeant in charge of a barracks or engaged on supervision duties. The head constable was in charge of a larger barracks or assisted the district inspector These ranks continued up to the dissolution of the force. From the 1860s onwards, there was an additional temporary rank of "acting sergeant'" whose members wore a chevron with two stripes and who assisted the sergeant in charge of a barracks and relieved him as necessary.

Textbooks Used by the Force

The principal professional reference book for the members of the force was *The Irish Constable's Guide* by Andrew Reed, who later became inspector general of the force from 1885 to 1900. There were several editions of the book to keep up to date with legislation. It was a substantial reference book consisting of over 500 pages, with the later editions running to over 700 pages. It contained all acts of parliament relative to the duties of the constabulary, details of cases stated in the higher courts, practices under common law and guidance to the constabulary as to procedures and investigations and the laws of evidence. *The Policeman's Manual*, which was a smaller and more compact book of about 150 pages, was issued personally to each member. The first twelve pages of the *Manual* set out the general principles of police duty and spelled out the standards expected from each member of the force. The *Manual* also provided a ready reference for the members on: the principal crimes; criminal investigations; arrests; summonses and warrants; general duties; duties in towns; the preservation of the peace; legal principles with definitions, etc.; aids in case of injury or sudden illness; abstracts of statutes and a schedule of offences. This was the most practical book available to members.

Relations with the General Public

In his book *Guardians of the Peace* Conor Brady accurately summarises the relations between the RIC and the Irish people during the latter part of the nineteenth century:

> It would be wrong to describe the relationship which pertained in those
> years between the Royal Irish Constabulary and the Irish people as one

of constant enmity and mutual antagonism. The relationship functioned on two levels. Individual policemen in their community were usually respected and even popular. They were the pick of the countryside's youth, athletic, intelligent and – relative to their neighbours – were better educated. They were good customers in small village stores, they could help out with official forms and documents which meant nothing to people who could not read nor write and they made reliable and desirable sons-in-law. But, on the other more basic level, they knew and the people knew that when a crisis would come the Peeler's first loyalty would be to the Crown. They were acceptable when things ran smoothly in the district, but when there was a whiff of disaffection in the air, they were the Castle's men and that basic factor underlay their affability. Inevitably there was enmity and antagonism, but as time went on its appearance became less and less frequent. The Peelers on a day-to-day level were welcome at weddings, parties or dances. If a Peeler were a good fiddler or dancer he was doubly welcome, and while his mingling too freely with the local population might prejudice his chances of future promotion, that was usually decided anyway by his religion and origins and did not therefore affect his everyday life.

Members of the force were encouraged to have good relations with the public without becoming too friendly with them. One ploy they used on patrol was to call to a house seeking a light for their pipe – even though smoking by members was prohibited except at night.

There was much antagonism towards members of the RIC during the Land War, and they were boycotted and reviled during the period and for some years afterwards. Life was made extremely difficult for them and their families. Things settled down during the 1890s, and with the dawn of the new century, newspapers all over the country carried reports on a weekly basis of generous presentations being made by the general public to members of the force when they retired or were transferred. A small number of members were elected to local authorities subsequent to their retirement. Ten years earlier this would not have been contemplated in the same part of the country. This was the general state of affairs until after the 1916 Rising and more especially during the Anglo-Irish war. There were of course a few areas of the country where excellent relations always existed between the force and the general public.

At any one time, there were between 10,000 and 12,000 Irishmen in the RIC Without considering members who had previously served or died in service, there was always an equivalent number of families who had a member of the family in the force. Another 7,000 to 8,000 families would have daughters married to RIC men.

Through their families and extended families, the force would have well over 200,000 close relatives throughout the community in Ireland at any one time. In many cases, two or three brothers from the same family were members.

District Inspector Thomas St G. McCarthy, Co-founder of the Gaelic Athletic Association

On 1 November 1884, seven men assembled at Hayes' Hotel in Thurles, County Tipperary, and founded an association which since then has been known as the Gaelic Athletic Association. The seven men were Michael Cusack and Maurice Davin, both of whom had organised the meeting, John Wyse Power, John McKay, Joseph Bracken, Joseph O Ryan and Thomas St George McCarthy. The latter was the district inspector of the Royal Irish Constabulary stationed at Templemore, County Tipperary. He was a native of Bansha in south Tipperary where his father George McCarthy, a native of County Kerry, was a constable (sergeant) in the Irish Constabulary. A noted athlete, he became a member of the Trinity College Rugby Club and played on the Irish rugby team against Wales in 1881. On deciding to join the RIC as a cadet, he attended a cramming school in Dublin run by Michael Cusack and after obtaining first place in the entrance examination, he joined the RIC as a cadet in November 1882, at the age of twenty. After six weeks' training he was appointed a sub-inspector, third class, and five months later he was allocated to Templemore, where he took charge of that district. One of the co-founders of the GAA – Joseph K. Bracken, a monumental sculptor – was also from Templemore, and his youngest son, Brendan, later came to prominence as a British cabinet minister and a close friend of Winston Churchill.

It is most likely that District Inspector McCarthy was invited to the meeting by Michael Cusack, who knew McCarthy exceptionally well from his academy in Dublin and through his keen interest in rugby and athletics. Regrettably there is no record of what transpired at that first meeting. There is a possibility that McCarthy attended a second meeting, but after that he appears to have had no further involvement in the new association. It is unlikely that any restrictions were placed upon him by the RIC authorities, as he would have had sufficient autonomy to be involved if he so wanted to. The troubled state of the country may have had a bearing on his cessation of involvement with the association, and in any case he left Templemore early in 1885. The Gaelic Athletic Association went on to become the biggest amateur sporting association in Ireland; when it celebrated its silver jubilee in 1934, the former District Inspector McCarthy was the only founder member then alive, which went practically unnoticed.

Serious Riots in Belfast in 1886

About 300 Protestant workers attacked a small group of Catholics working at Queen's Island Shipyard, Belfast, on 4 June 1886, and the only escape route open for many workers was to jump into the river Lagan. Ten Catholics were very badly beaten and a delicate eighteen-year-old Catholic youth – James Curran of Ballymacgarett – drowned in front of a hostile crowd while no effort was made to save him. The incident sparked off very serious rioting and nine people were killed, mostly as a result of shooting by soldiers and the police. A further thirteen people were killed on the weekend of 13/14 July when confrontations took place between marching Protestants and Catholic mobs. Riots continued into August when another sixteen people lost their life, and it was September before peace was restored.

Two thousand members of the Royal Irish Constabulary were drafted into Belfast, together with 200 cavalry and 1,000 infantry to augment the Belfast RIC force. They had a most difficult task in restoring peace and order. The total number of deaths exceeded fifty, hundreds were injured and thirty public houses were burned down. Over 100 arrests were made. A commission set up to investigate the riots published a 600 page report in 1887 on its findings. The 1886 riots in Belfast resulted in the biggest loss of life through civil disturbances in Ireland during the nineteenth century.

Expenditure on the RIC

During the years ending 31 March 1888, 1889. 1890 and 1891, the cost of maintaining the Royal Irish Constabulary force was as follows:

Details of expense	1888	1889	1890	1891
Superintending officers' salaries and allowances	£14,405	£14,379	£14,005	£14,546
Pay, extra pay and allowances	£1,016,340	£1,011,149	£1,010,271	£1,011,894
Arms, ammunition, accoutrements and saddlery	731	2,135	1,629	1,554
Clothing	31,513	32,262	27,017	33,515
Horses and forage	19,076	19,132	19,317	19,056
Rent of barracks, barrack furniture, fuel and light	28,870	30,910	31,758	32,224
Pensions and gratuities	286,629	289,884	296,244	298,927
Miscellaneous	12,890	13,096	12,440	12,814
TOTALS	1,410,454	1,412,947	1,412,681	1,424,530

Deployment of the RIC

The strength of the Royal Irish Constabulary on 30 September 1891 consisted of 1 inspector general; 1 deputy inspector general; 3 assistant inspectors generals; 1 surgeon; 1 veterinary surgeon; 1 barrack master and storekeeper; 1 town inspector [in Belfast]; 36 county inspectors; 229 district inspectors; 260 head constables; and 12,051 sergeants, acting-sergeants and constables.

The force was deployed as follows on 30 September 1891:

Counties	County inspectors	District constables	Head constables	Sergeants, acting sgts constables	Strength per 1,000 pop
Antrim	1	5	7	253	12
Armagh	1	4	4	198	14
Carlow	1	2	2	106	26
Cavan	1	5	6	226	20
Clare	1	9	9	491	40
Cork ER	1	12	14	577	27
Cork WR	1	9	9	380	26
Donegal	1	9	10	505	27
Down	1	4	5	272	12
Dublin	1	4	4	209	31
Fermanagh	1	4	4	158	21
Galway ER	1	6	6	355	34
Galway WR	1	8	9	309	34
Kerry	1	8	8	631	35
Kildare	1	4	6	195	28
Kilkenny	1	5	5	266	35
King's County (Offaly)	1	5	6	235	36
Leitrim	1	5	5	219	28
Limerick	1	7	7	528	43
Londonderry	1	3	3	143	12
Longford	1	3	3	166	32
Louth	1	5	4	150	26
Mayo	1	9	9	490	22
Meath	1	6	6	292	38
Monaghan	1	3	3	161	19
Queen's County (Laois)	1	4	4	191	30
Roscommon	1	7	5	328	29
Sligo	1	5	5	234	24
Tipperary NR	1	6	6	257	34
Tipperary SR	1	7	10	454	47

Counties	County inspectors	District constables	Head constables	Sergeants, acting sgts constables	Strength per 1,000 pop
Tyrone	1	6	6	234	14
Waterford	1	3	3	243	31
Westmeath	1	8	7	275	43
Wexford	1	5	6	258	23
Wicklow	1	4	5	185	30
Cities and Towns					
Carrickfergus	–			11	12
Cork	–	4	4	180	24
Drogheda	–	1	1	40	34
Galway	–	1	1	59	35
Kilkenny	–	1	2	32	30
Limerick	–	1	2	85	23
Londonderry	–	1	2	86	26
Waterford	–	3	2	61	30
TOTALS	35	211	225	10,728	
Belfast city	1	5	20	724	28
Reserve force	–	4	8	203	–
Depot	1	9	7	396	–
Force Total	37	229	260	12,051	–

These statistics relating to the distribution of the force and the numbers allocated per 1,000 population give a good indication of the more troublesome areas for policing towards the end of the nineteenth century. These areas had more members of constabulary per 1,000 population than others: Tipperary South Riding (47), Limerick and Westmeath (43 each), Clare (40) and Meath (38). At the other end of the scale, the lowest number of RIC members per 1,000 population were Antrim, Down, County Londonderry and Carrickfergus town (12 each); Armagh and Tyrone (14 each). There were far fewer policing problems for the RIC in the north-eastern counties of Ireland. The Land League was less active there, and that part of Ireland was also industrialised with very high employment opportunities. In 1895, Earl Cadogan took up office as lord lieutenant of Ireland, and on his first visit to Belfast, Lord Mayor McCammond in welcoming him said: "We are pleased to be able to assure your excellency of the peaceful and prosperous condition of our city and district and the full employment of our population and the continued development of our industries. During the past fifty years, the city has grown from a population of 70,000 to 300,000."

Changes of Inspector Generals

Colonel George Hillier was appointed inspector general of the RIC in 1876. He had been deputy inspector general for a number of years and replaced Sir Colonel John Stewart Wood, who had been inspector general for eleven years. In 1882 Colonel Robert Bruce took over from Colonel Hillier and served as inspector general for three years until 1885. Andrew Reed, who had been an assistant inspector general for a number of years and who had distinguished himself as the author of the *Irish Constables Guide* and the *Policeman's Manual* – both of which were essential text books for the force – was appointed inspector general in 1885 and served for fifteen years until he retired in 1900. All his predecessors had come into the constabulary from military careers, but Andrew Reed had joined the Irish Constabulary as a cadet and had progressed through the ranks. His rating as an inspector general was high and he was later knighted.

Marriages in the Constabulary

Through the lifetime of the Irish and Royal Irish Constabularies, very few issues created as much hassle or upset for individual members as romance and marriage. The code regulations and circulars issued on the subject indicate that the upper echelons of the force and the government would have liked to see all members of the forces remaining single during their service. Marriage appeared to have been definitely discouraged. However, members proved very attractive to eligible young ladies, and very many mothers desired them as sons-in-law. It would certainly have better suited the authorities to have all single men who had no family encumbrances and who could be moved at a moment's notice from one barracks to another without expense to public funds.

A member was not permitted to get married until he had seven years' service. He then had to seek permission from his authorities to do so. He had to satisfy them that he had at least £30 in savings, and his future wife had to be a woman of good character and receive the approval of the district inspector. For the rank-and-file there was no way of getting over these regulations.

Secret marriages – of which there were several – did nothing to alleviate the predicament and resulted in automatic dismissal if discovered. With a view to discouraging pregnant girlfriends, a serious disciplinary offence of "criminal intercourse" was created and reiterated in a circular of October 1876 by the inspector general. The penalty was automatic dismissal. In a few cases, members eloped with the daughters of wealthy farmers or traders. Some members who were dismissed for secretly marrying succeeded in joining the Dublin Metropolitan Police.

The Irish Constabulary had the lowest number of married members of any force in the United Kingdom, about 25 per cent of the rank and file. The marriage rate for head constables and officers was higher. Most members only married when they had twelve or fifteen years' service.

Married life for members and their wives was difficult – except for the higher ranks. A married member was obliged to reside in lodgings within one quarter of a mile of his barracks, later increased to a one-mile radius. The couple were forbidden to own any land, animals or poultry, or to work at any trade. From 1871 onwards, they were permitted to keep a pig and poultry, provided they didn't sell the produce, and they were permitted to have a garden not exceeding ten square perches. From 1905, member's wives were permitted to have lodgers, subject to certain conditions. The restrictions were relaxed somewhat in the early part of the twentieth century. Even though members were married, they were obliged to sleep in the barracks at night on a three-month rota system. Only one married man could sleep outside the barracks for every five men who actually slept in the barracks.

Many married constables and sergeants lived with their wives and families in accommodation within the barrack building. Their total married accommodation normally did not exceed two rooms, and the family shared the same hallway and stairway and very often the kitchen with the men attached to the barracks. In many instances they were obliged to share the lavatory which was used by the other barrack members as well as by prisoners who were detained. In rural areas the lavatory usually consisted of a dry closet in the rear barrack yard. The wife and children had to endure the noise, cursing and swearing of prisoners detained in the barrack cells overnight (a normal feature of ordinary barrack life) – often resulting in a total lack of sleep for all. The conditions in many barracks were deplorable and were the subject of complaints. How wives coped with them defies comprehension.

A member could not have more than four children in the barrack accommodation. Children of members reared in this environment were commonly referred to as "barrack brats" or "Peeler's pups". Prior to 1883, daughters of members were obliged to leave the barracks when they reached the age of fourteen years, later increased to sixteen years. Boys could remain until they were eighteen years. Conditions for children in this environment could not have been more difficult.

There was occasional friction between members, between constables and sergeants, or between the married family and single men residing in the barracks, which the wife had to endure. There were many serious incidents in these situations from time to time, but the worst occurred in November 1892 when a mentally deranged constable savagely murdered Sergeant Michael Rogan and his wife and four children at Ballinadrimna barracks, near Carbury, County Kildare.

The Contribution of the RIC to Other Police Forces

In addition to the role played in the establishment of some of the Canadian police forces (see p. 145), former officers of the RIC also made their mark in Australia. In *The Australian Police Forces*, G.M. O'Brien outlined the progress of one such officer, Major W. J. Cahill, who became commissioner of the Australian police in 1899:

> Major W.J. Cahill, an Irishman, who had served for years in the Royal Irish Constabulary, had migrated to Queensland in 1880 and had joined the public service. He was also prominent in the Queensland Rifle regiment. On his appointment as Commissioner, he made several changes in administration on the lines obtaining in the Royal Irish Constabulary, regarded then as the best disciplined and most highly trained British police force. He held office for twelve years and reported in 1910 that extraneous duties were seriously hampering the effectiveness of the police, particularly in the prevention of crime. "This," he said, "is most obvious in the country districts, where constant patrolling is neccessary to prevent stock stealing. Those thieves are acutely alive to the fact that the police in many places are tied down to office work for other departments when they should in fact be out patrolling the countryside."

Prior to this, a former member of the Irish Constabulary – Robert O'Hara Burke – had made a name for himself in Australia. With some years' service years in the Irish Constabulary he resigned and emigrated to Australia in the 1850s. On arrival there he was appointed as a magistrate in the state of Victoria. He later joined the police with the rank of inspector. He was given joint leadership of an expedition to explore central Australia and to cross the continent from south to north. With his team he set out from Melbourne on 20 August 1860 and succeeded in reaching the estuary of the Flinders river on the Gulf of Carpentaria. Having completed their mission, Inspector O'Hara Burke and his party set out on the return journey. They were unprepared for the return journey and the weather likely to be encountered, and unfortunately the entire party died of starvation and exposure on the way.

During the last half of the nineteenth century, former officers of the RIC were holding high-ranking positions or in charge of many of the police forces throughout the British Commonwealth. Their experience and service in Ireland with the RIC, qualified them for service anywhere. The Indian police force which was established in the 1860s was modelled on RIC structures and command. At the turn of the century, former officers of the force were serving as the commissioner of the London City Police and chief constables of Glasgow, Liverpool, Birkenhead, Birmingham, Cornwall and Newcastle-on-Tyne. In addition to high-ranking officers, very many former RIC members who left the force emigrated and joined the

English forces. Very many Irishmen with good old traditional Irish names could also be found in police forces in America, Canada, Australia, Great Britain or any of the Commonwealth countries.

John Cullen who was born in Ireland in 1851 joined the RIC and resigned in 1876. He emigrated to New Zealand and joined the New Zealand Armed Constabulary. Two years later he was promoted to sergeant and in 1897 he was promoted to inspector in charge of Nelson, Westland. He served as inspector in charge of Auckland up to 1912, when he was appointed commissioner of the New Zealand Police force. He held this position up to 1916 and had the distinction of being the first policeman to rise to the highest position in the force through the ranks in the New Zealand force. He was an extraordinary individual who led from the front, and his commissionership coincided with one of the most turbulent periods in the history of New Zealand, the Waihi strike of 1912 followed by a general strike in 1913. He was a rigidly upright individual, always prepared to discipline those who fell short of his high standards. During his tenure of office, he introduced several major reforms, including new uniforms for the force and new police regulations. On his retirement he was conferred with the King's Police Medal and was the first member of the New Zealand force to receive that distinction. By an extraordinary coincidence Commissioner Cullen was replaced as commissioner by another Irishman, John O'Donovan, a former schoolteacher who was born near Rosscarbery, County Cork, in 1858. He served as commissioner from 1916 to 1921.

Many officers from the Commonwealth countries underwent cadet and officer training courses at the RIC depot in Phoenix Park. While attending these courses, they wore the uniforms of their respective forces and provided a very colourful spectacle for onlookers whenever they paraded or drilled in the depot square. These courses for the colonial police officers continued well into the present century. Between 1907 and 1912 a total of 112 such officers underwent cadet courses at the the RIC depot. The countries from which they came, and the number of cadets from each, is as follows: Nigeria 47, Kenya 15, Ghana 12, Uganda 11, Trinidad 6, Guiana 5, Jamaica 4, Sierra Leone 3, Gambia 2, from other countries 7.

The courses included British criminal law, drill, police duties, musketry, physical training, equitation, fire drill, tropical hygiene, laws of evidence and accountancy procedures. The fact that the RIC depot was selected by so many police forces for the training of their future police officers was a tribute to the high quality of RIC training and demonstrates the esteem in which the force was held worldwide.

Developments in Transport

One of the biggest changes in the last decades of the nineteenth century was the revolution brought about by improved transport. Prior to that, the only means of transport were the trains, mail coaches, canal barges, horses and horse drawn transport and foot. The latter was the only means available to the members for performing their duties. The penny-farthing cycle or, more appropriately titled, the velocipede came into usage in the early 1870s. While a very small number of the constabulary acquired one of these machines they were a minority. In 1885 the bicycle in much the same format as it now exists – with two wheels of equal size and with the rear wheel driven by means of a chain from pedals operated by the rider – was invented. It provided great mobility for anybody who could afford one and its running cost and maintenance was negligible except for tyre replacements.

From a policing point of view, the advent of bicycles presented no problem until 1907 when the Lights On Vehicles Act (7 Edw. 7, c. 45) came into force and which made front white lights on bicycles obligatory. Carbide lamps (operated from gas generated within the lamp through the addition of a small amount of water to carbide) or paraffin oil bicycle lamps were obligatory from then onwards if one were to avoid the attention of the constabulary on night patrols.

The ownership of a bicycle for recreational purposes was the aspiration of every the rank-and-file member of the constabulary. They were targeted by the numerous cycle manufacturers and retailers who had emerged all over the country, and photographs of constables in possession of a new bicycle were used by dealers and manufacturers. One enterprising constable who was anxious to equip himself with the most up-to-date transport wrote as follows to Mr John Edwards, cycle dealer, Tralee, County Kerry:

> *RIC,*
> *John Street.*
> *Limerick. 20th April 1893.*
> *Dear John,*
> *I have not got a bicycle yet, and I am thinking of getting one now. As you and I know each other, I would like to deal with you.*
> *I saw the new list (Rudge) and I would fancy a model C.E, in page 11 of list, with cushion tyres. If I pay you in 12 months hence, what will the terms be and cost?*
> *Please write as soon as you can and you will oblige,*
> *Yours etc.,*
> *L.V. Wilson.*

Another constable from Lackenafooder, Knocknagoshel, Abbeyfeale, who already owned a bicycle sent his pedal for repair.

Steam-powered traction engines made their appearance on Irish roads in the 1890s, and their use on the public road was controlled by the Locomotives Act, 1865 (28 & 29 Vic., c. 83), otherwise known as the Red Flag Act, which obliged the users to have a man carrying a red flag walking in front of the steam engines as they proceeded through towns and cities. An early prosecution by the constabulary for a breach of the Red Flag Act was recorded at Nenagh, County Tipperary, petty sessions in 1896. The first motor car, a steam-powered Serpollet, made its appearance on Irish roads also in 1896. Motor cars were seen for the first time by many people in 1901 during the Grand Tour of Ireland, when a number of motor cars owned and driven by some of Ireland's wealthiest people left the Shelbourne Hotel in Dublin and travelled via Naas, Carlow, Kilkenny, Waterford, Cork, Bantry, Killarney, Limerick, Clare, Galway and then returned across the country to Dublin. In press reports of the event, tributes were paid to members of the Royal Irish Constabulary for the assistance they had given to the motorists who had got lost en route. District Inspector Hayes of the RIC was a passenger in a Daimler driven by Dr Coholan of Waterford during the event. The first legislation controlling the use of motor cars, which required them to be registered and fitted with registration plates, came into force under the Motor Car Act, 1903 – adding to the workload of the RIC and DMP. In anticipation of the successful development of the internal combustion engine, legislation controlling the sale and storage of petroleum was enacted as far back as 1871 with a number of subsequent amendments made to update it. From the early 1900s there was a gradual increase in the number of motor cars, motor lorries and agricultural tractors using the public roads.

Policing in the 1890s

Throughout the 1880s the demand for Home Rule for Ireland was being pushed by Charles Stewart Parnell and the Irish Party, and in 1886 Gladstone brought a Home Rule bill before the English parliament. The future of the RIC and the Dublin Metropolitan Police figured large in the provisions of the bill. Provision was made for the amalganation of both forces should an Irish parliament be set up. The bill was defeated. In January 1891 the bill was resurrected and, in an effort to appease the Irish Party, Gladstone gave certain guarantees in relation to policing and land. In relation to the RIC a five year plan was suggested, during which the force would become demilitarised and would be replaced with a civil police force. Parnell was insisting that the RIC should be abolished. He died some months later and the Home Rule movement lingered on for another twenty years, but no changes took place in the RIC or DMP.

Compared with the 1870s and 1880s, the RIC found policing in the 1890s less strenuous and more routine in nature. After the serious troubles and disorder arising from the Land League and the activities of the Moonlighters, the force settled down to give a more professional police service and succeeded in winning back the confidence of the ordinary people. As a result relations with the general public became more harmonious. In the early 1890s there were a few troubled spots for the constabulary in the country. In Arklow, County Wicklow, the Protestant rector of the parish engaged in street preaching and hymn singing each Sunday, and this raised the tempers of the local Catholics who saw it as a direct challenge to their religion. Technically the clergyman was not in breach of the law, as street-preaching was permitted in England, but in a small Irish town he was tempting fate through his actions. Sunday after Sunday, constabulary were drafted into Arklow to keep the peace, and their vigilance and tact prevented very serious disorder.

Trouble in Tipperary Town

In 1890 and 1891, there was a serious outbreak of violence in Tipperary town. It continued for a number of years and tied up huge numbers of the Royal Irish Constabulary, with a back-up of military and local troops, while it lasted. The trouble commenced with the refusal of tenants in the town of Tipperary and the adjoining estate of Arthur Smith Barry – later Lord Barrymore – to pay rents. At the instigation of William O'Brien, a new town was designed and built and named "New Tipperary". A senior RIC officer sent to Tipperary to take "executive charge" of the state of lawlessness there, wrote:

> There were all the usual accompaniments of Irish excitements – bombs of crude construction, made of the boxes of cart-wheels filled with powder and exploded with terrific noise, but with little effect. Mobs of men and boys parading with bands of indifferent music at weird hours of the night to "larn" those who were not in sympathy with the movement that they had better beware. Broken windows, threatening notices, revolver shots, excited curates, and patient, long-suffering parish priests. And last of all, the peripatetic politician gathering information to strengthen whatever side he belonged to in the Imperial Parliament, or to write articles, more or less correct of all he saw.

In the course of the disorder in Tipperary, the parish priest, Fr Humphries, assaulted Mrs Mullins, wife of an RIC sergeant in the town, and he called her a prostitute. He was brought before the petty sessions for the offence and was convicted and fined £20. The pregnant wife of Constable Linney, also stationed at Tipperary, was seriously assaulted in a separate incident and had a miscarriage as a result. Children of members of the force in the town were intimidated and the children of Sergeant O'Connor in nearby Cashel were stoned.

Maintaining the Protection Posts

One of the legacies left by the Moonlighters' activities to the constabulary was the maintenance of the protection posts at the homes of people whose lives had been threatened during the previous decade. Many districts where the worst disorder existed had at least one of those protection posts in addition to its established constabulary barracks. Several districts had between two and five such posts. Their around-the-clock maintenance put a severe drain on manpower, engaging members in excess of the ordinary policing needs. In most cases, the post consisted of a constabulary hut situated in a remote and lonely location, resulting in the protection duties for the members based there being repetitive and extremely boring. When members performing the duties were accommodated within or near the residence of the person being protected, it was a welcome break to the monotony of duty protecting a residence and its inhabitants when the person had to do some shopping in the nearby town or village, attend a funeral or a fair or other business, accompanied by fully armed menbers of the force.

The manning of the protection posts carried much responsibility. The members had to be prepared ready for an attack, and they were aware that their dismissal from the force was the most likely outcome should any succesful attack be made on the persons and property being protected by them.

Once established, the removal or closing down of one of these protection posts became very difficult. Those who had the benefit of protection for themselves and their property from the constabulary made every effort possible for their retention, even when the neccessity for the protection was past. Former inspector of the RIC, George Garrow Green, sheds some light on the retention of these posts in *In the Royal Irish Constabulary*:

> Apart from serious agrarian crimes which unfortunately have from time to time, given us so bad a name, there exists others of a second rate, also peculiar to the soil. Among such may be classed, threatening letters, maimings of cattle, burnings, and the like. I maintain, from long and practical experience, that at least fifty per cent of these are uncoupled from malice. For instance, I have known an estate-owner employ his steward to write him a threatening letter because a police barracks, his property, for which he received government rent, was about to be given up. Another wrote himself a similiar letter and fired a gun-shot at his own window because he wanted to retain two of our men stationed in his house whom he used to employ in various ways, and have driving about after him as a sort of guard of honour. Two land stewards wrote threatening letters to themselves to enhance their value in their master's eyes and to secure an increase in wages.

District inspectors and head constables were obliged to visit the protection posts frequently, particularly at night. Many of the posts were maintained up to the disbandment of the Royal Irish Constabulary, and a small number were retained subsequent to 1922.

Although the constabulary were still providing protection for sheriffs and bailiffs at evictions – their most hated and detested duty – the number of evictions was on the decline. From a total of 5,201 in 1882, they had dropped to 671 in 1895.

The Murder of a Suspected Witch

The RIC were highly praised for their investigations of murders of the most bizarre type, which received much press publicity, during the latter half of the 1890s. The first of these was the tragic murder of Mrs Bridget Cleary, aged twenty-six years, wife of Michael Cleary, a cooper, of Ballyvadlea, Drangan, County Tipperary. It occurred between Friday, 15 March, and Saturday, 16 March 1895. Bridget and Michael Cleary lived in a labourer's cottage, and Mrs Cleary's father, Patrick Boland, lived with them. She was described as a beautiful young woman and had no children. On Wednesday the 13th, she was sick in bed and was visited by the local curate Fr Ryan and by Dr Crean. The latter observed nothing about her that was likely to cause her death. On the following day, Fr Ryan was again requested to visit her but declined to do so, saying that he was busy, that he had anointed her on the previous day and that she did not appear to him to be in danger of death. Michael Cleary had, for some unknown reason, concluded that his wife was a witch. He enlisted the assistance of three of her cousins, Patrick, James and William Kennedy, her father Patrick Boland, another man named John Dunne and an old woman named Mary Kennedy to administer potions to and to torture Bridget for two days to rid her of an evil spirit. While rosaries were being recited, she was burned with a red hot poker and was finally burned slowly over the fire grate in the kitchen until she died. Her death was of the most horrific and gruesome nature.

Following her death, Michael Cleary and Patrick Kennedy took her body to a field about one mile away and buried it. The neighbours and friends were told that she had run away from home. Her disappearance came to the notice of the constabulary, and when Acting Sergeant Egan went to the Cleary home enquiring about Mrs Cleary's whereabouts, Cleary told him that she had left home at about 12 o'clock on the previous night. Acting Sergeant Egan was not satisfied about Cleary's story and, after making some enquiries, went back to the house that night. Finding the door locked, he gained entry through a window and found a burned nightdress in the house. An extensive search was carried out for the body of Mrs Cleary, whom the constabulary suspected had been murdered. Six days after her death their persistence was rewarded. In the course of a second search by them, her body was found by the constabulary where it had been buried. An inquest was held in a nearby house, but the injuries which caused Mrs Cleary's death were considered to be too gruesome for reporting. The constabulary buried Bridget Cleary that night by the light of a lantern in Cloneen churchyard after all efforts had failed to get any person to give a Christian burial to the unfortunate victim.

The constabulary investigation resulted in all those responsible being brought to trial. At the July assizes in Clonmel, charges of murder were withdrawn against all the accused. Michael Cleary was sentenced to twenty years' penal servitude for manslaughter; Patrick Kennedy, five years' penal servitude; John Dunne, three years penal servitude; William and James Kennedy, eighteen months imprisonment; Patrick Boland and Michael Kennedy, six months imprisonment each. When it came to Mary Kennedy, the judge said, "I will not pass sentence on this poor old woman." Judge O'Brien (a Catholic) was scathing in his remarks about all the people who should have done something, but did nothing, to prevent the death of Mrs Cleary. He said, "This case demonstrates a degree of darkness in the mind, not of one person but of several, a moral darkness, even religious darkness the disclosure of which had come with surprise on many persons." At the conclusion of the trial, Judge O'Brien praised the work of the RIC and complimented District Inspector Wansborough, who had been in overall charge of the investigation, and all his men for the excellent work done by them in bringing the difficult investigation to a successful conclusion.

Murdered Because of the Fairies

In March 1896 a strange murder took place in the village of Lisphelan, County Roscommon, for which blame was assigned to the fairies. The Cunningham family, consisting of a father and his four sons and daughter, lived in a comfortable house in the village. The second son, James, was a shoemaker by trade and the other brothers were employed on the land. The *Freeman's Journal* reported that "the inhabitants of the Lisphelan district were extremely superstitious and that on the night of March 6th, many of them including James Cunningham, were under the impression that evil spirits were hovering around their dwellings". Fr Gately, PP, branded this as "a calumny" and accused the correspondent for the *Freeman's Journal* "with slandering, with charges of belief in witchcraft and fairies in the whole locality". At the later trial, Fr Gately described the Cunningham's as "good honest, moral, respectable peasants" and asserted that for a few days before 6 March, James Cunningham was "religiously insane". In a letter to the *Freeman's Journal* on 13 March, Fr Gately wrote, "I saw him at home on Thursday in the presence of all members of his family, in whose hearing he told me that, for twelve days, the 'devil' had been tempting him to do away with himself but that God gave him grace to resist the temptation." The family pressed Fr Gately to take money and say masses for James Cunningham and he reluctantly did so. For a week prior to the murder, James Cunningham frequently visited an old ring fort near his home.

On the night of 6 March, the Cunningham family, believing they heard weird noises around their house, decided to sit up through the night until cockcrow. At midnight the family knelt and recited the rosary. While the family were still on their knees, James jumped up, caught his father around the throat and threw him on the ground. The rest of the family went to their father's assistance and dragged James away. A terrible fight ensued between James and his three brothers and sister. They overpowered James and battered him to death in a room off the kitchen. His body was subsequently described as "being terribly battered, chin cut away and teeth broken".

When James was dead, the remainder of the family claimed that they had heard a voice coming from the loft overhead which said, "Look out for yourselves now." They ran to the house of a neighbour who was reluctant to admit them, and after some delay they broke a window and let themselves in. They told the neighbour – William Cunningham – what had happened. They remained in William's house for the rest of the night "saying the rosary and making crosses". They told him that their own house "was filled with thousands of devils and that but for the Holy Water the devils would sweep them all in no time". They did not report the matter to the constabulary until the evening of the 7 March.

Sergeant Doyle and Constable Dalton were quickly on the scene and took statements. The constabulary arrested the entire Cunningham family and detained them overnight at Leecarrow RIC barracks. The constabulary spent the night trying to subdue the family, who broke down the cell door and wrecked the day room. They had to be handcuffed and their legs tied with ropes to control them. Sergeant Doyle said that "the talk about fairies and devils was kept up all the time. They were very violent. They could not be worse." On Sunday, 8 March, they were all removed to Athlone constabulary barracks and were followed by a jeering crowd through the streets. In Athlone barracks the family members prayed all night long to keep away the fairies. The inquest on James Cunningham was held on Monday, the 11th. The *Freeman's Journal* of 13 March reported: "Lisphelan village is almost exclusively inhabited by relatives and namesakes of the deceased, not one of them could be induced to lend assistance to the burial of the body. Father Mulready, the curate, personally requested most of the neighbours to assist the police but in vain." Eventually the constabulary, under the directions of a doctor, had to put the remains in a coffin, which at the last moment was found to be too small for the body and it was necessary to break the coffin to accommodate the body. The constabulary took the coffin in a horse cart to the cemetery where they dug a grave and buried it. No relative or friend assisted them.

All members of the family were charged with murder. The father and brothers were remanded to Tullamore Gaol and the sister and one brother were remanded to Ballinasloe Mental Asylum. The trial took place of the father and two sons in July at Roscommon assizes before Judge O'Brien. The father was acquitted and the two sons were ordered to be confined in a criminal lunatic asylum during Her Majesty's pleasure. A similiar sentence was passed on the third son in the following March.

The Tragic Killing of Four Children

On 29 November 1896, the tragic death of four young children took place at Cappawhite, County Tipperary. The Sadlier family lived in a comfortable farmhouse near Cappawhite. They had four children, aged four, three and two years and a baby of five months. Mr Sadlier got up at 3am and left for a fair at Bansha. When the family housekeeper heard no noises from Mrs Sadlier's room later in the morning, she went to investigate and found the four children dead and twenty-six-year-old Mrs Sadlier lying on the bed, looking quite normal.

The maid ran for assistance to neighbours and the constabulary were called. Sergeant O'Sullivan came quickly and found Mrs Sadlier lying quite still on the bed. She appeared to be dazed, but perfectly rational and conscious. Two of the children were at her side in the bed and two were on the floor of the bedroom. All the children were semi-decapitated, and Sergeant O'Sullivan found an open razor lying under a cloth at the foot of the bed. The sergeant informed Mrs Sadlier that he was arresting her and he gave her the usual legal caution. She volunteered a statement to him, which the Sergeant quoted from at the inquest on the four children:

> Well, I killed the four children in order that they may be with Almighty God, as I consider they were not capable of committing sin. I hope not. They were not up to the use of reason. I strove to destroy them before they would fall into the same sins I committed. I imagined I saw our Saviour this morning on a cross at the foot of the bed. I also saw my good acts and my bad acts in the balance, and I saw my bad acts over-balance my good acts and I thought I was damned, and sooner than put my children in hell, I destroyed them. Oh my God have mercy on me. I have consulted my spiritual adviser and have got Masses said for myself.

Mrs Sadlier was first detained at Cappawhite barracks and later remanded to Limerick Gaol. She preserved her calmness and demeanour throughout. The jail doctor certified that she was insane, "suffering from melancholia". By order of the lord lieutenant she was committed to Limerick Asylum.

Duty to London for Queen Victoria's Diamond Jubilee

The most prestigious duty performed by the Royal Irish Constabulary during the 1890s was on 29 June 1897 when a contingent of the RIC mounted troop performed duty in London for celebrations connected with Queen Victoria's Diamond Jubilee. An invitation had been extended to the inspector general to provide a mounted troop for the sovereign's bodyguard at the main Jubilee parade. Three officers, two head constables and twenty-four sergeants and constables were selected for the duty, as well as the best horses available to the force, with some reserves. They assembled at the depot in the Phoenix Park and trained and rehearsed for a number of weeks prior to their departure for London, under the direction of the troop leader, District Inspector John Tyson, who was in charge of the cavalry school. He was awarded the Queen's Jubilee Medal for leading the troop at the ceremonies. The fine turnout of officers, constabulary and horses drew the admiration of the world press and visitors who crowded London for the event.

Sport in the RIC

As times became more peaceful in the 1890s, members of the Royal Irish Constabulary had a greater opportunity to become involved in sports and athletics. As an organisation, the members had the finest physique and appearance of manhood in Ireland – or possibly anywhere in the world. With their strenuous duties, which involved much walking during daily patrols, and the plain diet of the time, they were extremely fit. In the early 1890s, many members took part in athletics and were very successful, but it was in team sports that they particularly excelled. In nearly every town, the local RIC party had a tug-of-war team. They competed with each other at district, county and inter-county level. In the 1890s, the Royal Irish Constabulary team took on all the international competitors and won the world tug-of-war championships. Over a number of years the team was unbeaten and it amassed a huge collection of trophies. There was always a great rivalry between the RIC and DMP teams and with the decline of the RIC teams, the DMP tug-of-war teams came in to prominence. Tug-of-war continued as a competition within the force up to 1920. RIC boxing teams also came into prominence over the same period. Boxing was not then organised on a national basis, but RIC teams were very successful against international police and army teams. Rowing was another activity engaged in by the RIC in some parts of Ireland, and their teams won many competitions at regattas. Football never appeared to be a popular game with members and perhaps the Gaelic Athletic Association ban on members may have been in some way responsible.

Introduction of Horse-Drawn "Black Marias"

During the 1890s, the RIC introduced enclosed horse-drawn vans for the conveyance of prisoners in the cities outside of Dublin. They were heavy, substantially built vehicles mounted on four wheels, drawn by one horse, and fitted with a turntable attachment for ease of manoeuvre. They were used to convey prisoners to and from courts and railway stations and to the bridewells from other city barracks. They were occasionally used for the transport of members of the constabulary when required. The use of the horse-drawn prison vans was phased out about 1916 with the introduction of motorised transport.

Visits of VIPs

The Duke and Duchess of York visited Ireland in 1897 and again in 1899 and travelled extensively throughout the country. A number of British MPs also toured Ireland during 1899, and the visits of all the VIPs over this period passed off without incident for the RIC The only major incident for the RIC before the end of the century took place in Derry city on 14 August 1899, when Archbishop Flood of Trinidad, a Dominican, visited the city. He was hooted and mobbed in his carriage by a crowd of Orangemen. One of the Catholic churches in Derry was attacked while confessions were being heard and the church had to be closed. The windows of a priest's house were broken and the priest was chased through the streets. There was much condemnation of the incident. Otherwise, Ireland was gradually settling down and the prospects for the Irish people and for the constabulary looked good as the twentieth century approached.

Developments in Administration and and Local Government

The Congested Districts Board was established in 1891. Its operations were spread over the poorer areas and it proved to be of immense benefit. Its area covered over three and a half million acres and included over half a million people. It received a grant of £126,000 for its disposal prior to 1894, and it received on-going grants during the following years. It alleviated the hardships of the worst off in the community, and on 2 October 1899, the Bishops of Tuam, Galway, Clonfert, Achonry, Killala and Elphin wrote a complimentary letter to Arthur Balfour, praising the work done by the Congested Districts Board. Agricultural output increased and grants became available for different projects. The fixing of rents and security of tenure given to the tenants was beginning to bear fruit, whilst the working of the Ashbourne Act, as it was commonly known, was enabling tenants to purchase their holdings and become independent. There was also an improvement in health welfare. There was an overall improvement in the lot of the Irish peasantry which had suffered so much prior to that. The population had fallen by one million between 1861 and 1891, when it stood at 4,704.750, of which Catholics accounted for approximately three-quarters. Emigration had been a huge drain in the population during the previous decades, and it was estimated that between 1851 and 1899, 1,981,443 men and 1, 814,688 women had emigrated.

Major advances were made under the reign of Lord Cadogan as lord lieutenant (1895–1900) by way of essential legislation and progress. The most fundamental legislation passed was the Local Government (Ireland) Act, 1898 (61 & 62 Vic., c. 83). Up to this point each county was controlled by the sheriff and grand jury. The grand jury, which had a representative from each barony, assembled each year to appoint a sheriff. The sheriffs, who were themselves grand jurors, were appointed by the lord lieutenant, on the nomination of the judge of assizes, acting on the recommendations of the grand jury for the county. The sheriff summoned the grand jury to meet twice a year, immediately before the spring and summer assizes, and these meeting were attended by the judge of the assizes. It met for two or three days until it was formally discharged by the judge. The grand jury had two spheres of duties: its fiscal or administration duties and its criminal duties. In its administrative duties it was responsible for levying rates and maintaining all the local government services in the county. Its criminal duties consisted of giving all criminal cases brought forward for trial at the assizes a first hearing, and the grand jury had in fact the power to prevent a trial from proceeding, if satisfied that there was no prima facie case against the accused.

Under the Local Government (Ireland) Act, 1898, the grand jury system of local government was abolished. Its duties in relation to administration was transferred to the newly created county councils, comprised of elected members and based on a successful system which had been operating in England for some years. The criminal role was transferred to trial judges with empanelled juries. One important aspect of the grand jury system, that relating to awards for compensation made to members of the constabulary and witnesses for injuries or malicious damage to property, passed to the county court judge rather than the county council. This act totally changed the local government system in Ireland as it entered the twentieth century.

Duties of the Various Ranks at the Close of the Century

Each county (excluding Dublin city) was under the control of a county inspector of the RIC. Counties Cork, Tipperary and Galway were each divided in two and had a county inspector in charge of each part, thereby accounting for the total of thirty-five county inspectors who reported upwards to the inspector general of the force. The county inspectore had total control and responsibility for all RIC operations, personnel allocation and resources within his county. He had authority to transfer members within the county or allocate them to special duties, as well as responsibility for maintaining the force discipline within the county. Once every quarter, the county inspector inspected all barracks under his control, during which he inspected all personnel attached to the barracks and their firearms and accoutrements etc. He examined the members on their knowledge of police duties, persons wanted for crime, etc. He also inspected their proficiency at drill, which was conducted under the command of the head constable or sergeant. He checked all barrack records and wrote a record of his inspection findings into an official inspection book in each barracks. In the course of his duties, the county inspector travelled around by horse-drawn sidecar, and he was provided with the full-time services of a constable to look after his horse and sidecar and to drive him. The rank of county inspector would equate with that of the chief superintendent in the Garda Síochána or the Royal Ulster Constabulary of the present time.

Each county was divided up into a number of districts – varying between four and eight per county. Each district, comprised of approximately six to ten sub-districts, was under the control of a district inspector, who was accountable to his county inspector. The district inspector was obliged to be in his office at 10am each morning and he had to inspect all the barracks in his district at least once a month, in addition to paying one monthly night visit to each. Men had to be frequently drilled and parades inspected. Each month he attended the petty sessions in his district and had to attend the county assizes for trials which had a connection with his area. Once a year he conducted target practice sessions for the men of his district at shooting ranges on headlands or remote country areas. Each of his men was obliged to fire twenty rounds in practice. Occasionally he attended at other districts to sit on disciplinary inquiry boards. He was responsible for ensuring that all members of his district force were paid their salaries and allowances due to them at the end of each month. At the start of each month he was responsible for submitting returns to his county inspector and the inspector general, giving details of patrols performed, outrages committed and the general state of peace in his district during the previous month. The maintenance of law and order in his district and the good conduct and discipline of all personnel under his control was his responsibility. In the course of his day inspections, he inspected all personnel attached to the barracks and examined the members on their knowledge of police duties, drill and persons wanted and described in *Hue and Cry* etc. He took charge of guards of honour for judges attending at assizes and for dignataries visiting his district. He was also obliged to attend at the scene of all disturbances or anticipated disturbances within his district. The district inspector normally travelled on horseback in the performance of his duties and employed a civilian to look after his horse and equipment. His office was situated at the district headquarters barracks. The rank of district inspector would equate with that of a superintendent in the Garda Síochána or in the Royal Ulster Constabulary. He was assisted by a head constable, who took charge of the district in his absence.

Head constables had charge of the larger district headquarters barracks and they were also allocated to other larger barracks situated within a district. They maintained day-to-day discipline and were consulted by sub-ordinates for advice and dealing with problems encountered by them. The head constable was always regarded as being vital to the organisation of the force and he had a pivotal position in its administration. The rank equates to the present-day rank of inspector. Sergeants who displayed exceptional ability were promoted to the rank and approximately one quarter of the head constables got further promotion to the rank of district inspector. The head constable was a non-commissioned officer of the force.

With the exceptions of the larger district headquarters barracks, sergeants were in charge of all other barracks. The sergeant-in-charge was usually assisted by another sergeant and/or possibly by one or more acting sergeants. The latter rank was temporary in nature, and constables who were efficient and displayed good potential were appointed as acting sergeants after they had passed the sergeant's or P examination. Many of the acting sergeants went on to become sergeants but some reverted to constable rank when they failed to make the grade. The strength of the smaller rural barracks was normally one sergeant and four or five constables. Constables interested in promotion to sergeant rank had the opportunity to undergo a promotion examination for the rank. Promotion to sergeant rank was slow; it usually took up to twelve years' service or more for a constable to reach the rank. The officer in charge of the RIC in Belfast subsequent to its amalgamation with the Irish Constabulary in 1865 bore the title of "commissioner".

Foot drill was always a high priority with the Irish and Royal Irish Constabularies. It was performed each morning in accordance with the code instructions of the force, under the command of a head constable or sergeant. It was directed that drill sessions should not exceed one hour in duration. The drill movements performed consisted of marching and changing direction left and right, marching in file, formation of squad, dressing, marching in squad, diagonal marching, turning about, reforming squad and forming fours. Drill was also performed with rifles, and loading and unloading of the weapons was practised under instruction. While drill was one of the para-military trappings of the RIC, it also served other useful purposes, such as maintaining a state of alertness amongst the members and maintaining a high level of fitness. Members of the force were nearly always extremely fit, and overweight or unfit members were rare.

The primary duties of the RIC at the turn of the century were the prevention and detection of crime and the protection of life and property. All their operational duties, day and night patrolling and intelligence gathering were designed to meet those commitments. The duties of a non-police nature (already described) were still being performed. There were over fifty separate acts of parliament for enforcement, the principle ones being the Offences Against the Persons Act, 1861 (24 & 25 Vic., c. 100), and the larceny laws. The former covered all conceivable types of attack or injury to the person, including abortion, and provided for penalties in accordance with the gravity of the crime or offence committed. Stealing was always a crime at common law, but the Larceny Act, 1861 (24 & 25 Vic., c. 92), made provisions for special classes of larceny which had not been covered by common law. This legislation was enacted for the protection of the landlords and privileged classes of society in Ireland and England. The Summary Jurisdiction Act, 1851 (14 & 15 Vic., c. 92), created numerous petty offences with small penalties and was obviously designed to deal with nuisances on roads and public places. One of the more serious offences created by the act was that "Any person riding any horse or animal, or driving any sort of carriage who shall ride or drive the same furiously on any public road or street so as to endanger any passenger or person, or who shall by careless or wilful misbehaviour cause any injury to any person or property, commits an offence." It carried a fine of £1.

The other legislation enforced by the RIC related to the protection of fisheries, vagrancy, pedlars, chimney sweepers, illicit distillation, the sale of intoxicating liquor, betting and gaming, sales of drugs and poisons, weights and measures, game poaching, control of dogs, bowling on the public road, wandering animals, etc. Also included was the most recently introduced legislation relating to the driving and lighting of locomotives, which heralded the arrival of the steam engine and motor car. During this period, the force produced several pocket-sized booklets on different aspects of legislation such as the fishery laws, the game laws and illicit distillation. They were produced in hardback cover and designed for convenient reference by members when on duty.

District Inspector Dagg of Lisnaskea, County Fermanagh, produced *The Road and Route Guide of the Royal Irish Constabulary* in 1893. This was an extremely comprehensive book of over 360 pages. Through the use of an elaborate code system, this book was probably the most detailed road and route guide ever published in Ireland. It included data relating to every RIC barracks and sub-district (excluding Dublin city), with a brief synopsis of the history and historical monuments in each sub-district. It was a unique publication.

Chapter Seven

1900–1916
A TIME OF CIVIL ORDER

The Royal Visit of Queen Victoria in April, 1900

The royal visit of Queen Victoria and members of her family during the month of April was the biggest event during the year 1900. Thirty-nine years had elapsed since her last trip to Ireland and there was great excitement in anticipation of her visit. On 3 April the royal yacht Victoria and Albert, accompanied by several other vessels, arrived in Kingstown harbour, and on Wednesday the 4th, Queen Victoria came ashore at Kingstown to a tumultuous welcome from a large crowd of ordinary people and VIPs. As she travelled the nine miles into Dublin city in an open horse-drawn carriage, huge crowds turned out to see her, and there were several military and civilian bands playing music along the route. At the Grand Canal bridge, the queen was presented with the keys of Dublin city. The procession continued through Dublin and on to the Viceregal Lodge at the Phoenix Park, where she stayed with her entourage for the duration of her visit.

The royal visit lasted until 26 April, and despite her advanced years, Queen Victoria had a hectic three weeks' stay. She hosted a party for 50,000 children in the Phoenix Park and visited hospitals – including the Mater Hospital – hospices, schools, colleges, convents and Artane Industrial School. She travelled to several parts of the city and its outskirts, while members of her family following different schedules also visited hospitals and charitable institutions. The goodwill and welcome shown for the royal visitors was exceptional. There was a perception that the Catholic hierarchy were deliberately shunning the queen, but Cardinal Logue did attend a dinner hosted by her at the Viceregal Lodge. The royal visit received much publicity and was regarded as very successful.

While travelling around Dublin, Queen Victoria had an escort of high-ranking military officers. A request had been made on her behalf for a low-key security, and the protection during the three week stay was discreet. Within Dublin city, police security was by the Dublin Metropolitan Police, while the Royal Irish Constabulary provided security outside the city limits. On leaving Kingstown, the queen said, "I am very sorry to leave Ireland. I have had an extremely pleasant time." She conferred titles on a number of distinguished public officials and prominent business people, and conferred the title of lord mayor on the mayor of Cork. One commentator observed, "Thus ended the Queen's memorable visit to Ireland, the most admirably conducted affair of its kind ever, perhaps, carried through in these realms." The police forces who provided security for the royal visit were complimented on their performance and awarded a commemorative medal. The following notice was later published in the *RIC Directory*:

> By command of Her Late Majesty Queen Victoria, and in gracious recognition of the services rendered by both Forces on the occasion of Her Visit to Ireland from 3rd to 26th April 1900, a commemorative Medal was granted to all officers and men of the Royal Irish Constabulary and of the Dublin Metropolitan Police who were then on duty in Dublin. The Medal is also held by the members of the civil service staffs of the Royal Irish Constabulary and Dublin Metropolitan Police offices, Dublin Castle.

This was Queen Victoria's last visit to Ireland as she died early in the following year. During her reign she made three visits and members of her immediate family visited frequently. No attempt was ever made on their lives and no incident of a serious nature occurred during any of these visits. Considering the on-going unrest and opposition to British rule in Ireland, the fact that these royal visits could be made without incident was surprising. The security arrangements and protection afforded by the Irish and Royal Irish Constabularies, the Dublin Metropolitan Police and the military was an important element in the security success of these visits.

Changes of Inspector General

Sir Andrew Reed, who had been inspector general of the RIC since September 1885, retired from the force in 1900. He had a distinguished career in the force and was the first, and only, inspector general to have progressed through the ranks from cadet. During part of his career he served as a resident magistrate. A former graduate of Galway University, he was author of the *Irish Constable's Guide* and the *Policeman's Manual*, both of which he revised many times and which were the principal textbooks for the Royal Irish Constabulary. During part of his career he served as a resident magistrate. He was succeeded as inspector general by Colonel Neville Chamberlain, who was sworn in on 1 September 1900. He held the post up to 1916 and was the author of *Rules and Regulations for the Control and Management of the Financial Department of the Constabulary of Ireland,* which he revised on several occasions. This was the ultimate authority for financial affairs within the RIC up to the time of its disbandment.

Claim for Pay Increase by the Royal Irish Constabulary

With an upturn in the economy and an improvement in the standard of living during the late 1890s, the RIC felt that they were again being left behind. There had been no pay increase since 1882 and many members remained dissatisfied with the increase given at that time. Meetings were held by members of the lower ranks at different venues through the country, and a decision was taken in 1900 to make a claim for a substantial increase in pay of £34 a year for constables and £43 for sergeants. The level of pay aimed for was that which was then being paid to the City of London Police force. The timing of the pay claim was not to the members' advantage. The 1890s had been relatively peaceful for the force compared with the previous decades and about 1,000 young eligible men wanted to join the force each year. Between 1891 and 1900, 1,000 sons of members of the constabulary or retired members of the force, had joined. For many young men, the RIC was an attractive career.

The government set up a committee of inquiry early in 1901 into the claims for pay increases made by the RIC. The committee members appointed were Colonel Sir Howard Vincent, MP KCMG, chairman; R.W.A. Holmes, CB, treasury remembrancer; and R.F. Starkie, RM. The committee commenced taking evidence on Monday, 20 May 1901, in the committee rooms, Upper Castle Yard at Dublin Castle. A total of sixty-two witnesses were called to give evidence, including representatives of each rank in the force up to assistant inspector general. The chief constables of the following British police forces gave evidence: Newcastle on Tyne, Essex, City of London, Aberdeenshire, Birmingham, Yorkshire West Riding, Cornwall, Shropshire and Birkenhead. Captain B. Munro, inspector of constabulary for Scotland, also gave evidence. A number of the chief constables who gave evidence had been officers in the RIC earlier in their careers, but their evidence did little to support any claims for pay increases made by their former colleagues. The members of the force who gave evidence were asked the most searching questions in relation to themselves and their wives and families and to account for every item of expenditure by them. All documentation submitted by them was examined and challenged. They were questioned in relation to any savings they had in the bank or post office, and production of their savings books was demanded in a number of cases. The fact that some had small savings formed the basis of contentious questioning for those who had been unable to save any money. The amount of "fortunes" (dowries) which their wives brought with them when they got married was discussed in a few cases. The demeaning and denigrating questioning by the committee members appeared to cause concern to some members giving evidence, who obviously felt harrassed. The following is a résumé of the evidence given by some members to the inquiry:

1. Constable Patrick Callaghan, Cork City

Constable Callaghan told the inquiry that he represented the constables from Cork city and that he was stationed there. He was forty years of age and had twenty years' service. He was married with three children and had been on the promotion list for over nine years. His weekly pay was 27s. and he had a beat allowance of 6d. per day while performing beat duty. With his wife and children he lived in a small house comprising of a sitting room and two bedrooms, for which he paid 5s. 6d. each week. He told the inquiry that the members he represented wanted an increase in pay on the same basis as the best paid of the English police forces as they considered themselves as good and their duties just as hard as any of the English forces. He said that the cost of living had increased since 1882 in respect of food, boots, clothing and labour, and would not accept that they were better off in Cork city than anywhere else. He gave details of his own family expenditure for the month and of another constable who had 6s.11d. left over on the previous January after providing food for his family. Another constable was in debt to the amount of 19s.7d. after buying food and provisions for his family in the same month. When questioned as to why so many members were retiring early from the force after twenty-five years' service, he replied that these were members stationed in backward country places who wanted to educate their children and who moved into places like Cork city hoping to get employment after their retirement. Of the 263 RIC pensioners in Cork city, there were 143 unemployed and 100 employed.

2. Constable Andrew McKelvey, Lisburn, County Antrim

Constable McKelvey was representing the 297 constables of Counties Antrim and Derry. He was forty years of age and had over fifteen years' service. He had been married for five years and his salary was £67 18s. per annum. He paid 3s. 6d. rent weekly. He itemised his own monthly household expenses, amounting to £4 18s. Another constable, who was married with nine children, spent £63 5s. a year on food, while his annual salary came to £69 3s. On the question of boot allowance, he told the inquiry that members engaged on outdoor duties got 6d. per week, which would purchase two pairs of boots each year, but this was not sufficient for members performing outdoor duties. He went on to say, "We say that our present pay is not sufficient to maintain us and keep us respectably, and keep us out of debt

– particularly the married men. These are the grounds on which we claim an increase in pay. We have got a great deal of praise for being the most efficient and intelligent force almost in the world. We have listened to that for a long time and we would like to get something now." He told the inquiry that the constabulary and the people got on well together in Antrim and Derry.

3. Sergeant Joseph Boyle, Naas, County Kildare

Sergeant Boyle told the inquiry that, with another sergeant, he represented the sergeants in Leinster. He was thirty-nine years of age and had twenty years' service. He spent his early service in County Donegal but had spent the previous thirteen years in different barracks in County Kildare. His pay was £80 12s. per annum, less a reduction of 1½ per cent for the Constabulary Force Fund. He owned his own house. He stated that he was married and had a family and that the pay he was getting was insufficient to support them in the condition in which a man of his position was supposed to live. He said that the RIC was the worst paid force in Europe, and added:

> We have been told over and over again by the highest officials in the land, that for efficiency, intelligence and physique we were the Model Force of the Empire. We believe that if these things were seriously meant, we at least ought to be paid as well as the best paid police forces. There has been no revision since 1882 of our pay and every class in the United Kingdom have got substantial increases since that date and although our pay was revised in 1882 there was no increase, practically, we have had no increase in pay since 1874 or 1875.

With regard to promotion, he observed that it was difficult to obtain as the vacancies were scarce. Regarding the nature of the duties performed by him, he told the committee members that when not on night duty he commenced work each day before 9am. He drilled the party for thirty minutes, followed by police duty instruction for another thirty minutes. He said that he was out frequently doing ten hours' duty per day and was often called upon at night. After six hours' outdoor duty he was required to perform clerical duties, keep records up to date and account for warrants. He drew attention to the force regulation which disallowed a man from being at his lodgings when off duty and prevented him being absent for more than two hours without leave. Sergeant Boyle compared prices of meats and foodstuffs in Naas with different English cities. He adverted to the fact that the constabulary had just completed the census returns for 1901, for which they got no compensation despite the amount of work involved. He answered a total of 234 questions and, despite the harsh questioning which he received, he acquitted himself very well.

4. Sergeant Michael Maguinne, Belfast

Sergeant Maguinne testified that he represented the 500 sergeants stationed in Ulster, excluding Belfast. He was forty-two years of age and had twenty-three years' service, including five years in sergeant rank. He was married with eight children, the eldest of whom was aged fourteen years. His yearly pay was £80 12s. Closely questioned about the night-watch allowance payable to members serving in Belfast, he explained that it amounted to 6d. per night. As members performed night duty one week in every four, they received the night-watch allowance for thirteen weeks each year. He told the inquiry: "I say my pay is insufficient. I say it should be increased in order to enable me to live – that I would be able to maintain the respectability of the service and be efficient. I cannot be efficient if I am dependent on the outside public. My pay should be increased by at least fifty-five pounds a year." When asked what he meant by saying that he was "dependent on the public", he replied:

> It can be proved that a great portion of the men in our service are in debt. I am sorry to admit myself, I am in debt. Of course I have a large family and do not wish myself to be taken as a criterion. I am a pledged teetotaller for life and also a non-smoker. I need eleven pounds per month to keep me in reasonable comfort. Of course that is altogether out of my power as I have only seven pounds and eight shillings per month. I pay twenty-two pounds rent per year as I need a large house for my family as I try to keep the boys and girls separate.

Sergeant Maguinne was questioned very closely on a detailed document before the committee of inquiry from Messrs Harland and Wolff, shipbuilders, Belfast, on the rates of pay for their nearly 10,000 employees, and the average rents paid by them: Sixteen classifications of workers were given from "platers" who were earning 39s. per week down to "tradesmen's assistants" who were receiving 19s.6d. per week. He pointed out that the RIC members worked far more hours than the shipyard workers, who also had an opportunity of further earnings, while the RIC had none. He said:

> I want to speak of the dangers we incur. I have had to serve in the country and carry arms, loaded, both day and night, for the protection of people unpopular through the agraraian struggles of the eighties. I went through the whole land trouble in the eighties, and in Belfast in the nineties we had to carry arms. I want to mention the collection of statistics. Statistics on which legislation is founded have to be procured through the constabulary. When we have to do work putting us on an equality with the best paid force, we want to point out the difference of the duties. I say, the duties rendered to the Government by the Royal

Irish Constabulary are such as should entitle them to a higher rate of pay, London even not being excepted.

Every allowance or benefit paid to the force was put in detail to Sergeant Maguinne (even that should he die at that time his wife and eight children would have a total pension of £27 10s. per annum on which they would have to live) and his views were invited. The volume of evidence given by him was considerable and he replied to over 300 questions.

5. Head Constable Daniel Gallagher, Londonderry City
Head Constable Gallagher was representing the head constables of Ulster. He was fifty-three years of age and had thirty-two years' service. He had been a head constable for twelve years, all of which had been spent in Londonderry city. His salary was £1 19s. per week, plus 1s. per week rent allowance. He lived in official barrack accommodation for which he paid 4s. 4d. rent per month. He was the senior head constable in the city, where there were four barracks and a constabulary strength of 108 members. He was responsible for supervisory duties over all four barracks in Londonderry, but was responsible for disciplinary matters only for the barracks to which he was permanently attached. He said:

> I will try and show you that the Head Constable is the hardest worked man in the establishment and that his duties are of a very responsible nature. From time to time the duties of a District Inspector frequently devolve upon him – very frequently – and he is then not only responsible for the superintendence of the duty within his sub-district but also for the work of the District Inspector; the financial arrangement of the district as well, and for this he, as of course you are aware receives no extra remuneration. In the absence of the District Inspector on leave or duty or otherwise, the whole work devolves on the Head Constable. I am responsible for the superintendence of of all the duties in Derry city, in addition to which I control a station of eighty-five men. When the District Inspector is on leave or duty, sometimes he is absent for prolonged periods, I have the responsibilities of his office on my shoulders in addition to my own work. I have to attend all the petty sessions and conduct all prosecutions in his absence. I begin work at 8.40 am. I parade the men on the first relief and then I am continually working from that on. The Head Constable is responsible that the parade is properly drilled and that the men have a fair knowledge of police duties. He has got hanging up in the dayroom of his barrack, a list of Acts of Parliament – fifty-seven of them – and the orders in connection with these things are that the list is to be exhausted every month.

This was a man of considerable experience who knew everything there was to know about the force and its administration and supervision by all ranks.

6. Head Constable Michael Masterson, Swinford, County Mayo

He represented the head constables of Connacht. He was forty-nine years of age and had thirty-one years' service, the last six of which had been in his present rank. His annual salary was £97 10s. but he was due an increase to £104 in a few months. He pointed out that inspectors in the City of London Police – a rank which compared with head constable in Ireland – were in receipt of £182 per annum and claimed that head constables should be paid a similiar salary here. When questioned if he had saved money before he married, he said that he had not, and when asked why not, he replied that he had friends at home who reared him and educated him and to whom he owed some duty. To further questioning he replied that he had contributed £50 or £60 to his family at home before he married. He was questioned about his wife's means and if she had a bank accoun. He replied that she did have some money in the bank, but that some of it had to be used when one of his children had an accident in their home and he had to take him to Dr Hayes, a specialist, in Dublin – otherwise the little boy would have been a hunchback. When asked why he would not consider retirement after twenty-five years in the force, he told the inquiry that the only reason why he stayed in the force was because he would get more money in pay than on pension.

One of the statements made by him in support of his claim for an increase in pay was that:

> ...all other classes in the community have had their incomes increased in proportion to the changes of the times except the Royal Irish Constabulary who have been left at a standstill and who have been in consequence, lowered in status and respectability, because people have gone away from us. We do not base our claim so much on this as on the increased cost of living, on account of the great rise in the general standard of comfort and consequent increased expensiveness of public taste; and to keep pace with the times has become as much of a neccessity with the policeman as with others. People are not now satisfied to subsist as they did twenty-five years ago. All classes live more expensively, not perhaps as much in food as in dress, and furniture, rent, fuel, the education of their children, increased cultivation of taste for literature, recreation, the interchange of social activities and the numerous other causes, all re-acting on one another, entail their proportionate increase of expense. The Head Constables feel that there is no justification for inferiority in our pay to that of the best paid police force in England. Our duties are

not less onerous or important, on the contrary they are more varied and important, and require as much intelligence, patience and tact, and involve greater responsibility than any force in the United Kingdom. The RIC can safely challenge whether there is in His Majesty's service another department which can show such an untarnished record of loyalty, fidelity and trust as we can. We are in fact an Intelligence Department as well as a garrison for maintaining the authority of the Government in Ireland.

7. District Inspector Henry Toppin, Dundrum, County Dublin

District Inspector Toppin was thirty-three years of age with ten years' service and had entered as a cadet. He was in charge of Dundrum district, which had a strength of one head-constable, ten sergeants and forty constables, and he had a total of nine barracks in his district. He said:

> It takes a man too long to come to his maximum pay, twenty years is too long. He should get his maximum pay after fifteen years service. I think a Constable beginning with one pound and one shilling per week gets enough, but the deduction for barrack accommodation should be done away with. What I have heard since I joined the force was that an increase in pay was given in 1883 [this should have been 1882] but that one shilling per week was deducted for barrack accommodation. I think a Constable is at his best after ten or fifteen years service. A Constable is as good then as he ever is and should get the maximum pay. Then I would like in order to stimulate the men of long service – they certainly seem to require some stimulant – to give some men good service pay at about twenty years service. I would suggest that sergeants should get more as compared with Constables than they do at present. An acting-sergeant should get three shillings per week more than a Constable on full pay and a sergeant should get three shillings more than an acting-sergeant. It is mainly the net amount they receive that men look at. They say to themselves "a man by not marrying loses so much per year". Regarding promotion, I do not think that it is at all as strong as it should be. I look upon promotion at present as practically non-existent in the County of Dublin. The average service for promotion is nineteen and a half years and then they are reaching their maximum service pay. There is another thing I should like to mention, it is rather an anomaly. My District joins the Dublin Metropolitan District, I should say that the constabulary man's work in Cabinteely is much the

same as the Metropolitan man's work at Kill-o-the-Grange, yet the
Metropolitan Constable on one year's service gets twenty-five shillings
per week and it takes my men twelve years to get that.

The district inspector debated various issues with the committee: head constables' performing relief duties for district inspectors; the merits of promoting constables directly to sergeants and doing away with acting sergeants; the salaries of
other UK forces; itemised costs of living produced by him; the neccessity for members of the constabulary to study and have a good knowledge of police duties apart
from preparing for promotion examinations and the neccessity for maintaining the
number of head constables.

8. District Inspector James Horigan, Listowel, County Kerry

District Inspector Horigan was a very experienced officer with thirty-three years'
service who had been promoted through the ranks from constable. He had served
in Counties Cork, Donegal, Clare, Mayo and Kerry. His responsibility at Listowel
covered eleven barracks and three protection posts. The police strength of his district was one head constable, fourteen sergeants, two acting sergeants and sixty-six
constables. While giving evidence he recalled the troubled period from 1879 to 1885
and he agreed that things were much quieter and much improved in 1901. The
monthly pay of a recruit was £3 and for a constable with five years' service it was
£4 15s. Mr. Horigan was adamant that there should be an increase on these rates as
well as for all ranks. He said that although constables in Listowel were paying up to
22s. per month for rent, they received a lodging allowance of only 4s. 4d. per month.
Some married men found it difficult to get accommodation and he recommended
that the rent allowance for a married man should be increased to £12 per annum.
Constables who stayed in the barracks had to pay 4s. per month for the accommodation. To keep a married man with five children in reasonable comfort cost £6 13s.
11d. per month. This included rent and the purchase of tea, sugar, milk, meat, flour,
fish and butter etc., as well as clothes for his family. He produced the mess book for
Listowel barracks. The cost of living per month for three constables availing of the
mess in three months worked out at, £1 17s. 5d., £1 15s. and £1 16s. He agreed that
a further 15s. per month would be a fair figure to cover the extra neccessities of life,
excluding drink, which cost another 4s. per month. On the subject of clothing, he
stated that members of the force were provided with uniform, but constables were
out of pocket for making up their uniform. They would need a suit of civilian
clothes every two years, costing between £3 and £3 10s.. Beef and mutton cost 8d.
per pound weight in Listowel.

Holidays were expensive, but some members of the force could not afford one
anyway. A month's holidays were given each year and single members, who normally

had some money in the savings bank, could afford them. It should be possible for single members to save up to £1 per month. Fees paid to the church amounted to about £1 per annum. Bicycles for recreation or duty were very useful. Very important captures had been made with bicycles, Mr Horigan stated, and a man could distinguish himself, but in the end he was forced to concede that a bicycle was not entirely essential.

The district inspector said that it was very hard for men in his district to live on their pay. A number of them were in debt; one man who had got into debt at an early stage of his life had never been able to extricate himself. The wife of an RIC constable made application to him to work as a dressmaker but she could not get permission from the authorities. Medical attendants allocated to the force were paid 2s. per man per month. The cost of doctors and medicine for his district force worked out at 6d. per man per week.

District Inspector Horigan was very critical of the pensions paid to retired members. He gave details of two retired members in Listowel district – one had nine children and the other had eight children. The pension of these retired members was £42 2s. 5d. per annum, on which they were expected to support their large families. There were twenty pensioners in the district, of which three were in employment, one had a small farm and nine had small businesses – mostly small shops. If they had the shop fittings, they could stock up on credit. One pensioner was earning 32s. per week in a flour store. One pensioner had to pay £24 a year for rent, half of that in advance.

On promotion, the district inspector said that sergeants should be promoted when they had about ten years' service and that the rank of acting sergeant should be abolished. He was under no illusion about the sergeant in charge of a barracks having much more responsibility than other sergeants and suggested that the sergeant in charge should get 10s. per month more for his responsibility. The average constable's service for promotion in County Kerry was eighteen to twenty years. He testified that policing in Kerry was severe in nature but not as harassing on the members as it had been. His district, which had been very disturbed at one time, was fairly quiet in 1901, except for an occasional outrage.

9. County Inspector William Arthur O'Connell, County Westmeath

County Inspector O'Connell had joined as a cadet in 1880 and had served as a district inspector in Counties Armagh and Meath, and in west Cork and south Tipperary. He had served for two periods in the depot, once in charge of a company and as adjutant during his second period there. He had an extensive knowledge of RIC operations and administration. The committee members went through the various allowances to which members of the force were entitled and the county inspector verified their accuracy. He told the inquiry that voluntary resignations from the force amounted to about one-half of a per cent. There was very keen competition amongst suitable young men for membership. On the question of retirement, he was of opinion that there should be compulsory retirement after thirty-one years' service, as members appeared to become stale after that. He submitted proposals relating to pension benefits which he felt would encourage members to serve out their full service. He favoured the retention of the acting sergeant rank as a probationary rank before a man was permamently appointed a sergeant. He calculated that the keep of a single man amounted to £51 17s. 6d. in a year. This figure included mess, underclothing, plain clothes, contributions to church, barrack rent, Queen's Jubilee Fund, blacking for boots, rashers for breakfast, tobacco and pipes. He considered that rent allowance should be increased to about £10 per annum for a married man.

When questioned as to whether young women marrying members of the force in County Westmeath brought dowries with them into marriage, he offered the opinion that they very often did. Wives of members were normally daughters of farmers, shopkeepers or school teachers. In reply to a question about the considerable accumulation of profits from the sale of intoxicating liquor at the depot canteen, he explained that some of it was allocated to the burial fund and some of it to the recreation room. He agreed that in 1881 only 32 per cent of the force had been married, while in 1901, 46 per cent were married, but he would not attribute that to the grant of lodging allowance for those with over ten years' service which was given in 1882. He felt that it was due to the times being more peaceful and members of the force now having more time to consider the subject.

The inquiry concluded on 31 May 1901. A total of 9,370 questions were asked by the members of the committee. Every possible aspect of the force and its operations were scrutinised, with an in-depth examination of the pay and allowances of the force as well as the cost of living down to the minutest detail. Never was the soul of the Royal Irish Constabulary laid so bare. The chairman, Colonel Sir Howard Vincent, was author of *Vincent's Police Code and General Manual of the Criminal Law*, of which there was at least sixteen editions. This book was the bible on policing for the London Metropolitan and other English police forces for almost half a century. He was an expert in police matters and could be relied on by the British government to have a conservative view of pay claims and to bear the interests of the government in mind. A most comprehensive report on all the evidence taken at the inquiry was submitted to both houses of parliament, but there was little joy in it for the Royal Irish Constabulary. Minor modifications were made to pay rates and a few of the allowances, but there was grave disappointment amongst the rank and file when they failed to get even a substantial part of the pay increase they sought.

Policing of a Motor Race in July 1903

The biggest policing assignment ever undertaken by the RIC – and possibly their most prestigious – was policing the Gordon Bennett Motor Race, held in Kildare, Carlow and Queen's County (Laois) on 2 July 1903. In 1900, James Gordon Bennett, owner of the *New York Herald*, donated a trophy for international motor racing, which became known as the Gordon Bennett Trophy. Open to all countries in the world, this was the first real international motor race and the competition for the honour of winning it was intense. The first motor race for the trophy was held in 1900. Thereafter the country who won it had the privilege of hosting the race in the following year. In 1902, the race was run between Paris and Innsbruck, and it was won by Selwyn Edge of Great Britain driving a British Napier car. Staging the race in England in 1903, however, ran into problems due to the strict regulations in force there relating to the use of motor cars, including a twelve miles per hour speed limit. Ireland was seen as the most acceptable venue. A special act of parliament, the Light Locomotives (Ireland) Act, 1903 (3 Edw. 7, c. 2), sponsored by John Scott Montague, received the royal assent in May 1903. The act remained in force for one year and authorised county councils to close roads for the purpose of motor racing or other motor sport activities.

Requests to stage the race were submitted by many county councils and a suitable circuit selected. The course was roughly shaped in a figure-of-eight, with the starting point at Ballyshannon crossroads, between Athy and Kilcullen, County Kildare. The race was run over alternate loops of the course for a total race distance of 386 miles. The outer perimeter of the circuit included the towns of Carlow, Athy, Kilcullen, Kildare, Monasterevan and Maryborough (now Portlaoise).

One commentator in describing the enthusiasm of the Irish people for the event said: "The entire Irish nation appeared to lose interest in everything except promoting a race between horseless carriages, these having the added fascination of being driven by foreigners." Most Revd Dr Foley, Bishop of Kildare and Leighlin, in whose diocese the event was being held, publicly welcomed it and sent a circular to all the priests in his diocese exhorting their parishoners to abstain from intoxicating liquor until the race was over and to warn them about the dangers of getting drunk on the day of the race.

The tasks of policing and crowd control for the event fell on the Royal Irish Constabulary. The inspector general, Sir Neville Chamberlain, gave an undertaking that the RIC were capable of taking on the challenge. He was given an immediate allocation of £1,000 towards the cost of policing it. The RIC planned the event with military precision. The military based at the Curragh covered the area across the Curragh plains from Newbridge to Kildare town. Outside of this section, the RIC provided crowd control and policing along the circuit. Arrangements were made to draft in extra constabulary. This was the biggest mustering of RIC personnel for any event during the lifetime of the force and created its own logistical problems in transporting, billetting and feeding of the members. Members were conveyed to the towns along the circuit by train and then to the outlying villages by horse and carriage.

The competing cars were scrutinised and weighed in at the Square at South Main Street, Naas, and received protection from the constabulary until the morning of the race. Thirty telegraph lines were installed at the start/finish location for the benefit of journalists who attended from all over the globe. Each of the competing nations had to paint their cars in a distinctive colour. Great Britain chose green for its cars in honour of the race's being held in Ireland and the colour "British racing green" has been used ever since. The French cars were painted blue, the United States' cars red, and the German cars were white.

For the purpose of police control, the entire circuit was divided into twenty "stations", each with an RIC officer in charge. Each station was divided into a number of "sections", ninety-two in total, each under the control of an RIC officer or head constable. The entire operation was under the control of Assistant Inspector General Thomas F. Singleton. A full-scale rehearsal took place on 1 July commencing at 2pm, at which time all members of the force were at the locations assigned to them. The Automobile Club drove a number of vehicles around the course for some hours by way of rehearsal. The members were directed to be at the same locations at 5.30am on the following morning for the race proper, which was due to start at 7am.

The entire circuit was closed to the public and to traffic from 6am on the 2nd. The constabulary took up positions at the mouth of every side road, boreen, avenue or access route of any kind along the entire length of the course. All gates leading to fields were checked and secured. They got very specific instructions to keep the public 200 yards away from each side of dangerous bends. The members were directed to stand on the fences or banks on either side and to impress on the public the very grave dangers which might arise not alone for spectators but for the car drivers should any persons or animals encroach on the circuit.

A novel feature of the race was that the cars were not permitted to race through the big towns at high speed. At the approach road to the town, a "control point" was set up and there the driver was obliged to bring his car to a halt at a white line across the road. Immediately he did so, a cyclist who was waiting in readiness for the car, took off at high speed. The driver of the car was compelled to drive behind the pedal cyclist through the town and stop briefly when he came to the "control point" at the exit. He then continued with his race at maximum speed.

There were twelve cars in the race. The first car got away from the start at Ballyshannon crossroads at 7am with the remainder following at intervals thereafter. The race lasted for several hours into the late afternoon and the eventual winner was a Belgian, Camille Jenatzy (otherwise known as "the Red Devil" because of his red hair) driving one of the German Mercedes cars. His average speed was 49.2 miles per hour. The event was a major success and generated much favourable publicity for Ireland. Glowing tributes were paid in all covering reports to the role played by the Royal Irish Constabulary. Their presence was so marked that in most reports the figure of 7,000 RIC was given, whereas the number employed was just short of 3,000. The £1,000 given at the outset to the inspector general did not cover the costs and a further substantial subvention in the region of £2,000 was paid, but nobody complained. The Gordon Bennett Race brought international fame to Ireland.

At least one RIC district inspector on duty on the day was fallible. The following account was subsequently published in the *Newsletter of the Irish Veteran and Vintage Car Club* (Summer 1993):

> When the last race car had completed the motor race, it was arranged that a motorcar would travel around the circuit carrying a flag and displaying a large notice that the race was over. This car duly did travel around the circuit as arranged. An over-zealous District Inspector on duty near the Moat of Ardscull, near Athy, failed to see the car passing by and steadfastly refused to allow any of the spectators leave the fields where they had been watching the race since early a.m. that morning, for almost two hours after the race had ended.

Control of Stores within the Royal Irish Constabulary

The most stringent control possible was exercised over stores and property issued to the RIC. There were annual issues of uniforms to members of the force. A member was permitted to retain his previous issue for official use, but the one prior to that had to be accounted for and returned to central stores. He could also retain one old trousers for "fatigues duties" at his barracks. A heavy overcoat was issued once every three years. Every item of uniform on issue to a member was carefully recorded and receipts required. There was very tight control over firearms, ammunition and accoutrements issued for the personal use of members, and they were inspected by a member of supervisory rank almost daily. After target practice, ammunition was checked and every round had to be accounted for. Each member had a "regulation black box" (trunk), in which he kept his full kit of accoutrements, and the contents of the box were subject to regular inspection. The control exercised over property issued to members was so tight that it was impossible for a member to lose or dispose of any item of property without being detected. Very tight control was also exercised over all items of "public property" such as furniture. Apart from details being kept in the barrack store book, the contents of every room in every barracks or at the depot was recorded on an inventory board, measuring thirteen inches by nine inches, which hung from a hook inside the door of each room, listing all the items of property in that room and enabling frequent checks to be made by supervisors. The following copy of an inventory board record indicates the level of control exercised.

ROYAL IRISH CONSTABULARY

Inventory of Barrack Bedding, Furniture and Utensils for the use of and to Remain Stationary in The Sergeants Quarters. Room No 11. No. 3 company at Depot.

1 Iron Bedstead.
1 Paillasse.
1 Bolster.
– Rugs.
3 Blankets.
2 Sheets.
1 Straps, Bed Leather.
– Tables, Officers – Tin Cans.
– Chairs, do.
– Tables, 6 feet.
1 Tables, 4 feet,
2 Iron Trestles.
- Forms, 6 feet.
1 Forms, 4 feet.
1 Constables Stool.
1 Pairs of Bellows.
1 Fenders.
1 Pokers.
1 Shovels.
1 Tongs.
– Coal Scuttles, copper
– Candlesticks.
1 Coal Boxes, wooden.
– Coal Boxes, 4 bushels.
– Arm Racks, six stand.
– Arm Racks, four stand
– Accoutremnent Racks, six set.
– Accoutrement Racks, four set.
1 Water Pail.
– Watering Buckets.

– Whitewash Brushes.
– Mops and Handles.
– Light Scrubbers and Handle.
1 Hair Broom and Handle.
– Hand Scrubbers.
– Black Lead Brushes.
– Tea Kettles.

– Tin Dishes.
– Fish Forks.
– Iron Ladles.
– Frying Pans.
– Grid Irons.
– Potato Trays.
– Coal Trays.
– Urine Tubs.
– Floor Scrapers.
– Passage Lamps.
– Window Lifters.
– Bed Wrenches.
– Notice Boards.
1 Inventory Board.
– Lanterns.
2 Keys.
– Metal Basins.
– Saucepans.
– Camp Kettles.
– Shovels, universal.
1 Wooden Press.

Certified: William S. Shoveller, Barrack Master. Dated: 21st February 1901.
SIGNED: W.S. Lowndes. District Inspector In Charge of Company

Eyes and Ears of the British Government

It has frequently been written that the Royal Irish Constabulary were the eyes and ears of Dublin Castle and of the British government in Ireland. During the lifetime of the force it specialised in the collection of intelligence as well as providing a police service. It inherited the practice from its predecessors, the Irish Constabulary, who made a determined effort to gather information following the Young Ireland insurrection of 1848. The Irish Constabulary were well prepared for the Fenian insurrection of 1867 due to the methodical collection and analysing of information and intelligence relating to the Fenians and their sympathisers. During the land agitation from 1879 until the mid–1880s, although the RIC had a considerable store of information on those responsible for outrages, witnesses were not prepared to give evidence and juries were not prepared to convict those brought to trial. Without hard facts and evidence, the belief that some individual was responsible for an outrage was not sufficient. There was a considerable network of barracks outside Dublin city and the ratio of constabulary per 1,000 of population – depending on the peace of the district – varied between twelve and forty-seven. The RIC had knowledge of every family in Ireland from their ordinary dealings with the force.

All census returns were collected every ten years between 1821 and 1911 by the constabulary, who visited every house in their sub-district to deliver and collect them. In most cases, the forms were completed after census night by the constabulary members, as the level of illiteracy amongst the population was very high. In the mid-nineteenth century, the constabulary began taking particulars of each household from the census returns collected by them and recording them in a special "householders register". (A rough form of the register had been kept by the constabulary since the early 1820s.) A new register was completed after each census. The register was kept by electoral district and the townlands within it. It was divided into columns which provided for the surname of the family; the Christian names of the family members; the date of birth of each member; the relationship of each person to the head of the household; and the occupation of each member of the household. Through this register, the constabulary had a pen picture of every member of every family within its sub-district. Between census returns, the constabulary kept the register up to date by crossing off people who died or left the area and by entering details of any new families taking up residence. It was methodically kept, and was examined and initialled by inspecting officers. If deaths or departures of people were not being recorded, it brought a comment from the inspecting officer to the effect that the register was "too healthy to be accurate".

This was the key record of people kept by the RIC. The practice of keeping it continued in use with an Garda Síochána for fifty years, until it was realised that there was no legal basis authorising its use. One extraordinary and ironic feature of the census returns was that in some parts of Ireland, members of the RIC did not enter their own full Christian names or surnames in the census forms completed in respect of their own barracks. Only the initials were given. Presumably this was in the interests of security, but it would not have served much purpose in rural Ireland where the names of all RIC members were well known. Other essential details were given.

The constabulary were also responsible for collecting agriculural statistics on an annual basis, and this again gave the force the opportunity of visiting farmers and all landholders at least once a year to get the neccessary return of livestock and land usage. New members to a barracks were assigned to this duty as it enabled them to obtain a good local knowledge of their sub-district.

Considerable information was circulated through the conference patrols. As mentioned earlier this was a system whereby a constable from each of three or four barracks met every day at a specified time and a prearranged location, normally a crossroads, to exchange information about crime, suspects, movements of criminals, etc. The constables returned to their respective barracks and reported details of the happenings in the adjoining sub-districts. The system was simple but it worked very well, especially in rural areas without telephones.

The force gathered much information through the tremendous powers of observations of its members. Through their intensive system of foot patrols and later cycle patrols they covered their areas each day and nothing untoward went unnoticed by them. They were also very good at meeting and talking with people, frequently using the excuse of getting a light for their pipes to gain entry to a house. The majority of the force were the sons of small farmers and had much in common with the rural inhabitants. The members were always on the look-out for strangers to their areas. Many people travelled on foot from one workhouse to another. Their descriptions were carefully noted and recorded in the barracks in a register of "tramping vagrants". The RIC maintained very close links with other government agencies, particularly the Coastguard Service, the local military and staff of wireless stations where they existed, and information relevant to each agency was exchanged. There was also close contact with the post office service and with postmen.

At any one time there were several thousand retired members of the RIC throughout Ireland. They were obliged to report once a month to their local RIC district inspector to sign for their pension. It was expected that they would supply information on any subject on which the force should be informed, and they were at all times a most useful and reliable source of intelligence to the RIC.

The landlords and their agents were also a good source of information for the force, as some were under protection and many feared for their lives from 1880 onwards. Close contact was always maintained with the landed classes. Publicans were normally co-operative with the constabulary, who apart from being steady customers also had the power to close down licensed premises – a fact of which the publicans were very conscious.

The *Hue and Cry* [see Chapter 3] gave details of persons wanted for crimes in all the counties of Ireland or in the United Kingdom, if relevant. Circulated every Tuesday and Friday, it was filed safely at each barracks and studied in detail by the constabulary.

Paid "informers" also had a role in supplying the RIC and its predecessors with information in relation to suspect individuals or groups, but the numbers of such informers always tended to be exaggerated. The threat of an insurrection or upheaval of some kind against the government frequently existed. This possibility, exercised the mind and thinking of the constabulary throughout its existence and information on anything which might in any way contribute to such a happening was of prime importance. Consequently, very particular attention was given to individuals or groups who displayed any marked "nationalist" tendencies. The Gaelic Athletic Association clubs, the Ancient Order of Hibernians, the Irish National Foresters and clubs and associations of a similar nature were monitored. The attention paid to detail in the following copies of returns available for year ending 31 December 1901 indicates the high priority and the very methodical attention given to this aspect of intelligence gathering locally by the Royal Irish Constabulary, which was then being collated at national level.

Approximate Numerical Strength of Secret Societies and other Associations for year ending December 31st 1901, in respect of County Limerick.

IRB

Number of Circles	5
Total Estimated Membership	2,050
Estimated Number of Members of Good Standing	165
Ancient Order of Hibernians	None

Gaelic Athletic Association

Number of Branches	5
Number of Members under Fenian Control	230
Number of Members under Clerical Control	None
Total Number of Members	700
Estimated Number of Good Standing	470

United Irish League

Number of Branches	2
Number of Members	100
Number of Members of Good Standing	60

Young Ireland Society

Number of Branches	1
Number of Members under Fenian Control	65
Number of Members under Clerical Control	None
Total Number of Members	65
Total Number of Good Standing	29

Gaelic League

Number of Branches	7
Total Number of Members	340
Number under Fenian Control	180
Number under Clerical Control	160

Irish National Foresters

Number of Branches	1
Number of Members	86

Trade and Labour Associations.

Number of Federated Trades & Labourers Branches	16
Number of Non- Federated, ditto	3
Total Number in both	1,019

Other Information – LIMERICK CITY only

Number of RIC Pensioners under 60	64
Approximate Number of Active Loyalists who might serve as Special Constables	264
Total Number of all Loyalists	1,592
Number of Light Vehicles for Fast Service	553
Number of Four-Wheeled included in Last Line	83
Number of Carts or Wagons for Heavy Traffic	510
Number of Four-Wheeled included in Last Line	69
Number of Hardware Stores	18
Probable Number of Spades kept in Stock in H/Ware Stores	190
Probable Number of Picks kept in Stock in H/Ware Stores	48

Leisure Time Activities Within the RIC

Very severe restrictions were placed on the leisure time of the RIC. The objective in the constabulary code was to have members tied down to duties for the greater part of every day when not performing night duty. They were obliged to be up at a fixed time each morning, followed by parade at 9am. From 9am to 10am was spent on drill instruction and police duties. There was a roll-call of all members, married or single, at 11pm each night, and even those who had performed their actual duties for the day were obliged to be in barracks for it. Such regulations could not have been complied with except that, at all times, the majority of members were single.

Fishing was the big seasonal activity, and every member without exception became involved in this pastime at one time or another – a pastime which many of them enjoyed long after leaving the force. The fishing rights of rivers and lakes all over the country which were the preserves of the landlords and the wealthy were made available to the local RIC members. In return for this favour, they were expected to enforce the fishery acts during the closed seasons. By their presence at the rivers and lakes during the open seasons, they made life very difficult for poachers who felt that they had a God-given right to fish as they pleased. Where poaching was prevalent, special patrols were performed night and day by the RIC to prevent it. Sea fishing was also popular for those stationed near the coast. One former member, who had spent many years in the force, had no hesitation in stating that the most enjoyable days of his life were spent fishing on the river Slaney between his barracks at Clonegal, County Carlow, and Newtownbarry (now Bunclody), County Wexford, and from Clonegal bridge when the river was in spate.

A letter written by a member of the force to a dealer in fishing tackle and equipment, indicates the urgency on his part for fishing:

> RIC Dingle,
> County Kerry.
> April 25th 1898.
> Dear Sir, Kindly send me by first post, two dozen trout hooks (tied). I require them for a small river. Send them to suit. Will send amount on receipt.
> Yours Faithfully,
> John Mitchell RIC.

Some members were very involved in game shooting. They had free access to shooting rights over lands, bogs and mountains during the open seasons, and again they could be depended upon to protect the deer, pheasant and other game. The deerparks were the most protected areas within estates, and the existing high stone-and-mortar walls of the old estates which still stand bear testimony to the value and importance placed on the deer herd by the landlords.

Reading was a favourite pastime. Many members were very well-read and familiar with the best-known classics. This love of reading may very well have had an influence on the families of members, many of whom achieved very prestigious positions later in life. The newspapers read were selective and very much pro-British, and there were standing orders for English newspapers at all the central locations.

Some members were accomplished musicians and played the concertina, violin, tin whistle and bagpipes. The violin was the most favoured instrument, and on the disbandment of the force, many members were observed carrying their violin case amongst their luggage. The members who played music were very much appreciated by their colleagues as their music brightened up and shortened many a long, dull and dreary night in barrack accommodation. They were also very welcome at weddings, parties and house dances, and their musical instruments gave them a passport to events to which they would otherwise never have been invited.

While there was a prohibition on the playing of card games for stakes in the barracks, card games – particularly "nap" – and dice games were popular.

From the early 1890s, the ambition of every junior member in the force was to acquire a bicycle. By the early 1900s most members had bicycles, and this gave them a freedom which they had not previously enjoyed. It was even possible for them to take their bicycles on the train when travelling home on holidays. Bicycles were expensive, but favourable easy-term payments made it affordable for those who were barely able to make ends meet due to family commitments. Advertisements in constabulary magazines indicate that RIC members were targeted in a big way by cycle dealers and by jewellers for the sale of watches.

When bicycles came into common usage, there was a relaxation in the police code regulation which compelled members to remain in barracks when off duty. They could be given leave of absence from their barracks for a defined period of time "to improve their proficiency in cycling". When cycling patrols were first recognised by the RIC authorities, members were obliged to travel at least twice the distance of a foot patrol over the same period of time.

Many members drank intoxicating liquor and they were regular customers at local public houses, where their custom was always appreciated. The constabulary code was very strict on members' indulging to excess, and it was always accepted that the most likely cause for being dismissed from the force was through drunkenness or addiction to drink.

Members found many other unusual ways to enjoy their leisure time. On display at the Heritage Centre on Valentia Island off the Kerry coast is a heavy slate slab, on which is carved in relief a large badge of the Royal Irish Constabulary. It appears to have been carved with a sharp instrument such as a penknife or wood chisel. It is a splendid work of art, painstakingly executed, which must have taken a year or more for a number of members to complete. It was found some years ago buried in the garden of the former RIC barracks on the island and is in a perfect state of preservation.

The Role of the Royal Irish Constabulary from the 1890s until 1916

From the early 1890s until 1916, the Royal Irish Constabulary led a normal existence like any civil police force. In the absence of civil disturbances, the force had
allowed itself to develop into a fully integrated civil police force. It had lost much
of the semi-military trappings associated with it prior to the 1890s. As this pattern
of policing had so firmly established itself by 1916, it left the force somewhat vulnerable when endeavouring to cope with the violence following the 1916 Rising. The
force enjoyed the friendship and confidence of the people, who appreciated the
work, help and service rendered by it. Only on rare occasions did members of the
force consider it necessary to take their firearms with them on patrol, as there was
no evident threat to their lives or welfare. When members of the force went to
Banna Strand on Good Friday 1916 to investigate the landing of Roger Casement
and found revolvers on the beach, they had to return to Ardfert barracks for their
rifles and cycled back to Banna Strand again before carrying out a search of the area.

In 1902, the *United Irishman*, edited by Arthur Griffith, had kind words to say
about the Royal Irish Constabulary and their involvement with the community:

> The Royal Irish Constabulary is a body of Irishmen, recruited from the
> Irish people. They are bone of their bone, and flesh of their flesh. The
> typical young constabularyman is Irish of the Irish, Catholic and (as the
> word goes) Nationalist; the son of decent parents; his father a Home
> Rule farmer; his uncle a patriotic priest; his cousin a nun; his sweetheart
> the daughter of a local Nationalist District councillor and patriotic pub-
> lican; her uncle being chairman of the local "league" branch and a
> friend of the eloquent and patriotic member for the Division, who asks
> questions on the floor about the young constabularyman's prospects and
> grievances. The young constabularyman subscribes liberally to the
> Church; he is smiled on by the Irish clergy; he is smiled on by the Irish
> girls; he is respected by the young fellows of the street corner and the
> country crossroads.

There were few major disturbances other than riots associated with strikes in
Belfast in 1907, and the RIC coped exceptionally well with the policing events of the
period. One indicator of the excellent relationships which existed between the RIC
and the people up to 1916 was the considerable number of presents given to the
members in the local barracks at Christmas time by way of drink, potatoes, turkeys,
geese and chickens and groceries. Members who served during the period proudly
commented on this generosity bestowed on them by the people at Christmas time.

King Edward VII came to the British throne after the death of Queen Victoria
early in 1901. He visited Ireland in July/August 1903 in what was officially titled the

"Royal Progress". Extraordinary security measures were taken by the RIC for the visit. The king went on a motor tour of the Connemara area. The police precautions taken there were recorded by Sir Henry Robinson, who accompanied the king:

> It would never have done to have had an enormous display of force, still less would it have been to have the King molested, so he [the inspector general] had collected an enormous force of constabulary from all over the country. He spread them all along the roads disguised as tourists, under the impression that as the King's visit might be expected to attract tourists, this guard would not be noticed. But what rather spoiled the precaution was that every man dressed alike, straw hat, Norfolk jacket, watch chain from breast pocket to buttonhole, knickerbockers and bicycle. Every man was exactly the same distance apart, 100 yards or so, and all were lying in a carefully rehearsed loose and careless attitude beside the road in the character of the weary cyclist. But what rather spoilt the effect was that when the King's car was passing, each man sprang to attention, clicked his heels and saluted smartly, and then resumed his full length attitude until the king was out of sight, when the bicycles were mounted and the procession of straw-hatted tourists wended their way towards Westport. I was travelling in the motorcar with the King and Queen and he asked me who these men were who kept jumping up. I was saved from having to make an explanation, as at that moment we suddenly turned a corner and the village of Tully came into view, where an enormous crowd attended.

The royal visit passed off without incident, and bronze medals struck to commemorate the visit were presented to all officers and men of the RIC and DMP who were on duty in connection with the visit and to the civil service staffs on duty in the RIC and DMP headquarters at Dublin Castle. The obverse side of the medal bore an effigy of Edward with Latin inscription, while the reverse side was identical to the medal issued for Queen Victoria's visit in 1900, other than that the date was 1903.

In 1901, an event in County Clare caused much embarrassment to the RIC. A Sergeant Sheridan arrived on transfer to the county from Leitrim. He had an extraordinary reputation for crime detection in County Leitrim where he had served for three years and in County Limerick where he served for eight years prior to that. On arrival in Clare, his reputation at solving serious crime again took off, but suspicions were aroused when he gave evidence at a trial that he had seen a beggarman posting threatening notices. It was proved that the beggarman was incapable of such an act and he was found not guilty. It was suspected that Sergeant Sheridan had committed perjury, and methodical investigations carried out into previous crimes "detected" by him in Counties Limerick and Leitrim discovered that many of the crimes were manufactured by him. He was charged with perjury and dismissed from the force. One of his accomplices was also dismissed and another constable and sergeant resigned as a result. This was one of the very few occasions during the lifetime of the RIC that any of its members were found to be involved in corruption.

Following the reverses sustained by the British forces in the Boer War in 1899, an appeal was made for members to join the forces fighting the Boers. The essential qualifications were that "members should be able to shoot well and ride horses". A small number of officers and rank-and-file members did volunteer and resumed their former positions or higher ranks in the RIC on their return.

Old-age pensions became payable in 1908 and for the purpose of verifying the eligibility of applicants, the constabulary were given an important role. When the pension books were issued they were delivered personally by members of the force to the recipients. This practice persisted thereafter for the lifetime of the RIC. Their role in assisting applicants in completing the necessary forms and safely delivering the pension books endeared them at least to the elderly in the community.

In the early 1900s, eviction duties became a thing of the past as tenants acquired rights to their properties and there were fewer problems with the landlords. However, on 12 October 1904, a Murphy family was evicted from their holding at Mitchelsfort near Watergrasshill, County Cork. The bailiffs were accompanied by District Inspector Mulliner, Head Constable Blessing and a party of RIC from Fermoy. The eviction met with stubborn resistance from an organised mob of men, women and children. Paving stones and boiling water were thrown at the constabulary and a nearby bridge was blocked with fallen trees to prevent the arrival of reinforcements. Among the leading supporters of the Murphy family were two MPs – Mr D.D. Sheehan for Mid-Cork and Captain Donnellan for east Cork.

Prosecutions against a big number of persons followed the incidents at the eviction, and they came before Riverstown petty sessions one week later. County Inspector Rogers, District Inspector Wade of Queenstown and District Inspector Webster were in charge of a large assembly of RIC for the court hearing at Riverstown Courthouse. Thirty members formed a cordon across the main road to cut off the huge crowd of spectators from getting too near the courthouse. At the entrance to the court, a constable manhandled Captain Donnellan and this started a riot which reached serious proportions. Three priests were present and rendered spiritual assistance to those seriously injured and a local doctor had to treat twelve casualties following the event. As events such as these had become rare at the time, they received a lot of publicity.

In 1907, the king granted permission to the French government to decorate members of the RIC for bravery in County Clare. The members were authorised to accept and wear the medals conferred on them for their daring rescue of crew members from the wrecked ship *Leon XIII* off Quilty, County Clare, on 2 October 1907. The members were District Inspector James Reid, Sergeant James Brien, Sergeant Daniel Comerford, Constables Patrick Doran, Thomas Gillman, Michael O'Shea, John Giles, Owen Kerrigan, William McBride, James Harrington and Timothy McCarthy.

On 27 August 1907, the counties deemed to be in a state of disturbance were reviewed, and from then onwards Counties Clare, Galway and Roscommon were the only counties declared. This authorised an additional establishment of constabulary to them.

King Edward VII died on 6 May 1910. His son King George V was crowned king on 22 June 1911. He paid an official visit to Ireland that year and 100 officers and 1,000 men of the RIC, all over 6 feet tall, were selected for duty in connection with the royal visit which passed off without incident. The RIC members on duty were later presented with a silver medal to commemorate the visit, as were members of the Dublin Metropolitan Police. In addition to the medal, each member of the RIC received a voucher from the officer in charge entitling the recipient to one pint of porter in the depot canteen.

RIC Mutiny in Belfast

In January 1907, James Larkin, the Dublin-based trade union activist, went to Belfast to organise the National Union of Dock Workers. Dockers who were trade union members refused to work with non-trade union members and went on strike, as did carters and coal workers. The strike continued for months, and dockers were brought in from Liverpool to replace those who were on strike. The dock authorities refused to negotiate, and it became very ugly and troublesome during the month of May, by which time a total of 2,500 dockers, coal workers and carters were on strike. Additional constabulary assisted by a large contingent of soldiers were drafted into the city to control the situation. In July, Larkin turned his attention, to the constabulary on duty, who were working prolonged hours each day of the week in policing the dock strike and its associated problems, and offered them his full support.

The constabulary called a meeting to discuss the extra duties being performed by them and for which they were receiving no extra pay. They outlined their grievances in a document which they submitted to their authorities, but they got no satisfaction. A decision was taken to have another meeting to air their grievances. They were warned in advance by the acting commissioner of the Belfast constabulary that any further meeting would be illegal, and that disciplinary action would be taken against members attending. The meeting went ahead in the parade ground of Musgrave Street barracks on Wednesday, 24 July, attented by about 500 members. When the acting commissioner, Inspector H. Morrel, ordered the embers to disperse, he was punched and hassled and had to make a hasty retreat. He then told the two leaders of the demonstration that they were being suspended from duty.

One of those suspended was Constable William Barrett. Following some short rousing speeches, Constable Barrett was carried shoulder high from the parade ground on to the public street and to the Custom House steps, followed by the whole group of constabulary, all of whom were in uniform. Barrett was the hero of the day and reports circulated that an attempt was made to arrest him but failed. This was later denied by the authorities, who endeavoured to play down the affair, worrying about the unwelcome publicity in the midst of the whole chaotic situation caused by the ongoing dockers strike. The authorities fearing an all-out mutiny by the constabulary, approximately 2,000 troops were drafted into Belfast on the following day and placed on standby. The strike affecting coal workers finished on 25 July but the dockers and carters remained on strike.

On 27 July, another meeting held at Musgrave Street barracks was attended by bigger numbers of constabulary than the previous one. The striking dockers and carters and the general public also joined in the proceedings. A demand was made for the reinstatement of Constable Barrett. The acting commissioner again addressed the gathering but was heckled and booed by the crowd. Constable Barrett addressed the assembled members of the force and was again paraded shoulder high. The strikers pledged their support for the constabulary, saying that they were all united in seeking better pay for the work which they performed. Messages of support came from RIC barracks all over the country.

The developments which followed are described by Seamus Breathnach in *The Irish Police*:

> Five members of the RIC had signed a petition which they pressed "strongly and with the greatest possible respect for a definite assurance within a week that our case will be favourably dealt with forthwith". This latter part of the petition was construed as a threat neccessitating the "complete re-establishment of discipline" before any grievance could be considered. The authorities took swift and decisive action. By the 6th of August the mutiny was completely suppressed. Six RIC men were suspended and no less than 300 were transferred, some with wives and children. Some were reduced in rank and Constable Barrett was dismissed from the force. After his dismissal, Constable Barrett held a meeting at the Custom House steps where he replied to the official decision. Uniformed men sent to keep order looked on, some sheepishly, others truculently. The man who had been carried shoulder high not long before was now alone. As they were no longer united, the police were scattered and

defeated. By 7th of August, the soldiers had taken over the traffic protection and now that police discontent was snuffed, the employers, assisted by a very biased and sensational press, thought it high time to force the trade unions to their knees. 7,000 soldiers had been drafted into the city. Larkin acknowledged that the authorities were placing batallions of troops on the Falls Road in order to invite sectarian conflict and thereby break the protestant and catholic unity which throughout the strike had held firm. On 12th August sometime after 7 p.m. the military, under the orders of Major Green, fired on a crowd of people in the Falls Road, Maggie Lennon, a mill girl aged 22, and Charles McMullan, an iron turner aged 24, were killed. Twelve others were injured, five with gunshot wounds, three very seriously. On that occasion, Major Thackeray read the Riot Act before his comrade gave the order to fire.

The Belfast strike and the agitation which accompanied it was the most serious disturbance handled by the RIC during the decade. The mutiny was a very sad saga in the history of the force, but with hindsight it was almost inevitable, with the grievances about the inadequacy of pay and the disappointing result of the inquiry into pay and conditions of 1901. A few years later, the Belfast constabulary had complained about grievances which they had in relation to their service there but they were ignored. Having to work sixteen or eighteen hours a day during months of the dock strike, without any extra pay, finally caused the members to rebel. They were in a difficult and vulnerable position, well aware that it was contrary to their police regulations to go on strike or hold demonstrations. The underlying discontent over a number of years on their pay issue, the pressure under which they were working at that time and the prompting of James Larkin about their pay and conditions resulted in matters coming to a head. Once the first demonstration was held, what followed was inevitable in view of the very rigid stand taken by the authorities, who asserted their authority as soon as military reinforcements were safely in place. It was a tragedy for the RIC and a personal tragedy for Constable Barrett.

Allowances and Pay in the early 1900s

A constable's pay while in training was £39 per annum and increased by increments to a maximum pay of £72 16s. after twenty-five years' service. An acting sergeant was paid £75 16s., sergeants on maximum pay got £78, and head constables received a maximum of £104 per annum.

For overnight absences from their barracks, constables, sergeants and acting sergeants received an allowance of 3s. 6d. per night and head constables received 4s. 6d. per night. Subsistence allowance for temporary absences from barracks for a period not less than twelve hours was 1s. 6d. for constables, acting sergeants and sergeants, and 1s. 6d. for head constables. For absences exceeding eight hours, head constables received 1s. 3d. and the lower ranks received 1s. A marching allowance was payable for every eight miles traversed by members outside their sub-districts, and for which head constables received 1s. 3d. and the lower ranks received 1s.

A "charge" allowance of 2s. per week was paid to sergeants and head constables who were in charge of barracks. Lodging allowance of £5 4s. per annum was payable to all married members who were not residing in barracks.

An allowance of 6s. per annum was allowed for repairs to arms and accoutrements. The straw allowance for bedding was 3s. per annum. Boot allowance was £1 6s. per annum. The provision of uniform and medical attendance were free.

District inspectors' salaries commenced at £125 per annum and rose in increments to £225. The salary of county inspectors varied from a minimum of £400 to a maximum of £500.

The following extract from the *Constabulary Gazette* dated 23 August 1913 indicated that the members were still seeking a substantial increase in their pay twelve years after the committee of inquiry sat to examine their case:

> The Post Office employees had in seven years, two Inquiries into their wages and conditions of service, while the RIC had only one Inquiry in their existence and that was twelve years ago. Yet Mr Birrell, the Chief Secretary says it is too soon to open up the subject as the police got an increase in wages in 1908 – a paltry increase of one shilling – but he should remember that the increase in 1908 was the result of the 1901 Inquiry, therefore, the unfortunate men were seven years waiting for it. Is this justice or anything like fair play?
>
> Looking back on the matter from another standpoint, everyone knows that since 1901 the prices of foodstuffs and the cost of living generally, have gone up over thirty per-cent. Everybody living in Dublin knows that since the cattle embargo of last year, the price of meat has gone up from 15 to 20 per cent, and the price of coal has gone up steadily for the last eight years, culminating with the coal strike last year, when coal which could be got a decade ago for one pound per ton, cost twenty-seven shillings and remained since then fixed at that price, no matter how fine the summer – because it used to be the custom of Dublin coal merchants to substantially reduce their price during the summer months. The cost of living in country districts is very little cheaper. Now, in face of this incontravertible statement as to the present high cost of living, how can any man, or any Government with a spark of humanity resist the demands of the RIC for better pay and

better conditions of service? The young blood of the force, after being trained and having a few years experience in it, are leaving it and joining Police Forces in Canada, Australia, South Africa and other places where they get immensely better pay, have more attractive conditions of service, winding up with pensions which makes the home policeman's mouth water.

The same feature expressed dissatisfaction with the officers in the RIC and at sergeants who weren't retiring quickly enough:

The Ornamental Section, as the officers have come to be called, is maintained at full strength and at enormous cost, the supposed reason being, to give a loyal spirit to an armed and conceivably disloyal force.

Can any reader say, why there are so many time-expired sergeants in north Tipperary? Not a few of them have over 32 years' service and no sign of them going. Great prospects for Constables in this country.

After several years of agitation, the members succeeded in getting toecaps on their boots in 1913. Moustaches beame very much the fashion from about 1910 onwards, and at one time almost the entire force wore moustaches. This led to competition and friendly rivalry amongst members as to how they maintained them, and fancy waxed moustaches were very popular.

A government inquiry was held into pay and conditions of the RIC in 1914. There were two reasons it was needed. First, there was serious dissatisfaction within the force with pay and conditions. Also, a big reduction in recruits for the force during the previous decade had resulted in the force's being considerably under strength. While being an RIC member was still a good job during the period of relative peace since the early 1890s, the pay and conditions of the force were unattractive. Not only were there fewer recruits applying, but the standard of those applying was dropping. There were now more work opportunities available for young men who might otherwise have joined. The sons of farmers, who had always been the mainstay and backbone of the RIC, were not as interested in joining the force as they used to be, and there was even a big reduction in the number of sons of serving or former RIC members applying, even though the entrance requirements for this category were less rigid. The number of labourers, grooms, craftsmen and gardeners applying for membership trebled in number. Evidence given by officers of the force shed very interesting light on the problems of recruiting at the time. A Belfast officer complained to the committee of inquiry that he was obliged to take whatever recruits he could get.

The Clare county inspector said, "I won't say exactly that they come from a different social class, but we are not even getting the pick of that class. In the past we have got the best of those men." A district inspector stationed in County Mayo took advantage of the inquiry to air his grievances: "Mayo is not a desirable place for a District Inspector as there is very little society for him in it, the County is very poor and there are no hunting grounds there." Evidence was given to the committee about the improved relations between the RIC and the general public and that it was no longer customary for members of the force to carry firearms while on duty. Again there were complaints about the pay rates and expressions of disappointment about increases given following the 1901 inquiry. The committee of inquiry on this occasion saw merit in the claims made for extra pay and better conditions for the force and recommended a pay increase. Since the Great War had commenced, the military strength in Ireland was very depleted. As a result, the government were depending on the RIC to maintain peace and tranquillity in Ireland. In 1915 it was found necessary to introduce the Police (Emergency) Provisions Act (4 & 5 Geo. 5, c. 54) to control resignations from the force and to suspend retirements for the duration of the war, except for those members who wanted to enlist in the British army.

One of the most important recommendations made by the committee of inquiry was that in the future pay increases should be given to the RIC without having to implement legislation each time. This was a major breakthrough and was long overdue. The committee congratulated the force "on being so well integrated with the community".

Protection Posts Maintained in 1912

By 1912, the number of protection posts had been considerably reduced. Those that remained were a grim reminder of the activities of the Moonlighters in the 1880s.

In June 1912, protection posts were maintained in the following townlands:

> County Cavan at Tullygullion.
> County Clare at Cappanakilla, Leeds, Coolmeen, Woodfield, Claremount, Ballinahinch and Clooney.
> Cork East Riding at Cahergal, Mitchelsfort, Snugmore, Longstown and Knocknahorgan.
> Cork West Riding at Coolkerrane and Curraclough.
> Galway East Riding at Colmanstown, Woodlawn, Hollypark and Loughrea Square.
> County Kerry at Cragg, Bunglasha, Ballygarrett, Bungasha, Gurrane and Knockanish.
> County Offaly at Russelspin.
> County Longford at Killeen.

County Mayo at Lowvalley, Liskillen, Knocknagaraun, Valley and
  Bundorragha.
County Meath at Stahalmog.
County Roscommon at Ardkeenagh.
Tipperary North Riding at Tulla [Nenagh].
County Waterford at Crushea.
County Westmeath at Ballinlassy and Curry.

The Petty Sessions

The petty sessions were the courts of summary jurisdiction to which the Royal Irish
Constabulary summoned minor offenders who broke the law. Serious criminal cases
which were tried at assizes before a judge and jury. The petty sessions had other
functions as well, such as the granting of liquor licences and special exemptions to
sell intoxicating liquor at places other than in licensed premises, such as race meetings and other sporting fixtures. Civil cases relating to trespass or assault between
individuals were also dealt with. They were held in every town and in most villages
throughout Ireland at weekly or monthly intervals and they were presided over by
a resident magistrate who sat with one or more justices of the peace. Their number
in Ireland varied between sixty and seventy, and each covered a designated petty
sessions district. With the exception of the monthly fair, the petty sessions was the
most important event held in any town or village and provided a source of entertainment, drama and amusement for the general population. Tales of cases dealt
with, excuses given, perjury committed, the performance of solicitors and the liti-
gants who thrived on regular appearances are legendary.

In Memories of a Resident Magistrate 1880–1920, Charles P. Crane, who was a resident magistrate for many years in different parts of the country, gives an objective
and amusing view of petty sessions as he observed them from the bench:

> And now I must take my readers in imagination to the scene of the
> labours of the magistrates of Ireland – the court of petty sessions – the
> people's court. It was here that the public congregated week after week,
> or month after month, to enjoy the strivings of rival solicitors, to ripple
> with laughter at the answers elicited and to feel the glow of satisfaction
> or otherwise, according as one side or the other worsted or won in a bat-
> tle of words – and oaths. The perjury committed in these courts beg-
> gared all description. It was flagrant. The fluency with which a man or
> woman would lie to gain the smallest advantage over an adversary was
> such that it bewildered the brain. Sometimes when hearing a publican's
> case, I have wondered whether the whole thing – offence, prosecution

and defence – was not a dream; whether the door as described "as open your Honour" by the police and closed by the defendant, had really any existence in fact. Whether the man "just after having a pint of porter" according to the police and according to a witness "not a tint good nor bad" had any existence either. In numberless small cases involving at most a fine of sixpence or a shilling, the excuses made were often ingenious. When the "lighting-up order" was vigorously enforced it was a common thing for men in charge of carts to keep their lamps lighted just long enough to last through the zone affected by the police patrols in a town, and then blow out the light and plod the weary way in darkness till the next zone of constabulary activity was approached, when the cart light would again flicker up on the right shaft of the cart. If caught unexpectedly, the light had always "just quenched, your Worship" or the delinquent was just about to light it when the sergeant came up. The stolid sergeant in these cases would frequently upset the whole defence by saying, without the movement of a muscle, "There was no wick or oil in the lamp" or no candle as the case may be. The excuse that the lamp was lost between the place where the sergeant met the offender and the last town he had left, became the usual and too frequent cause of excuse, until it was pointed out to a defendant that the road must be literally paved with lamps. This excuse then became less frequent, but another, equally ingenious was soon found.

The dullness of the everyday life in the country was enlivened and rendered more interesting by attempts to outwit the constabulary, and the payment of a small fine was money well spent, for the entertainment of an hour's law; hearing the solicitor for the defence brow-beating the sergeant of police and making an impassioned appeal to the bench on behalf of his client "squandering his carcase on the bench" as one litigant put it. The courts in which all this amusement occurred varied in size and dignity, from the somewhat pretentious, corinthian – pillared edifice guarded by two guns captured at Sebastopol, which graced the County town, where Assizes, Quarter Sessions and petty sessions were held, to the little whitewashed thatched cabin in the country district, with its mud floor and bare rafters, and in winter weather, its pungent smell of turf smoke mingled with wet frieze. It was to these little courthouses that people flocked once a month to hear the law, and where at times they became so excited and eager that they would bend over the table and spill the ink. It was in these little courts that one often had to make sure of an interpreter, who was sworn in the following words, "You shall well and truly interpret the Irish language into the English language, and the English language into the Irish language, to the best of your skill and ability. So help you God."

In latter days, the kissing of the book was dispensed with, the Oath having been made to sound more blasphemous than it used to, making perjury seem still more awful. There is no doubt that the kissing of the book was open to much abuse, and I doubt very much whether its abolition is not a benefit. "Watch Jerry O'Sullivan when he is taking the Oath, he will kiss his thumb and not the book at all." Such was the anonymous scrawl which was handed up to the bench on one occasion. The extraordinary remarks one heard years ago tried one's sense of humour to the utmost.

These remarks were not confined to the clients or the more ignorant country folk, but came from solicitors and sometimes magistrates on the bench. "You will answer my questions," said an excited solicitor to an unwilling witness, "or before you leave that place you will find yourself somewhere else." This was said in all seriousness at a remote sessions. "He hit me on the back of the head, your Worship," said another aggrieved person. "And what did you do?" asked a magistrate. "I turned about and knocked the silence out of him, your Worship," was the reply. It was often hard to maintain a judicial gravity on occasions when excitement took possession of the witnesses. The law was so cheap in Ireland, and the people naturally so litigious, that the number of cases at far away sessions was sometimes enormous. Often, I have travelled many miles to hear a few cases of trespass of a goat, or of a few hens in a neighbour's haggard. The assessment of damage to crops in such cases was out of all proportions. But one always had to keep in mind, that trivial as these little things appeared to the magistrate, they were of vast importance to the people themselves, but it was always wise to hear their cases with great patience.

An extract from the court book kept by the clerk of petty sessions in Carlow town in respect of the petty sessions held at Carlow on Monday, 5 October 1915, indicates the wide variety of cases and prosecutions brought before petty sessions of this period:

1. Constable Gavin -v- Patrick Kelly. Charged with being drunk in charge of a horse. Convicted and fined ten shillings with two shillings in costs.
2. Constable Meighan -v- John Byrne. Charged with being Drunk. Convicted and fined seven shillings and sixpence and ordered to pay one shilling and sixpence in costs.

3. Ditto -v- Patrick Kelly. Charged with being Drunk and Disorderly. Adjourned for 8 weeks.

4. Constable Weakley -v- William King. Charged with Simple Drunkenness. Convicted and fined seven shillings with one shilling and sixpence in costs.

5.Constable Weakley -v- Mary Comerford. Allowed ass to wander on public road. Warned and case dismissed without prejudice.

6. Constable Warrington -v- Joseph Purcell. Refusing to quit licensed premises of Michael McDonnell. Adjourned for seven days.

7. Sergeant Callaghan -v- Patrick Hutchinson. Charged with leaving horse unattended. Convicted and fined one shilling and one shilling and sixpence costs.

8. Ditto -v- Joseph Purcell. Charged for using an unlighted cart. Convicted and fined sixpence with one shilling expenses.

9. Constable Corr -v- James Fitzpatrick. Charged with Cruelty to a horse. Convicted and fined ten shillings and sixpence.

10. Constable Jackson -v- James Fitzpatrick. Charged with cruelty to a horse. Convicted and fined five shillings.

11. Constable Gavin -v- Patrick Ward. Charged with Cruelty to a Jennet. Convicted and fined thirty shillings.

At the same petty sessions, there were four cases taken by the rate collector for arrears of poor rate and decrees for amount due were given in all cases. There was one application taken privately for liberty to take possession of premises. There were three private prosecutions taken for assault. There were two prosecutions for breaches of attendance orders made under the Education Act, 1882. There were five prosecutions taken by an employee of Carlow Urban Council whose title was "town constable" – one was for "simple drunkenness" and four were for "riotous and indecent behaviour". All five defendants prosecuted by him were females. The petty sessions were in every sense "the people's courts", to which people had easy and cheap access to seek redress for wrongs done to them.

The district inspector of the RIC, or in his absence, the head constable, conducted the prosecutions on behalf of the RIC. The members summoned offenders to the petty sessions and were frequently complimented on the fairness of their evidence. Fines imposed were generally very small and those convicted appeared to bear no grudge against the constable or prosecuting member. The resident magistrates carried out their duties in a fair, professional and impartial manner. This is evident from press reports on petty sessions proceedings. They were salaried, independent individuals who had no business other than the administration of justice to the best of their ability. Resident magistrates differed very much from the local justices of the peace. Wealthy landlords or members of the local aristocracy appointed by the lord lieutenant to what amounted to an honorary position, their decisions at petty sessions were often looked upon with suspicion by the underpriviliged sections of society. On the foundation of the new state, the petty sessions were replaced by the district courts, with the old petty sessions areas remaining intact.

The *Lusitania* Disaster

On Friday afternoon, 7 May 1915, a single torpedo from a German U.20 submarine crashed into the engine room of the *Lusitania*, the flagship liner of the Cunard Line, a short distance off the Old Head of Kinsale, County Cork, while it was en route from New York to Liverpool. Following the initial torpedo impact there was a massive explosion in the liner, and within twenty minutes the giant ship had sunk over 100 metres to the bottom of the sea. World War I was in progress at the time and controversy surrounds the motive for torpedoeing the liner and as to whether it was conveying explosives or ammunitions in addition to its complement of passengers.

The sinking of the *Lusitania* resulted in the biggest ever single disaster involving loss of life in Ireland. Despite frantic efforts to rescue passengers, 1,195 people lost their lives. The victims were of all age groups and from all walks of life. Many of the bodies were never recovered. Queenstown (now Cobh) was used as the headquarters for dealing with the tragedy. Temporary mortuaries were set up for the doctors examining and attempting to identify the hundreds of bodies which were recovered for days afterwards all along the west Cork coast at Kinsale, Glandore, Crookhaven, Baltimore and Skibbereen, and as far away as Coumeenole Strand near Slea Head in County Kerry. In many cases identification proved impossible. Providing sufficient coffins at short notice created a difficulty. Mass graves were dug at Queenstown to bury the dead.

In addition to dealing with the victims, there was the added problem of coping with the panic, anxiety and grief, as well as the physical needs of the 764 survivors, many of whom had lost family members in the tragedy.

Press reporters from all over the world turned up to cover the disaster and its aftermath. Inquests were held on the victims at the military barracks in Queenstown, before the coroner, John Horgan, and at a later stage an inquiry was held. The bulk of the work and responsibility relating to the tragedy fell on the RIC, who were busy for months afterwards in dealing with it. They were assisted by the British navy based at Haulbowline and by the military at Queenstown in searching for and recovering bodies. Extra constabulary were drafted in from outlying districts and from Cork city. The constabulary involvement went on by night and day for several weeks, and the valuable contribution made by the force in the aftermath of the tragedy was highly commended by the various authorities. The sinking of the

Lusitania was the direct cause of bringing the United States into the war in Europe on the side of the Allies. The loss of the *Lusitania* and its 1,195 passengers ranks as one of the greatest maritime shipping disasters of all time.

"Memories of the RIC 70 Years Ago"

Con Casey, former editor of *The Kerryman* newspaper, recalled his memories of the RIC during the period from 1900 to 1922 in a feature in the *The Kerryman* on 26 August 1983. His career as a journalist and renowned newspaper editor spanned more than half a century.

> I grew up in Bridge Street, Tralee, a little more than a stone throw from the Royal Irish Constabulary (RIC) barracks in High Street. Like all small boys, I became familiar with my surroundings and the people residing in them. The RIC barracks with its concentration of uniformed manpower had an attraction all of its own for youngsters though we did not go into it, or were not allowed to do so.
>
> To us the movements of the police coming on duty and going off duty at regular intervals was commonplace. You could set your watch by them if you were old enough to have one.
>
> If you were around the lower end of the town and was so minded, you could not fail to see the RIC sergeant and three or four constables marching up Bridge Street to take up duty. The sergeant who might have been accompanied by one of the constables, usually the most junior, patrolled the main thoroughfare. The others went off in different directions to show their presence in the side streets and suburbs. Tralee was then a more compact town than what it is now. From time to time the sergeant took up position at the Munster and Leinster bank corner at Denny Street and there he received reports from the constables before they moved off again to patrol other areas.
>
> It was foot patrolling so methodically ordered, that it left no doubt on the public that the policemen were vigilantly on their job. Very little escaped their notice as they moved at the regulation three miles an hour through their beat. This procedure was repeated two or three times during the day until the "watchmen" took over for the night hours.
>
> Other constables were out on bicycles keeping the rural portions of the Tralee police district under supervision. They were prepared to dismount and chat and when the time came for taking the annual return of livestock and crops they had access to every farm house in their charge and became acquainted with the occupants.

All in all, it was a quiet but most effective way for keeping tabs on everybody who lived and on everything that went on in Tralee and its rural surroundings.

Nor could you enter or leave Tralee without being observed. There were attached to the force, policemen who were never seen in uniform, they were detectives. One of their duties was to be present at the railway station to take note of anybody of consequence or suspicion who was arriving or travelling.

Law enforcement was the RIC man's duty and he performed it literally. Cycling without a light or a bell; cycling on the footpath; playing a ball on the street; throwing stones at the cups on telephones or telegraph poles; not having your name and address on your cart or a light on it; staggering drunk; cruelty to animals – usually a donkey; raiding an orchard; owning or keeping an unlicensed dog and other petty offences attracted their attention.

Any one of these offences could lead to your name being entered in a policeman's note book and to a summons, to appear before the magistrate's court. The court which sat every Monday was composed of a Resident Magistrate who presided, a British appointee who was salaried – in my experience Mr E.M.P. Wynne – a tall English bachelor – and an unpaid Justice of the Peace, prominent local citizens who liked to have the initials J.P. after their name and to be saluted by the RIC as they passed along the streets.

The enforcing of the licensing laws was not a popular function of the RIC. The opening and closing of licensed premises was defined by law – I do not think there were any extensions then, but I do recall the furore that was caused when a local organisation or club contemplated or succeeded in applying for a temporary licence for a bar at their annual dance. Anybody found on licensed premises outside of stipulated hours was fined and so was the publican for whom it was a serious matter as three endorsements on his licence could put him in danger of losing it and his way of living.

In those days a publican was a grocer as well. In the front part of the premises was the shop, in which he sold tea, sugar etc and through which one passed on their way to the bar.

The RIC also had among its duties the supervision of Weights and Measures. A senior man, usually a sergeant, performed the duty for the whole county. Scales were then almost the only means of establishing the weight of an article for sale. Weights were numerous, from the ounce or less to the 56 lbs, the half hundred. They had to be verified, stamped and inspected at intervals to ensure that they were not tampered with. Similarly, with measures of liquids of different kinds. Giving a customer short weight or measure led to prosecution.

The RIC also enforced the Foods and Drugs Act. Samples of milk were taken on the way to the creamery to ensure that water was not added to it. Similiarly, samples of spirits were taken and analysed to ascertain if they were of legal strength. Butter offered for sale with excess in moisture could, as in the case of milk or spirits lead to prosecution and unwelcome publicity.

Youthful offenders got short shrift from the RIC. One or two appearances in court could lead to the adnministering of three strokes of a birch rod and if he persisted in his waywardness he could find himself in a Reformatory school where discipline was strictly enforced. There were not many such cases and the boys usually came from deprived homes with indifferent parents. The Reformatory and the birch rod used to be spoken of as deterrents. They are no longer part of the laws that deal with juveniles.

I would venture to say that Ireland was never as governable from the British point of view as it was during the first decade of this present century. The Royal Irish Constabulary, manned for the most part by native born stalwarts, mainly from farming stock, seemed to have law and order in their grip. There was of course an occasional serious crime. Their detection rate was high, their intelligence system was in good shape, they were regarded as "the eyes and ears" of Dublin Castle, as an English Secretary for Ireland declared. They obeyed their officers, of different stock to themselves with unfailing obedience and discipline. Never was England served so well anywhere as it was by the Royal Irish Constabulary in Ireland.

Ireland was quiescent in the first decade of the twentieth century; poverty, unemployment and emigration had sapped her virility. The Wyndham Act of 1903 ended the land agitation. Local Government put power, formerly held by the Grand Jury into the hands of elected representatives. The only stirrings of nationalism were in the Gaelic League and the Gaelic Athletic Association. The Irish Party, recently united under John Redmond, dominated the political life of Ireland. It hoped that the liberals, who came to power in England in 1906 would give Ireland Home Rule in return for it's support to the British House of commons. The eyes of the Irish people for the most part were turned towards Westminister and the Irish daily newspaper carried long reports detailing at length what transpired in the Parliament there. A member of the Irish Party telling his British listeners how law abiding rural Ireland was and that the "police spent their time fishing and courting". An exaggeration no doubt.

Attached to the RIC barracks in High Street was a coachyard and stables in charge of a sergeant and three constables, each with a horse. They had side-cars on which they drove the County Inspector and the District Inspector on their inspection tours. They also turned out, as one might expect, in full rig, armed with swords, mounted on horses groomed to the nines, to escort the judges to assizes when they came to hold court in Tralee twice yearly, with great pomp and ceremony.

Mention of the County Inspector and the District Inspector (the D.I.) reminds me to recall that the officers of the RIC came to their rank through the Cadet system. Their background was different to that of the young men who served in the ranks and was more akin to the British army officer in peace time. It was seldom that a man from the ranks became an officer in the RIC. The officers were for the most part Protestants and the men in the ranks, Catholics. The method of selecting or appointing RIC officers produced a caste or class system and was in keeping with the military character of the force. On formal occasions, in field dress, the RIC officers carried swords as British army officers did.

The men in the ranks of the RIC had, for the most part, rural backgrounds and were splendid physical specimens selected after strict medical examination and conforming to regulation height and chest measurements. They were of good farming stock and needed local recommendations before being accepted for the six months intensive training at the Depot in Dublin. How in the short time they were turned from easy-going country lads into efficient and stern instruments of British law enforcement in their native country was remarkable. A good brain washing job must have been done. The conditions of the time attracted into the RIC, the second and other sons of farmers who might have emigrated or become apprentices to the drapery, grocery or hardware trade in their nearest town. To enter these callings, a premium had to be paid to the employer before being accepted as an apprentice for a term of years. The value of money in the first decade of the century is well illustrated when it is realised that an experienced police constable was regarded as well paid at a pound a week. There might have been a few perks such as boot or bicycle allowance. Yet there were families reared on that wage or a little more.

The unmarried constables lived in the barracks. They were not permitted to marry until they had served a fixed number of years and if they married local girls a transfer to another county followed. Married or unmarried, RIC men were not stationed in their native county.

Promotion was slow and had to be earned after years of loyal and active service. Acting sergeants (they carried two chevrons on their sleeve) and sergeants were well established men of status in the force while a head constable in a barrack like Tralee was the pivot around whom the organisation turned. He prosecuted cases in the local court and the opinion of "the Head" carried as much weight with the bench of magistrates as his orders did in the barracks His rank was about the highest to which most policemen could aspire and which only few attained. Occasionally an outstanding head constable was promoted to District Inspector.

The high wall surrounding the rear of Tralee barracks contained a fair piece of ground. At times one could hear the sound of firing emanating from it. It was the police at target practice which was in keeping with their role as a military as a well as a civil force.

Once a year there was a great flurry of excitement within and outside the barracks. The surrounds always kept in good order were smartened up and so was everything and everybody.

It was in preparation for the annual inspection of the Inspector General, when he or his deputy came to have the officers and men parade before him and to ensure that good order and discipline abounded throughout the force. A paragraph in the local papers recorded the visit and an expression of his satisfaction with the conditions that prevailed at the barracks.

The sons of married RIC men who came to school in my day, as far as one could see and looking back on them, came from well run homes. Not that they were any different from the rest of us but again looking back, one sensed that they were a liitle more disciplined, that their shoes and person were clean and tidy, that they showed more respect for the brothers, or lay teachers authority, than what we did. It may have been otherwise but that is the way I remember it.

This recollection of mine was forged long after schooldays and after the RIC was disbanded for years, to read the notice of deaths of former members of the force, how many of them had priests, nuns and religious orders in their families. Did not one of the RIC men who mutinied in Listowel barracks rather than accept the ruthless direction of a British military divisional commander, become a priest and subsequently a bishop in the foreign missions? His was not the only late vocation.

Behind the bottle green or blue/black uniform and the baton, and the roughness and rigour displayed in the enforcement of law in all its details and the reputation they fostered among the public and neighbours of being loyal to England rather than to Ireland, there must have been sown in the homes of many RIC men the seeds of nationalism. I have read that in the first Dáil Éireann which made the declaration of allegiance to the Irish Republic and gave official recognition to the IRA as the army of the Republic, fourteen of its members were sons of RIC men.

What happened to the RIC in the seven years between then and 1921 is another and much more vivid story. The RIC attempted to hold the line for the British against the IRA (as the volunteers became known in January 1919) and the will of the majority of the people, and failed. Their reinforcement by Black and Tans and Auxiliaries changed the RIC from a native Irish force, to one infiltrated and dominated by Englishmen who were a law unto themselves and left stinking memories behind them.

I am adding a personal note with some difference. Very few know that I was once a police officer. In the autumn of 1920, I was appointed by the Brigadier Paddy Cahill as the officer in charge of the Republic's police in the Tralee Battalion area. I held the appointment until the day of the Truce in 1921 when I was promoted. During this duration I spent a term in Cork Jail. The regular RIC, the Black and Tans and the auxiliaries hated the Republican police, looking on them as unsurpers to whom the people looked for what redress they could obtain through the Republican courts.

On Christmas morning 1920, I and two or three others of my section raided a home where there was a man in bed under which there was a quantity of stolen whiskey. The whiskey was seized and returned to Twomey's shop at the Mall. The receipt for the whiskey is among the few souvenirs I have of the period.

With me on that Christmas morning were Christy Ryan, son of a respected RIC sergeant, Big Dan O'Sullivan, a well known and popular Rock Street baker, and maybe John (Gal) Slattery, who afterwards played football for Kerry. They and I were members of D (Rock Street) company of the IRA. They and the officers of the Tralee battalion staff, of which I was the junior member and the youngest, are all dead now, God Rest them.

Con Casey died in 1996 aged 99 years.

Edward Carson and the Ulster Volunteer Force

The Liberal government took up office in 1906. In the general elections of 1910, when it lost its majority in parliament, it became dependent on the votes of the Irish

Party to remain in office. To appease the Irish Party, the British government re-opened the case for Home Rule in Ireland. The Ulster Protestants feared Home Rule and made it quite clear that they were unwilling to accept a Dublin-based government. They were encouraged in their view by the British Conservative Party. The Northern Ireland Unionists had earlier shown their muscle against the Wyndham "devolution" proposals, causing the proposed scheme to be dropped and forcing Wyndham out of office. Edward Carson, born in Dublin in 1854, a prominent barrister and MP, became leader of the Irish Unionist Party in February 1910 and vigorously opposed Home Rule in parliament. He was a very dominant leader and from September 1911 he organised a mass movement in Ulster in opposition to the proposed provisions which he then saw as being inevitable. His staunchest ally in Ulster was James Craig, a forty-year-old MP and wealthy industrialist. On 23 September 1911, a mass meeting was held on Craig's estate at Craigavon, which was attended by at least 100,000 Protestant Unionists. Several more rallies were held throughout Ulster until 200,000 Unionist men had signed a pledge to defend Ulster. The Orangemen had already discovered a loophole in the law, whereby drilling could be legally authorised by two justices of the peace, and commenced drilling.

By January of 1913, the Ulster Volunteer Force was formed, with an initial target of 100,000 men. It set up its headquarters in the Old Town Hall in Belfast. Within a year the UVF had grown into a powerful army. The force, which was committed to making an armed resistance to the implementation of Home Rule in Ulster, set about acquiring arms, for which it had collected over one million pounds. A massive consignment of arms, consisting of 35,000 rifles and five million rounds of ammunition were smuggled in from Germany through the ports of Larne, Bangor and Donaghadee. They were quickly and efficiently distributed throughout the whole UVF membership, without the constabulary becoming involved, and the British government appeared powerless to do much about it. As a further boost to the UVF, fifty-eight high ranking military officers based in the Curragh Camp under General Hubert Gough, officer commanding the 3rd Cavalry Brigade, gave notice that they would resign rather than obey orders to coerce the Ulster Protestants into accepting Home Rule. (This became known as "the Curragh Mutiny".) After several years of failed attempts, Home Rule eventually became law in 1914. Civil War was averted only by the outbreak of the World War I on 4 August 1914. Another statute immediately followed, suspending the introduction of Home Rule until the war was over.

The Ulster Volunteers enlisted in the British army and formed their own division (the 36th Ulster Division) and suffered enormous losses at the Battle of the Somme. Due to delay and weak leadership on the part of the British government, allied to the threat from the military officers at the Curragh, Carson and Craig were permitted to get away with open flouting the law and engaging in actions which could only be described as treasonable. Members of the Royal Irish Constabulary would later say that they saw this as the beginning of the end, resulting in serious developments for the worse in Irish history. Had the government persisted and conceded Home Rule to Ireland, even belatedly in 1914, the awful tragedies of the next eight years might have been averted.

The observations made by Resident Magistrate C.P. Crane in *Memories of a Resident Magistrate* about the activities of Edward Carson summed up this difficult period:

> But I confess I did foresee some very awkward complications as a result of the arming and drilling on the part of the Orangemen in the North. To me as an official and with no politics, it seemed to be a direct incitement to all and every class of people who did not approve of the laws made by the King, Lords and commons of the British Parliament, to resist by force of arms, and I formed the very strong opinion that no matter what the result, the leaders of the movement ought to have been brought before a competent tribunal to answer for their conduct. Rebellion against oppression may or may not be justified – according as it is successful or otherwise, but to arm and drill in defiance of the law in view of a possible or even probable oppression, seemed to me to be quite unjustifiable. If once it is admitted that rebellion against prospective laws are justified, there is an end to constitutional government. But the leaders of the Ulster movement, to their credit be it said, made no bones about the illegality of their actions. They defied the government openly and said in effect "Prosecute us – we know we are acting illegally – but be strong and put us down." But the government of the day did not dare to do it, and from that day, when they flinched from their duty, the British Government in Ireland, sunk to the depths of contempt in the minds of the people it professed to govern.

The Recruiting Campaign for the Great War

With the outbreak of the Great War of 1914–1918, recruiting for the British army commenced. Buntings, flags and recruiting posters hung outside recruiting offices, which were opened in the major towns and cities. Military bands gave public musical performances on a daily basis outside the larger centres. Recruiting posters were distributed to every RIC barracks where they were permanently displayed on the external notice boards. A good number of young Irishmen, who had little interest in the political intricacies of the situation at that time, joined at an early stage.

Employment was scarce and, as they saw it, the British army offered an opportunity to see the world, and some excitement, compared with the dull lives they were leading at the time.

Lord Herbert Horatio Kitchener, British secretary of state for war, a native of Gunsboro, Listowel, County Kerry, looked out, appealing for recruits from the thousands of posters bearing his picture displayed in all public places. Kitchener told John Redmond leader of the Irish Party, that if he got 5,000 recruits from Ireland he would say, "Thanks," and that if he got 10,000 he would take off his hat in salute. The Nationalist organisations discouraged young men from joining the British army, but many looked to John Redmond, who saw the British cause as the Irish cause as well, for guidance. Initially he did not express a firm opinion on the subject in public, but at a speech made by him at Woodenbridge, County Wicklow, on 20 September 1914, he urged the Irish Volunteers to join the Irish regiments in the British army.

Redmond's speech split the Irish Volunteers. The larger group – in excess of 150,000 – which remained loyal to him, became known as the National Volunteers, and several thousand of them did join the British army on Redmond's advice. The National Volunteers did not take part in the Easter Week insurrection.

Approximately 100,000 Catholic Irishmen joined the British army and fought in the Great War. They were placed in the vulnerable positions in many of the battles, where they fought bravely but suffered very severe casualties. The deaths of the thousands of Irishmen brought grief and tragedy to thousands of homes in Ireland between 1914 and 1918. Members of the RIC were encouraged to seek recruits for the British army at the time, a responsibility which some took very seriously, although others did not.

A plea made by the inspector general for members themselves to volunteer for service, supported by the officers in the force, met with a good response. Approximately 800 members of all ranks volunteered. One county inspector and thirty-three district inspectors volunteered. (Five of the DIs were killed in action and a number were wounded.) The remainder came from the lower ranks of the force. They suffered very severe casualties. One quarter of the total were wounded and almost another quarter were killed in action. Seventeen were declared as missing and about twenty were made prisoners of war. They served in different regiments of the British army, with the majority serving in the Irish Guards regiment. They fought with distinction at the front and their bravery and fighting spirit were very favourably commented on by their commanding officers. A small number were promoted to higher ranks in recognition of their outstanding service. Less than half of those who volunteered were able to resume their normal policing duties with the RIC.

With the outbreak of the war, the enforcement of the British Nationality and Status of Ireland Act, 1914 (4 & 5 Geo. 5, c. 17), other known as the Alien's Act, became a priority. All foreigners arriving in the country had to report to the constabulary, and close attention was paid to the movement of strangers in each sub-district. In 1915, the British parliament passed legislation which became known as the Defence of the Realm Act (5 & 6 Geo. 5, c. 8). Its provisions related mostly to the defence of Great Britain and its vital installations such as road and rail links, bridges, canals, etc., but the provisions also applied to Ireland. Orders made under the act were circulated on a regular basis to the RIC, even though they appeared to be of little relevance to the country at that time.

THE GROWTH OF NATIONALISM

The Irish Republican Brotherhood

Following the dynamiting campaign in England in the 1880s, only the remnants of the IRB organisation survived at the end of the century. Tom Clarke, released from prison in 1898 after serving fifteen years for his part in bombings in England, again became one of the central figures in the organisation. The other leaders were Major John McBride, Westport, County Mayo; Dr Patrick McCartan, County Tyrone; P.S. O'Hegarty of Dublin; Denis McCullough from Belfast; and Sean Mac Diarmada from Leitrim. Their newspaper, the *Irish Freedom,* founded in 1910, voiced very militant and republican views, which were also the views of Mac Diarmada and Clarke, who in time became the undisputed leaders of the organisation. The IRB very carefully recruited new members, all infused with new militant ideals and ready to take advantage of any opportunity presenting itself. The IRB infiltrated other nationalist organisations through which it could gain influence without betraying its militant presence. Even though its membership stood at little over 2,000, it was a well organised and directed organisation as 1916 approached.

The Gaelic League

The Gaelic League was founded by a County Roscommon Protestant, Dr Douglas Hyde, in Dublin on 31 July 1893. The co-founder was Eoin Mac Neill, an Irish scholar and history professor, from County Antrim. Founded primarily out of love for the Irish language and Irish culture, it never had any military or violent aspirations. Under Douglas Hyde's influence, the Gaelic League was declared to be non-political and non-denominational. It attracted individuals who had a passionate interest in the revival of the Irish language. The Gaelic League had phenomenal success, employing full-time organisers; establishing branches in America, Great Britain, New Zealand and Australia; and founding a total of nineteen colleges in

Ireland solely for the training of teachers in Irish. These colleges had a total capacity for about 2,000 students. Although its aim continued to be the promotion of the Irish language and culture, it was infiltrated by members of the IRB, including Padraig Pearse, Sean Mac Diarmada and Thomas Clarke, who saw its potential to fulfil their aspirations. At its Ard Fheis in Dundalk in July 1915, a motion was passed at the instigation of the IRB members which altered the aims of the Gaelic League. Douglas Hyde, who was president, resigned in protest and his place was taken by Eoin Mac Neill. From that point onwards, the Gaelic League's priority was to obtain a free and united Ireland. The organisation became one of the vehicles through which the 1916 Rising was launched, and most of those who took part in the rising were members of the Gaelic League.

The Gaelic Athletic Association

The Gaelic Athletic Association was founded in Thurles, County Tipperary, on 1 November 1884, for the purpose of preserving the cultural and national Irish pastimes and games. Shortly after its foundation, Charles Stewart Parnell and Michael Davitt were elected patrons, along with Dr Croke, Archbishop of Cashel. During the early years of the association there was no indication of any militant tendencies within the organisation. It spread to every corner of Ireland, and within a short period, practically every parish in the country had a GAA club with teams competing at local level in the national games.

The association was infiltrated by Fenians at an early stage and later by the IRB, who saw its national organisers and members as potential recruits. Members of the association were sworn into the IRB and in later years many of its active members joined the Irish Volunteers.

Sinn Féin

Arthur Griffith and others founded Sinn Féin on 28 November 1905 to cater for what Griffith described as a new brand of nationalism, less militant than the IRB, and with a view to bringing all nationalist clubs and societies together. Other prominent members were John Sweetman, William T. Cosgrave, Sean T. O'Kelly, Sean Mac Diarmada and Countess Markievicz. Griffith's personality and the organisation's financial situation created problems in the early years. Griffith used the *United Irishman* newspaper to bring together all the diverse national organisations into an awareness of a common purpose. While the organisation was weak in numbers, its name caught on, and in a short time members of the organisation were referred to as "Shinners" by the British military and press. It did survive and when the Irish Volunteers were formed they were known as the Sinn Féin army. Likewise the

Easter Rising of 1916, was frequently referred to as the Sinn Féin Rising. It was after 1916 that Sinn Féin grew into a powerful political organisation.

The Trade Union Movement

Following the Trade Union Congress of 1894, the trade union movement was built up under the leadership of James Larkin and James Connolly. Connolly wanted to link nationalism with the Labour movement all over the country but socialism did not find favour with the IRB or Arthur Griffith, so he went his own way following his own ideology. Dublin industrialists and employers under the leadership of William Martin Murphy formed an association to fight the trade unions, and this resulted in the very bitter strike and lock-out of 1913. The Dublin Metropolitan Police, in endeavouring to maintain the peace, got caught up in the strike situation, and striking workers were baton charged on a number of occasions. It was alleged that the police were acting on the side of the employers. The affair led to much bitterness against the DMP, and until the force was amalgamated with the Garda Síochána in 1925, it had a black mark against it. The strike resulted in a victory for the employers; the workers had to return to work after many months as they were close to starvation. The strike left the workers in a very militant and defiant mood, and the solidarity of their protest moulded them into a closely organised group. In November 1913, Connolly founded the Irish Citizen Army, consisting of 200 striking workers, to prevent imported "blackleg" labour being employed and to keep them fit and with a sense of unity and purpose while on strike. After the strike finished, the Citizen Army continued in existence with regular training under the control of James Connolly and playwright Sean O'Casey. It later became actively involved in the 1916 Rising.

The Irish Volunteers

The nationalist organisations in the south of Ireland had seen Carson organising his huge Ulster Volunteer Force in Ulster. When the British government took no action against him or the Ulster Volunteers, they concluded that if the British government was in no position to take action in northern Ireland, there was no reason why a Volunteer Force should not be organised in the south. As a consequence, the Irish Volunteers were established on 25 November 1913 at the suggestion of Eoin Mac Neill, professor of Irish history at University College Dublin. Over 3,000 men were recruited at the outset, including members of the IRB, the Gaelic League, the GAA and other nationalist organisations. IRB members had a big influence in the leadership of the Volunteers. MacNeill himself was chosen as president of the Volunteers and chief of staff; Bulmer Hobson was elected secretary and The O'Rahilly and

Roger Casement were placed in charge of finances. Eamon de Valera was amongst the recruits who joined. By the summer of 1914, over 100,000 men had joined the Irish Volunteers. They regularly met and openly trained in drill, using hurling sticks but no guns. By the end of the same year over 180,000 men had joined. Padraig Pearse was one of these and he maintained a very outspoken militant stance with which all the Volunteers did not agree. John Redmond, on seeing the growth of the Irish Volunteers, endeavoured to keep them on his side and he called upon them to join the British army to prove Ireland's right to full nationhood. When the Volunteer movement split, the minority which sided with Eoin Mac Neill and Labour's Citizen Army provided the Volunteers who took part in the Easter Rising of 1916.

The Royal Irish Constabulary took very little action against the Irish Volunteers, as they openly drilled in fields with their hurley sticks or openly marched in file along the public roads throughout the country. In the early stages of the Volunteer Movement the attitude of the authorities was that this was a passing phase and would collapse, as had happened to so many other movements in the past but their attitude changed following the Howth gun running in 1914. The standing instruction to the RIC at the time was that they were to keep the Volunteers under observation, record the numbers involved, and identify those taking part, particularly the leaders. The approach was low key.

They were of course to ensure that no breach of the peace took place. Apart from keeping the Volunteers under observation – and occasionally cycling around after them – while they were at their drilling and marching, the RIC did not take their activities very seriously. Members of the force would later say that after these drilling sessions, they often ended up drinking with the Volunteers in the local public house that night and they frequently played cards together until the early hours of the morning.

The Howth Gun Running

The Irish Volunteers needed firearms, and the purchasing and smuggling of these was arranged by Erskine Childers and Darrell Figgis. On Sunday, 26 July 1914, a total of 1,500 rifles and 45,000 rounds of ammunition were landed from the trawler *Asgard* at Howth, County Dublin. Up to 800 Volunteers assembled to get the arms ashore and have them distributed. A party of the Dublin Metropolitan Police was despatched to Howth by tram, but allegedly received no instructions as to why they were being sent there or what they were to do when they arrived. On arrival at Howth Junction they met the Volunteers carrying the smuggled rifles, but took no action, and indeed some of the police party gave loud cheers for "The Irish Volunteers".

The Volunteers were intercepted by another party of police under Assistant Commissioner Harrell and about eighty British soldiers at Clontarf. In the absence of the chief commissioner, Mr Harrell was in charge of the Dublin Metropolitan Police. On his own responsibility, he sought the assistance of the military, and two companies of infantry accompanied the small number of DMP members. There was a confrontation between them and the Volunteers, but whatever actually took place or what compromise was arrived at, the Volunteers succeeded in getting away with only the loss of nineteen rifles.

Three members of the DMP were dismissed by their authorities for refusing to take action against the Volunteers, but from fear of an all-out mutiny by the DMP as well as political pressure, they were reinstated four months later. One of the three DMP men – Andrew O'Neill, a native of Myshall, County Carlow – later resigned from the force in 1918. Assistant Commissioner David Harrell, who was also forced to resign, was not reinstated.

Later on the same day, the company of British soldiers was marching back to its barracks along Bachelor's Walk in Dublin city when it was jeered and stoned by a crowd along the street. The soldiers opened fire on the crowd and charged the crowd with their fixed bayonets. Three people were killed and thirty-eight people were injured. It was suggested that the soldiers had opened fire due to a misunderstanding of orders. There was a huge turnout for the funerals of the three victims, and the funerals were used as an occasion for a big nationalist demonstration. The shooting tragedy had repercussions in the British parliament.

The Funeral of O'Donovan Rossa

Jeremiah O'Donovan Rossa, a native of Rosscarbery, County Cork, who was a prominent Fenian and had served terms of imprisonment, died in August 1915. His funeral to Glasnevin Cemetery was used as a militant demonstration of strength by the nationalist elements and as a platform to announce the likelihood of an early insurrection. Padraig Pearse, dressed in the full uniform of an Irish Volunteer officer, delivered a moving and passionate graveside oration, which left those present in no doubt but that an armed insurrection at that time was very imminent. It was a well known before this that Pearse was bent on an armed insurrection to gain freedom for Ireland.

Preparations for 1916

By mid–1914, Protestant Ulster was armed and defiant and Volunteers were joining up in large numbers. Huge numbers were also joining the Irish Volunteers in the south. By the end of the year, there were two strong rival organisations, one very heavily armed and the other partially armed. One writer described the situation at this time as "being pregnant with disaster". The Royal Irish Constabulary had its finger on the pulse and was very much alert to the situation and concerned about it, as reflected in the following confidential report sent by the inspector general to Mr Birrell, chief secretary, on 15 June 1914:

> In Ireland, the training and drilling to the use of arms of a great part of the population is a new departure, which is bound in the not too distant future to alter all the existing conditions of life. Obedience to the law has never been a prominent characteristic of the people. In times of passion or excitement the law has only been maintained by force, and this has been rendered practicable owing to the want of cohesion among the crowds hostile to the police. If the people became armed and drilled, effective police control would vanish. Events are moving. Each County will soon have a trained army far outnumbering the police, and those who control the Volunteers will be in a position to dictate to what extent the law of the land may be carried into effect.

This report was like an inspired prophecy of the following eight years. Its contents were also highlighted later by the royal commission on the 1916 rebellion.

In May 1915, a military council was formed, consisting of Padraig Pearse, Joseph M. Plunkett and Eamon Ceannt. In the following September, Sean Mac Diarmada and Thomas Clarke joined and early in 1916 James Connolly and Thomas McDonagh were co-opted to it. These were the most militant of the Irish nationalist leaders. The Rising was orginally planned for the autumn of 1915 – this was strongly indicated by Pearse's oration at Glasnevin – but support expected from Germany did not materialise and it was decided to postpone it until Easter Week 1916.

The government knew that an insurrection was planned but not what form it would take. The situation differed from the Fenian Rising. Now the responsibility for putting down the rebellion rested with the military rather than the constabulary. The policy was that military force would be met with military force, and it was known that thousands of rifles were in the hands of the Irish Volunteers. The role of the RIC and the DMP was minimal in the contingency plans made. Both forces continued to gather intelligence on the activities and movements of the nationalist organisations and their leaders, and dossiers were built up on all those with militant tendencies.

Rumours were rife throughout 1915 and early 1916 that Germany was about to send substantial reinforcements of men and armaments to the Irish nationalist movement. The RIC, DMP and coastguards, very much on the alert for this possible development, kept special watch on the coastline, harbours and piers. There were reports of some unrest, but it was confined to Ulster, Dublin and a few other locations. Early in 1916, there was little indication in some parts of Ireland that an insurrection was imminent. Former constable Con Sullivan, who was stationed in a small barracks in County Carlow at that time, related that the entire station party, consisting of one sergeant and four constables, left their barracks and cycled forty miles to Punchestown Races for a day's recreation. As they approached Punchestown they had a discussion as to who had secured the barracks before they left; none could remember having attended to it. The sergeant put their mind at ease, saying, "I know the people in the village well enough and everything will be all right until we get back." They enjoyed their day at Punchestown and arrived back to their barracks after midnight to find the front door open, all the rifles safely on their racks and nothing touched or disturbed in the barracks. The situation would change drastically throughout the country in the following twelve months.

The oldest known photograph of an RIC party.

RIC constable's helmet as worn from 1881.

Badges of the Irish Constabulary and the RIC.

THE
Police  Gazette,

OR
HUE-AND-CRY.
Published for Ireland on every Tuesday and Friday.

All Notices intended for insertion in the Hue-and-Cry, are to be transmitted under cover addressed to the Inspector-General of Constabulary (the words Hue-and-Cry to be written on the left hand corner of the Envelope). No Description can be inserted unless an Information shall have been Sworn; but it is not necessary to forward the Informations to the Inspector-General.
As the Law (48 Geo. 3, c. 140, s. 44,) only permits the insertion of Notices respecting Felonies, no other description of Notice can be inserted in the Hue-and-Cry.

DUBLIN, FRIDAY, JANUARY 22, 1864.

English Police.

ABSCONDED from Sunderland, on the 4th instant, charged with stealing a cheque of the value of £15, which he got cashed at Messrs. Blackhouse, and Co.'s Bank, after committing a forgery:—Julius Oppenheimer, a Jew by birth, about 30 years of age, 5 feet 8 or 10 inches in height, black hair, large prominent nose, and generally wears spectacles; dressed in black, and wears a white tie; professes to be converted to Christianity, and has been preaching in Dissenting chapels in this town.

Information to be given to J. Stainsby, Chief Constable, who holds a Warrant for his apprehension.

Central Police Station, 11th January, 1864.

Scottish Police.

John Morrison (forgery) not arrested; Hue-and-Cry, 7th October, 1862.

Dublin Police.

G DIVISION.

Margaret Sands (convict, whose ticket of licence has been revoked) not arrested; Hue-and-Cry, 1st December, 1863.

Margaret Donnelly, alias Devlin, alias O'Hara (convict, whose ticket of licence has been revoked) not arrested; Hue-and-Cry, 20th March, 1863.

Henry Baldwin (convict, whose ticket of licence revoked) not arrested; Hue-and-Cry, 20th March, 1863.

Alexander M'C... been revoked) not ... ber, 1863.

Rose Byrne (convict, whose ticket of licence revoked) 2nd October, 1863.

Michael Delany (convict, whose ticket of licence has been revoked) October, 1863.

William Manning (sheep stealer) not arrested; Hue-and-Cry, 27th November, 1863.

William Harry (sheep stealer) not arrested; Hue-and-Cry, 24th November, 1863.

James Driscoll (felonious assault) not arrested; Hue-and-Cry, 10th July, 1863.

Michael Flynn (felonious assault) not arrested; Hue-and-Cry, 23rd June, 1863.

Timothy Connor (cow stealer) not arrested; Hue-and-Cry, 9th June, 1863.

Patrick Collins (felonious assault) not arrested; Hue-and-Cry, 29th May, 1863.

John Bohan (sheep stealer) not arrested; Hue-and-Cry, 20th March, 1863.

David M'Clements, a native of Kilmore, Down, and Michael Kinealy, a native of Rathcormac, Cork (prison breach) not arrested; Hue-and-Cry, 14th April, 1863.

Patrick Hogan (serious assault) not arrested; Hue-and-Cry, 14th April, 1863.

Donegal.

Dominick M'Elwain (rape) not arrested; Hue-and-Cry, 3rd July, 1863.

Down.

Francis Hale (rape) not arrested: Hue-and-Cry, 14th July, 1863.

Kildare.

Patrick Ryan (assault endangering life) not arrested; Hue-and-Cry, 13th October, 1863.

James King (robbery) not arrested; Hue-and-Cry, 11th September, 1863.

Kilkenny.

Patrick Jackman (homicide) not arrested; Hue-and-Cry, 14th November, 1862.

Thomas Fleming (homicide) not arrested; Hue-and-Cry, 7th November, 1862.

King's.

John Regan (house attack) not arrested; Hue-and-Cry, 29th Dec., 1863.

James Carey (cattle stealer) not arrested; Hue-and-Cry, 24th November, 1863.

Oliver Griffin (embezzlement) not arrested; Hue-and-Cry, 23rd October, 1863.

Bernard Warren (grievous assaults) not arrested; Hue-and-Cry, 16th October, 1863.

Thomas Feeny, native of Roscrea, county Tipperary, and Patrick Hickey, native of Gorteen, county Tipperary (cattle stealers) not arrested; Hue-and-Cry, 9th June, 1863.

CON...

William John...
the night of the...
from the Malone...
arrested; Hue-an...
James M'Keen...
and-Cry, 10th No...

John Brown (rc...
14th July, 1863.
Owen Moan (fe...
and-Cry, 13th Fe...

Michael Crooks...
glary) not arre-te...
1863.
Thomas M'Le...
arrested; £20 rew...
Hue-and-Cry, 3rd...

James Mullins...
endangering life)...
August, 1863.
Thomas Grady...
and-Cry, 3rd Mar...

Thomas Rouse...
and-Cry, 5th Jan...
Daniel Buckley...
gering life) arreste...
Michael Buckle...
arrested; Hue-an...
Michael Fing (...
and-Cry, 8th Dec...

THE
Police  Gazette,

OR
HUE-AND-CRY.
Published for Ireland on every Tuesday and Friday.

All Notices intended for insertion in the Hue-and-Cry, are to be transmitted under cover addressed to the Inspector-General of Constabulary. No Description can be inserted unless an Information shall have been Sworn; but it is not necessary to forward the Informations to the Inspector-General.
As the Law (48 Geo. 3, c. 140, s. 44,) only permits the insertion of Notices respecting Felonies, no other description of Notice can be inserted in the Hue-and-Cry.

DUBLIN, TUESDAY, APRIL 30, 1867.

By the Lord Lieutenant-General and General Governor of Ireland.

A PROCLAMATION.

WODEHOUSE.

Whereas James Stephens has been an active Member of a Treasonable Conspiracy against the Queen's authority in Ireland, and escaped from the Richmond Prison on the Twenty-fourth day of November last. Now We, being determined to bring the said James Stephens to Justice, do hereby offer a Reward of One Thousand Pounds to any person or persons who shall give such Information as shall lead to the Arrest of the said James Stephens; and a further Reward of One Thousand Pounds to any person or persons who shall arrest the said James Stephens. And We do hereby offer a further Reward of Three Hundred Pounds to any person or persons who shall give such information as shall lead to the Arrest of any one whomsoever who has knowingly harboured or received, or concealed, or assisted or aided in any way whatsoever in his Escape from Arrest, the said James Stephens. And We do also hereby offer a Free Pardon, in addition to the above-mentioned Reward, to any person or persons concerned in the Escape of the said James Stephens who shall give such Information as shall lead to his Arrest as aforesaid.

Given at Her Majesty's Castle of Dublin, this Twenty-sixth day of January, 1866.

By His Excellency's Command,

THE POLICE GAZETTE, OR HUE-AND-CRY, APRIL 30, 1867.

Dublin Police.

G DIVISION.

John Kirwan (treasonable practices) not arrested; Hue-and-Cry, 26th April, 1867.

Ticket-of-leave convicts whose licences have been revoked, not arrested:—James Ryan, Hue-and-Cry, 16th March, 1866. Bernard Reilly, Hue-and-Cry, 29th June, 1866. Michael Reilly, Hue-and-Cry, 14th August, 1866. William Joseph Cooper, Hue-and-Cry, 29th August, 1866. William Smith, Hue-and-Cry, 1st March, 1867. Richard Stanghanssy, Hue-and-Cry, 20th April, 1867.

CONSTABULARY.

Antrim.

Samuel Christy (serious assault) not arrested; Hue-and-Cry, 1st February, 1867.

by an armed party, wounded by a gun-shot, and robbed of his land, tod., etc.

His Excellency, for the better apprehending and bringing to justice the perpetrators of this outrage, is pleased hereby to offer a reward of £500 to any person or persons who shall, within six months from the date hereof, give such information as shall lead to the arrest of the person or persons who committed the said outrage.

And also a free pardon to any person concerned in the said outrage who shall give such information as aforesaid, except the person or persons who actually fired the shots.

By His Excellency's Command,

THOS. A. LARCOM.

The above reward will be paid, on conviction, by Daniel J. Cruise, Esq., the Resident Magistrate at Killarney, to those who may become entitled to it under the conditions of this Proclamation.

gray eyes, thin nose, fair hair, wore a black jerry hat, blue pilot coat, tweed trousers and vest. Roscrea, Sept. 28, 1866. (s. 63328—19556.)

Michael Darmody (sheep stealer) not arrested; Hue-and-Cry, 15th February, 1867.

John Ross (homicide) not arrested; Hue-and-Cry, 1st February, 1867.

James Shea (felony) not arrested; Hue-and-Cry, 20th June, 1866.

King's.

DESCRIPTION of James O'Brien, native of King's county, who stands charged with having, on the 24th of April, 1867, in the barony of Ballyboy, parish of Killoughy, robbed his master, Pat Duffy, of Gorbally, by picking his pocket and stealing a purse containing 10s. in silver, and a Nineteen Prayer-book; and also for taking away an I absconding with his master's son, a lad under 12 years of age, ... ars of age, 5 feet ...

RIC party, Tralee, 1894.

All the uniforms worn by the RIC.

A young district inspector in full dress uniform.

A sergeant of the RIC on sentry duty.

A district inspector of the period 1903–1922.

Acting-Sergeant Martin Begley, "Champion Boxer of the RIC" with his Aston cycle. (Photograph: Courtesy of Mr Patrick Houlihan, Old Photographs Collection, Killorglin.)

Sergeant William Clarke, Service Number 45155 who was stationed in Cork city, pictured in 1899; he retired in 1920. He is wearing a pre-1900 style tunic and cap.

Sergeant Thomas O'Rourke, of Kiltyclogher, Co. Leitrim, who served as a constable at Fenit, Co. Kerry and as a Sergeant at Ardfert, Farranfore and Tralee; he retired in 1920.

Constable Tim O'Leary, of Bantry, Co. Cork.

RIC members lead the 'Corpus Christi' procession along New Street, Killarney Co. Kerry in 1913. (Courtesy of Paddy McMonagle, Killarney.)

District Inspector Luxton in his office, with his clerk, Constable Con Sullivan; Cashel RIC barracks Co. Tipperary, 1919. Note the old trestle table, files, ink and glue bottles, office stamps, pin cushion, reference books, aladdin oil lamp and Suttons Coals calendar. (Courtesy of Con Sullivan.)

Mulgrave RIC Barracks at Lady's View, on the Killarney–Kenmare Road; its two watch-towers facilitated the prevention of game poaching. (Courtesy of Mr and Mrs O'Shea, Lady's View Stores, Killarney.)

A farcical collage postcard depicting an RIC raid for poteen at around the turn of the century. (Courtesy of Paddy McMonagle, Killarney, Co. Kerry.)

A lone RIC constable armed with a carbine stands by as the bailiffs demolish a dwelling with their battering ram.

Onlookers viewing the damage to Listowel Barracks after its destruction by Anti-Treaty forces following vacation by the RIC in August 1922.

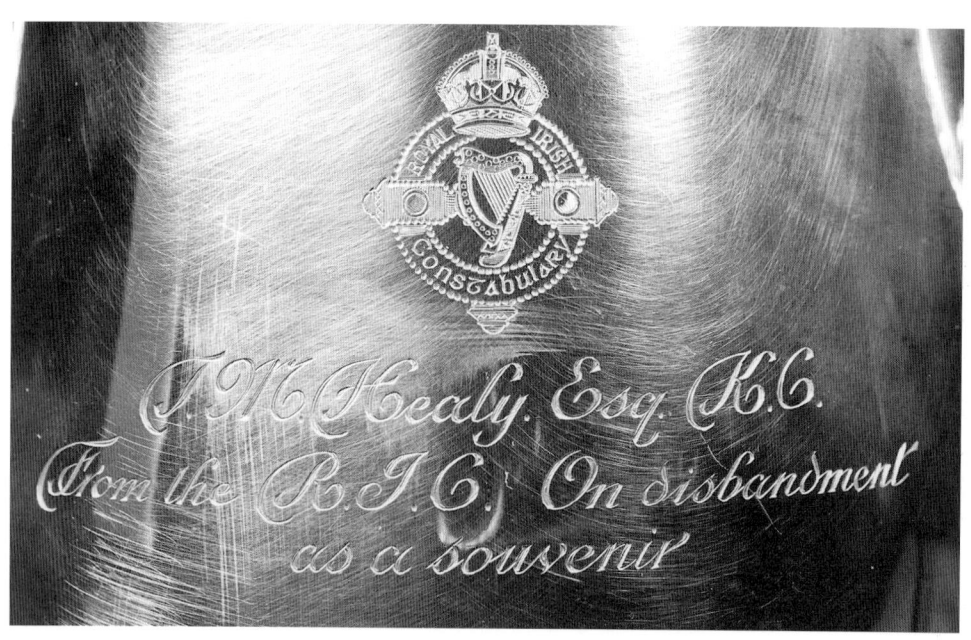

Lord French inspecting the RIC at Phoenix Park Depot 1920. (RTÉ, Cashman Collection.)

Badge and inscription on the Cup of Peace.

Chapter Eight

1916–1919
THE WAR OF INDEPENDENCE

Events Leading up to the Easter Rising, 1916

Late on Good Friday night 21 April 1916, a motor car with four male occupants approached Killorglin town in County Kerry from the Killarney direction. Instead of following the Cahirciveen road, it took a wrong turning to its right along a minor road which led to the unprotected Ballykissane pier. The driver saw the danger too late and was unable to stop the car before it reached the end of the pier and plunged into the tidal river Laune, which was in full tide. Local residents went to the scene and rescued the driver, who gave his name as Thomas McInerney and said that he was from County Limerick. He was later active during the War of Independence in Limerick and died as a result of an accidental shooting in 1922. He told the rescuers that there were three other men in the car with him whom he did not know as he was only acting as a driver for them. When the car was recovered some time later, there were no bodies in it. Two bodies were recovered the following day and one a number of days later. Following the accident, McInerney was taken to the nearby house of Timothy O'Sullivan where he got a change of clothing. Two members of the RIC from the local barracks quickly came to the scene and then visited the house where McInerney was to take details of the tragedy from him. McInerney also told them that he did not know who the passengers were or what their business was. It later transpired that McInerney had a revolver which was resting on a chair in the house after he had changed his clothes, but one of the onlookers present sat on the revolver while the constables were present. The RIC dealt with the occurrence as an ordinary accident.

The three casualties were later identified as Charles Monahan, Belfast; Donal Sheehan, Newcastle West, County Limerick; and Con Keating of Cahirciveen, County Kerry. All three were based in Dublin and were members of the Gaelic League and the GAA. Keating was buried in Cahirciveen and Sheehan and Monahan were interred in the local Derravalla cemetery. There were no military trappings at any of the funerals.

They had left Dublin to travel to Valentia Island, off the Kerry coast, where their mission was to seize the wireless station. They had a knowledge of wireless telegraphy and Admiralty charts and were planning to send out messages to the British warships off the west coast to decoy them away from the German vessel the *Aud*, which was expected there on that weekend to land guns. The *Aud* had arrived in Tralee Bay on the previous day and was waiting for a pilot boat. The RIC had no reason to suspect the type of mission on which the three deceased were engaged, and it was several days afterwards before the pieces began to fall into place. Ever since the Fenian Rising of 1867, however, the protection of the transatlantic wireless station at Valentia Island had been a high priority for the RIC, and on that Good Friday, a number of RIC members conducted a checkpoint at the entrance to Cahirciveen town on the Killorglin road. Monahan, Keating and Sheehan were the first casualties of the 1916 Easter Rising.

The Arrest of Roger Casement and the Seizure of the *Aud*

For more than a year before the Easter Rising, Roger Casement was in Germany acquiring a shipment of arms and provisions from the German government to supply the Irish Volunteers. He was joined there in 1915 by Robert Monteith, an Irishman and a Boer War veteran who had been dismissed from the Ordnance Service at the Phoenix Park, Dublin, in 1914 because of his involvement with the Irish Volunteers. He had moved from Dublin to Limerick, where he trained local Volunteers before departing for Germany. A large consignment of arms and ammunition was acquired by Casement and Monteith from the German government, and it was despatched to Ireland on board the *Aud*. The vessel was of 1,400 tonnage and was originally a British ship named *Castro*. It had been seized by the Germans and renamed the *Libau*. As it left German waters it bore the latter name but en route was renamed the *Aud* and given the appearance of a tramp steamer bearing Norwegian identity and relevant papers and loaded with timber. It was under the command of Captain Carl Spindler. The vessel carried 20,000 Russian-made rifles; ten Maxim machine-guns; a quantity of ammunition to suit both weapons; 1,000,000 rounds of ammunition to suit the rifles already brought ashore at Howth in 1914; and a quantity of explosives.

The German government decided to send Casement, Monteith and a Sergeant

Beverley to Ireland on board a submarine. They left the port of Wilhelmshaven on the morning of 12 April, changed to a U.19 submarine at Heligoland and, having experienced very bad weather, reached Tralee Bay on Thursday, 20 April. There was no pilot boat to meet the submarine as was expected, and after cruising around for several hours, the commander of the submarine decided to put Casement, Monteith and Beverley ashore in a small boat. In the early morning of Good Friday, 21 April, they came ashore at Banna Strand. All three were hungry, miserable and wet, and Casement was suffering from diarrhoea. They buried their revolvers, holsters and other items in the sand close to where they had come ashore. Monteith and Beverley decided to leave Casement in a nearby fort while they went to Tralee – a distance of about eight miles – to hire a car to convey Casement to Dublin.

Local residents observed the three men in the vicinity of the beach and a local farmer discovered the boat a short distance out from the shore and, with the help of neighbours, dragged it ashore. (The little boat is on display at Ballyheigue Maritime Museum.) It contained a dagger and other items. Three revolvers were found nearby and a bag containing maps, a flash lamp and a number of other articles. One of the men went to the nearby village of Ardfert and reported the matter at the RIC barracks.

Sergeant Hearn and Constable Reilly cycled to the beach where a large crowd had assembled around the boat. The RIC men returned to barracks to arm themselves and then made a search of the area. Sometime after 1pm they entered an old fort where Casement was hiding and Constable Reilly covered him with his rifle. Casement gave his name as Richard Morton, and told the constable that he was an artist from Buckinghamshire. The sergeant on observing that the legs of Casement's pants were wet arrested him, and they set off for Ardfert barracks on foot. On the way they met a boy driving a pony-trap and the sergeant ordered the boy to take Constable Reilly and the prisoner to Ardfert barracks. A local boy later found a document in code which Casement had dropped and handed it up to the constabulary. It was subsequently submitted as vital evidence at Casement's trial. After examining the documents and evidence from the boat and strand at Ardfert barracks, the sergeant decided to transfer Casement to Tralee. He was taken there by horse and trap and detained overnight at the Tralee RIC headquarters.

Head Constable John Andrew Kearney, in charge of Tralee barracks, who was aware of Roger Casement's international reputation, as well as his debilitating illness at the time, ensured that the prisoner was treated with every humanity and dignity. The head constable took Casement to his private family accommodation, where Mrs Kearney (the head constable's wife) cooked a steak for Casement – even though it was Good Friday. Casement was kept overnight in the kitchen of the barracks rather than in the detention cell, which would have been the routine procedure. While in custody, Casement was visited by a local priest of the Dominican order and by a doctor. He gratefully acknowledged the humane treatment he had received from Head Constable Kearney and the members of the RIC while he was in custody at Tralee RIC barracks.

As a token of his appreciation, he left his watch behind with the Kearney family, but John Kearney returned the watch about six weeks later via George Gavan Duffy, who was defence counsel for Casement.

On Easter Saturday, Casement, without handcuffs, was escorted by the RIC through the streets of Tralee and by train to Dublin. From Dublin he was rushed to Dun Laoghaire and put on board the mail boat. He arrived at Euston Station in London under heavy escort on Easter Sunday morning.

The instructions issued to Captain Spindler, skipper of the *Aud*, were that he was to arrive in Tralee Bay on Good Friday, where he would meet the submarine. A pilot boat would be waiting for him and appropriate lamp signals were agreed upon. The *Aud* left Lubeck on 9 April with its cargo of rifles and ammunition, but no wireless. As it negotiated the west coast of Ireland, there was considerable activity by British naval cruisers. It reached the mouth of Tralee Bay on Holy Thursday night, but there was no sign of a pilot boat or submarine. Having waited for several hours, Captain Spindler displayed his signals, but there was no reply. On Good Friday morning, the *Aud* was boarded by the commander and a party from the British naval cruiser *Shatter 11*. Having checked out the *Aud*, they were entertained to drinks and cigars by Captain Spindler and his crew. The naval personnel, obviously satisfied with the *Aud* and the story given to them by Captain Spindler, allowed the *Aud* to proceed.

The *Aud* remained in Tralee Bay for the greater part of Good Friday and went close to shore on a number of occasions, but there was no sign of a pilot or the expected signals. Some hours after the first encounter with the British cruiser, the cruiser again approached the *Aud*. Captain Spindler, realising that his vessel was probably under suspicion, got up to maximum speed and headed straight out into the Atlantic, where he was stopped and questioned by a British warship the *Bluebell*. He was then ordered by the naval officer of the *Bluebell* to follow the warship to Queenstown, after a warning shot had been fired across the bow of the *Aud*. Realising that he was trapped with all the naval vessels around him, Captain Spindler complied and proceeded around the south coast of Kerry and Cork under escort. As the *Aud* neared Queenstown Harbour, Captain Spindler and his crew donned their German uniforms, raised the German flag and made preparations to scuttle the vessel. When it was about fifteen minutes journey from Queenstown Harbour, the *Aud* was stopped and blown up as Captain Spindler and his crew safely took to their lifeboats. Within minutes, the *Aud* and its consignment of arms had sunk to the seabed. Captain Spindler and his crew were arrested by the British naval escorts.

It later transpired that a message had been sent to Captain Spindler directing him to arrive in Tralee Bay on Easter Sunday rather than on Good Friday, but with no wireless on board he did not receive it. Those in charge of the operation in Kerry expected the *Aud* to arrive in Tralee Bay and the rifles to be unloaded at Fenit pier early on Easter Sunday morning. Controversy still exists about the mix-up in the arrival date. On 18 April, the American Secret Service raided the offices of the German Embassy in New York and discovered the German plans for sending assistance to Ireland. The American authorities passed this information immediately to their British counterparts, which accounts for the heavy concentration of naval cruisers and destroyers off the west coast of Ireland to intercept the suspected vessel. The RIC was not given a major role in the affair and the responsibility for intercepting any vessel carrying arms rested with the British navy. The coastguard stations would in the ordinary course also be on the alert for suspicious vessels close to the coast.

The Easter Rising

Even though he was chief of staff of the Irish Volunteers, it was only during Holy Week of 1916 that Eoin Mac Neill became aware of the decision taken by the Military Council to have an armed insurrection during Easter Week. The Military Council was made up of the most militant leaders of the Volunteers and the IRB, and Mac Neill realised that he had been deceived by the group for some time prior to that. On hearing of Casement's arrest and the capture of the *Aud*, Eoin Mac Neill saw the futility of going ahead with a rising, and on Easter Saturday (22nd) he issued a command – through a network of messengers – to all branches of the Irish Volunteers, directing that no action be taken by the Volunteers in relation to plans made for Easter Sunday. He also inserted a notice in the *Sunday Independent* of Easter Sunday prohibiting all Volunteer movements on that day. The Military Council met on Easter Sunday and decided to go ahead with the Rising on Easter Monday evening, in the full realisation that it would then be confined to Dublin only. The countermanding of the plans made for the involvement of the Irish Volunteers at several centres throughout the country caused much confusion, and Volunteers who had assembled were instructed to return to their homes. As a result, the Easter Rising had little significance outside of Dublin city.

The British authorities were aware that an insurrection had been planned, but in the light of Mac Neill's directions to the Irish Volunteers and the capture of the *Aud* and Roger Casement, the danger of an insurrection had apparently evaporated once Easter Sunday was passed. (Neither was there any trace of any German officers or military personnel whose arrival had been openly expected to assist the Volunteers with their plans for insurrection.) Coded messages with relevant information and instructions were relayed to the RIC members throughout the country who had been alerted in advance of the likelihood of an insurrection. The threat appears to have been taken more seriously in some areas of the country than others, as the precautions to be taken were ultimately left to the discretion of the local RIC authorities acting on local intelligence. In some counties, the smaller RIC barracks were closed down for the week, with the personnel attached to them being moved to reinforce larger centres. Elsewhere no advance precautions were taken.

The Rising in Dublin

In Dublin, the Rising commenced on Easter Monday, 24 April, and several detachments of the military were engaged during the week in putting it down. The members of the DMP were confined to their barracks in the city to secure their buildings against attack. A small number of DMP members were on duty in plain clothes gathering information. Three members of the DMP force were killed during the week. Constable James O'Brien, 168B, who was on duty at the gate of the Upper Castle Yard, was shot dead on Monday. Constable M. Lahiff, 125B, who was on duty at the Grafton Street entrance to Stephen's Green, was shot dead on Monday when he tried to prevent armed insurgents' entering Stephen's Green. Later in the week, Constable W. Frith, 174C, was shot dead by a sniper through one of the windows in Store Street police station. Six members of the DMP were seriously injured. It was rumoured that the RIC depot had been taken over by the Volunteers during the week, but no attempt was in fact made to do so. The depot was highly fortified by the fully armed Reserve and other available staff members. Fifty members of the DMP from the adjoining area took refuge there for the week.

Incidents in County Galway

There were a number of attacks on RIC barracks outside of Dublin city during Easter Week. At 7am on Tuesday morning a party of Volunteers attacked Clarenbridge RIC barracks in County Galway with gunfire and bombs. The attack went on for a number of hours, but the small RIC party of five members held out and only one member of the force was slightly injured. On the same morning, another group of Volunteers laid siege on Oranmore, County Galway, RIC barracks for several hours. Other groups of Volunteers joined in the attack. Reinforcements of RIC and military from Galway arrived and a gun battle took place. The barracks were not taken by the Volunteers, but a small number of RIC members were taken prisoner and later released. The Volunteers withdrew from the scene after a number of hours. Differing accounts were given by the Volunteers and the military of losses sustained in this attack. Also on Tuesday, Volunteers who took up position in a house opposite Athenry RIC barracks and attacked the barracks with gunfire, were forced to retreat after running out of ammunition.

Early on Wednesday morning, a strong force of RIC under District Inspector Heard and some military personnel travelling in motor cars came upon a group of

Volunteers at Cairn More Cross in County Galway and an exchange of gunfire took place. RIC Constable Patrick Whelan was seriously wounded and subsequently died from his injuries. On the same day another exchange of gunfire between Volunteers and RIC members took place at a protection post at the Model Farm, Athenry, but there were no casualties. The vacant RIC barracks at New Inn, County Galway, were entered by Volunteers and documents and records found there burned.

On Thursday, Kinvara RIC barracks was attacked by the Volunteers, but the attack was unsuccessful and after some hours the Volunteers withdrew. On learning on Saturday that the Rising in Dublin had failed, the different units of the Galway Volunteers dispersed.

During the week, a detachment of 100 extra military were landed in Galway and about 200 prominent Sinn Féin members in the county were arrested and sent by mine sweepers moored in the bay to England. In addition to the military support-ing the RIC in County Galway, detachments of RIC from other counties were trans-ferred there. A party of constabulary from as far away as Belfast, under the command of District Inspector Hernden, performed temporary duty in the county in late April and early May 1916. The very high level of activity of the Irish Volun-teers in County Galway during Easter Week could be attributed to their organiser in the county, Liam Mellows, a dedicated and committed republican activist.

County Wexford

At Enniscorthy, County Wexford, the Volunteers assembled on Wednesday of Easter Week and on the following day took over the Athenaeum in Castle Street, where they remained until the following Monday. The RIC were confined to their bar-racks. Although the Volunteers directed sniper fire at the building over a number of days, expecting the police to surrender, they did not do so and the barracks was not captured. One RIC constable was injured during the attacks.

County Kerry

At Firies, between Killarney and Castlemaine, County Kerry, Constables Michael Cleary and Thomas McLoughlin who were engaged in putting up notices declar-ing the proclamation of martial law were shot at and injured.

County Louth

The County Louth Volunteers mobilised on Easter Sunday and set out for Dublin to take part in the Rising. At Ardee they seized a number of rifles and a quantity of ammunition from the local National Volunteers. On Easter Monday, one section marched back towards Dundalk through Castlebellingham, where they blocked the road and stopped and seized motor cars. A small number of unarmed RIC men and military personnel who came on the scene were arrested, lined up along a railing and fired at by the Volunteers. Constable Charles McGee, a very young constable, was murdered and a military officer was wounded. Some of the Volunteers reached Dublin and took part in the Rising.

County Dublin

On Wednesday of Easter Week, the RIC barracks at Swords and Donabate came under attack from the north County Dublin Volunteers under the leadership of a Kerry-born schoolteacher, Thomas Ashe. No shooting took place at Swords, but at Donabate the RIC returned the fire before they were forced to surrender. The few constables at each of the barracks were disarmed and their firearms taken by the Volunteers. On 27 April, the Volunteers raided the unoccupied barracks at Garristown, but there were no firearms or ammunition in that building.

The "Battle of Ashbourne", County Meath

The same group of Volunteers, numbering forty-five in all, under the command of Thomas Ashe with Richard Mulcahy (later general) second in command, travelled on bicycles to Ashbourne, County Meath, on Friday and laid siege on the RIC barracks there close to the crossroads on the Dublin/Slane road. The constabulary had erected a barricade in front of the barracks and replied with rifle fire when called on to surrender. The Volunteers took up positions at strategic locations around the barracks and attacked the building with gunfire and grenades. There was a prolonged battle and eventually the constabulary indicated that they intended to surrender. As this was about to happen, RIC reinforcements under County Inspector Alexander Gray arrived on the scene in motor cars from Slane. Intelligence reports had been received by the RIC that Thomas Ashe and his party of Volunteers were heading for Ashbourne, but arrived too late for the reinforcements to reach there before the start of the siege.

The battle recommenced with greater ferocity than before. The RIC personnel arriving on the scene drove straight into an ambush. The RIC under County Inspector Gray were totally surrounded by the Volunteers, who were under good cover in their positions. Six rank-and-file members of the RIC – Sergeants Young and Shanaher, Constables McHale, Gormley, Hickey and Clery – and District Inspector Henry Smyth were killed. County Inspector Alexander Gray was mortally wounded. (In the late 1880s, County Inspector Gray had become notorious as a district inspector in the Dingle Peninsula arising from his ongoing confrontations with the Irish National League, during which period he was known as "Baby Gray".) Several other constables were seriously injured in the ambush.

Two of the Volunteers were killed and five were injured. The RIC unit fought bravely but eventually surrendered when their supply of ammunition was exhausted. The Volunteers seized all the firearms as well as the ammunition of the dead and wounded members of the RIC. The event, commonly referred to as the "Battle of Ashbourne", was the most serious incident of the Rising outside of Dublin, with great loss of life to the RIC. This was the first major loss of life sustained by the Royal Irish Constabulary in one incident.

Fatal Shooting of Two Members of the RIC at Tipperary

On 25 April, a few days after the Rising, a search was being carried out by the RIC for a Tipperary Volunteer named Michael O'Callaghan, arising from an incident near Tipperary town on Easter Monday. Sergeant Thomas O'Rourke and Constable John Hurley went to the home of Peter Hennessy, a relation of Michael O'Callaghan, at Moanrour, Kilross, outside Tipperary town. The sergeant and constable entered the kitchen and Sergeant O'Rourke told Michael O'Callaghan that he was arresting him. O'Callaghan, who had a loaded revolver in his possession, instantly shot Sergeant O'Rourke dead, and before Constable Hurley had time to draw his revolver, he too was shot dead in the kitchen by O'Callaghan. O'Callaghan made his escape from Hennessy's house and went to America shortly afterwards.

The Resistance by the Kents at Castlelyons, County Cork

The final event in the Easter Rising series took place on 2 May 1916 at the home of the Kent family at Bawnard House, Castlelyons, near Fermoy, County Cork, when the house was surrounded by a large detachment of military and RIC The Kent family had been very prominent in nationalist activities since 1913 and its members were amongst the first to join the Volunteers. Thomas Kent was a leader in the Volunteer movement and his three brothers, Richard, David and William, hoarded ammunition and firearms at their home in anticipation of the Easter Rising. Some of the brothers had not been staying in the family home for some time, but they were all at home on the night of 1 May. When Head Constable William Rowe announced to the family that they had come to arrest some of them, Thomas Kent replied that they were soldiers of the Irish Republic and were not prepared to surrender. The Kent brothers took up separate firing positions within the house, while their eighty-year-old mother distributed ammunition to them and helped at reloading their guns. In the gun battle, Head Constable Rowe was shot dead and other members of the RIC and military were wounded. David Kent was also seriously wounded. When the Kents' ammunition supply ran out, Richard Kent, who was an athlete, made a run for safety from the house but was mortally wounded as he did so. Thomas and William were taken in handcuffs in military custody to Fermoy. David and Richard were taken to a military hospital and Richard succumbed to his injuries a few days later. Thomas and William were later court-martialled. William was acquitted and Thomas was sentenced to death and executed on 9 May. David was later tried and sentenced to death, but the penalty was subsequently commuted to penal servitude for life and he was released from custody in 1917. William Kent later served as a member of Dáil Éireann for several years.

Eamon Ceannt, and the RIC Connection

One of the signatories of the "Proclamation of the Irish Republic" in the Easter Rising of 1916 was Eamon Ceannt. He was born in 1881 in the RIC barracks at Ballymoe, County Galway, where his father was a head constable. His father moved on transfer to Dublin, and Eamon attended O'Connell Schools and later University College. He was employed as assistant treasurer with Dublin Corporation. He was gifted with a brilliant intellect and at a very early age developed a love for the Irish language. When he got married in 1905 he insisted that his marriage ceremony should be conducted solely in Irish. He joined the Gaelic League and remained a staunch member until his death. He also became fluent in French and German. He learned to play the bagpipes at an early age and became very proficient. At an athletic meeting in Rome in 1908, which had been arranged to celebrate the Papal Jubilee, he led the Irish athletes on to the field with his bagpipes. He was invited to the Vatican on the following day to entertain Pope Pius X, and turned up dressed in his full kilted uniform. A most imposing figure when wearing his kilt, as he was exceptionally tall and athletic in appearance, he caused something of a sensation as he entered St Peters Square and the Vatican, playing Irish airs on his bagpipes. He also entertained a number of Irish priests who were studying for the priesthood in Rome at the time.

His political views were socialist and he was very critical of Sinn Féin for not backing Jim Larkin or supporting the cause of Irish trade unionism. He immersed himself wholeheartedly in any cause which he believed to be just – particularly the Irish language, his support for the working classes and Irish nationalism. His strongly held ideals led him to his involvement in the 1916 Rising and subsequent execution. During the Rising and his subsequent court martial he bore himself with dignity and pride, and in a letter which he wrote after being sentenced to death he said, "I leave for the guidance of other revolutionaries, who may tread the path which I have trod, this advice, never to treat with the enemy; never to surrender at his mercy; but to fight to the finish."

Eamon Ceannt was executed on 8 May 1916 by firing squad. The RIC barracks where he was born is now the Garda Síochána station for the locality. On 8 May 1966 – on the fiftieth anniversary of his execution – the commissioner of the Garda Síochána, William P. Quinn, unveiled a fine plaque on the building, commemorating the birthplace of the RIC head constable's son and 1916 revolutionary.

The Aftermath of the Easter Rising

There was very little sympathy or support for the Easter Rising or for those who brought it about. In parts of Dublin city, the Volunteers who had taken part in the Rising were jeered by onlookers as they were marched through the streets in custody. In the greater part of Ireland outside of Dublin there was indifference to the action taken by the Irish Volunteers. The total casualties of the Rising were approximately 450 people killed and 2,600 wounded. Of those killed, 132 were members of the police and military, as were 397 of the total wounded. Total damage to property amounted to £3,000,000; 3,500 persons were arrested, of whom 1,840 were deported to England for internment there. The total number of RIC men who lost their lives during Easter Week and immediately afterwards was twelve, including one county inspector, one district inspector and one head constable. Lieutenant-General Sir John Maxwell, who was in over-all control of military affairs in Ireland, dictated the manner in which the Rising was to be brought under control and how those arrested in connection with it should be dealt with.

Courts martial commenced immediately the Rising was over. The issue of the *Irish Independent* covering the period (26 April to 4 May 1916) carried an "Official Notice":

> Revolutionary Leaders. Three Tried and Shot – Pearse, Clarke and McDonagh. Three signatories of the notice proclaiming the Irish Republic, P.H. Pearse, T. McDonagh and T.J. Clarke, have been tried by Field General Court Martial and sentenced to death. The sentence having been duly confirmed, the three above-mentioned men were shot this [Wednesday] morning. The trial of further prisoners is proceeding.

These three executions were followed by another twelve, in twos and threes, up to 12 May. Pleas for clemency were made to the British government by Irish leaders, the most notable being by John Dillon to a hostile House of Commons when he said: "I am proud of these men. I am proud of their courage; it is not murderers who are being executed, it is insurgents who have fought a clean fight, a brave fight, however misguided." John Dillon also prophesied that the British government was "letting loose a river of blood by executing these men". Pleas for leniency fell on deaf ears. General Maxwell felt strongly that an example should be made of them. In all, ninety were condemned to death as a result of the Rising, but seventy-five of these sentences were commuted to penal servitude for life. While the population at large had not supported the Easter Rising, the execution of the fifteen leaders resulted in their being immediately regarded as martyrs and caused outrage, anger and indignation amongst the majority of the Irish people.

RIC Reports on the Easter Rising

That the feelings of the people were manifest in many ways is particularly reflected in the following synopsis of confidential reports submitted to Dublin Castle by the Royal Irish Constabulary from each county following the Rising.

The county inspectors for Wicklow and Leitrim reported that the people in their counties had no sympathy with the rebels. There was no activity in either county related to the Rising.

The county inspectors for Armagh, Cavan, Kildare and Kilkenny reported that there was a marked falling off of recruits for the British army as a result of the Rising. The county inspectors for Antrim, Carlow, Clare, Donegal, Down, Fermanagh, Londonderry, Monaghan, Longford, Kilkenny, Limerick, Cork West Riding, Tipperary North and South Ridings, Roscommon, Mayo, Sligo and Waterford reported that there had been no interest by the people of those counties prior to the Rising; that there was no activity or participation by people from their counties in the event; but, that there was now much sympathy for the rebels after the executions, and disloyalty and resentment were evident towards the British government.

The acting county inspector for Meath submitted a lengthy report, outlining in detail the tragic events which had taken place at Ashbourne and which had resulted in the death of County Inspector Alexander Gray and District Inspector Smyth and six members of the constabulary.

The county inspector for Louth reported on fifty armed men marching out of Dundalk on Easter Sunday, picking up various contingents along the way and seizing rifles and ammunition belonging to the National Volunteers at Ardee. He outlined the activities of the group on Easter Monday when they returned via Collon, Dunleer and Castlebellingham, and fatally wounded young Constable Charles McGee and seriously wounded a military officer, Lieutenant Dunville.

The county inspector for Tyrone gave details of the activities of Dr McCartan, dispensary doctor at Gortin, and three Catholic curates. On 22 April, 140 Sinn Féiners assembled at Coalisland, but dispersed later and hid their arms and ammunition. He added:

> When the news of the Rebellion reached Tyrone, and for a few days
> after, the feeling amongst Nationalists generally was one of

condemnation, not from patriotic motives or the injury done to the Empire, but because it was thought that the action of the Sinn Féiners has seriously damaged the cause of Home Rule. Then came the visit of the British Prime Minister to Ireland, his statement in the House of Commons, the announcement that Home Rule must be immediately granted, followed by Mr Dillon's speech in the house, eulogising the rebels, and finally the letters from the Bishop of Limerick. These things changed the whole feeling of the people. The Sinn Féiners from being objects of contempt and derision became heroes. The punishment of the rebels accentuated the ill-feeling.

The county inspector for King's County (County Offaly) reported on an unusual incident which had occurred prior to the Rising relating to a serious clash in Tullamore between the Sinn Féin members and the wives of the British army billeted in the town. Some Sinn Féin members had to be escorted by the RIC to a meeting held in the Sinn Féin Rooms. Shots were then fired from the windows of the Sinn Féin building into the crowd of protesting women and children outside. When the constabulary went to the Sinn Féin headquarters to seize the weapons held by them in the building, the constabulary were fired on, and the county inspector and Sergeant Ahern were lucky to escape without injury.

The report for County Kerry detailed the arrest of Roger Casement and the interception of the *Aud* on Good Friday in Tralee Bay. It also stated that more than 300 Volunteers had mobilised in Tralee on Easter Sunday to bring the rifles and ammunition ashore from the *Aud* at Fenit Pier. On hearing of Casement's arrest and the interception of the *Aud*, they all dispersed and returned to their homes on Easter Monday.

The county inspector at Wexford detailed the events in his county during the week. Train services had been suspended in the county and trade had suffered generally. At Enniscorthy and Ferns, goods, motor cars and firearms were commandeered by the rebels. His report included an aspect not referred to from other parts of the country, to the effect that "large numbers of people assembled under arms to assist the police in the towns of Wexford, New Ross and Gorey".

The report for Cork East Riding detailed the events at Bawnard House and the murder of Head Constable Rowe. A few other minor incidents were recorded, but apart from that, there was little other activity in the district and none in Cork city itself.

The report for County Dublin gave details of the attacks made on the RIC barracks at the northern side of the county and the theft of a quantity of dynamite from a quarry near Brittas. A railway bridge on the Northern Railway near Donabate had been blown up by the rebels. The county inspector reported that the Sinn Féin movement attracted many sympathisers after the rebellion, especially young members of the Catholic clergy. He also adverted to the fact that recruiting for the British army had been badly affected.

There were many incidents in County Galway during Easter Week, including the death of a constable. Some were of a very serious nature and many of a minor nature. Details of these were given in the reports submitted by the county inspectors for Galway West Riding and Galway East Riding. In addition to attacks on the different RIC barracks, attempts were made to blow up bridges, railway lines were torn up and telegraph wires pulled down. During the attack on Clarenbridge barracks, the local parish priest, Fr J. Tully, called to the RIC barracks twice asking the party there to surrender, but they refused to do so. The county inspector for Galway West reported that on Easter Monday night, Sinn Féiners took over Athenry town hall for bomb-making. When the Volunteers from west and east Galway joined forces towards the end of the week, the RIC estimated their total number at 1,000. They then dispersed in groups, leaving behind the five RIC constables whom they had earlier taken as hostages and who to the credit of the Volunteers, were unharmed.

Increased Support for Sinn Féin

Following the 1916 executions there was a considerable increase in support for Sinn Féin. Young men who prior to 1916 would never have thought of joining a Sinn Féin club queued up to join later in 1916 and 1917 during the huge swell of sympathy and anger which followed the executions after Easter week. While they may not have all been prepared to die for Ireland, they were emotionally attracted to Sinn Féin, and it was a disciplined organisation which provided good leadership. It also provided an opportunity for excitement for healthy young men. Apart from participating in the national games, there were few other pastimes available to them. There was a considerable decrease in the number of men who wished to join the British army, which was still deeply involved in the Great War. When several hundred of the prisoners arrested after the Rising, who had never in fact been charged with any crime or offence, were released from detention at Christmas 1916, there were tremendous celebrations. Their welcome home as heroes to tumultuous receptions everywhere provided a further boost to the Sinn Féin recruiting campaign.

In 1917 four by-elections took place, all of which were contested by Sinn Féin candidates. Eamon de Valera, who had been convicted and sentenced to death for his part in the Easter Rising and later had his sentence commuted to penal servitude, won the County Clare by-election. William T. Cosgrave, who also took part in the 1916 Rising and was condemned to death but had his sentence commuted, was elected in Kilkenny. Count Plunkett, father of Joseph Mary Plunkett, who was executed in 1916, won the Roscommon by-election, and J. McGuinness was victorious in Longford. These victories for Sinn Féin strengthened the political platform for the movement, generating more publicity for its existence and aims, and created a certain amount of panic for the British government. The election results reflected the nationalist feelings of the community at that time.

Thomas Ashe, who had led the north Dublin Volunteers' raids on the RIC barracks in north County Dublin and at Ashbourne, County Meath, was arrested following the Rising, court-martialled and sentenced to death. The sentence was later commuted to penal servitude. He served his sentence in different English prisons and was released in 1917 on the eve of the Clare by-election. Ashe was a charismatic individual. He was a native of Kinard, Lispole, County Kerry, and was a primary schoolteacher at Corduff in County Dublin. He founded the Black Raven Pipe Band and was prominent in the Gaelic League and Gaelic Athletic Association before joining the Volunteers and IRB. Following his release he gave an address at the Roger Casement anniversary commemoration.

A few days later he made a speech at Ballinalee, County Longford, which was reported on by the RIC. As a result of that speech he was again arrested, sentenced to two months' imprisonment and was lodged in Mountjoy Gaol. While in prison, he rebelled against the prison regime, was deprived of benefits and went on hunger strike. After a few days he was removed to the nearby Mater Hospital where he choked to death while being forcibly fed. His body lay in state with a guard-of-honour for four days in the Mater Hospital and later in the Dublin City Hall. Thousands of people formed a steady stream of mourners as they paid their respects. His funeral through Dublin city was one of the biggest and most impressive manifestations of nationalist sympathy ever witnessed. He was buried in Glasnevin Cemetery, and the oration at his graveside was given by Michael Collins. The circumstances of Thomas Ashe's tragic death proved to be one of the greatest boosts for the cause of Sinn Féin and the other nationalist organisations. He was looked upon as a hero after the attack on Ashbourne barracks and his subsequent imprisonment. The particular circumstances of his death aroused nationalist feelings and anger, probably on an even greater scale than the executions after the 1916 rebellion. He was regarded as a martyr.

Michael Collins was born at Woodfield, Clonakilty, County Cork, in 1890, and in 1906 commenced work in the London Post Office. In London he was sworn into the Irish Republican Brotherhood by Sam Maguire, a Protestant and a native of Dunmanway, County Cork, whose memory is now commemorated with the All-Ireland Sam Maguire Cup for Gaelic football. Collins returned to Ireland and took part in the 1916 Rising and was later imprisoned. This was his first high-profile appearance. He was destined to become one of the principal leaders in the military and political life of Ireland over the following five years.

Another important event occurred on 25 October 1917 at the Sinn Féin Ard Fheis, when the IRB and the Volunteers came together with Sinn Féin. A common policy was agreed upon between all three. Arthur Griffith stood down as leader of Sinn Féin and Eamon de Valera was unanimously elected president of the organisation. On the following day at the annual Volunteer convention, he was elected president of the Volunteers. Cathal Brugha became chief of staff of the Volunteers and Michael Collins was appointed director of organisation. There was a strong IRB presence in Sinn Féin and the Volunteers.

Sinn Féin had by this time become a powerful organisation, and before the end of 1918 had approximately 1,500 Sinn Féin Clubs all over Ireland, despite its suppression in the meantime. The Volunteers were unarmed, but they were kept together and moulded into a disciplined organisation through regular meetings, marching, drilling and parading. They were employed marshalling crowds during the 1917 by-election campaigns and at other nationalist activities. In rural parts of Ireland, Sinn Féin and the Volunteers became active in the division of farms and estates owned by absentee landlords and farmers and encouraged local smallholders to plough the lands and sow crops. There were occasional confrontations between those involved and the RIC but none of a very serious nature.

The Role of the RIC from 1916 to 1918

From the Easter Rising until January 1919, no member of the RIC was killed on duty, but there were a small number of incidents where they sustained personal injuries. Following the Rising, an assessment was made of the overall policing situation in the country. The security at barracks was reviewed and tightened up, with all doors being barred and secured at night. Telephones were installed in many of the barracks which did not have that facility. A small number of barracks were closed down, and by the end of 1918 a total of about 1,200 barracks were occupied by approximately 10,000 members of the force.

The constabulary carried on with their normal policing duties as they had done prior to 1916. In many counties, they experienced no difficulties and they continued to patrol and perform outdoor duties unarmed during daylight hours. In some areas they went about in armed groups of twos or threes during night duties. Immediately following the Rising, the inspector general issued a very specific instruction to the RIC that they were to carry their revolvers at all times while on duty, even in barracks. The members knew that the firearms held by them were the prime targets of their local nationalist activists who might attack them for the guns they carried.

On 3 May 1918, Sean Treacy, who was in charge of the south Tipperary Volunteers, issued the following instructions relating to proposed attacks on barracks in County Tipperary:

I don't think it possible to do anything about Tipperary military barracks, except to try and keep them inside. Barricade all roads leading to the town with felled trees. Build stone walls across roads. Smash down bridges. Burn station house at Tipperary and destroy railway, wires etc. Make all approaches to the town impassable. Snipe barracks from surrounding hills with rifles and shotguns. Soak sods of turf with petrol, oil or tar and throw them lighting on the huts to set them ablaze. Hit the enemy every way you can. The companies at Donohill and Solohead should be responsible for Limerick Junction RIC barracks and railway. Tear up rails, cut wires. Smash down Junction bridge, or use gelignite if procurable. Destroy signal cabin. And also at Grange crossing, Donaskeigh co-operate with Golden. Mount Bruis company to be responsible for Lisvernane and Glenbane RIC barracks and co-operate with Galbally. Bansha to be responsible for Bansha RIC barracks. All other companies to be responsible for their respective RIC barracks, if any. The gunmen under cover should cover the windows while stormers smash in the doors. Take the enemy by surprise. Hit first and don't let him hit you. Burn barracks. Use gelignite bombs if procurable. Show no mercy to resisters.

On 10 January 1919, Treacy sent further instructions to the officer in charge of each battalion of South Tipperary Brigade:

You will have all barracks, Police and Military, in your areas examined and watched with a view to raiding them. some of the points to remember are:

1. Number of men in all barracks – number who sleep in and are in at different times – Number who go out on patrol, to church, on outside duty etc. 2. Time of leaving on Patrol. Routes taken and time of Return. 3 Precautions taken at night in opening doors. (Send someone to try.) 4. Where arms are kept. If kept loaded. 5 Position of telephone and telegraph wires to barracks or local Post Office. 6. Best way and time to take barracks by surprise. Have reports covering all above-mentioned points and any others you may think necessary, sent in to Brigade H. Qrs by Sunday 19th June next.

Following the Easter Rising, there was a marked difference in the mood of the people towards the force, a coldness, but having lived with this attitude towards them through the 1880s, they felt that they could do so again. As the nationalist movements progressed in 1917 and into 1918, the atmosphere gradually got worse. While the members would not agree that the attitude of the people to them amounted to hostility, they conceded that it was at least "uncivil" in nature. Many people were still glad to avail of the assistance which they had always received from the Royal Irish Constabulary in helping them to fill up forms and to assist them with applications for pensions etc. There was no diminution in the services which they had always given to the public. The situation was not helped by the attitude of the government which believed that it could contain the situation against the escalating level of nationalism. Those actively involved in Sinn Féin, the IRB or Volunteers were treated with suspicion and were arrested and charged with offences which at times appeared to be trivial. There were numerous arrests and summonses for illegal drilling.

Those charged at the petty sessions turned their backs to the Bench, surreptitiously smoked cigarettes during the proceedings and were generally disrespectful to the court. They invariably informed the magistrates that they were soldiers of the Irish Republic. Their attitude usually earned them a two months' sentence of imprisonment and being then bound over to keep the peace. Escorting them to prison took up a lot of police time, and the whole affair would make heroes of the defendants in the episode.

The *Irish Independent* of 27 November 1917 carried a report under the heading "Constable Hands in Gun" relating to the dismissal of a Constable Thomas O'Leary, who was attached to Cloontumper police hut near Claremorris, County Mayo. It was alleged that he was recently found to be in breach of RIC regulations regarding the collection of agricultural statistics and was due to be dismissed. He wrote a letter to his authorities, stating that his sympathies were with Sinn Féin and the executed leaders of Easter Week and saying that he could not serve two masters. He was dismissed from the force and the local Sinn Féin group arranged a farewell party for him.

Rumours of a "German Plot" involving IRB and Sinn Féin leaders circulated in mid–1918. Many of the principal leaders including de Valera and Arthur Griffith were rounded up and taken to England where they were interned without trial until the early part of 1919. In furtherance of the policy adopted against militant nationalist activists following 1916, the total of house searches carried out by the RIC during the years 1917, 1918 and 1919 numbered 12,589. Every action taken by the constabulary against the nationalist leaders was resented by the majority of the people and aggravated the worsening situation.

Some members of the RIC found it difficult to comprehend their exact role. While they were arresting and prosecuting members of Sinn Féin for illegal drilling and carrying out searches for firearms, explosives and seditious literature on a daily basis, there were Sinn Féin processions carrying Republican flags and a Sinn Féin parliament meeting in Dublin. With the law of the land being openly brought into contempt and the position and standing of the RIC deteriorating rapidly, it was surprising that the events of the time did not sap the morale of the force.

Very specific instructions were issued to the force regarding the action to be taken by them in the event of a landing being made by German troops in the country. It was instructed to evacuate all residents within a twenty mile radius of such landing and to destroy all crops within that area pending the arrival of military reinforcements. The arrangements made to deal with this eventuality were always regarded with light-hearted humour by the members, and of course it never happened.

Resident Magistrate C.P. Crane, who had a passionate love for and interest in Ireland where he had lived for forty years, observed in *Memories of a Resident Magistrate* on his return to Ireland in June 1918 after three years war service:

> What a change one found on all sides. The old Ireland of previous days seemed to have disappeared. The beauty of the hills alone remained as a memory of past times. A sulky, anti-British spirit prevailed all over the country. The rates had risen. Prices for all necessaries of life had gone up, and though the farmers and prosperous traders in the towns were living in affluence, there was widespread discontent on the part of the earning class, and Sinn Féin with its futility was rapidly sapping the vital energies which go to making healthy life. Numbers of young men who ought to have been in the army doing service for their country loafed about the corners of the streets, feeding their fertile imaginations on the past wrongs of Ireland, grasping at every straw as an excuse for not doing their duty to their country.
>
> For the Irish people generally, all through my forty years of experience in the country, I have always felt the deepest and most true affection. But for Irish politics and Irish politicians I could feel nothing but the most profound contempt, touched with indignation. And what made all this so much more hateful to an Englishman was the feeling that the degradation of Ireland was in a great measure due to his own countrymen. For there is no use blinking the fact that it was owing to the party politics of the British and to the want of any real knowledge on the part of the British administration that Ireland had been allowed to slip downhill. I say want of real knowledge, for I cannot believe that any responsible person with a real knowledge of the conditions prevailing in Ireland would have been content to allow events to proceed as they did during these years.

Bad publicity for the RIC resulted from the shooting dead of a man named Daniel Scanlon by an RIC member at Ballybunion, County Kerry, in July 1917. A large noisy group of people marched through the streets in Ballybunion celebrating de Valera's victory in the Clare by-election – just across the Shannon from

Ballybunion. The marchers assembled outside the RIC barracks and attacked it with stones, breaking most of the windows. Members of the RIC within the barracks became fearful for their lives and fired a number of shots to frighten off the attackers. Daniel Scanlon, who was an innocent spectator, was unfortunately hit by one of the constabulary bullets and killed. Another event which created ill-feeling occurred at Listowel Races on 10 October 1917 when a simple altercation between the constabulary and a number of people developed into a full-scale riot. The RIC fired shots to quell the disturbance and one person was seriously wounded.

The Campaign Against Conscription and the 1918 Elections

Early in 1918, the war was going very much against England, the English forces were badly depleted and replacements were needed. Conscription was already in operation in England. Sir Henry Wilson, chief of the imperial general staff and a native of County Longford, convinced the British cabinet that conscription should be extended to Ireland, where many young men were unemployed and could not emigrate. In April 1918 legislation was passed to enforce conscription in Ireland. The Irish Parliamentary Party in the House of Commons strongly opposed the measure, despite Lloyd George's promise to the party of the early reintroduction of Home Rule. The party, under John Dillon, who had taken over the leadership of the party following the death of John Redmond in March of that year, withdrew from Westminster and organised resistance to the proposed conscription measures. There was immediate and outright opposition to conscription by everybody, with the exception of the Ulster Unionists. Sinn Féin launched a comprehensive campaign in opposition to it, and at a conference held in the Mansion House in Dublin, Sinn Féin, Labour and a number of other organisations drew up an anti-conscription pledge which undertook to resist conscription by the most effective means at their disposal. The Catholic hierarchy also condemned the proposed conscription measures.

The day fixed for signing the pledge was 21 April and a one-day strike was organised for 23 April. Faced with the outright opposition to the measure by the majority of the people and by the Volunteers, who numbered in excess of 100,000 at this time, the British government backed down and the order bringing the measure into operation was never signed. Sinn Féin got more than its fair share of the credit from the Irish people for the success of the anti-conscription campaign. Considering the political and nationalist climate prevailing at the time, the proposed introduction of conscription was politically ill-conceived. Some members of the RIC and DMP opposed the introduction of conscription and a small number of RIC constables resigned as a protest in 1918. In *Memoirs of Constable Jeremiah Mee, RIC,* edited by Fr J. Anthony Gaughan, the editor refers to these resignations:

The national campaign against conscription, caused a number of resignations from the RIC. For instance on 24th April 1918, John P. Lydon (1887–1974), Hugh O'Donnell (1892–1973) and William Riordan (1895–) tendered their resignations in protest against the attempt by the British authorities to impose conscription in Ireland. The reaction of the authorities to this development indicated how serious they regarded it to be. At 2 a.m. on the following morning the three constables were replaced at Murrisk, County Mayo, by three others and were taken under arrest to the County Headquarters at Castlebar, where they were held for three days before being released. (Information from William Riordan.) One of the other constables who resigned from the RIC at this time in protest against the proposal to impose conscription on Ireland was Denis Tuohy, of Kenmare, County Kerry. On May 1st 1921 he was arrested by the Crown Forces, taken to a temporary prison in Kenmare and, while there, assassinated. On May 11th an official statement was issued to the effect that Tuohy had been shot while "attempting to escape".

While Sinn Féin was at the zenith of its popularity following its successful campaign against conscription, a general election was fixed for December 1918. Earlier in the year, legislation had been enacted which substantially increased the number of persons entitled to vote – from a figure of just over 700,000 in 1910 to almost two million voters in 1918 – as a result of the franchise's being separated from property ownership. Sinn Féin, who had seven outgoing seats, put forward a big number of candidates. The party promised not to take their seats in Westminster, but to set up an Irish government in Dublin, to be known as Dáil Éireann. Before the general election, the Irish Parliamentary Party had seventy-eight seats in the House of Commons, but after the election it was reduced to six seats. Sinn Féin ended up holding seventy-three seats, making a nett gain of sixty-six. Twenty-five of the seats gained by Sinn Féin were uncontested. The party received more than 47 per cent of the votes cast. Twenty-six Unionists were returned in the election, twenty-three from north-east Ulster. Sinn Féin was surprised at the extent of its own electoral success. More than half the candidates put forward by Sinn Féin for election were either in prison or on the run, which proved to be more of an asset than a hindrance to them, as they received a huge sympathy vote.

The First Attack on an RIC Barracks since 1916

On Saturday night, 13 April 1918, the first attack on a RIC barracks in Ireland since 1916 took place at Gortatlea, County Kerry, about five miles from Tralee and a short distance off the main Tralee/Killarney road. The Ballymacelligott company of the Irish Volunteers, under Captain Tom McEllistrim, decided to raid the barracks to obtain arms for the purpose of resisting conscription while two members of the RIC party were out on their usual night patrol. There were seven Volunteers in all in the raiding party and they had their faces masked. Two of the Volunteers had shotguns, two had batons and Tom McEllistrim had a revolver. A Volunteer monitoring the activities of the RIC party from the nearby railway line saw Sergeant Martin Boyle, who was in charge of the barracks, and Constable Patrick Fallon leaving the barracks on their patrol. He then passed the information to the raiding party, who went to the barracks at 10.25pm and found the door locked and secured. After knocking at the door, one of the Volunteers convinced the constable on duty in the barracks that the caller was a friend and the door was opened. The raiders burst in and, after a fierce hand to hand struggle, overpowered Constables John Considine and Michael Denning. Considine was injured in the attack. The constables were placed facing the wall with their hands up while some of the raiders collected firearms and ammunition in the barracks.

One of the Volunteers, suddenly realising that Sergeant Boyle and Constable Fallon had returned and were outside the building, shouted at his colleagues to fire. Sergeant Boyle, armed with a pistol, and Constable Fallon with a carbine, exchanged gunfire with the Volunteers who were inside. One of the Volunteer raiders, James Browne, was shot through the temple and killed instantly as he stood guard over the two constables in the barracks with a shotgun. Richard Laide, another of the Volunteers, was badly wounded and died from his injuries on the following day. Apart from Constable Considine who was injured in the first attack, none of the other RIC men were injured. Five raiders escaped, leaving their dead and injured colleagues behind. The funerals of both Volunteers were attended by large crowds a few days later and generated a lot of local sympathy.

The members of the RIC party were transferred elsewhere shortly after, but it became known to the Volunteers that Sergeant Boyle and Constable Fallon would be in Tralee on 14 June 1918 to give evidence in a court case. The survivors of the raid on the barracks made elaborate plans to shoot Sergeant Boyle and Constable Fallon as they walked from Tralee Courthouse. The would-be attackers waited in a public house for word that the RIC men were leaving the court. Both RIC men passed along the far side of the street and two Volunteers ran across the street carrying shotguns. As they did so, somebody shouted to the RIC men to watch out. They turned around and threw themselves on the ground. Fallon was hit with a shotgun blast in the back, but the shots fired at Sergeant Boyle missed. The street was crowded with people and the attackers then fled. Arrests were made after the shooting but those who had actually taken part were not arrested. The buckshot was removed from Constable Fallon's wound and he made a full recovery and was later promoted to sergeant. Sergeant Boyle was not injured and was awarded the King's Police Medal. He was later promoted to head constable. Constables Fallon, Considine and Denning were later awarded the Constabulary Medal for valour.

The raid on Gortatlea RIC barracks heralded a new and dangerous approach by the Volunteers. It was the first organised attack on an RIC barracks since Easter Week 1916 and signalled the start of a series of attacks on RIC barracks. It became clear that the Volunteers were making a determined effort to secure arms and the rural RIC barracks were regarded as soft targets. A short while after the attack on Gortatlea. the isolated barracks at Eyeries in the Beara Peninsula, west Cork, was raided while temporarily vacant and four police rifles and ammunition was taken.

Reaction by the RIC to Attacks

The Gortatlea attack sent a very ominous message to members of the Royal Irish Constabulary: what had happened there could again happen at any time. There was a further review of barrack security. Doors were reinforced with bars and heavy steel shuttering with small apertures through which rifles or carbines could protrude were fitted to the ground floor windows of barracks. This work went on in the latter part of 1918 and through 1919, until many barracks in Ireland became virtual fortresses. Full sandbags were distributed to the smaller country barracks to form a barricade around the doorway. Wire mesh was also put in place around barracks to prevent grenades striking the buildings. All barrack doors were firmly secured during the hours of darkness and passwords were used by members of the force to gain admission. Members no longer patrolled on their own and again resorted to carrying firearms, particularly at night. There was gradual withdrawal of patrols from remote country areas, and through 1919 a policy existed of closing more country barracks in rural locations. This left large stretches of rural areas unpoliced and allowed Sinn Féin and the Volunteers to march and drill without much risk of detection in remote areas. Naturally, the level of intelligence available to the RIC also declined.

First Meeting of Dáil Éireann in 1919

The Sinn Féin representatives elected in the December election of 1918 met at the first meeting of Dáil Éireann at the Mansion House in Dublin on 21 January 1919. Elected members of the Unionist and Irish Parliamentary parties refused to attend. A total of only twenty-eight elected members of Sinn Féin attended, because the remainder were either in prison or on the run. The meeting lasted for two hours, and much business was transacted under the chairmanship of Cathal Brugha. It confirmed the continuity of the objectives of the Easter Week insurgents and ratified the setting up of an Irish Republic. It also approved a provisional constitution, sanctioned the transmission of a message to all the free nations of the world and endorsed a declaration of independence. It also appointed delegates to attend the forthcoming Peace Conference to be held at Versailles in France. Though the attendance was small, the meeting was an historic one.

In the following month, Eamon de Valera escaped from Brixton Prison and returned safely to Ireland. Due to a serious outbreak of influenza in England in March 1919, the British authorities released most of the Irish prisoners then being held in English prisons and detention centres. This provided another opportunity for large gatherings and welcome-home ceremonies for the prisoners, who were hailed as heroes.

The second session of Dáil Éireann took place on 1 April and it was attended by fifty-two elected representatives. Eamon de Valera was elected president, and he appointed a cabinet of eight, all of whom had been involved in nationalist affairs for a number of years. De Valera went to America two months later to raise funds and to win recognition for the Irish Republic and did not return until the end of 1920. He raised one million pounds in the USA, and Michael Collins, who was minister for finance, raised £350,000 in Ireland by way of a Dáil loan. The Dáil initiated many measures and developments until it was suppressed and declared an illegal body in September 1919. After that, it rarely met and then only in secret. Its plans and policies were being implemented insofar as they could be by the cabinet ministers appointed by de Valera.

Murder of Two RIC Constables

On the first day – 21 January 1919 – that Dáil Éireann met at the Mansion House in Dublin, two RIC constables were shot dead at Soloheadbeg, near Limerick Junction in County Tipperary. Explosives were tightly controlled over this period due to the unrest in the country and the gelignite for use in the large stone quarry at Soloheadbeg was stored at Tipperary military barracks. The explosives were conveyed by a horse and cart with a driver and attendant who were county council employees. Armed protection was provided by two members of the RIC travelling on foot alongside. The RIC members escorting the hundredweight of gelignite (112 lbs) on the morning of 21 January were Constables James McDonnell and Patrick O'Connell from Tipperary town. Constable McDonnell was in his mid-fifties and was a widower with a large family, some of whom were still young. He was a native of Belmullet, County Mayo, and was due to retire from the force a short time later. Constable O'Connell was in his early thirties and was a native of Coachford, County Cork. As the horse and cart, the driver and the two constables approached the quarry, eight armed Volunteers, under the command of Dan Breen and Sean Treacy, lay in wait, concealed from view behind gate piers and fences. They shouted to the constables to put their hands up, and there was an immediate burst of gunfire from the Volunteers. Both constables were shot dead. They had not used their weapons and, according to the witnesses to the event, they had no opportunity of doing so. The weapons of the dead constables were seized by Dan Breen and his party, some of whom drove away at speed in the horse and cart with the gelignite in the direction of Doonaskeigh, County Tipperary.

The *Irish Weekly Independent* of 25 January 1919 carried the story of the shooting on its front page (ironically in the column immediately adjacent to the leading three columns which gave details of the first meeting of Dáil Éireann). The report was headed "Police Shot, Tragic Affair in Tipperary" and went on:

> Constables McDonnell and O'Connell were shot dead by masked men while conveying a quantity of gelignite to Soloheadbeg Quarry about three miles from Tipperary town. The Government has determined to proclaim the district as a military area immediately.
>
> The gelignite was being taken in a horse cart from the Military Barracks, Tipperary, to the quarry for blasting purposes. The two constables walked beside the cart with loaded rifles accompanied by Patrick Flynn, an employee of the County Council who was in charge of the explosives. The driver of the cart was James Godfrey. According to a statement made by Flynn to our correspondent between 12.30 and one o'clock in the day, a dozen masked men, jumped over the roadside fence near the quarry and shouted "Hands Up". At the same moment he heard a report and the two constables fell on the road. One of the men got into the cart and drove away in the direction of the quarry with the gelignite. The others took the policemen's rifles and ammunition and went away in the direction of Coffey's forge. Flynn came back to Tipperary and reported to the police barracks. Later particulars indicate that Constable O'Connell's body was found about 18 yards from that of Constable McDonnell. In the afternoon, several persons saw a cart being furiously driven towards Dundrum. In the cart there were two men with masks and a third man lying behind. Possibly the third man was wounded and this would point to some kind of struggle between the constables and their assailants. The missing horse and cart minus the gelignite was found by District Inspector Poer O'Shee, Clonmel, and Sergeant Horgan, Tipperary, on the road at Alleen creamery near Dundrum.
>
> Dr Charles Ryan and Revd D. Egan C.C. went to the scene of the occurrence but found life extinct in both constables. Constable McDonnell aged about 50 was a widower with four or five children and was

from Belmullet. Constable O'Connell was aged about thirty and was unmarried. He was a native of Coachford, County Cork. The following official announcement was issued on Tuesday: "In view of the murder of police constables at Tipperary today, the Irish Government has determined to proclaim the district a military area immediately".

While the proclamation of the district as a military area lasted, it caused much hardship to the inhabitants, as no fairs, markets, sports fixtures, parades, processions or other event attracting a large crowd of people could be held. There was outrage and shock amongst the general public at the shooting of both constables. It was condemned by the newspapers who described the killings as brutal murders. The clergy, the politicians and everybody who opposed violence described the shootings as murder. Some of the eight Volunteers in the ambush later said that when the constables were asked to put their hands up, they reached for their carbines. Others in the ambush party believed that the constables thought that it was a practical joke.

There was never any justification for shooting both men dead. They were outnumbered by four to one and if the real objective was to acquire the box of gelignite, it could be taken, as well perhaps as the arms and ammunition of the two RIC men. Dan Breen in *My Fight for Irish Freedom* indicated the frame of mind of himself and his companions prior to the ambush:

> We expected that there would be an escort of six fully-armed police, and if they put up an armed resistance, we had resolved not merely to capture the gelignite, but also to shoot down the escort. This action of ours would proclaim to the world that there still lived Irishmen who had made up their minds not to allow free passage to an armed enemy.

In describing his feelings on seeing the horse-and cart approaching with the two county council employees, followed by the two RIC constables, he observed: "I felt that I could take on single-handed, a squadron of those fellows. What were they but a pack of deserters, spies and hirelings?"

The shooting of both constables caused horror and indignation amongst the townspeople of Tipperary, where both constables were well liked and regarded as quiet, harmless men. There was particular shock and disbelief at the killing of Constable McDonnell, a man who had already suffered more than his share of tribulations in his domestic life and who had acted the role of father and mother to his young family since his wife died. He had been looking forward to retirement in a few months to look after his children full time. At least some of those who shot him were believed to have known him very well. At the subsequent inquest, the coroner said that it was evident that both constables had been "nailed" on the spot, and he said that the tragedy was one of the saddest happenings in County Tipperary or in any part of Ireland for many years. He knew the deceased constables well and said that Constable McDonnell had spent thirty years in Tipperary, and a quieter or more inoffensive man he had never met. The medical evidence was that Constable McDonnell had been shot in the left side of his head and through the left arm. Constable O'Connell was shot through the left side; he had been fired on from behind, and the track of the bullet indicated that he had been in a stooping position.

The shooting took place just three hours before the commencement of the first Dáil session at 3.30pm It is accepted that the happening of both events on the same afternoon was coincidental. There is no evidence linking any responsibility for the Soloheadbeg affair with any of the elected representatives attending that Dáil Éireann session and none of them knew about it that afternoon.

The murder of Constables McDonnell and O'Connell signified the commencement of what became known as the War of Independence or the Anglo-Irish War. After the publicity about the Soloheadbeg killings had died down, the Volunteers continued their activities with attacking RIC barracks, shooting dead and wounding police constables, raiding houses for arms and taking action against people whom they believed to be police informants. They continued with their activities as Volunteers, receiving some support for their activities from some members of Dáil Éireann until they later became known as the Irish Republican Army.

Relationship Between Dáil Éireann and the Volunteers

The exact relationship existing between the Volunteers and Dáil Éireann during 1919 and early 1920 is rather vague. They were not under the direct control of Dáil Éireann. Some members of the Dáil, particularly those with IRB connections, were definitely on the side of the Volunteers and gave their tacit agreement to the activities. Other members of Dáil Éireann did not agree with their actions and voiced their disapproval at the killing of the constables. Others were ambivalent. In *My Fight for Irish Freedom*, Dan Breen complained about the lack of support for himself and his group by Dáil Éireann following the Soloheadbeg affair and right up to December of 1919. The Volunteers, who appear to have been following their own agenda, continued with acts of violence.

On 31 January 1919, ten days after Soloheadbeg, *An tÓglach*, the official organ of the Volunteers, proclaimed that every Volunteer was entitled to use "all legitimate means of warfare against the soldiers and policemen of the English usurper, and to slay them if it is necessary to do so to overcome their resistance".

In April 1919, Eamon de Valera made a proposal to Dáil Éireann advocating a policy of ostracism against the Royal Irish Constabulary. He said: "Their history is a continuity of brutal treason against their own people. They must be shown and made feel, how base are the functions they perform and how vile is the position they occupy."

In *Ireland in the Twentieth Century*, Professor John A. Murphy writes:

> In the struggle which was to mount in intensity up to the 1921 Truce, the Volunteers could feel a sense of legitimacy which was to be denied to their counterparts in other lands later on in the century. They could claim to be the military arm of a political order which had been established by popular vote. They were fighting within a democratically established framework and this not only enhanced their own morale but was in part responsible for the support extended to them in their rural "theatres of war". But this must not be taken to mean that the Volunteers were subordinate to, or controlled by, Dáil Éireann. The relationship remained a vague and ill-defined one throughout. The Volunteers were in many ways independent of Dáil and Cabinet, and, as well as this, tended to act on their own initiative in their own localities without being greatly troubled by control from Volunteer headquarters. Independence of action was enhanced by the lack of agreement among Dáil members and at their own headquarters to what course Volunteers should pursue. Cathal Brugha, though Minister for Defence, never had anything like the authority and influence which Michael Collins enjoyed with the Irish Republican Army, as the Volunteers came to be called. Nominally Brugha's subordinate, Collins's various "military" roles as Adjutant General, Director of Organisation and Director of Intelligence, placed him in a commanding position, while as Minister for Finance he was a vital member of the Republican cabinet. Between him and Brugha there developed a hostility which was to become public later on. Again, it must be remembered that the IRB continued to exercise a powerful, if as yet undetermined influence on the course of events down to the Civil War. The fact that some Volunteers were members of the secret Brotherhood while others were not, was a source not only of confusion but of danger. Brugha himself an ex-IRB man, was fearful of its influence with the Volunteers and worked to bring the latter under the control of the Dáil. Collins's prominent membership and later Presidency of the Supreme Council, made the IRB all the more suspect in Brugha's eyes.

In *Ireland Since the Famine*, Professor F.S.L. Lyons summarises the complicated issue of the period:

> Yet however weakened they might have been, by past events, the RIC stood full in the path of the revolutionaries and must expect to bear the brunt of the coming storm. They were vulnerable on two counts –

because theirs was the primary responsibility for maintaining law and order and because they were the nearest and most accessible source for the arms and ammunition which the Volunteers so desperately needed. It was this latter fact which gave Mr de Valera's denunciation of the police its deadly significance, for what was said in the Dáil could not go unnoticed at Volunteer Headquarters.

When Cathal Brugha, who had been chief of staff of the Volunteers, became minister of defence, he worked to bring the Volunteers under the control of the Dáil and to counteract the influence of the IRB on them. In April 1919, de Valera himself admitted to the Dáil that the minister of defence "was in close association with the voluntary military forces which are the foundation of the national army", indicating that no civil control had as yet been established. In August of that year, Cathal Brugha succeeded in winning the approval of the Dáil for a resolution imposing on all members of that assembly and of the Volunteers the same oath of allegiance to the state. Each Dáil deputy and each Volunteer had to swear "... to support and defend the Irish Republic and the Government of the Irish Republic, which is Dáil Éireann against all enemies, foreign and domestic ..." It was intended at the time to summon a Volunteer convention to endorse this action, but the danger of mass arrests was too great. Although the Volunteers took the oath as individuals, their organisation never formally ratified the change in status which the oath implied. In effect, their status was recognised by Dáil Éireann and they were now the standing army of the republic, in recognition of which they came to be called the Army of the Irish Republic.

Piaras Béaslaí, in volume one of *Michael Collins and the Making of a New Ireland,* briefly refers to the status of the Volunteers early in 1920:

> By this time the curious title "IRA" had come into common use. Strictly speaking, this popular name had no justification. The official title of the body so designated was always "Óglaigh na hÉireann" or, in English "The Irish Volunteers". On the election of Dáil Éireann, however, which the Volunteers recognised as the lawful authority of the country, and the submission of their control to a Minister of Defence elected by the Dáil, "An tÓglach" began to refer to the Volunteers as "the Army of the Irish Republic" and this phrase became popularly transmuted into "Irish Republican Army" and regularly abbreviated to "IRA".

In late 1919 when Michael Collins was a member of the Dáil cabinet, he took up an ambush position with a number of Volunteers in the first of a number of attempts made by them to assassinate Lord French, the British viceroy. This was a definite indication of Collins' support and backing for the Volunteers.

Shooting of Police Escort at Knocklong, County Limerick

Following the Soloheadbeg shooting on 21 January, the eight Volunteers who took part went on the run for over three months. The *Hue and Cry* during the following months carried notices about the atrocity and offered a reward of £1,000 for the capture of any of those involved. Photographs of the leaders were also published and those, along with the reward offer, were publicly displayed throughout the country. On 11 May, Sean Hogan, one of the wanted men, was arrested near Thurles, County Tipperary, and was detained at Thurles RIC barracks. Two days later he was conveyed by train to Cork Prison, escorted by Sergeant Peter Wallace and Constables Michael Enright, Ring and Reilly. All five were in the same rail carriage. Word had been passed on by a Thurles lady to the west Limerick Volunteers that "the greyhound is on the train". At the quiet, isolated railway station at Knocklong, County Limerick, the train was ambushed when it came to a halt by a group of eight men, including Sean Treacy and Dan Breen. A short vicious struggle took place in the carriage, during which Sergeant Wallace and Constable Enright were shot dead and the prisoner Sean Hogan was rescued. Four of the rescuers were injured in the course of the rescue.

There was much condemnation of the incident in the newspapers in the days that followed. Messages of sympathy were sent by the lord lieutenant to the families of the dead sergeant and constable, and their killings were denounced by church and state leaders. As a result of the Soloheadbeg murders and the rescue of Sean Hogan at Knocklong, Dan Breen, Sean Treacy, Seamus Robinson and Sean Hogan were the four most wanted men in Ireland. Their descriptions and photographs were published in *Hue and Cry* over the next few years, with a reward of £1,000 offered for each.

Further Events of 1919

During the following month the RIC at Thurles were to sustain another tragedy when District Inspector Michael Hunt – for no apparent reason – was shot dead at Liberty Square in the middle of Thurles town on 23 June 1919. District Inspector Hunt was the first RIC officer shot dead during the War of Independence. His death was taken so seriously by the British government that Sinn Féin was proclaimed in County Tipperary and it indicated the seriousness of the situation in that county.

On 6 April 1919, a wounded Volunteer named Robert Byrne was receiving treatment at the workhouse infirmary in Limerick city following a short hunger strike. Volunteers entered the building to rescue Byrne and during the attempt, Constable Martin O'Brien was shot dead and two others were badly wounded. The prisoner Robert Byrne was also shot in the course of the rescue and later died from his injuries

On 31 March, J.C. Milling, the resident magistrate of Westport, County Mayo, was shot dead in the hallway of his home. It was believed that Mr Milling's death resulted from unpopular decisions which he made at petty sessions relating to local republican activities. His murder resulted in the Westport area's being proclaimed. He was a very popular and fair-minded individual who, early in his career, had been a most efficient officer of the Royal Irish Constabulary while serving in County Donegal. The murder caused much concern to the authorities at Dublin Castle and to other RMs, who feared that it might be the start of a murder campaign against magistrates, but this did not materialise. Nobody was tried for the murder of the magistrate.

On 20 April, the RIC barracks at Araglen, County Cork, was attacked by Volunteers, and six rifles and a quantity of ammunition was taken. There was only one constable on duty in the barracks at the time of the attack and no resistance was offered.

In July and August 1919, there were armed attacks on RIC barracks and protection posts in County Clare at Inch, Connolly, Moyfadden, Scariff, Bodyke and Moyne. An RIC patrol was ambushed at the Illaunbawn protection post, in the course of which Constable Michael Murphy was shot dead and Sergeant John O'Riordan was mortally wounded. The barracks at Newmarket-on-Fergus was raided, and six rifles and five revolvers were taken. Another raid took place on a barracks in County Cork. A two-man RIC patrol was ambushed near Lorrha, County Tipperary, where Sergeant Philip Brady was shot dead and Constable Foley was seriously wounded.

In what was the first attack on the British military, a group of Volunteers at Kilbrittain, County Cork, waylaid a small party of military and disarmed them on 16 June 1919. One soldier and one Volunteer were wounded. The Volunteers seized five rifles, a revolver and a quantity of ammunition.

On Sunday, 7 September 1919, the British military were again the target of attack by the Volunteers, when a group of soldiers from Fermoy military camp walking to attend service at the Wesleyan church in Fermoy were ambushed and attacked by a group of Volunteers under the command of Liam Lynch. One soldier was shot dead and four were seriously wounded. The Volunteers seized all the weapons being carried by the soldiers and then sped away in waiting cars. An inquest was held into the death of the soldier on the following day. The jury refused to bring in a verdict of murder and found that the deceased had died from bullet wounds "fired by some person unknown". The colleagues of the dead soldier, obviously displeased with the verdict result, went into Fermoy town that evening and caused £3,000 in damage to shops and premises belonging to the members of the inquest jury.

The most alarming incident during 1919 took place on 19 December when a very serious effort was made to assassinate the British viceroy, Lord French. The Volunteers had nothing personal against Lord French, but knew that his assassination would produce big publicity, as had happened following the murder of Lord Cavendish in 1882. The responsibility for the protection and security of the viceroy rested with the Dublin Metropolitan Police. A police informer for the Volunteers inside the Castle communicated the movements of the viceroy in advance. Several ambushes were set up by a group of Volunteers who had assembled in Dublin from different parts of the country to assist a small unit of the Dublin Volunteers. These attempts failed for different reasons, but principally because of last-minute changes of plans by the viceroy for security reasons.

It was learned that he was returning from a holiday on his estate in County Roscommon by train on the morning of 19 December. He normally left the train at Ashtown railway station, a small quiet station convenient to the Phoenix Park, and was driven to the Viceregal Lodge in a motor car accompanied by at least two other vehicles. The Volunteers set up the ambush at the exit from the railway station where a lone member of the DMP was on duty. Two carloads of military arrived on the scene just as the viceroy arrived. As the motorcade emerged from the railway station, a grenade was thrown at the DMP constable, but it bounced away from him and he was only slightly injured. The first car in the motorcade was allowed through and gunfire and grenades were aimed at the second vehicle, in which the viceroy was presumed to be travelling. In the gun battle between the Volunteers and the military who had come on the scene, one of the ambush party, Martin Savage from Ballisodare, County Sligo, was shot dead and Dan Breen of Tipperary sustained a leg injury.

Lord French was in the first car leading the motorcade and escaped unscathed. In the second motor car, on which the attack was concentrated, Constable O'Loughlin of the Dublin Metropolitan Police and the car driver McEvoy were badly wounded. They both recovered from their injuries, and some time later Constable O'Loughlin resigned and went to America. A most extraordinary feature of the event was that the Volunteers, who left their dead comrade behind in Kelly's pub at Ashtown, left the scene on pedal cycles and cycled into Dublin city without being accosted by police or military en route.

The Volunteers, displeased with the uncomplimentary headlines which they received in the newspapers of Saturday, 20 December – which referred to them as murderers and assassins – decided to carry out reprisals. On Sunday, 21 December, a number of Volunteers entered the printing offices of the *Irish Independent*, smashed the printing presses with sledges and wrecked the printing room. They caused £16,000 worth of damage, but the newspaper managed to get a printing facility elsewhere and was on sale on the next day.

The RIC Situation

Despite the 1916 Rising and the events which followed in 1917 and 1918, the majority of the RIC were convinced that that violent period would pass over if the Great War ended and Home Rule was granted to Ireland. While their own position as a semi-military police force was very much in doubt in the event of Home Rule's being conceded, they accepted this and felt that they would have an opportunity of enlisting in any civil police force which replaced the RIC. The success of Sinn Féin in the 1918 general election did not scare them, as they regarded many of those elected as being reasonable people who had never shown an inclination for violence. The views of the RIC radically changed with the murders of Constables McDonnell and O'Connell at Soloheadbeg on 21 January 1919. The members realised that everything had changed for the worst when the Volunteers saw fit to shoot two of their members dead for the purpose of acquiring one hundredweight of gelignite.

Constable Con Sullivan's arrival on transfer at Cashel RIC barracks in south Tipperary coincided with the Soloheadbeg shootings. He had eight years' service in Counties Wexford and Carlow. In interviews with the author in later years he said that he found the members of the force in Cashel and the adjoining areas, "devastated, numbed, angered and horrified" by the occurrence. They had known the dead constables, who had served in the adjoining district of Tipperary, very well. There was particular disbelief and anger at the shooting of Constable McDonnell, who was known to his colleagues in the force and to the public at large as a very decent and inoffensive man who had already suffered serious tragedies in his life. Apart from occasionally expressing anger, very little was being said about the tragedy, but the members when off duty sat brooding and reflecting over their personal situations in the light of what had occurred. Each member understood what the thoughts of his colleagues were on the tragedy and what it signified for them. For several weeks after it took place, searches went on incessantly day and night to apprehend those who were responsible. The duties of the members were not made easier by a heavy fall of snow in the area – including the Galtee mountains – during the latter part of January.

There was unbelievable commitment by the men during these difficult conditions. For their own safety it was essential that they patrol and carry out their searches while fully armed and in groups of not less than four. In addition to the Reserve force despatched from the depot in Dublin to the Tipperary district, the military were called upon to assist, and RIC reinforcements were brought into the area from adjoining districts. After long tours of day duty, they volunteered to go out at night on "ambush patrols" on roads many miles away from their barracks which they thought might be used by those wanted for the crime. Their intelligence system had been quite good, and within a day of the shootings they knew exactly who had been involved. They had their exact descriptions, and photographs (where available) circulated in the *Hue and Cry* and displayed on posters at all public places. However, communications were slow and the wanted men moved quickly from place to place over a wide area, rarely staying in any one house for more than one night. The RIC search parties, on a few occasions, arrived only minutes or within an hour after their departure. The continuous search operation helped to occupy the minds of the members but their lack of success generated bitter disappointment, especially after the arrest in Thurles and escape of Sean Hogan, with the deaths of two more RIC members.

Constable Sullivan experienced a major difference within the ranks of the force itself – between those who were married and those who were single. Single men were determined to remain in the force, to support each other and to see out the apparent crisis which was presenting itself. The married members were worried about their wives and children and feared for them much more than for their own personal welfare. They were living in small communities; everybody knew where they lived and where their children went to school. There was no anonymity for them compared with the single men. From that point onwards, the lives of wives and children of RIC men became a worry and a preoccupation as they waited up into the night for the safe return of their husbands at the end of their day's duty. At this early stage in the troubled period, some married members made arrangements for their wives and children to go back to live with the wives' relations. Many of those who were married and entitled to a full pension took it. Constable Sullivan had never previously experienced such a high *esprit de corps* as existed amongst the members of the Royal Irish Constabulary after January of 1919, and it remained rock solid within the force right up to its disbandment.

In *Voices and the Sound of Drums*, Patrick Shea, a retired Northern Ireland senior civil servant and son of an RIC man stationed in Athlone during the period, wrote:

> What was happening in Dublin or what was being argued in the inner councils of the Republican organisation meant nothing to me. I was eleven years of age. My father's occupation had become a dangerous one; the fiery speeches had led to the killing of two men who had done no wrong. I was filled with a fierce anger towards everyone associated with the new patriotism.
>
> Soloheadbeg was followed by further shootings. Unarmed policemen were shot in the streets or from behind ditches as they walked or cycled along country roads. If father was late coming home, we lay awake and listened for the sound of his step. He became the centre of all our thoughts; we were frightened and sorry for him. We knew that he was not made of the stuff of fighting men but we also knew that he was not likely to come to any sort of a compromise with what he believed to be wrong.
>
> Republican apologists have made much of the point that the RIC was a semi-military force. It was, it is true, organised on military lines, its hierarchy was comparable to a military unit, many of its officers were

recruited in a cadet class and its members were trained in the use of arms with which they maintained familiarity by firing twenty-one shots at a target once a year. But police and military duties are very different and any military indoctrination received during training in the police depot was lost in the day-to-day job of being a policeman. They sometimes carried arms on ceremonial occasions and but for the I.R.A. campaign, a contemporary of the Soloheadbeg victims could have gone through all of his service without ever being armed on duty.

Although its members were not without grievances, they really believed that the Royal Irish Constabulary was an exceptionally good force and they bitterly resented allegations that they were oppressors in their own country. They were of the people; they were almost to a man, believers in Home Rule for Ireland.

A few days before we left Athlone [in June 1920] I saw one of the new English recruits. He wore khaki trousers and cap and the dark green jacket of the Royal Irish constabulary. He was wheeling a bicycle along Barrack Street and he was very drunk. Within weeks, the name "Black and Tans" was given to these imported reinforcements.

Our journey to he North took one whole day. Father had to leave some weeks earlier and had quickly found a house for us at Rathfriland. Before leaving he had made arrangements for the transfer of the furniture and settled our travel arrangements.

During the late 1890s and up to 1916, the Royal Irish Constabulary had been operating as a civil police force, rarely wearing firearms and working closely with the local people. After so many years of patrolling without firearms, members found it very difficult to comply with the firm instruction issued by the inspector general following the 1916 Rising that all members should carry their revolvers. The vast majority of the population trusted the force and depended on it for advice; for completing application forms for grants and pensions; for giving references to young people emigrating or seeking work; for assisting small shopkeepers with their accounts; for co-operating with the clergy in parish affairs; and in several other ways which were above and beyond the call of duty. The RIC sergeant and the parish priest were the two most influential and powerful personalities in any town, village or country area. It was accepted that if the RIC did have a leaning, it was towards the poor people of the community to whom they were generous with their time and assistance and occasionally with financial help.

Over 80 per cent of the members were Roman Catholics, and they set headlines insofar as church attendances were concerned and paid their church dues without fail. Likewise, the Protestant members of the force dutifully attended their own churches and had a close association with the clergy and members of those churches.

The performance of ordinary, traditional, operational police work ceased in 1919 when the force became preoccupied with searches for persons wanted for murder and other serious crimes. Checks for dog licences, gun permits, sheep dipping offences, raids for poteen makers and cock-fighting: all routine matters which had kept the constabulary busy in the past, and which had kept them in close touch with the people were, apart from routine patrolling, now in abeyance and with the progressive worsening of the overall situation would not be renewed up to its disbandment. As the force entered 1920, the safety of its members and the protection of its barracks became its primary concerns, and from this time until its disbandment its role was semi-military.

The Police Union

With the direction that events had been taking since the 1916 Rising, it was natural that the members should have misgivings and concerns about the future. Many members saw themselves as being in the front line of the confrontation with subversive, nationalist elements. With the general deterioration of law and order since the Rising and the force, which for all intents and purposes had been a civil police force, again taking on a semi-military role, it became evident to the members that the role of the force was destined to change radically in the years ahead. The National Union for Police and Prison Officers in England had received recognition from the authorities in August 1918 after ongoing agitation and a strike there by police for better conditions and pay. The question of union membership was first discussed by RIC and DMP members who met in Dublin in 1918 to voice their anxieties about, and objection to, the conscription measures. Now they looked to the protection of the English union, and a branch office was opened at No. 8, D'Olier Street, Dublin, in December 1918. Notwithstanding the recognition of the union in England, the authorities here perceived it as a threat, and the lord lieutenant issued a directive to the effect that he could not see his way to permitting members of the RIC or DMP to join the union. An instruction was then issued to all members of the RIC prohibiting their joining on the grounds that, as a semi-military force under the direct control of the Crown, they were subject to the same discipline as the military.

Many members joined the union immediately, one third of the force in the first three months. Prior to suppression in February 1919, practically all members of the DMP had joined, as well as about 3,500 members of the RIC and the majority of prison officers.

A conference of the union was held in London in March 1919. It was attended by delegates representing the RIC, DMP and prison officers, under the leadership of Sergeant Thomas J. McElligott, a young weights and measures inspector stationed at Trim, County Meath, and Sergeant John Brennan of Sligo. A regular bulletin was issued by the union leaders to all RIC barracks and DMP stations, keeping members up to date on all its developments.

There were union members in most barracks spread throughout the country, and the only location where it never gained strength was in Ulster, particularly in the north-eastern counties. In a letter to the *Freeman's Journal* of 25 May 1920, Thomas J. McElligott repeated the objectives of the union on behalf of the RIC which were:

1. The abolition of the cadet system.
2. That all promotions in the force should be made from the ranks.
3. Disarmament of the force.
4. The amalgamation of counties and abolition of the existing county system.
5. A demand for Catholic Emancipation of the force.

There was nothing new in these demands, all of which had been made at some stage or another over the previous three or four years and all of which could be regarded as reasonable. With a number of other named RIC and DMP members, McElligott went about organising a national police conference to take place in August 1920, but the conference did not materialise.

A general conference of the union was held in Dublin on 29 and 30 April 1919, and Thomas J. McElligott was elected as chairman. Copies of resolutions passed at the conference were sent by McElligott to the inspector general of the RIC, commissioner of the DMP and to the chief secretary.

The authorities, apparently concerned with the growing strength of the union despite its suppression by the lord lieutenant in February, singled out the leaders of the union. McElligott was directed to move on transfer from Trim to Belmullet, County Mayo. He refused to do so and resigned instead. On tendering his resignation he is quoted in *Memoirs of Constable Jeremiah Mee* by J. Anthony Gaughan as stating:

> The efficiency of a Police Service is dependent on national goodwill which, if secured, could create what is wanted in Ireland, the same feeling between police and people as exists in Great Britain. The experience of a century proves that under the present system we cannot bring about a reasonable understanding whilst we have a semi-military force, maintained not as peace officers but as a garrison for the firm government of Ireland. I am leaving the force with no regrets after eleven years service. I am leaving, rather with pride to serve the union (of which you say I am a member), the force, the men whose interests and whose welfare I have at heart and the country I love.

Two other active leaders of the union who were stationed in County Galway – Constables Edward Tarpey and Patrick J. Maguire – were also forced to resign in May 1919. Despite the forced resignations of the leaders, the union survived and at one period had over 4,000 subscribers from within the RIC. There was a perception amongst members – and with justification – that life was deliberately made very difficult by the authorities for members who displayed interest in the union or who encouraged members to join it or take an active part in it.

From its suppression, it did not have access to publicity in the official *Constabulary Gazette*. Thomas J. McElligott remained the principal activist following his resignation. He used the newspapers of the day to air grievances on behalf of the union and was a frequent contributor to newspaper debates under the nom de plume of "Pro Patria". Some of the newspapers eventually refused to publish any further correspondence from him on issues relating to the suppressed union. Early in 1920 a collection taken up from members of the RIC and DMP on behalf of McElligott, Maguire and Tarpey raised over £5,000.

Thomas J. McElligott, who was the son of a small farmer from Duagh, County Kerry, and the second eldest of a family of sixteen children, joined the RIC in 1907. After service at different locations in County Cork, he was promoted acting sergeant in November 1914 and allocated to the depot Reserve force. He was appointed a weights and measures inspector and transferred to Trim, County Meath, early in 1917 and was promoted to the rank of sergeant on 1 February 1918. His progress through the lower ranks was rapid compared with the usual trend of the time.

Following the 1916 Rising and the growth of nationalism throughout the country he anticipated problems for the RIC in the years ahead and aired his views and fears at every opportunity. He possessed natural leadership qualities, and following his resignation, he travelled extensively throughout the country encouraging members to join the union and setting up branches. He used his home in Duagh, County Kerry, as a base for his activities, but stayed mostly with friends and acquaintances as he had fears for his safety. He was in regular contact with Michael Collins and other members of Dáil Éireann on issues relating to the RIC. He continued with his activities all through 1920 and worked unselfishly not only on behalf of members of the union, but also for others who encountered difficulties. In 1921 he made arrangements to set up an association of RIC and DMP members who had been dismissed or resigned, and was promised the full support and encouragement of Michael Collins and Dáil Éireann in doing so. On 24 January 1922, at a delegate conference which took place in Dublin, he praised those members who had resigned rather than co-operate with the British, and he was very critical of the members of the RIC who had served in the force until its disbandment.

He was consulted by Michael Collins on setting up a new police force to replace the RIC, but when his appointment to the Civic Guards was later proposed,

Commissioner Owen O'Duffy, who did not trust him, objected. McElligott was dissatisfied with the terms of the Treaty and supported the Irregulars. In late 1922 he was arrested and interned. He was released after about three months, but was rearrested a few months later and again interned at the Curragh. During this period of internment he went on hunger strike with other internees and had to receive medical attention at the Mater Hospital, Dublin. He got married in 1924. He supported Eamon de Valera and his policies and was appointed to a number of government-sponsored bodies when de Valera took up office. He took up farming in County Kildare and, on the formation of Clann na Phoblachta, he left Fianna Fáil and became active with the new party. He kept up correspondence with newspapers on numerous diverse and controversial issues until he died in 1961.

A committee of inquiry under the chairmanship of Lord Dessborough was set up by the British government on 1 March 1919 to review the pay and conditions of service of the police in England after a Strike by some of the English police forces. The authorities were concerned about the success which the National Union for Police and Prison Officers was having there in the early stages of its existence and hoped to diffuse the tensions and unrest in the British police forces at the time. This committee was more favourable to the demands of the police than any of its predecessors and made generous and long overdue recommendations. The committee also recommended that the union should be suppressed but that a representative association for all ranks of the force up to the rank of chief inspector should be established. The Police Federation came into existence in England later in 1919. The Police Act, 1919 (8 & 9 Geo. 5, c. 53), outlawed the union. Following publication of the recommendations of the Dessborough Committee, the inspector general of the RIC authorised a meeting of members of the force from each county to consider the findings of the committee and to give their views as to whether similar recommendations would be acceptable to the RIC.

This was followed by the setting up of a committee under the chairmanship of Sir John Ross to look into matters affecting the pay and welfare of the RIC and DMP. The Ross Committee made favourable recommendations for the forces in Ireland along the same lines as the Dessborough Committee had earlier made in England, and these were again accepted later on in 1922 in establishing the pay and conditions of the Royal Ulster Constabulary and the Civic Guard when these forces replaced the Royal Irish Constabulary.

Establishment of Republican Courts

In late 1918, Republican-controlled courts were established in County Clare to determine civil matters. Republican police appointed from amongst the Volunteers at parish level took on a law enforcement role. Prominent members of Sinn

Féin or the Volunteers in the area were nominated to adjudicate in much the same manner as magistrates in the established petty sessions. The first Republican courts were deemed a success by Dáil Éireann, who gave them its blessing on 17 June 1919 and authorised their extension to other areas in the country. In some locations these courts became very popular. Solicitors appeared at these courts and represented clients, and people with civil grievances resorted to them and accepted their findings. Persons were also brought before the courts by the Republican police for criminal matters such as theft or house or store breaking and sentences were meted out. Michael Staines, who later became the first commissioner of the Civic Guards, was in charge of the Republican police who enforced the Republican court system. The Republican courts were only as strong as the local republican movement in the locality. In some areas they were influential and persons ignored them at their peril, while in a large part of Ireland they were non-existent or had little influence.

The ordinary established petty sessions continued to function, and while a number were discontinued at the most rural locations – principally due to the closing down of the rural RIC barracks – they continued to exercise their functions in some form until the end of 1921. In most parts of the country the existence of the Republican courts did not pose serious problems for the RIC, but where they did function on a regular basis, they constituted a threat to the administration of government and challenged its authority. Occasionally, those very actively involved in the promotion of those courts were arrested and charged. Raids were frequently made on offices used by the Republican courts, and documents were seized and destroyed. In areas where they had little impact, their existence appears to have been ignored. As the situation deteriorated, many justices of the peace resigned from their posts and a number of resident magistrates eligible for pension retired. With the exception of the murder of J.C. Milling, the resident magistrate in Westport in March 1919, there were few attacks on magistrates, but it was understandable that they should be concerned about their safety. C.P. Crane, resident magistrate for south Kerry, writing about his experiences at petty sessions in a remote rural area in February 1920, illustrated the rapidly deteriorating state of affairs pertaining at the time in relation to rural petty sessions:

> In February I went, as usual, round my large district, where I never saw a policeman on patrol and where I was ever reminded of retreat before the forces of lawlessness in abandoned police barracks and burnt out court houses. At one outlying sessions I arrived to dispense justice, and having taken my seat on the bench in solitude, a young man walked into court with his cap on and smoking a cigarette. I ordered him out, but on looking around I saw no one to carry out my orders. The police were not

present, and all I could do was to order the fellow out. Which order was eventually obeyed! But I could do no more than adjourn the sessions, and console my wounded feelings by going to the river, where the getting of a nice fresh run ten-pound salmon acted as a balm.

The Closing of RIC Barracks

Towards the end of 1919, the constabulary withdrew more and more to their barracks. As it became necessary to patrol in bigger groups, this could only be done in the larger barracks where personnel was available. As attacks became more frequent, the rate of closure increased towards the end of 1919 and through 1920. A total of 327 rural RIC barracks closed down during 1920. In County Limerick alone, thirty-one barracks were abandoned that year; thirty closed in County Mayo; twenty-six closed in Galway West Riding; twenty-two closed in Roscommon; twenty in Clare and nineteen in Meath. Without local policemen in these areas, the flow of intelligence relating to subversive activities dried up. In some counties where there was little disturbance, the numbers closed were small, and in a small number of counties none were closed down.

The closure of these rural barracks – many of them adjoining each other – left huge tracts of countryside without a barracks, facilitating the IRA with its drilling and other activities. Some of the rural barracks closed down could have been thirty to fifty miles from the nearest central RIC barracks, so that patrolling these areas on bicycles was out of the question due both to distance and the high risk to members. After 1919 the only visits made to these locations by the RIC were by motor transport.

The RIC had acquired its first motor vehicles in 1916 – small Ford Model T open trucks and vans – but they were not on general issue to the force as the early vehicles were all attached to the depot at Phoenix Park. From 1916 onwards, there was a practice of hiring motor hackney vehicles for special duties or to attend special events. With a view to curtailing the activities of Sinn Féin and the Volunteers, a government regulation came into force in 1919, directing all motor drivers to obtain permits from the RIC. The effect of this was that in nationalist areas of the country, drivers refused to drive resident magistrates, members of the RIC or government officials. Official motor vehicles of various types were then issued to the central RIC barracks, and the Leyland and Crossley tenders, which could carry up to twelve members, became the most commonly used vehicles during 1920 and 1921.

As soon as the barracks were evacuated by the RIC the Volunteers/Irish Republican Army burned or otherwise damaged them to prevent their being reoccupied by the RIC or by the military. Up to the end of June 1920, 450 evacuated barracks had been made unusable. During the first six months of 1920, fifteen occupied RIC barracks were attacked and destroyed, and in the same period, twenty-five barracks were badly damaged. Isolated courthouses became the target of attack by the IRA in late 1919 and during 1920. They were, of course, unmanned and were soft targets. Their destruction was intended to prevent the holding of petty sessions and other courts, thereby giving more status to the Republican courts. In most cases they were set on fire, resulting in varying degrees of destruction. In Caherdaniel, County Kerry, the local courthouse keeper was shot dead by the IRA. His apparent crime was that after the RIC had evacuated the local RIC barracks, he had stored bicycles belonging to a few of the constables in the local courthouse. The IRA campaign to destroy courthouses resulted in protection being given to the more prominent of these buildings by the RIC.

Chapter Nine

1920–1922

THE FINAL DAYS OF THE ROYAL IRISH CONSTABULARY

The Events of 1920

The outlook for the Royal Irish Constabulary was very bleak as 1920 dawned. Eighteen members of the force had been killed by the Volunteers/IRA during 1919, barracks had been attacked and some members had sustained very severe injuries. The proclamation in An tÓglach of 31 January 1919 and de Valera's proposal to Dáil Éireann in April amounted to a declaration of war on the RIC. Its members were the most vulnerable arm of the British government, being isolated in small groups throughout the country, unable to move freely through their districts without fear of attack and being shot at from behind hedges and fences. They were easily identifiable targets because of the uniforms which they wore, while their assailants went about wearing ordinary clothes and giving no indication that they had weapons concealed on their persons. Despite the gloomy outlook, the RIC, the force that had put down the Fenian Rising in 1867 and had brought the large-scale disorder of the 1880s under control, were still reasonably confident that they could succeed in restoring law and order.

The major problem faced by the force was that of maintaining an effective strength. Many members eligible for retirement had taken that option and many others had resigned. Recruits were still joining the force but not in sufficient numbers to counteract the wastage. Eligible young men who showed an interest in joining the force were threatened and intimidated by the local Volunteers/IRA; many of them got letters warning them not to join. Parents got threatening letters and messages to dissuade their sons from joining the force. Those who did persevere in joining as recruits left their homes at night and travelled to meet trains many miles away. Having arrived at the depot for training, there were no more visits home for them other than at the peril of their lives. There were many letters to the newly attested members from their mothers pleading with them to leave. These letters were either inspired by the natural anxiety of their mothers about the future or as a result of pressure from the local IRA units. These men made a huge sacrifice in their choice of career, as many were destined never to go home or see their parents again. As the RIC moved into 1920, more than 75 per cent of the force had joined it in relative peacetime and had not experienced the dangers and hardships of the 1880s. In reality they were unprepared for what lay ahead. In the next two years they would be preoccupied with their own safety and the protection of their barracks rather than providing a regular policing service as they had for the previous twenty-five to thirty years.

The concern of the heads of government in Dublin regarding their own security and of the overall situation then prevailing is reflected in an account given in *Memoirs of a Resident Magistrate 1880–1926* by C.P. Crane, a friend of the viceroy and a serving magistrate, who was also a former RIC officer and a veteran of the Boer and Great Wars, when he paid a visit to the viceroy in January 1920.

> I was sent for to Dublin early in January, and stayed a few nights at the Viceregal Lodge with the Viceroy, Lord French. A more humiliating condition of things I never beheld. All the officials, heads of police and other departments connected with the maintenance of order were virtually prisoners in the Castle. The Viceroy was unable to go to Church, without the protection of an armoured car, with soldiers as an escort and the whole route lined with the members of the Dublin Metropolitan Police. When I saw this, and then thought of the police in the country districts behind their sand-bagged barracks, the ostentatious abandonment of the whole loyal population, handed over to the forbearance of the Sinn Féin leaders, I wondered if ever British prestige had suffered a greater blow. I felt it so much, I could hardly bear to think of it. But there was even greater humiliation in store. I saw very clearly at that time, that this abandonment of Government would lead to disastrous consequences and I felt strongly the necessity for active measures for the prevention of crime. Great numbers of well-disposed and law-abiding people throughout the country, were waiting to see what was going to be the strongest, the legitimate government or the usurping Sinn Féin government, and now, if ever, was the time for active

work. It has always been my theory that in proportion as you lessen the power of the civil law by putting in force exceptional measures, and using (except for the protection of the peace) the military power, so much you lessen the morale and prestige of your civil power. As long as civil law prevails, it should be supported and protected by every means possible, military law should not be used in a half-and-half way. If things come to such a pass that civil law is of no weight, and cannot be carried out, then it may be necessary to supersede it and rely entirely on the military forces to maintain order. But in January 1920, things had not come to that state, and the one object of the executive might have been to strengthen the civil power.

While Dáil Éireann and some organisations had been proclaimed at this time, martial law had not yet been introduced. Some parts of the country still posed no problems for policing, and members of the force in these areas began to be transferred on a temporary basis to more disturbed places. The military was to help the civil powers maintain law and order.

January 1920

There were many serious incidents during January. The IRA attacked Carrigtwohill RIC barracks near Cork city on 3 January. After several hours of rifle and grenade attack, the building was eventually captured and all arms and ammunition taken. None of the RIC members were killed, but two were injured. Four RIC barracks at different locations in the country were attacked on the 4th and another on the following day. On 8 January the home of a prominent justice of the peace at Bodyke, County Clare, was raided by the IRA, who took a number of firearms and quantity of ammunition. A well-organised plan by the IRA to attack Castlehackett RIC barracks on 9 January was foiled when a number of RIC constables attacked the attacking party from the rear. The IRA members were lucky to escape without serious casualties. There was a lull in hostilities in mid-January due to local elections, for which Sinn Féin had many candidates.

On 20 January RIC Constable Luke Finnegan was shot dead in Thurles, County Tipperary. Six months earlier, District Inspector Hunt had been shot dead in the town, and one month prior to that Sergeant Enright and Constable Wallace, also from Thurles district, were shot dead at Knocklong railway station while escorting Sean Hogan to Cork Prison. The murder of four of their colleagues in a space of seven months was obviously too much for some members of the RIC stationed in Thurles to accept, and they took retaliatory action. In the first of a series of what became known as "reprisals", a number of the RIC went into Thurles town centre with a party of military and indiscriminately discharged their firearms. The RIC reprisals, which got much publicity, was rather exaggeratedly described as "the sacking of Thurles". The RIC members and military involved smashed two shop windows, fired their weapons indiscriminately on the street and broke eleven panes of glass in the local Sinn Féin hall. Shots were fired through the windows of the home of Mr Denis Morgan, chairman of the local urban district council. Fortunately nobody was killed or injured.

Michael Collins had assembled a group of hand-picked men in Dublin city in July 1919 for special duties and assignments. They had been involved in the failed attempt on the life of Lord French in December 1919 at Ashtown. This group was commonly referred to as "the Squad" and during 1919, 1920 and 1921, they were responsible for the shooting of alleged spies, policemen and military who were seen as threats to the IRA or those involved in the "fight for freedom" during that period. On 21 January, as Assistant Commissioner William C. Redmond, who was responsible for the Detective Division of the DMP, was returning to his hotel from his office in Dublin Castle, he was shot by the Squad in Grafton Street. A reward of £10,000 was offered for information leading to the arrest and conviction of those responsible for his murder. A reward was also offered for similar information in connection with the earlier shootings of four DMP detectives and nine members of the RIC. The British authorities also offered £10,000 for Michael Collins "dead or alive". He was regarded by the authorities not only as the man responsible for organising the deaths carried out by the Squad, but also as the director of IRA activities throughout the country. Narrowly evading arrest on numerous occasions, he nevertheless led an active life in Dublin city during the period. He recruited a number of DMP and RIC members working within Dublin Castle who were friendly disposed to the Republican cause, as contacts. What he learned from them proved invaluable in the work he was pursuing and saved his life on a number of occasions.

February 1920

The first curfew of the period was enforced in Dublin from 12 midnight to 5am commencing on 5 February 1920. On 14 February, the RIC barracks at Castlemartyr, County Cork, was attacked by an IRA unit and after a gun battle lasting for some hours the barracks and its firearms and ammunition were captured. On the same night the barracks at Ballytrain, County Monaghan, was attacked by a large party of IRA – more than 100 – and after a gun, grenade and mortar attack which lasted for several hours, the RIC sergeant and five constables were finally forced to surrender when the entire end wall of their semi-detached building was blown open by explosives. One of the IRA officers in charge of this operation was General Owen O'Duffy who in 1922 became commissioner of the Civic Guards. A number of other unsuccessful attacks were made on RIC barracks during the month. In the course of a raid for arms by the IRA on a farmhouse in Enniscorthy on 14 February, the raiders shot dead the farmer's wife.

Throughout 1919 and 1920 the Roman Catholic clergy were consistent in their condemnation of the attacks made by the Volunteers/IRA on RIC members and their barracks, and more particularly where members of the force were shot dead or badly wounded. The hierarchy – with the notable exception of Dr Fogarty, Bishop of Killaloe – presented a united front in denouncing the actions of those involved. Bishop Daniel Coholan, Bishop of Cork, condemned out of hand the activities of the IRA in his Lenten pastoral issued during February. In a message which received much publicity in the national press, he threatened those responsible for the atrocities being committed with the sanctions of the Catholic Church. In what may been a response to the Catholic Church and its views on the actions of the IRA, Constables Charles Healy and John Roche were shot dead while returning to their barracks at Toomevara, County Tipperary, from mass in the local Catholic church. At Holycross, in the same county, a constable who was keeping company with a local girl was waylaid while in her company. He was stripped and abused while his girl friend had her hair shorn off.

March 1920

March 1920 was an eventful month for the Royal Irish Constabulary. The murder of Thomas McCurtain, lord mayor of Cork city, on the night of 19 March, allegedly by members of the RIC, created public outrage and revulsion towards the force. Thomas McCurtain, who was also commandant of the Mid-Cork Brigade of the IRA, was in bed in his home when armed raiders with masked faces entered, brushed his wife aside when she opened the door and shot him dead in his bedroom. The inquest jury, inquiring into the death of Thomas McCurtain, returned the following verdict:

> We find that Alderman Tomas MacCurtain, Lord Mayor of Cork, died from shock and haemorrhage, caused by bullet wounds, and that he was wilfully wounded under circumstances of the most callous brutality; and that the murder was organised and carried out by the RIC, officially directed by the British Government. We return a verdict of wilful murder against David Lloyd George, Prime Minister of England; Lord French, Lord Lieutenant of Ireland; Ian McPherson, late Chief Secretary of Ireland; Acting-Inspector General Smith of the RIC; Divisional Inspector Clayton of the RIC; District Inspector Swanzy and some unknown members of the RIC.

The verdict went far beyond the usual inquest jury verdict. It was a damning indictment of the RIC and was based on circumstantial evidence available which indicated that a number of RIC members under District Inspector Swanzy were responsible for the murder. It was never proved conclusively that members of the RIC had actually committed the murder, and nobody ever went public claiming responsibility or admitting participation in the deed. Other theories were put forward but the general public believed that RIC members were responsible. The sensational murder of the lord mayor received national and international publicity. It shocked the country. The sympathy it generated for the nationalist cause proved a very timely and welcome boost for IRA propaganda. For the RIC, it was a disaster, creating suspicions about the force and undoubtedly causing the loss of some public support. District Inspector Oswald Swanzy was transferred immediately after the murder from Cork city to Lisburn, County Antrim, but Michael Collins directed that he should be tracked down and executed. Some months later, on 22 August 1920, District Inspector Swanzy, still serving as an RIC officer, was shot dead in a church at Lisburn, County Antrim, allegedly by members of the IRA from Cork city. Following his shooting in Lisburn, there was severe retaliation by Orangemen against Catholics living in the Lisburn area. Very serious rioting lasted for several days, during which Catholic homes were burned down and many Catholic families were forced to leave.

In County Donegal, a British army officer, Major Johnstone, was shot dead through the window of his home. One week after the murder of Thomas McCurtain, an elderly, respectable Dublin resident magistrate, Alan Bell, was murdered in Dublin by the IRA in broad daylight. For some weeks prior to that he had been assigned the task of investigating links between some banking institutions and the Sinn Féin organisation, relating to its funds. Mr Bell, who was in his seventies, was travelling to his office at Dublin Castle from his home at Monkstown by tram, and when it stopped at Merrion, six young men armed with revolvers boarded it. One of the men tapped Mr Bell on the shoulder and said, "Come on, Mr Bell, your time has come." He was bundled out on to the roadway and shot a number of times. Although the cruel murder took place in full sight of the remaining tram passengers and passers-by, nobody made any attempt to stop it. The murder of Mr Bell, which received much publicity both at home and abroad, was denounced by people of all shades of opinion.

On 10 March, Michael O'Brien, a land steward employed by the Rattoo estate near Ballyduff, County Kerry, was attending the monthly fair at Rathkeale, County Limerick. He was receiving full-time police protection at the time and was escorted by Sergeant George Neazer and Constable Garrett Doyle, both in civilian clothes. All three were having a meal at Ward's Hotel in Rathkeale when a number of IRA men entered the dining room where the men were seated and ordered them to raise their hands. Sergeant Neazer drew his revolver and was instantly shot dead. Constable Doyle was shot and badly wounded, but O'Brien was not injured in the attack. The revolvers and ammunition of both RIC men were taken by the IRA.

In east Clare, the IRA attacked Newmarket-on-Fergus RIC barracks, and in one of the very few incidents of its kind during the 1919–1922 period, the barracks and all its firearms and ammunition were surrendered to the IRA by Constable Patrick Buckley. He immediately joined the IRA and was very actively involved with it in his native County Kerry until the Truce. After the outbreak of the Civil War he took the Republican side, was arrested in February 1923 in County Kerry by Free State troops and detained at Ballymullen barracks, Tralee. Following a booby-trap ambush which killed two officers and a number of Free State soldiers near Knocknagoshel, Patrick Buckley and eight others were taken by Free State soldiers to Ballyseedy, outside Tralee, where they were handcuffed and tied together with rope and wire around a land-mine which was then exploded. Buckley and seven others were killed outright and one man – Stephen Fuller – escaped death. Considering that he had been a member of the RIC for a number of years, Patrick Buckley met his death in most extraordinary circumstances. There were attacks on a number of other barracks throughout the country during the month but they yielded no major successes for the IRA.

Leadership Changes in the RIC and Military

Dramatic changes came about in the leadership of the RIC and British forces during March 1920. In the RIC, Sir Neville Chamberlain, who had been inspector general of the force from 1 September 1900, was replaced by Brigadier General Sir Joseph A. Byrne on 1 August 1916. The latter, who held the position until January 1920, was the only Roman Catholic inspector general of either the Irish Constabulary or Royal Irish Constabulary. Highly regarded for his ability, he had an excellent relationship with the officers and rank and file in the force. He was known to strongly oppose conscription for Ireland. Brigadier General Byrne, the tenth inspector general of the constabulary and RIC, was a much decorated veteran of the Boer War. His removal from office early in January 1920 was reported in the *Daily News* (13 January 1920) as being due to "the spread of Republican sympathies among the men of the RIC and the generally unsatisfactory perfomance of the force." The announcement of the removal of the inspector general came as a shock and a disappointment to many members of the force, the Catholic membership of which at this time was around 80 per cent. Apparently he and the viceroy, Lord French, disagreed on the deployment of the RIC. The inspector general did not want to close the smaller rural RIC barracks throughout the country. He felt very strongly about this and gave a number of reasons as to why an RIC presence should be maintained at these locations, including:

1. That to vacate the smaller barracks would leave large areas open to the IRA and their activities.

2. That people who had no sympathies for the IRA or Sinn Féin would now be isolated with the closure of the smaller barracks.

3 That the absence of the RIC from rural areas would result in a very serious loss of intelligence and information to the force and the authorities.

Lord French favoured the policy of closing down all the smaller barracks and bringing the RIC into the larger, fortified barracks. When the disagreement came to a head, the inspector general was given an indefinite "leave of absence". He was never officially dismissed. He continued to draw his full salary, was awarded the King's Police Medal for his services to the force, and later went on to perform very prestigious work in the colonial services.

On 11 January 1920, a large number of representatives of all ranks of the RIC, mostly from Leinster, met at the depot in Phoenix Park and held a protest meeting against the removal from office of the inspector general. Their action was contrary to police regulations but they took the risk. The meeting had been organised by former members of the suppressed Union of Police and Prison Officers. It made no difference to the situation, and it is believed that Inspector General Byrne appealed to the organisers not to proceed further with their protest. There were few who could disagree with the strong beliefs held by the former inspector general as to how the force should be deployed. As a result of the policies embarked upon by Lord French, the force virtually became a military force, confined to the larger barracks, which were heavily fortified and sandbagged, and preoccupied with its fear of attack rather than taking a pro-active policing role. Another theory put forward for the removal of the inspector general from office was that he was being blamed for not putting down the police union following its suppression. The allegation about the spread of Republican sympathies may have had its origins in the short-lived success of the union.

Inspector General Byrne was replaced on 11 March by Sir Thomas J. Smith. He had joined the force as a cadet in 1882 and served at a number of locations as district inspector. Following his promotion to county inspector in December 1905, he served for periods at east Galway, County Roscommon and as commissioner at Belfast. Smith was regarded as having strong Orange and Carsonite sympathies. The government's expectations of him were very high, as he had earned a reputation for being tough and for having the ability to get things done. He failed to halt the slide into which law and order in Ireland was plunging, and instead of the situation improving, it got worse. It is known that he too had differences of opinion with the authorities during his term of office, which lasted less than nine months. He retired from the RIC on 5 December 1920, and his reasons for doing so were not published. He was awarded the King's Police Medal. He was not replaced as inspector general and on his departure, overall responsibility for both the RIC and for the DMP was assumed by Major General Sir Henry Hugh Tudor. In May 1920, the latter was appointed by Lloyd Georges's Westminster government as the "Police Adviser to the Viceroy on the Royal Irish Constabulary and Dublin Metropolitan Police".

There were changes in all the top rank positions within the force during the year: Charles A. Walsh became deputy inspector general on 13 March; Edward M. Clayton was appointed assistant inspector general on 15 April; Lieutenant Colonel Ivon H. Price, was appointed assistant inspector general on 1 October; George B. Heard was appointed commandant of the depot on 24 April and District Inspector George A. Mordant was appointed private secretary to the inspector general on 18 December 1920. Early in the year, six county inspectors were called upon to retire. In April, the retirement of three serving assistant inspectors general – Flower, Tyacke and Pearson – was announced. It was believed that they had also been called upon to retire, but this was not made public. All the changes made in the higher rank structure of the Royal Irish Constabulary during the first six months of 1920 amounted to a virtual purge of all the serving officers in the higher ranks.

Lloyd George made other changes which he hoped would strengthen the administration in Ireland and create a more effective government for the country. Sir Hamar Greenwood was appointed chief secretary. General Sir Neville Macready was given command of the regular military forces on 23 March 1920. He had served as commissioner of the London Metropolitan Police since 1918 and it was originally intended that he should control the RIC as well as the military. He refused to accept responsibility for the RIC, however, and he convinced Lloyd George about his views on the matter. In any case, Macready was known to favour direct military rule for Ireland. He later wrote that he accepted the appointment with reluctance and would not have done so but out of loyalty to his friend the viceroy, Lord French. Overall control of the Royal Irish Constabulary and the Dublin Metropolitan Police was now in the hands of Major General Tudor.

The Partition Bill

In addition to making sweeping changes of personnel in the Irish administration with a view to strengthening it and taking a tougher line with the IRA, Lloyd George was also pushing a bill through the British parliament, known as the Bill for the Better Government of Ireland – more commonly referred to as the Partition Bill. It proposed two separate parliaments for Ireland: one for the six north-eastern counties and one for the remaining twenty-six counties. A Council of Ireland was proposed to co-ordinate the workings of both governments, and all members of both parliaments would take an oath of allegiance to the Crown. The bill was not acceptable to the Republicans in the south, who claimed that the whole of Ireland should have its own parliament; and it was not acceptable to the northern Unionists, who saw themselves being cut off from Great Britain. The Unionists, eventually realising that they would at all times have a clear majority over Catholics in the six selected countries, reluctantly accepted the proposed parliament for northern Ireland. The acceptance by the Unionists there of a separate parliament created fear and apprehension amongst the Catholic population. With the involvement of the IRA, there were ongoing disturbances on a large scale throughout the summer and autumn of 1920. There was very serious rioting in Londonderry, and Belfast had its worst ever sectarian rioting, resulting mostly in Catholic casualties. The Ulster Volunteers were reorganised, and Edward Carson promised to use them in the defence of the six counties against Sinn Féin. Many Catholic families were driven from their homes and the communities divided along traditional Orange/Catholic lines. Over sixty people lost their lives in the serious incidents which took place, and about 200 people were seriously injured. Before the proposed parliament was set up, very firm lines were drawn dividing both communities in the six counties. During this period of disturbances, the RIC in the six counties in question were not attacked by the IRA to the same extent as their southern colleagues. They were, however, fully stretched in dealing with riots and disturbances and endeavouring to keep both communities separated. They suffered casualties in the course of their duties, but were not as isolated as members of the force were elsewhere. RIC strengths were high in the larger centres in the six counties, and there was a very strong military back-up available to them.

Recruiting for the Black and Tans

During 1919 and the early months of 1920, members of the RIC who were eligible for pension retired from the force in large numbers. The strength of the force was already depleted. Many members had joined the British armed forces during the 1914–1918 war and resignations from the force were high. Recruits were still joining, but far too few to bring the strength of the force up to a reasonable or practical level. In January 1920, Field Marshal Henry Wilson, who was chief of the General Imperial Staff, made a plea to the British government to double the strength of the RIC instead of supplying more troops, as he felt that it was the only way to restore law and order. In late February and during March 1920, posters appeared in public places in the bigger English cities seeking recruits for the RIC in Ireland. This was a totally new development. Recruiting offices were opened at Scotland Yard and in Liverpool and Manchester, with RIC officers sent there to oversee the recruiting.

The recruits selected in the initial stages met the criteria laid down for ordinary membership of the RIC but many of those recruited in the later stages would not have been accepted as recruits in normal times. Those selected had previously served in the Great War and since their demobilisation had been unemployed, as job opportunities in Great Britain were almost non-existent. The majority of them had never worked in ordinary employment and their job experience amounted to trench warfare and a high proficiency in the use of firearms. Many of them were very demoralised, feeling that they had been badly let down by the British government as soon as the war had ended, and saw service in the Royal Irish Constabulary as an opportunity for adventure and excitement for which they would receive £3.10s per week, as well as uniform and cost-of-living expenses. Contrary to reports in many publications on the subject, they did not have criminal records, nor had they obtained early release from prison to come to Ireland, because there was no shortage of recruits from amongst the former soldiers.

There was little delay in getting them organised for transfer to Ireland. The first contingent of the new recruits arrived at the North Wall, Dublin, on 25 March 1920. Regular contingents followed at frequent intervals thereafter. The training of this large influx of recruits created major problems for the RIC administration. Ordinary RIC recruits at the depot were transferred to the Curragh Camp to complete their training there and make room for the English recruits at the depot. The military camp at Gormanstown, County Meath, was taken over by the RIC and most detachments of the new English recruits received their training there, with some later sent to the Curragh for their training course.

The standard training course for the new English recruits was of six weeks' duration (as compared with the standard six months for ordinary RIC recruits). Already expert in musketry and the use of firearms and proficient at drill, they received little instruction in these subjects. They received only the most elementary instruction in police duties, amounting to little more than outlining their powers of arrest at common law and under statute and their powers of search and detention, as well as the differences between the principal felonies and misdemeanours. They also received instruction on some provisions of the RIC Code and familiarised themselves with the types of armaments and bombs being used by the IRA.

On 30 March 1920, five days after the arrival of the first new recruits, war was declared on them through a proclamation issued by the "General Officer Commanding the Irish Republican Army", which stated:

> Whereas the spies and traitors known as the Royal Irish Constabulary are holding this country for the enemy, and whereas said spies and bloodhounds are conspiring with the enemy to bomb and bayonet and otherwise outrage a peaceful, law-abiding and liberty loving people; wherefore we hereby proclaim and suppress the said spies and traitors, and do hereby solemnly warn prospective recruits that they join the RIC at their own peril. All nations are agreed as to the fate of traitors. It has the sanction of God and man.

The new recruits were sworn in as members of the RIC and given regular warrant numbers. As members of the force it was essential that they should be identified by wearing the official "rifle-green" uniform, but the huge influx of English recruits resulted in a shortage of RIC uniforms. They were all issued with khaki service uniforms and each was issued with some of an RIC uniform: tunic, pants or cap. The end result was a strange mixture of uniforms, with some of the recruits wearing an RIC tunic and cap with khaki pants; some wearing RIC pants and cap with khaki tunic; some wearing RIC cap with an entire khaki uniform; and a further group wearing civilian hats or caps with either RIC tunics or pants. The new recruits wore the standard black belt of the RIC.

They became known as the Black and Tans, named, it is believed, after a pack of hounds in south Tipperary when they arrived on the streets of Limerick in their motley uniforms. It was a title which would come to inspire terror, fear and hatred in many people and gain them an infamous place for ever in Irish history.

The first of the new recruits were allocated to RIC barracks in the last days of April 1920. By the end of May, 1,500 had completed their short training course and were on duty on the streets in the most troublesome locations in the country.

Allocation of Black and Tans to RIC Barracks

The Black and Tans were allocated to RIC barracks throughout the country. Large numbers were first sent to the bigger centres in the more troublesome areas, where RIC strengths were badly depleted. The general policy otherwise was to send them in pairs or in small numbers to other barracks in the disturbed areas. In the quieter areas they were dispersed to smaller barracks. As local officers had some reservations about their serving in large groups, this was avoided as much as possible. The majority were allocated to the south and west of Ireland where the IRA was most active.

The reaction of the regular RIC members to the arrival of the new recruits was mixed. They were welcomed with open arms at barracks which had depleted personnel strengths and which were likely targets for attack by the IRA. As the RIC members at these barracks felt extremely vulnerable and would have welcomed assistance from any quarter, the expertise of the Black and Tans in the use of firearms was seen as an asset. While they were welcomed as a support group for the force, they were at the same time, because of their backgrounds and the fact that they only underwent a crash training course, viewed with some suspicion by the established members. RIC members had a considerable pride in their force, and from the outset, they looked on the Black and Tans as lower grade or inferior policemen.

It very soon became apparent that they were not policemen with a vocation and that they did not think or act like policemen. They had received no training or experience in routine police work and had evidently been recruited only because of their skill and knowledge of firearms. This was very much in contrast with the senior RIC members who, during a relatively long period of peace, had gone stale in the handling of weapons. These senior members were a high risk in confrontational situations both to themselves and their colleagues. The Black and Tans were, basically, trained soldiers, and their reaction to threats on their lives was to shoot all round them. They were never regarded as individuals likely to settle down to perform police work.

The culture of the established RIC was totally different from that of the new recruits. The force had one of the strictest discipline regimes of all time: when head constables or more senior officers gave orders they were carried out; when sergeants gave instructions, they too were complied with without question. The RIC Code was regarded as the bible for the conduct of the force. The Black and Tan recruits found it difficult to conform to this rigid discipline and to the well-established standards and work ethics of the force. They found it difficult to get out of bed in the mornings or be on time for parade at 9am They were late returning to their barracks at night and weren't available for urgent duties when required. They were very often drunk. These and a host of other problems led to friction with supervisors and fellow constables. All of the new recruits held the rank of constable; none was employed in a supervisory capacity. When performing outdoor duties they were always accompanied by an experienced constable who knew the law and had a good local knowledge, and when in groups they were under the control of a sergeant.

With the arrival of the Black and Tans, the established members of the RIC who were in the force prior to their arrival immediately became commonly known – in most parts of the country, affectionately known – as the "Old RIC" to single them out from the Black and Tans. They were the members of the force whom people knew and trusted and had had dealings with for generations past. The RIC men themselves did not object to the term and appreciated the distinction, especially later in their retirement.

A minority of the Black and Tans were regarded by their colleagues as decent, pleasant and honourable individuals, who maintained high personal standards and who had obviously come from good family backgrounds. They got on well with everybody and created no problems. They were cultured individuals who read a lot in their spare time, and some of them joined local church choirs where they were stationed. The majority were troublesome in one way or another and, considering their backgrounds, perhaps this was not surprising. They had fought under terrible conditions in the trenches during the Great War and they were lucky to have survived. They were young, highly strung men, most still in their twenties, who had failed to come to terms with ordinary living when the war ceased. Their standards of personal behaviour and personal esteem were very low.

Their biggest problems were connected with excessive drinking. They fought between themselves and with civilians in bars, and on their return to barracks, they insulted and fought with colleagues and supervisors. Their pay day and the days following were not looked forward to by either their colleagues or supervisors. Sergeants frequently had to intervene and take possession of their revolvers. Bouts of fisticuffs were not uncommon, but the established members were far bigger and heavier and came out best in these encounters. (It was said that the Scots that were worse than the English.) Some of them frequently refused to pay for their drink in public houses. The theft of drink and groceries was not beyond the low standards of some. The senior constables were often in fear of them and, before their disbandment, many had come to hate them. Other former members simply considered them damned nuisances. On disbandment of the force RIC members refused to serve in the Palestinian Police with disbanded members of the Black and Tans who had already gone to serve there. From a management and supervisory aspect, they posed huge problems for sergeants, head constables and district inspectors who were already overburdened with work.

In *Memoirs of Constable Jeremiah Mee, RIC*, Fr J. Anthony Gaughan describes the actions of two Black and Tans who arrived on transfer at Listowel barracks. After a short period, they were found to be unsuitable for service there and were transferred for duty to a protection hut in Newtownsandes (now Moyvane), County Kerry. The sergeant at the latter location was terrified of both members and cautioned the other members of his party to be wary. One day in the absence of the sergeant, a discussion arose about the security of the police hut. Both Black and Tans took Constable Mee to a fence some distance away from the hut and from the shelter of the fence they riddled it and its contents with bullets. Stories were also told of near misses within barracks when firearms were discharged by them either accidentally or deliberately, and bullet marks were visible in ceilings of barracks day rooms for many years afterwards. Senior management in the RIC, at an early stage, endeavoured to control recruitment into the Black and Tans, insisting on adherence to the Code of Conduct for the force and seeking a more rigid recruitment policy, but their views were ignored. Rather than matters improving, they became steadily worse. The relationships within most barracks between the "old" RIC personnel and the Black and Tans were constantly strained, and it was only the constant threat of attack posed by the IRA which held the members from the different backgrounds and cultures together up to the time of disbandment.

The Boycott of the Royal Irish Constabulary

During April 1919, Dáil Éireann on the proposal of Eamon de Valera, approved of the boycotting or "social ostracism" of the Royal Irish Constabulary. De Valera made a very long and emotive speech, in which he said:

It is scarcely necessary to explain what is meant by this motion. The people of Ireland ought not to fraternise as they often do, with the forces which are the main instruments in keeping them in subjection. It is not consistent with personal or national dignity. It is certainly not consistent with safety. They are spies in our midst. They are England's janissaries. They are the eyes and ears of the enemy. They are no ordinary civil force, as police are in other countries. The RIC, unlike any other police force in the world, is a military body, armed with rifle and bayonet and revolver as well as baton. They are given full licence by their superiors to work their will on an unarmed populace. The more brutal the commands given them by their superiors the more they seem to revel in carrying them out, against their own flesh and blood be it remembered.

Their history is a continuity of brutal treason against their own people. From their very foundation they have been the mainstay of the privileged ascendancy and the great obstacle to every movement for social as well as for national liberty. I need not remind you of their record during the tithe and land wars or of their recent outrages at Ballybunion for which not a man of them has been punished. Punishment by their British masters – not likely. They are patted on the back, praised and encouraged. The British Minister McPherson, to whom they are most directly responsible, speaks of their wonderful fidelity – there have been no Curragh Mutinies in the RIC – and promises that he and his government will back them up, with all their resources, in everything they do and in every action they take. Very well, they have undoubtedly merited the praise of their paymasters, but the Irish people have a duty to themselves.

If Mr McPherson may incite the police, the Irish people, as an organised society, have a right to defend themselves. The social ostracism which I propose, and which I ask you to sanction, is a first step in exercising that right. These men must not be tolerated socially, as if they were clean, healthy members of our organised life. They must be shown and made feel how base are the functions they perform and how vile is the position they occupy. To shun them, to refuse to talk or have any social intercourse with them, or to treat them as equals, will, give them vividly to understand how utterly the people of Ireland loathe both themselves and their calling, and may prevent young Irishmen from dishonouring both themselves ands their country by entering that calling.

In early 1919 the "social ostracism" had no effect on the force, but from late 1919 onwards, Sinn Féin and the Volunteers/IRA spearheaded the boycott campaign against the Royal Irish Constabulary. In the greater part of the country it had little or no effect on the force. In the counties where the IRA were strongest and most active, it did have a limited effect. Shopkeepers and publicans were ordered not to serve RIC members; hackney owners were ordered not to drive them; public transport services were ordered not to convey them; milk, coal and vegetable suppliers were advised not to serve them. Churchgoers were advised not to share pews in church with the members, or even attend the same mass normally attended by them. When refused hackney car services, RIC members had authority to commandeer motor vehicles in cases of urgency. They occasionally availed of this authority. Some hackney operators were glad to have the excuse that their vehicle had been "commandeered" as the RIC were good customers and always paid.

The boycott was not as successful as claimed in IRA propaganda. Members of the force had always been good customers in their local shops and public houses, and their custom was still needed by many. The majority of publicans and shopkeepers ignored the warnings. When they came under pressure from the IRA not to deal with the RIC, a system was devised to get around the boycott. The members entered their local shops with a shopping list, took all the items required from the shelves, helped themselves to their meat, bacon or other requirements, and ticked off the list. The list was then handed to the shopkeeper who priced each item, and either the shopkeeper or member totted up the total which the member then paid. No conversation may have taken place, but both parties were happy with the transaction. In public houses, they pulled their own pints or served their own drinks and placed the money on the counter. Touts might inform the IRA that they were serving the RIC but with the system devised, shopkeepers and publicans could always maintain that they were in no position to refuse. There were a number of incidents in Republican areas during 1920 and 1921 where publicans refused to serve RIC members. When refused service, they turned on the taps of porter barrels and whiskey measures and having left them running, then left. When the they called again they were invariably served.

Barrack cooks and cleaners were intimidated and came under much pressure at some locations and many did leave their employment. They were normally people in poor circumstances such as widows, and were dependent on the few pounds which they earned. In one particular case, the IRA took their instructions relating to the boycotting so seriously that they shot a donkey which was used for taking a regular supply of turf to the local RIC barracks. In another instance they cut off a donkey's tongue in a revenge attack after its elderly lady owner was seen speaking to a member of the RIC who was good enough to stop and fix a puncture on her bicycle.

At the other end of the scale, there was no boycott in operation against the force in approximately twelve counties. While the boycott did cause some inconvenience to members of the force in certain parts of the country, they managed to survive it.

It was not the big success against the RIC which its instigators had hoped for, or claimed it to be.

In 1920, a very intensive campaign was embarked upon by the IRA to encourage members to resign. This pressure was exerted through the member's family or his local Catholic clergy. Some members did resign as a result of the pressure put on them, and many later regretted it as they were left without a pension or other remuneration. Sinn Féin and the IRA failed to live up to promises made by them that they would look after the members following their resignations.

April 1920

The IRA burned down about 325 RIC barracks which had previously been evacuated by the force during April 1920. The authorities apparently received information that Sinn Féin and the IRA intended to hold large-scale commemorations of the 1916 Rising in the cities and towns on Easter Sunday. Elaborate preparations were made by the RIC and the military to prevent this, and barricades were erected on all main roads leading into cities and towns. Whether the information received was incorrect or the precautions taken by the RIC and military forced the organisers to change their plans, the commemoration ceremonies failed to materialise.

An unusual happening occurred at Millstreet, County Cork, on 25 April. The RIC learned that a large contingent of armed men was approaching the town, and they withdrew to their barracks, expecting an attack by the IRA but no attack materialised. It transpired that the IRA had entered the town to "arrest" criminals who had allegedly robbed a bank, and they recovered the £18,000 which had been stolen. This operation indicated the weakening of ordinary police work in investigating serious crime by the RIC and the increasing influence of the Republican police. The incident was a major display of force by the IRA.

On 28 April the RIC barracks at Ballylanders, County Limerick, was attacked by the IRA and after a spirited defence by the constabulary it was captured and burned down. The firearms and ammunition were taken and three constables were wounded in the attack.

May 1920

Income tax offices became the target for destruction by the IRA, along with RIC barracks, during May, and approximately 1,000 unmanned offices were burned. Cloyne RIC barracks, County Cork, was attacked and captured on 8 May and there were no casualties. The isolated barracks at Hollyford, County Tipperary, came under attack from the IRA on 11 May and it was a spectacular one. Large quantities of paraffin oil had been brought to the scene by the IRA. They climbed ladders to the roof, made a hole in it, poured the paraffin in and lit it. The battle between the IRA and the RIC lasted from 12 midnight until 7am when the IRA were forced to abandon the attack after a stout defence by the small RIC party.

In west Cork, two RIC cycling patrols were ambushed and shot at near Timoleague village and at Innishannon. Four members of the RIC – almost the entire station party – were shot dead in the Timoleague ambush. There was much criticism of the IRA for these four murders. Their condemnation by Most Revd Dr Kelly, Bishop of Ross, who described them as being murderous and cowardly, received much international publicity.

A highly organised attack was made on Kilmallock RIC barracks on 28 May. IRA members were drafted in from Clare, Tipperary, Kerry and north Cork to assist the Limerick Brigade of the IRA The same barracks had been subjected to a prolonged attack by the Fenians in 1867, but the constabulary had held out and the Fenians were forced to retreat having suffered casualties. It may have been for historical reasons that such a determined attack was now being made by the IRA to take the barracks. The attacking force numbered over sixty. The RIC strength in the barracks was two sergeants and twenty-two constables, under the command of Sergeant Tobias O'Sullivan. The attack was a methodical and comprehensive one; commencing at 12 midnight, it went on until daybreak.

The IRA had taken up vantage points in a nearby hotel and in other adjacent premises. A hole was made in the roof of the building by the IRA and paraffin was poured in and then set alight. Grenades were also thrown in through the hole in the roof. When eventually the roof and barracks caught fire, the RIC party retreated to an outbuilding where they steadfastly continued to defend their position. The IRA failed to dislodge them and, after daybreak, called off the attack. An IRA officer from Kerry was killed, Constables Moreton and King were killed and Constable John Barry sustained a serious head wound. In recognition of the valiant defence of the barracks by the RIC which he had directed, Sergeant O'Sullivan was promoted to the rank of district inspector and was awarded the Constabulary Medal. While serving at Listowel, County Kerry, as district inspector he was shot dead on 19 January 1921 in a cowardly manner less than fifty yards from the Listowel RIC barracks – presumably for his successful defence at Kilmallock in the previous May.

The events of May caused much apprehension amongst the people, who saw law and order breaking down although not to the extent reported in *The Irish Times* of 1 May that: "The King's Government has virtually ceased to exist south of the Boyne and west of the Shannon."

An important conference of ministers was held in London on 11 May relating to the Irish situation. General Macready was present and outlined the problems being encountered by the RIC. It was decided to send another eight battalions of troops to Ireland to augment the thirty battalions (approximately 30,000 troops) already there. It was also decided to increase the number of vehicles available to troops in Ireland from 190 to 420. There would be more troops available in Ireland than in Great Britain itself.

June 1920

A number of RIC were ambushed a few miles from Bantry, County Cork, on 12 June, and Constable Thomas King, a native of County Galway, was killed. In a follow-up operation after the shooting in Bantry town by the RIC, Black and Tans and military, a young crippled man was shot dead. Near Leap in County Cork, an attempted ambush on a party of RIC and Black and Tans failed and a number of the ambushers were arrested.

On 15 June, District Inspector Percival Lea-Wilson was shot dead near Gorey, County Wexford. (His widow, a medical doctor and daughter of a Charleville solicitor, some years later presented a painting to the Irish Jesuit community which she had purchased in Scotland shortly after her husband's death. In the 1990s, this painting was identified as a priceless masterpiece by Caravaggio and now hangs in the National Gallery.) The RIC barracks at Drangan in south Tipperary came under attack, and after a seven-hour battle during the hours of darkness, the building was captured and set on fire. In this attack a pump had been used to pump paraffin from containers on the ground through a hole made in the roof of the building before setting it on fire. All firearms and ammunition were taken. There were no serious casualties on either side. A few nights later an attack made on Cappawhite barracks in south Tipperary was unsuccessful when the RIC party held out and fought off the attackers. There were several other attacks on RIC barracks and personnel during the month in the Munster area.

A secret session of Dáil Éireann took place on 17, 18 and 19 June in Fleming's Hotel in Dublin. Approval for IRA activities is recorded in *Michael Collins and the Making of a New Ireland* by Piaras Béaslaí:

> With regard to the Department of Defence, Cathal Brugha gave only a verbal report which was a model of brevity, giving the members no information save that all was going well and that the army was carrying on gallantly in the face of many difficulties. No member opened his mouth to ask any questions or criticise any action of the Army or the Ministry of Defence, and this silence constituted a complete vote of confidence in both. All the other departments submitted elaborate reports, typed copies of which were supplied to all the Members.

On 26 June, Brigadier General Lucas, who was the officer in charge of the British troops at Fermoy, was kidnapped while fishing on the river Blackwater.

Another officer – Colonel Danford – who was also kidnapped was later injured in a struggle with his captors and was left behind for medical attention. The kidnappings had been carried out by a number of IRA personnel under Liam Lynch, and it was intended to hold them until certain IRA prisoners had been released from custody. The kidnapping caused a sensation. Over the following month General Lucas was detained at different locations, mostly in County Clare. After a month he escaped from his captors and turned up at Pallasgreen RIC barracks in east Limerick. Following the kidnapping of General Lucas, a big number of soldiers from Fermoy military barracks, led by officers in civilian clothes and with blackened faces, entered Fermoy town, damaged and looted property and wrecked a number of business premises.

The RIC Mutiny at Listowel, County Kerry, June 1920

One of the most publicised events relating to the RIC took place at their Listowel barracks on 19 June 1920 and became known as the Listowel Mutiny. The law and order situation in Munster had broken down badly, with an increase in attacks on RIC barracks and personnel and on military personnel. In an effort to gain control of the situation in Munster, Colonel Gerald Bryce Ferguson Smyth was appointed a divisional commissioner for Munster on 3 June 1920. He was thirty-five years of age and had joined the British army in 1905. He was decorated for bravery and had lost an arm in combat during the Great War. He decided on some radical changes, principally to have the larger RIC barracks taken over by the military and to have the RIC from these larger barracks dispersed to the smaller barracks which still remained open within the same county. A small number of RIC men would stay on in the larger barracks to act as guides for the military and to pass on their local knowledge. On 16 June, a direction was received by the district inspector at Listowel to the effect that the military was taking possession of the barracks on the following day, and directing that fourteen members attached to the barracks be transferred immediately to small outlying barracks in the county. When the message was communicated to the lower ranks in the barracks, they held a meeting and decided that they were not prepared to agree. A spokesman for the fourteen constables was elected unanimously to communicate their objections to the proposal to the authorities. He was Constable Jeremiah Mee, a fairly junior member with nine years' service who had only arrived in Listowel a short while previously. He was a native of Glenamaddy, County Galway, where his father had a small, twenty-acre farm.

Like other events of the period, many versions are given of the mutiny, but the details as related by Jeremiah Mee in *Memoirs of Constable Jeremiah Mee RIC*, edited by Fr J. Anthony Gaughan, must be regarded as the most authoritative account of the event. Jeremiah Mee wrote down his version of the events soon after they happened. In his memoirs, he relates that on being appointed spokesman for the group of fourteen members, he informed the local district inspector and head constable at Listowel. Later that night, he also informed the county inspector at Tralee, John M. Poer O'Shee, who notified his intention of visiting Listowel at 10am on the following morning. On 17 June, the members paraded at 10am as directed and were addressed by the county inspector. Constable Mee told him that he represented the fourteen men. When asked by the county inspector if he was disobeying the orders of the divisional commissioner, he replied, "Yes I refuse to obey the order." The county inspector then said, "Then you had better resign," to which Mee replied, "Accept my resignation now." He then enquired if any others wished to resign, and thirteen other constables stepped forward and said, "I resign".

The county inspector endeavoured to reason with the men but to no avail. After a while he left the day room and went to the district inspector's office. The district inspector then tried to reason with the men, but again to no avail. The military did not take up occupation of the barracks at the appointed time of 12 noon on that date. There were no developments on 18 June other than a direction to the effect that all members were to parade again in the barracks at 10am on the 19th. The constables reviewed their situation and decided to maintain the stand which they had taken. Amongst the fourteen constables were two Black and Tans who had been allocated to Listowel a short while previously.

On the morning of 19 June, three Crossley tenders laden with RIC and military personnel arrived at Listowel barracks. Amongst them was County Inspector John M. Poer O'Shee, the newly appointed divisional commissioner, Colonel Smyth, General Henry H. Tudor and his adviser, Colonel Leatham. There were also some other high-ranking military officers present. The meeting commenced with the withdrawal of the extra military officers after objection was taken to their presence by Constable Mee.

Colonel Smyth then addressed the members at some length and allegedly made the following points:

1. That he was responsible only to the British Prime Minister.
2. That martial law was coming into operation.
3. That he was getting 7,000 troops from England.
4. That in the event of a police barracks being burned down by the IRA, the best house in the locality should be commandeered for use as a barracks.
5. That military and police would patrol the country roads on five nights each week.
6. That hunger-strikers would be allowed to die in gaols.
7. That the more Sinn Féiners the police shot, the better he would like them.
8. That he gave a guarantee that no policeman would get into trouble for shooting anybody.

9. That police were to lie in ambush and shoot any person who refused to put up their hands when requested to do so.

10. That he sought the assistance of all members in wiping out Sinn Féin.

When Colonel Smyth then asked the members present if they were prepared to co-operate, each constable replied that Constable Mee was their spokesman. When the colonel addressed Constable Mee, the latter replied, "By your accent I take it you are an Englishman. You seem to forget that you are addressing Irishmen." Colonel Smyth replied that he was in fact an Irishman from Banbridge, County Down. Constable Mee took off his cap and laid it on the table in front of Colonel Smyth and said, "This is English. You may have it as a present from me." He then put his belt and his bayonet on the table.

Colonel Smyth directed that Constable Mee be placed under arrest. He was linked out of the day room by District Inspector Flanagan and Head Constable Plover and taken to the kitchen of the barracks. When Colonel Smyth had left the day room and gone to the district inspector's office, Constable Mee was permitted to return from the kitchen and rejoin his colleagues in the day room. Before leaving the barracks, General Tudor spoke to the men and pleaded with them to co-operate, but they refused. He also told them about the substantial pay increase which was due to the force shortly, as well as improved promotion prospects. He also undertook to close down the police protection huts in the district, of which the members had complained.

All the high-ranking RIC and military officers left the barracks some time later, and the takeover of the barracks by the military did not materialise. There were no developments in the matter over the next three weeks and a stalemate situation developed. The RIC received a substantial increase of 14s. per week which had been promised some months earlier. Constable Mee and the other constables involved prepared a written report on the affair and gave it to Fr Charles O'Sullivan, CC Listowel, for transmission by him to Sinn Féin headquarters and to the media.

The group of fourteen members who had rebelled failed to stick together during the weeks that followed, and on 7 July, Constable Mee, with Constables Patrick Sheeran, John O'Donovan, Thomas Hughes and Michael Fitzgerald, left the RIC barracks at Listowel without having been dismissed or formally handing in their notices of resignation from the force. They left the Listowel area by train for different destinations. Constable Mee returned to his native Glenamaddy and shortly afterwards travelled to Dublin. He and some of the other constables took their official service revolvers with them. The two Black and Tan members who were in the original dissenting group of fourteen remained on in the force with the others. Constable Thomas Hughes was the district inspector's clerk at Listowel barracks. After leaving the RIC he attended Galway University and, having graduated there, went on to study for the priesthood. He became a Catholic bishop for the diocese of Ondalarin in Nigeria many years later.

Questions were asked about the mutiny in the House of Commons on 14 July 1920. The British government denied that the details as given by the constables of the event, which by then had got much publicity in the United States and Great Britain, were accurate. There was general agreement that the only way to get to the bottom of the matter was through a tribunal of inquiry. Many influential politicians were of the opinion that Colonel Smyth was only voicing the inner views of the British government when he spoke as he did at Listowel barracks, and that the new appointments of Colonel Smyth and others as divisional commissioners a few weeks previously indicated a change of policy and direction in tackling the IRA problem. Lloyd George was so concerned about the events which had taken place at Listowel that he summoned Colonel Smyth to meet him in England to discuss the matter.

While based in Cork, Colonel Smyth lodged at the Cork County Club off the South Mall in Cork city. Following a tip-off by a waiter at the club that Colonel Smyth was drinking in the lounge bar there, an armed unit of the IRA entered the premises at about 10pm on 17 July 1920 and shot Colonel Smyth dead. He was accompanied at the time by County Inspector George F. Craig of the Cork East Riding RIC, who was wounded.

On 15 July 1920, ex-Constables Mee and O'Donovan had been interviewed by Michael Collins, Erskine Childers, Countess Markievicz and others at 32 Lower Abbey Street, Dublin. Although Mee was not impressed by Michael Collins at that first meeting, he had two subsequent meetings with him. The oath of allegiance to the Irish Republic was later administered to ex-Constable Mee by Countess Markievicz. She told him that she, as minister for labour, was setting up a bureau to cater for resigned or dismissed members of the RIC and DMP, and that she was putting him in charge of it as he would know and understand the needs of such men. While he worked hard in his new job, his efforts met with little success and he appeared to find his work frustrating. In 1922 he changed jobs on a number of occasions. He later married and settled down and raised a family. He kept up a campaign with successive Irish governments for a better deal for members of the RIC who had resigned or been dismissed during the Anglo-Irish War, but met with limited success.

The Listowel Mutiny is part of the Royal Irish Constabulary folklore and the differing versions of the event given depended on the allegiances and viewpoints of different people. The majority of serving members of the RIC at that time were annoyed and disgusted with the mutiny and the publicity and propaganda which followed it, as it gave the impression that the force was caving in under pressure and that morale was lacking. From the early 1920s, there were many former members of the force who, for the purpose of rehabilitating and integrating themselves with the community at large, claimed to have been involved in the mutiny at Listowel. If they had all been present, a large military barracks – not alone an average sized police barracks – would have failed to accommodate them.

The attacks on RIC barracks had now established a very definite pattern. In most instances they began around midnight and continued for a number of hours, often up to 5 or 6am. The attackers left under cover of darkness, secure in the knowledge that the RIC party was unlikely to give chase or that anybody was likely to identify them. Under the threat of these attacks, the RIC parties had to remain on a state of alert throughout the night and sleep during daylight hours, making them virtual prisoners within their barracks. There were forty attacks on manned RIC barracks during the first half of 1920 and a total of fifteen were destroyed. Of the vacated barracks, 350 were burned down by the IRA and 105 others were seriously damaged.

The Arrival of the Auxiliaries

To further augment the strength of the RIC and Black and Tans, a further group of men who were specially recruited in England arrived in late July 1920. They were the Auxiliary Division who quickly became known as "the Auxies". Older on average than the Black and Tans, they were very intelligent and had all trained and served as army officers in the British regiments abroad. They were paid £1 per day for their service in Ireland in addition to cost-of-living expenses. They were under the overall control of Brigadier General Crozier and were generally tough and fearless men, more daring than the Black and Tans. They wore their own distinctive, dark blue uniform and glengarry-style caps. A familiar feature of their dress in uniform was that each carried an ammunition bandolier across his chest and had a revolver strapped to a holster midway between the knee and hip.

Unlike the Black and Tans they were not actually part of the RIC force, even though their mission to Ireland was to augment the force. Their rank title was cadet, but they were not assigned RIC warrant numbers. They maintained their own separate identity and did not live in or work from RIC barracks. They were allocated to the most disturbed areas, with the majority going to the south of Ireland. They were based in the larger towns, in numbers of up to 100 or more, where they took over large houses or hotels and used them as their bases from which they operated. Their brief was to act as a mobile strike force against IRA units or flying columns.

They had five bases in Dublin city and one base each at Boyle, Trim, Castleblayney, Cork city, Galway, Macroom, Corofin, Dunmanway, Tralee, Innistiogue and Waterford city. They patrolled daily in motor vehicles, usually open Leyland lorries or Crossley tenders. The numbers patrolling varied, but occasionally as many as five or six vehicles travelled in convoy. Each unit was very well armed and had seven personnel carriers and a number of motor cars allocated to it. As, technically, they were performing their duties "in aid of the civil power", to justify and validate this they were always accompanied on patrol by an RIC head constable or sergeant, who was also essential to them for his local knowledge of areas and suspects. The Auxiliaries were under the command of an officer at each of their locations, and he liaised with the RIC county inspector for the respective county. An RIC constable was allocated to the Auxiliaries at each centre for clerical work. Other than this, they had little contact with the RIC on a day-to-day basis and regarded themselves as superior to the ordinary constable or sergeant. They carried out searches for IRA suspects and activists. They searched dwelling houses on a regular basis and checked all occupants against the mandatory list which every householder was obliged to keep of the identity of all family members and persons staying on the premises. They set up road blocks on a daily basis and checked the identities of persons passing through. When they found trenches or dykes cut across roads by the IRA, they would round up a number of local men and direct them to fill in the trenches and dykes, which kept the IRA from planting landmines in the trenches.

A favourite ploy of the Auxiliaries was to pick up one or two innocent men as hostages when leaving town each morning and to keep them on the lorries as they travelled about. In doing this, they felt that there was less likelihood of being ambushed. They frequently concentrated their activities in the towns and cities and were capable of a reign of terror when in a bad mood following an ambush on them or other activity of the IRA.

In time the Auxiliaries became more feared than the Black and Tans. They were totally unpredictable and had no compunction about shooting innocent people dead if they felt in the mood. They were cavalier and insolent in their attitude to the people and endeared themselves to few. They had no feelings whatsoever for the Irish people and had no understanding of the Irish culture or way of life. Like the Black and Tans, they too had fought through the Great War, and army life was the only life they knew anything about. They were fond of drink and capable of doing anything when drunk. Their policy was to take reprisals for any attacks made on them, and they were responsible for a sizeable number of atrocities during their stay in Ireland. They were answerable to nobody and had a relatively free hand. Their commanding officer, General Crozier, eventually resigned his position, stating that he could not go on leading a drunken and insubordinate body of men.

The RIC, who felt that the Auxiliaries and their activities had brought their own force into disrepute, had little respect for them. That the Auxiliaries' role was totally in aid of the police and not the British army was clearly a well-thought-out British strategy. In following this line, the British government was refusing to concede that there was actually a war in progress in Ireland, as claimed by the IRA, and not merely a state of disorder calling for stronger police measures. The permanent

British military forces in Ireland were not dragged into the events of 1919–1922 except on very rare occasions in aid of the civil power.

At the end of May and in early June 1920, several troop ships arrived at ports all along the south coast bringing several thousand troops in to that area. Two thousand troops came ashore at Bantry alone. The troops were dispersed all over Munster and large houses and suitable premises were commandeered to accommodate them as the existing military barracks were already staffed to capacity. Some of the troops were accommodated under canvas near large towns. The IRA, with a few exceptions, was not prepared to take the military on in combat, due to their superior strengths and military resources, and the British government appeared to be adamant that it would not give the status of "war" to its confrontation with the IRA The RIC, in small numbers in their barracks or on patrol, were softer targets with a greater prospect of acquiring rifles and ammunition for the use of the IRA.

Organisation of the IRA

In mid–1920, the IRA established a command structure for its operations. In the south and west of Ireland each county was divided up into a number of "brigade areas". Small operational units known as "flying columns", each consisting of between twenty and fifty Volunteers under a commandant, operated in each brigade area. The normal strength was about thirty men. They were on full-time active service and moved around from place to place in the brigade area, carrying out ambushes on police and military, attacking RIC barracks and carrying out reprisals. Where one of these columns would not have been sufficient on its own for an operation, it could receive assistance from one or more other columns from within or outside the brigade area. There was a well-organised system of "despatch runners" between the columns themselves and their command hierarchy, usually local Volunteers in the different brigade areas.

The members of the columns were billeted in safe houses or in dugouts in farm sheds or fields. They moved frequently, sometimes on a daily basis, from one place to another. Sympathisers provided them with food and clothing; they were well looked after by the people in the more nationalist areas in which they were most active.

As the active service members wore ordinary civilian clothes, they were able to dispose of their weapons, integrate with a crowd and, within minutes of an operation, be lost in anonymity. This made their detection extremely difficult. The police, who had experienced it for many years, understood the situation; The Black and Tans and Auxiliaries, on the other hand, could never come to grips with it. They had been used to fighting in trenches and in open combat against easily identifiable enemies, who wore uniforms, fought in large groups with recognisable armaments, banners, etc., so to them the IRA was always the "unseen army". The IRA conducted a guerrilla-warfare campaign, and in the southern counties were likely to strike at any one of thousands of targets at any time. The IRA threat tied down the security forces, as besides protecting their barracks around the clock, they were also compelled to patrol in large numbers in the interests of their own security.

Female Republican activists formed an association known as Cumann na mBan which provided support and back-up for the IRA. The members provided clothing, food and laundry for the column men. They organised safe houses, nursed injured members and carried despatches from one brigade area to another. They proved very valuable to the active IRA units during the War of Independence.

Stronger Measures

With the arrival of the Black and Tans and the Auxiliaries, General Macready pressed the English government for the introduction of martial law to Ireland. In May, he also made a strong case for the erection of reinforced blockhouses at strategic locations all over the country and recommended that they be manned by motorised garrisons of up to fifty soldiers armed with machine-guns. He recommended the further fortification of RIC barracks with suitable machine-guns and that demobilised military personnel should be deployed for their defence. His arguments failed to convince the British cabinet, which opted instead in early August to strengthen the general's hand through further legislation: the Restoration and Maintenance of Order in Ireland Act, 1920 (4 & 5 Geo. 5, c. 17). The new legislation gave authority for the arrest and imprisonment without trial of anyone suspected of IRA or Sinn Féin activities. It authorised the trial of prisoners by courts martial rather than by the ordinary courts. It replaced the coroner's inquests into deaths through violence with a military inquiry. The act legalised the arrests and searches carried out by the Black and Tans and Auxiliaries and included a number of useful provisions to strengthen General Macready's hand and broaden the role of the RIC, Black and Tans and Auxiliaries. It was seen as the official British response to the Irish problems.

On 28 June, Field Marshal Sir Henry Wilson, who attended most of the cabinet meetings dealing with problems in Ireland at the period, noted in his diary: "I am very unhappy about Ireland. I don't see any determination or driving power in the Cabinet and I really believe we shall be kicked out." At loggerheads with the British prime minister about the way affairs were being managed in Ireland, on 11 July, Sir Henry advised Winston Churchill, who was in charge of the War Office and Air Ministry at that time, that the present policy on Ireland was suicidal, that it would lead to the British being put out of Ireland, that strong measures should be taken or that they should retire, and that if the latter course was taken, the Empire would be lost.

Another response to IRA attacks and acts of terrorism was also evident from mid–1920 onwards: reprisals, carried out by those charged with enforcing and maintaining law and order. This was regarded as the unofficial approach to the problem. In a debate in the House of Commons, Winston Churchill advocated them for all acts of violence perpetrated on the forces. The diary of Sir Henry Wilson indicates that the taking of reprisals by the Crown forces were supported by the prime minister and Winston Churchill, but that Wilson himself and Macready opposed them. The level at which reprisals were authorised or condoned in Ireland is not very clear, but there were some extremely serious incidents of reprisals during the second half of 1920, including the destruction of community services such as creameries and stores. At the end of October 1920, Sir Henry Wilson was disturbed by a letter which he received from Macready, who declared in it that more drastic action was imperative if reprisals on the part of troops in Ireland were to be prevented. On 2 November he told Winston Churchill that Macready intended taking more severe disciplinary action against the commanding officers involved, which did not please Churchill.

July 1920

On the evening of 2 July, three RIC constables accompanied by Sergeant Robert Tobin were cycling between Dualla and Ballinure, County Tipperary, returning from collecting their pay at Cashel barracks, when they were ambushed by an IRA unit. Sergeant Tobin was shot through the heart and died instantly and Constable Brady was seriously wounded. The other constables escaped injury. Sergeant Tobin, who had volunteered for service during the Great War and suffered from a disability as a result of wounds he had received, left a widow and six young children.

In early July it was evident that the IRA campaign had been stepped up all over the country. The newspapers of 4 July reported on fourteen outrages being committed in eleven counties during the previous two days. In addition to the attacks on the RIC or Crown forces, all types of criminal activity of a serious nature, such as bank and post office robberies (more than 100 during the first half of the year), robberies of trains, assaults on postmen and theft of their mailbags etc., were happening. Despite all the problems of the period, race meetings and other sporting events went on as usual throughout the country.

The Irish Times of 5 July commented on the millions of pounds being paid out in compensation for malicious injuries arising from the troubles of the period and posed the question "Can the Ratepayers Pay?" At the Clare assizes on 3 July a total of £11,400 was awarded for malicious damage to eight RIC barracks in County Clare arising from IRA attacks, and the jury members expressed their concern about the situation.

On 4 July, for the second time, Holycross barracks in County Tipperary came under sustained attack from the IRA, at 2am. The RIC party of Sergeant John Geoghegan and his constables again successfully defended the barracks and beat off the attackers. At Bookeen, County Galway, the RIC barracks there was also attacked and eventually set on fire, but the seven members of the force who manned it escaped without serious injury. At Mohill, County Leitrim, a lorry carrying furniture from an RIC barracks which had been evacuated broke down and was left overnight on the roadside under military protection. The military personnel protecting the vehicle and furniture were attacked during the night and disarmed and the lorry and its contents burned by the IRA.

On 5 July two intoxicated RIC men entered a public house at Ferns, County Wexford. An argument developed between them and other customers, and the licensee refused to serve the RIC men as he considered them to be too drunk. They left the premises and a further row developed on the street. A thirty-five-year-old man named James Dunne, a native of Courtown Harbour, who worked in Bolger's Mills nearby, was shot dead by Constable Henry Linehan. At a special court held in Wexford on 6 July, Constable Linehan was charged with the murder and remanded in custody.

On the night of 11 July 1920, Rear Cross RIC barracks in County Tipperary was attacked by a strong party of IRA under Sean Treacy, Dan Breen and Ernie O'Malley. The RIC garrison put up a very stubborn resistance and a very bitter fight continued for more than five hours. Gunfire, homemade bombs, grenades and petrol bombs were used in the attack. Sergeant J. Stokes, who was in charge of the barracks, was shot dead when he emerged from the building while the attack was taking place; a Black and Tan defending the building was also killed. A number of the attacking party were injured. In spite of the barracks being set on fire, the occupants did not surrender, nor were any weapons seized by the IRA.

During July, the IRA embarked on a new activity of raiding the coastguard stations which were strategically situated around the Irish coast. For the IRA they were very soft targets and the raiders met with little resistance. Over a few nights in July, twenty-five coastguard stations were raided for their rifles and ammunition. On the 13th, Constables Michael Linehan and George Roche were shot dead in an ambush at the Cloghane end of the Connor Pass on the Dingle Peninsula and District Inspector Fallon was seriously injured. On 20 July, serious reprisals and shootings were carried out by Black and Tans and Auxiliaries in Tuam, County Galway, after an RIC constable had been shot dead by the IRA.

In Bandon, County Cork, the shooting of RIC men reached a new low, when Sergeant William Mulhearn was shot dead in the porch of the Catholic church as he left after attending mass. Dr Coholan, Bishop of Cork, publicly excommunicated those responsible. The shooting caused revulsion in the local community, who regarded it as totally inexcusable.

At the end of July organised attacks by Orange mobs were made on Catholic workers in Belfast and at a few other locations in northern Ireland. During vicious attacks on Catholic workers in the shipyards, some of them were thrown into the water. Mobs entered the largest Catholic area in Belfast and drove people from their homes, which they looted and burned. A number of Catholics were killed and many were injured in the attacks. The RIC in Belfast were stretched to the limit in trying to maintain law and order, but the task was too great. Numerous families had no option but to get out of Belfast, and a great many of them came to Dublin, creating a minor refugee problem in Dublin city during August. Following these events, Dáil Éireann declared a boycott on Belfast businesses and manufacturers which met with some success. To enforce the boycott, "Boycott Patrols" of IRA/Sinn Féin members were organised. Rioting kept the RIC and military busy in Belfast and Londonderry right up to the end of the year, during which sixty-two people were killed in Belfast and twenty were killed in Londonderry.

August 1920

One of the most notable events of August was the arrest of Terence McSwiney, lord mayor of Cork city. He represented Mid-Cork in Dáil Éireann and was a commandant in the IRA. He had been unanimously elected lord mayor of Cork following the death of Thomas McCurtain. Following his arrest he was tried by court martial for possession of seditious documents. He refused to recognise the court martial and declared that he was prepared to fast to death. He was removed to Brixton Prison in England, where he continued with his fast until he died on 25 October. There were daily newspaper reports on the progress of his hunger strike, and it evoked a lot of public sympathy, not alone from nationalists but from all shades of public opinion. Although not officially authorised by IRA headquarters, his hunger strike proved to be a powerful propaganda weapon for the IRA and Sinn Féin.

About 2,000 railway workers were dismissed from their employment due to their refusal to handle trains or railway wagons conveying firearms or ammunition for the RIC and military forces. This refusal had been ongoing for a number of months. They had no option but to go back to work before the year ended. On 21 August Sergeant Partrick O'Reilly and Constable John Flaherty of Kill barracks were shot dead at Greenhills, near Naas, County Kildare. Following the shooting dead of an RIC district inspector at Patrick Street, Templemore, County Tipperary, the Black and Tans burned down the town hall, the urban district council offices and the market hall. The damage caused was considerable.

On 30 August, a number of RIC men from Ballinasloe, County Galway, wrote to Sir John Anderson, a prominent British civil servant, setting out the situation in which members of the RIC found themselves. They recommended that the force should be disbanded as the state of affairs in Ireland at the time amounted to a state of war. They were realistic in their comments: "We consider that it is almost impossible for us to carry out our functions as a civil police force under the pressure of the present circumstances. The strain on the force is so great, that we are now useless as a civil police force. We as a body of men are not able to restore law and order." The letter was a cry from the heart and it probably reflected the feelings and thoughts of many members of the RIC throughout Ireland at that time.

The report of the divisional commissioner for Munster to the inspector general, dated 31 August, pointed out the hopelessness of the situation for the constabulary at that time: "For want of transport, they are shut up in their barracks, watching nightly for attacks, murdered if they go out singly, ambushed if they go out in parties, liable to be shot in the back at any time by innocent civilians, unable to get exercise or recreation except at the risk of their lives." In his monthly report for the previous month (July 1920) the same officer had stated that the IRA were now stronger and better organised, and by cutting communications would force the constabulary to concentrate still further. He said that it was becoming a military, not a police job. He commented further:

> He is conducting warlike operations against us and we are not permitted to do so against him. He also enjoys the usual advantages of guerrilla warfare without suffering any of the penalties attached to it. We have to act largely on the defensive, for we have no one to take the offensive against. As far as we possibly can we take the offensive but our blows fall on empty air, as the enemy forces at once take up the role of innocent peasants whom we cannot touch.

September 1920

The month of September was noted for large-scale reprisals carried out by Crown forces, the most notable taking place in Balbriggan, a town in north Dublin. On the evening of 20 September, two brothers named Burke met for a drink and a meal at a public house in the town. Peter Burke was a head constable in the RIC. His brother had been promoted in his employment a short while previously, and they had arranged to meet for a celebratory drink and meal. The head constable was recognised by members of the local IRA and as the two men went to their car after leaving the pub, they were shot at. Head Constable Burke was killed and his brother badly wounded. The IRA had used dumdum bullets in the shooting, which resulted in terrible injuries to the bodies of both men.

Word of the shooting and the injuries inflicted reached Gormanstown Camp, the training headquarters for the Black and Tans, about three miles away. The Black and

Tans there got into a number of lorries and drove to Balbriggan bent on carrying out reprisals. They first attacked a public house, smashed the doors and windows, looted drink from the premises and then set it on fire. They broke into and set fire to three other public houses, a stocking factory and nineteen private houses. They wrecked another thirty houses. They shot and killed two local men whom they suspected of being members of the IRA. The burning and looting went on for a number of hours before the Black and Tans returned to Gormanstown Camp. The incident, which became known as "the Sacking of Balbriggan", was debated in the House of Commons. The reprisals received so much publicity that the terrible fate which befell the Burke brothers on what was to be a joyous occasion went almost unnoticed.

On the following day, an IRA flying column ambushed a Crossley tender conveying a number of constabulary and Black and Tans between Ennistymon and Lahinch. The party, which was fired on at very close range as the vehicle climbed a steep hill, suffered many casualties. Dumdum bullets were again used, ripping the bodies of the dead apart. A party of RIC and Black and Tans, obviously horrified by the nature of the terrible deaths sustained by their colleagues, went berserk. They drove to Milltown Malbay where they shot an old man driving a cart and burned down eight houses. They then went to Ennistymon where they shot dead a man suspected of having been involved in the ambush. They burned a drapery shop and four houses in Ennistymon. A boy endeavouring to put out one of the fires was shot at and killed. In the early hours of the following morning, Black and Tans and RIC went to Lahinch and set fire to the town hall and six houses. The IRA officer believed to have been in charge of the ambush was burned to death in his house in Lahinch.

Some days later, on a Sunday morning, the IRA attacked Trim RIC barracks in County Meath. The RIC were caught off guard, as most of the barrack party had left to attend mass. The IRA succeeded in overpowering the few members who were left in the barracks. The building was burned and all firearms and ammunition were taken. One constable was very seriously wounded. A belief persisted after the event that an RIC constable attached to the barracks had "set up" the attack for the IRA by deliberately leaving a rear door of the barracks unbolted. That night a large party of Auxiliaries and Black and Tans invaded the town of Trim, looted shops and burned down a number of dwelling houses and businesses.

The IRA in County Clare kidnapped Captain Lendrum, a resident magistrate and a native of County Tyrone. The IRA shot him in the head, but the executioner botched the job, leaving the resident magistrate seriously wounded. He was then taken to a farmyard and dumped on a manure heap. When the IRA returned that night to find him still alive, they took him to a sandy beach and buried him up to his neck in sand to await the incoming tide. The following day, it was found that the tide had not reached him and that he was still alive. He was dug out from that position and taken further out the beach, reburied up to his neck to await his terrible end. This was one of the worst atrocities committed during the period.

A daring raid was carried out on Mallow military barracks by an IRA flying column under the command of Liam Lynch. The barracks had only a skeleton strength at the time, as most of the troops were absent on exercises. An army sergeant who was orderly in charge was shot dead by the attackers, and the soldiers working in the barracks were locked into a shed. About twenty rifles, two machine-guns and a quantity of ammunition were taken. Late that night, soldiers from the barracks went on a rampage of destruction in Mallow town and burned down the town hall, a large creamery, shops and a hotel. The townspeople were terrified. An unusual feature of these reprisals was that the Black and Tans tried to stop the destruction and to bring the military under control. This was the only military barracks captured by the IRA.

On 20 September a group of IRA members attacked an unescorted military rations van near Monk's bakery in Dublin. The IRA members engaged in a shoot-out with soldiers who came on the scene. One of the soldiers was killed instantly and two others received serious wounds from which they later died. One of the IRA Volunteers was an eighteen-year-old medical student named Kevin Barry. He was later tried by court martial and condemned to death for killing the young soldier during the attack. Because of his youth, his case received a lot of publicity and was used as propaganda by the IRA. Calls were made by members of Dáil Éireann to foreign governments to intervene. The British argued that the IRA had killed two soldiers in Cork who were a year younger than Kevin Barry without having any regard to their ages. The inspector general of the RIC threatened to immediately resign from his post if the sentence was commuted. Even though much sympathy was whipped up for Kevin Barry while he awaited execution and numerous pleas made by church and other authorities, he was hanged at Mountjoy Gaol on 1 November 1920.

On 22 September, a Mr John Lynch, Kilmallock, County Limerick, arrived in Dublin with £23,000 which he had collected in the Kilmallock area of County Limerick for Michael Collins' National Loan fund. He stayed at the Exchange Hotel, and in the early hours of the morning the hotel was raided by a party of British military officers and police, some wearing uniform and others in civilian clothing. John Lynch was shot dead as he lay in bed. It was believed at the time that he had been mistaken for Liam Lynch, an IRA officer from north Cork. Inquiries resulting from his death indicated that an official "death squad" made up of British army officers, RIC and DMP was active in the Dublin area and operating on much the same lines as Michael Collins' own squad. Michael Collins took a particular interest in identifying those responsible.

As the month ended on 30 September, a large party of the IRA ambushed a lorry conveying RIC members and Black and Tans near Tubbercurry, County Sligo. The lorry managed to get away from the ambush scene, but District Inspector James J. Brady of the RIC was shot three times with dumdum bullets and died instantly. One RIC constable received facial injuries and another had his leg blown away by an expanding bullet. Three lorryloads of military and Black and Tans were despatched from Sligo to investigate the incident. They set fire to a number of shops and burned down Tubbercurry creamery. The RIC tried in vain to restrain them.

October 1920

On 4 October, the RIC barracks at Schull, County Cork, was raided by IRA men who knew the password for admission ("Kilmallock"), and thirteen rifles, twenty revolvers, a quantity of Mills bombs and ammunition were taken. There were no casualties. Later in the month an IRA flying column under the command of General Tom Barry ambushed a party of the Essex Regiment at Tooreen, near Kinsale, and seized eight rifles. The military lorry was set on fire by the IRA. On 11 October, the home of Professor Carolan, at Whitehall, Dublin, was raided by military and British intelligence officers. Dan Breen and Sean Treacy, both prominent IRA officers who had been involved in the Soloheadbeg shooting of two constables in January 1919, were staying in the house at the time. A gun battle ensued in which two of the intelligence officers were killed. One of these officers was Major Smyth, a brother of Divisional Commissioner Smyth, whose address to the RIC in Listowel caused the mutiny there in June 1920 and who was shot dead a few weeks later. Sean Treacy was shot dead a few days later when surrounded by troops in a Dublin street. Several civilians on the street were either killed or wounded, as well as a member of the DMP. Two days later, RIC Sergeant Daniel Roche of Tipperary was shot dead in Dublin by the IRA after he had travelled to the capital to identify the body of Sean Treacy.

Terence McSwiney's prolonged hunger strike in Brixton Prison throughout the month eclipsed most other happenings during October. He lapsed into unconsciousness on 21 October and died in the early morning of 25 October on the seventy-fourth day of his hunger strike. His final days and death evoked sympathy from all quarters. On 28 October his funeral procession took place from Southwark Cathedral to Euston Station in London. Thousands of people lined the street, and the funeral party included a detachment of IRA members wearing uniform. The plans were to have the remains arriving in Dublin, but General Macready would not accede to this. When the coffin arrived in Holyhead, it was placed on a boat for Cork rather than Dublin. His funeral passed off quietly and with dignity. Arthur Griffith gave a short oration at the graveside. Shopkeepers and business people were directed by the IRA to close down for the day. In Borris, County Carlow, William P. Kennedy, a businessman, refused to close his premises as directed. He was at first boycotted and later shot dead, along with his solicitor, Michael O'Dempsey, for his failure to comply with the order. In sympathy with Terence McSwiney, a number of prisoners in Cork Prison had also gone on hunger strike. Two of the prisoners died. After McSwiney's death, when Arthur Griffith, acting president of Dáil Éireann, contacted the remaining prisoners and requested them to come off their strike, they did so.

Black and Tans and RIC members travelling in tenders called to Abbeydorney village in County Kerry, raided the local creamery and beat up the manager before setting it on fire. On 30 October a party of military based at Templemore military barracks left the barracks and went on a rampage of destruction through the town. They set fire to a public house and looted a draper's shop. The RIC, assisted by a number of Black and Tans, arrived on the scene, got the situation under control and had the soldiers returned to their barracks. These reprisals were sparked off by an ambush on a lorryload of troops from Templemore military barracks at Thomastown in south Tipperary on the 28th, when the commanding officer was killed and a number of soldiers wounded. Templemore Urban District Council publicly thanked the Black and Tans for their action in getting the military under control and back to their barracks. (Ironically the same Black and Tans had burned down the town hall and urban district council offices during reprisals carried out by them in the previous August.)

There were serious disturbances in Tralee, County Kerry, on the same night. Five Black and Tans had been killed by the IRA, and on the previous day Constable Patrick Waters (a native of Spiddal, County Galway) and Constable Ernest Bright (a Black and Tan) had been kidnapped by the IRA. Notices were posted up in the town by the Crown forces, demanding the safe return of the two kidnapped constables and threatening reprisals if they were not returned unharmed within a specified time. Business premises were also ordered to remain closed for a few days by the Auxiliaries. A very tense situation prevailed. After two days, there was no trace of the two missing constables. Their safe return at that stage was impossible, as it was believed that they had been thrown alive into the huge furnace attached to the gas works in the centre of the town. When the missing men did not turn up, the Black and Tans and Auxiliaries carried out reprisals in the town as they had threatened to do and burned down the county hall and a local shop. The military intervened to control the situation and helped the fire brigade to put out the fires.

Sergeant Henry Cronin, aged forty-eight years, was shot four times after he had left his home at Tullamore, County Offaly. The dying man was found by his wife after she heard the shots.

A district inspector of the RIC was shot dead in very strange circumstances in Granard, County Longford, on 31 October. A native of Macroom, County Cork, where his father was an eminent doctor, District Inspector Philip Kelleher had been a military officer holding the rank of captain during the Great War, in which he served with distinction and gained honours for gallantry. When he returned to civilian life he accepted a position as a district inspector of the RIC. He had only been in the RIC for a short period and had been in Granard for a few months. He was a fine athlete and an excellent rugby player of international standard. In Granard he was well liked and respected and got on well with all sections of the community. He was twenty-three years old. On 31 October he went to the Granville Arms Hotel, and while he was playing billiards with three other men there, a gunman entered the billiard room and shot District Inspector Kelleher a number of times in the back, killing him instantly. The military inquiry into the death was held a few days later, coroner's inquests having been dispensed with at this time. The principal witness, who had been playing billiards with the district inspector, was brought to the inquiry in a military lorry. Members of the press were not admitted to the inquiry and when it concluded, the principal witness was quickly whisked away in the military lorry.

The results of the inquiry into District Inspector Kelleher's death were never published, and his family were never notified officially as to the exact circumstances surrounding his death. One theory put forward was that he was shot by a Black and Tan or Auxiliary, as they did not like the friendships which he had with people of different political views – particularly Republicans. Another theory advanced was that Michael Collins had specially arranged the killing because he was jealous of a friendship developing between the deceased officer and Kitty Kiernan, who was Michael Collins' fiancée and whose family owned the Granville Arms Hotel.

November 1920

Kevin Barry was hanged at Mountjoy Gaol on 1 November. On the same day, Constable Peter Cooney was shot dead while returning off leave to his barracks at Granard, County Longford. Constables Evans and Casely, who were also returning off leave near Killorglin, County Kerry, were ambushed and shot dead. Another RIC man was shot in Dungannon, County Tyrone. The RIC barracks at Ballyduff in north Kerry came under attack from the IRA, and Constable George Morgan was shot dead. On 3 November, Constable William Maxwell was shot dead at Cloughjordan, County Tipperary. No fewer than fifty-two attacks were made on the RIC and military on the same weekend.

Early in November an ambush on RIC and Black and Tans took place at Granard, County Longford. On 5 November a large detachment of Black and Tans and Auxiliaries were despatched to the area from Gormanstown and Dublin. On their way back through the village of Ballinalee, they were ambushed by a party of about twenty IRA members under the local commandant, Sean McEoin. In a very bloody battle, a number of the Black and Tans and Auxiliaries were killed and seriously wounded. No official figures were given by the British for their casualties. The IRA claimed that up to twenty members of the Crown forces were killed, but this claim could not be verified.

The events of Bloody Sunday – 21 November 1920 – overshadowed the other happenings of the month. Michael Collins, who had been keeping a sharp eye on the operations of a number of individuals working for the British intelligence service in Dublin, had information that a large scale strike was about to be made by them against prominent members of Dáil Éireann and Sinn Féin. The Squad were given instructions to assassinate all of those involved. Early on the morning of 21 November a total of fourteen men were shot dead in their beds at different locations all around Dublin. That afternoon, in retaliation for these assassinations, Black and Tans, Auxiliaries and military went to Croke Park, where Tipperary and Dublin footballers were playing. A warning shot was fired by some spectator in the crowd to warn of their arrival. Recklessly and indiscriminately, the Black and Tans and Auxiliaries fired shots into the crowd, causing panic and a stampede. When the shooting finished, eleven spectators and Michael Hogan, one of the Tipperary players, were dead. Murders for the tragic day ended with the deaths of two prominent IRA officers arrested in Dublin that morning – Dick McKee and Peadar Clancy – who were allegedly killed while trying to escape at Dublin Castle. Also killed with them was Conor Clune, a County Clare Volunteer who had also been arrested while on a visit to Dublin. With twenty-nine deaths, Bloody Sunday was the worst day for killings during the Anglo-Irish War.

On 21 November, the dead body of a young Galway priest, Fr Michael Griffin, was found in a bog with a bullet wound through his head. He was very active in the revival of the Irish language and was very friendly with the IRA Volunteers in the area. He had been kidnapped some weeks earlier, and it was believed that the Auxiliaries were responsible for his murder. A few days after Bloody Sunday, a sergeant attached to the RIC depot named Michael Staines was shot as he alighted from a tram at North Circular Road. He was mistaken for a prominent IRA officer of the same name who became the first commissioner of the new Civic Guards in 1922.

On 28 November, two lorryloads of Auxiliaries travelling from Macroom Castle towards Dunmanway, County Cork, were ambushed by an active flying column of about thirty men under the command of General Tom Barry at an isolated, twisty section of road at Kilmichael. In the vicious gunfight which followed, the lorries having been immobilised by bombs thrown by the IRA, fifteen Auxiliaries were killed, one was seriously wounded and one was reported as missing. Three captains, one major, ten cadets and one temporary constable were killed. The wounded and missing officers were cadets. All armaments were seized by the IRA and both lorries were set on fire. Three IRA Volunteers were killed during the ambush when they exposed themselves after the Auxiliaries pretended to surrender. This was one of the major successful ambushes carried out by the IRA over the period, resulting in the biggest loss of life for the Auxiliaries in any one incident during the War of Independence.

A plan to kill Bishop Fogarty of Killaloe and dispose of his body, drawn up by the Auxiliaries, accidentally came to the notice of General Crozier, their commanding officer, who took steps to ensure that it did not take place. Bishop Fogarty was a trustee of the first Dáil Loan and was openly sympathetic to the IRA and Republican activities. Drunken Auxiliaries killed Captain Nicholas Prendergast, a very popular retired British army officer in Fermoy town, by throwing him over a wall in to the flooded river Blackwater after they had assaulted him in the Royal Hotel. Another local man living near the hotel was also thrown into the river before his home was set alight and burned, but luckily he was swept on to the riverbank downstream.

During the month of November, the IRA decided to extend its activities to mainland Great Britain. On 28 November, seventeen large warehouses were destroyed by fire on the Liverpool Merseyside docks, and there were other isolated attacks on property in England.

December 1920

Early in December, martial law was imposed by the government in Counties Cork, Kerry, Tipperary and Limerick. General Macready had been seeking it for six months prior to this, but the British government showed a marked reluctance to introduce it until all other methods had failed. Most Revd Dr Clune, Archbishop of Perth, Australia, was very active in trying to mediate a peaceful resolution to the Irish problem between the members of Dáil Éireann and the British government. While his efforts met with some success, he failed to make a breakthrough in the situation. On 3 December, Galway County Council passed a resolution deploring the IRA's campaign of violence and the reprisals being carried out by the Crown forces. It also called upon Dáil Éireann to appoint three delegates to negotiate an honourable truce between both countries.

On Saturday evening 11 December, a Cork IRA flying column attacked two Auxiliary tenders with grenades and gunfire when they slowed down at a sharp bend at Dillon's Cross at the north side of the city. One Auxiliary was killed and ten or eleven were injured. A group of Auxiliaries then went into the centre of Cork city, stopped all trams, ordered the passengers off and then searched and abused them. After curfew, Auxiliaries raided a number of dwelling houses near the earlier site of the ambush and set fire to some of them. Later that night they called to the home of a Delaney family at Blackpool and shot dead twenty-four-year-old Joseph

Delaney. They then shot and seriously injured his brother Cornelius, aged thirty, and their uncle William Dunlea, a man of about fifty years.

The reprisals perpetrated by the Auxiliaries in Cork city that night constituted the biggest act of destruction and vandalism to property carried out by the Crown forces during the War of Independence. The *Cork Examiner* of the following Monday carried details of all the happenings under fifteen separate headlines. Under one headline – "Cork in Flames. Night of Terror. Patrick Street Ruined" – details of the damage and terror caused were summarised:

> Cork has never experienced such a night of horror as that of Saturday. The residents in every part of the city were terrified by the rifle and revolver firing, bomb explosions, extensive outbreaks of fire, the breaking and smashing of windows and business premises and crashing of walls and buildings. The alarming incidents were in progress until the break of dawn and it was then found that portions of the city were masses of smouldering ruins. Valuable business premises had been razed to the ground while many other establishments had been brought to a state of ruination. Between half past nine and ten o'clock volleys of musketry reverberated through the city and created considerable alarm and when several explosions followed, a feeling of intense anxiety was created. The people sought their homes, extinguished all lights and then passed through many hours of suffering and pain. Ten o'clock had only arrived when a serious conflagration broke out in the fine premises of Messrs A. Grant & County in Patrick Street. The flames raged with great intensity and within an hour the building was reduced to ruins. The sensation coming from the huge fire illuminating the sky as a result of the conflagration at Messrs Grants establishment had scarcely died down when there was another alarming outbreak of fire and at this time it was presumed that the Munster Arcade and other premises towards Patrick's Bridge had been fired. With remarkable suddenness the valuable premises of Messrs Cash & County and the Munster Arcade burst into flames. There were two terrific outbreaks and as the flames shot towards the sky, they could be seen for many miles around the city – in fact the entire city and county was illuminated. It was approaching six o'clock when it was found that the work of destruction continued. At that time, the City Hall and the Carnegie Library became ablaze. Both of these buildings were gutted, only the walls being left standing. The upper portion of the City Hall including the clock tower fell in.

The *Cork Examiner* went on to give details of the damage caused to Patrick Street, which was almost totally destroyed along its full length on one side, and the destruction of shops in Oliver Plunkett Street and Merchant Street. The British authorities claimed the City Hall and the Carnegie Library had caught fire from sparks coming from Patrick Street, almost a quarter of a mile away, with the river Lee intervening. Nobody, however, had any doubt but that Auxiliaries had burned and destroyed Cork city. They even cut the hoses of the fire brigade units endeavouring to control the fires. The regular RIC, who were providing assistance to the fire crews and endeavouring to control the situation, were totally outnumbered. Most of the Auxiliaries were drunk and they looted many of the premises which they later set on fire. Fortunately, no one was killed and it would appear that only one person was admitted to hospital, because the destruction occurred during curfew when nobody would then have been on the streets. Apart from the destruction of the City Hall and Carnegie Library, a total of forty shops in the city had been totally destroyed while another twenty were badly damaged. The cost of the damage was estimated as being between three and five million pounds.

On the following Tuesday, the burning and sacking of Cork city was raised in the House of Commons. Sir Hamar Greenwood denied emphatically that the Auxiliaries or Black and Tans had been involved or that they had cut the hoses of the fire brigade units. He put the origin of the fires down to incendiary bombs which he claimed the Crown forces did not possess. General Macready defended the Auxiliaries' role, and commented that the excesses of a few should not result in the condemnation of the Auxiliary Division as a whole.

Following the burning of Cork, Bishop Coholan of Cork issued an edict, in which he said: "Any Catholic who shall within this Diocese of Cork, organise or take part in an ambush, or in kidnapping, or otherwise who shall be guilty of murder, or attempt at murder, shall incur by that very fact the censure of excommunication." He stated that the killing of police was morally murder and politically useless and that the burning of barracks was simply the destruction of Irish property. Dr Coholan based his condemnation on the futility of armed resistance on the suffering and unemployment which it was causing to ordinary people and on the fact that, as a result of one single ambush incident, the city of Cork was in ruins. He was never forgiven by the Republicans for having issued such a decree, and it did not deter them from carrying on with their activities.

On 16 December, General Strickland, GOC of the southern forces in Cork, opened a military inquiry into the burning of Cork city, but refused to allow legal representatives on behalf of interested parties attend. The inquiry closed five days later with nobody aware of what format it had taken or who had given evidence – if anyone. The findings of the inquiry were never published, nor made available to interested parties. The company of Auxiliaries based in Cork at the time, and who were known to have been responsible for the burning of the city, were transferred to Dublin a short while afterwards, where they wore burnt corks on their glengarry caps when on duty. When members of the British Labour Party came to Cork and conducted their own inquiry into the burning of Cork and took statements from numerous witnesses, the Auxiliaries threatened to shoot them. They had no hesitation in informing the prime minister and British parliament that they were satisfied that the destruction of Cork city had been caused by the Auxiliaries.

The Government of Ireland Act, 1920 (10 & 11 Geo. 5, c. 67), received the royal assent on 23 December. It provided for two parliaments in Ireland, one for the twenty-six southern counties and one for the six north-eastern counties. No Irish peer had voted for it in the House of Lords, but the representatives from the six counties had supported it as the better of two poor options.

On 15 December, a fifteen-year-old boy named Tadgh Crowley and Canon Magner, the local parish priest at Dunmanway, County Cork, were shot dead by an Auxiliary on the main road near Dunmanway. The circumstances which led up to the shooting were extraordinary. Patrick Sarsfield Brady, a resident magistrate, was travelling to his petty sessions at Skibbereen when a tyre on his car punctured. Canon Magner came on the scene and requested Tadgh Crowley to assist Mr Brady in changing the punctured wheel. While this was going on, two lorryloads of Auxiliaries arrived. An Auxiliary cadet named Harte dismounted from one of the lorries and approached the three people on the road. When Canon Magner remonstrated with him for his aggressive behaviour towards young Crowley, he shot Tadgh Crowley dead. He then shot Canon Magner before being restrained by his fellow Auxiliaries. The shooting of Canon Magner caused revulsion throughout the country, but particularly in west Cork where the canon was well known and liked. Mr Brady insisted on an inquiry into the shooting. At a court martial held in Cork in the following January, Cadet Harte was deemed to have been suffering from delirium tremens and to have been insane at the time of the shootings.

1920 in Retrospect

Although 1920 ended with talks about peace through intermediaries between Irish and British representatives, nothing firm was in place. De Valera returned from the United States where he had been on a fund-raising mission since April 1919. Martial law was in force in Counties Cork, Kerry, Tipperary and Limerick from early December. This area continued to be the most troublesome part of Ireland, with some activity in Dublin city, Counties Galway and Clare and a few other locations. During 1920 there was virtually no activity by the IRA in thirteen counties. Additional Black and Tans continued to arrive up to the end of December to augment the RIC. They were all based in the RIC barracks and continued to work within the RIC structures.

The established "old" RIC men noted that the standards of the Black and Tans had deteriorated further with the addition of new arrivals to the force. The original intention was that 1,500 Black and Tans would be recruited to bring the depleted RIC up to strength, but they kept arriving at Gormanstown Camp at the rate of about 200 per week, and by September approximately 2,000 had joined up. The Black and Tans had their own weekly bulletin, the *Weekly Summary*, the first issue of which appeared on 5 May 1920. Designed to keep up the morale of the Black and Tans, it generated much hatred towards the Irish people, particularly Sinn Féin and the IRA. Gormanstown Camp, which was controlled by the RIC for the training of the Black and Tans, had a management/training team led by thirteen RIC officers. The officer in charge was County Inspector C.F.F. Davies and his assistant was County Inspector Gerald R.E. Foley. The other officers consisted of ten district inspectors, each having a specific responsibility: adjutant, police duty instruction, musketry instruction, company officers and other miscellaneous duties. There were more officers deployed in training of the Black and Tans at Gormanstown Camp than at the depot in Phoenix Park during the second half of 1920.

The total strength of the Royal Irish Constabulary in September 1919 was 9,656 men. By the end of 1920, the strength of the "old" RIC had dropped to approximately 8,000 men. The total number of Black and Tans recruited was in excess of 3,000. The total number of Auxiliaries was 2,210, and remained consistent at that figure. The strength of the British military in Ireland was about 40,000 members. There are no definite statistics available for the strength of full-time, active IRA members, but it is believed to have been somewhere between 3,000 and 5,000.

In the *Royal Irish Constabulary Directory* of January 1921, three district inspectors and sixty-five rank-and-file members of the force are recorded as having died (been killed) during the year 1920. A total of 556 members resigned, 746 were pensioned and thirty-six left the force on gratuity (resulting from serious injuries sustained) in that year. These statistics do not include Black and Tan or Auxiliary casualties. The Dublin Metropolitan Police also suffered a big number of casualties. The *Directory* also indicates that there were less than 1,000 RIC barracks functioning in the country by the end of 1920, with 327 having closed during the year. The military casualties for 1920 were fifty-four killed and 118 wounded. It was a bad year for the RIC, particularly the second half. In about twelve counties they continued to provide a police service, albeit a limited one. In the remainder of the country their role was almost totally military. Due to depleted numbers the RIC had had to accept the Black and Tan reinforcements from England and the assistance of the Auxiliaries a few months later, and then things went from bad to worse. The period from July to September were the worst months of the year for attacks on RIC personnel and barracks and for serious incidents.

The apparent "unofficial" policy of carrying out reprisals following attacks on Crown forces did not help the position or credibility of the police. While members of the RIC were implicated in a number of the reprisals, they had not participated in the major ones, and in the latter part of the year were known to have made every effort to stop the Auxiliaries and Black and Tans. After reprisals by the Crown forces, the IRA would respond with further reprisals – principally by burning down the homes of Protestants and people known to be loyal to the Crown. Many of the loyalists fled the country after receiving death threats, and some of the finest mansions in Ireland were burned to the ground. These were the people who had always staunchly supported the constabulary in trying to maintain law and order.

Confidential reports to the inspector general from the county inspectors at Waterford and Kerry during the second half of the year indicate the huge problems faced by the force in trying to maintain a policing service. In the confidential report for July from County Waterford, the county inspector recommended withdrawing the RIC from further barracks in the county, to which the divisional commissioner added the following comments:

> From the foregoing it will be seen that none of the barracks has an adequate force for effective patrolling and defence, should disturbances arise. On the other hand, the demand for men in more important centres is urgent and cannot be met without some such scheme as this. This demand for men is the more urgent as the winter approaches, and as events are going now, the holding of such stations means the cooping up of a number of men for defence of isolated posts where they might be used far more effectively as an active force. This of course again means the handing over of tracts of country to the enemy. But the situation has to be faced, and taking all into consideration, I would recommend that the County Inspector's suggestion be at once sanctioned. I hesitate to carry out so large a scheme without reference to you. The County Inspector wishes to carry this scheme into effect at once, and I can see no object in delaying the inevitable till later days make it more difficult. May this matter be treated as urgent please, so that I can have it carried into effect.

To this, Inspector General Smith replied:

> Ardmore. – I should have thought that 10 police and 25 marines would be able to look after themselves, even in a bad locality. Is the idea in reducing the strength merely to provide men for other stations? I am very reluctant to give up territory if it can be avoided. Have not special measures been taken for the defence of Ardmore?
>
> Ballinamult – This barracks will be burned down if vacated. Could the strength in any way be increased?
>
> Kill might go.

There would be a big tract of country between Waterford and Dunmore East without police if Passage East be given up. Can nothing be done?

The confidential report to the inspector general for the month of August 1920 from Major Beanney, county inspector for Kerry, was most revealing and factual. It indicated the dire straits in which the force found itself; the rapidly deteriorating situation indicated the very bleak future which lay ahead for it. The report read:

County Inspector's Office,
Tralee, 30th August 1920.

I beg to report that there is no improvement in the condition of the county; the reverse is rather the case. The Dingle Peninsula is the worst part, being in a most lawless condition, except in the town of Dingle. The withdrawal of the stations at Annascaul and Camp has left the greater part of the peninsula without police or military control and, as a consequence, all the able-bodied men in that region have adopted the most aggressive attitude, and arrange with very short notice to attack on the return journey any police or military transport that passes which they do not deem too strong for them. As reported, they had a mine on the road, and after exploding it under a military lorry, they attacked the escort with rifles, shotguns and revolvers, wounding four and overcoming the whole party. They then took all their arms, ammunition and equipment. This trap was laid between the passing of the lorry to Dingle and its return journey. Between 100 and 150 men took part in the attack. For the rest, the northern part is more disturbed than the southern, though in the latter, the feeling is bitter, and is increasing against the police. On the 14th, four constables from Aghabeg were fired on and one was wounded though not seriously. Two attempts were made to blow up Milltown old barracks and, in addition, information has been received that an ambush was laid for a Crossley car, which was expected to pass near Beaufort, carrying out a transfer (the car did not return that day), and also that other ambushes are being prepared. The worst Districts are Dingle, Tralee, and parts of Listowel, Castleisland and Killarney. In Kenmare and Cahirciveen there has not been much activity. There is everywhere a desire to boycott the police, and commandeering has to be resorted to in many places. For this reason motor transport has to be used for supplying some of the stations, especially Causeway and Brosna. There is hostility to the police everywhere and through a great part of the county, I do not regard it as safe for a single police vehicle – even a Crossley tender – to travel.

The feeling as regards the Lord Mayor of Cork is pretty tense – qualified by a firm belief that he will be liberated before he gets too bad – and there is no doubt but that there will be grave danger of serious disturbances if he dies. Sinn Féin Courts are held, but the places are varied, and, if the police go to a house or hall where it is expected that one is to be held, no person appears. Intimidation on behalf of Sinn Féin is rife throughout the country. Almost all local magistrates have resigned their commissions, a good number of them through fear of terrorism, which is rampant. The same terrorism prevents people from prosecuting their cases at petty sessions and drives them to the Sinn Féin Courts. The local press is, of course, strongly Sinn Féin, but the paper which does most harm throughout the country is the 'Independent'. There is no industrial trouble between landlord or tenant, farmer and labourer. The recent fine weather is enabling the farmer to save his crops. The harvest seems to be, on the whole, very fair. I attach lists of the different political associations. It is not possible at the present time to do more than give approximate numbers of these. But it may be taken for granted that nearly all the young people of the county are Sinn Féin, and that a large proportion of the young men are Irish Volunteers. Between them, these two associations are controlling the whole life and action of the county, and every person, whether loyal or disloyal, is afraid to run counter to their wishes.

In *An tÓglach* a few weeks later, the IRA commented on the situation as it saw it at that time:

It is significant that it is in those parts of the country where the warfare on the armed spies of the RIC was in the most part feeble and insufficient, that the worst reign of terror is now being instituted. The secret of this is obvious. In the West the guerilla warfare was not sufficiently energetic to greatly relax the grip of the old RIC on the countryside; and they are now striving desperately to regain their hold, with the aid of foreign reinforcements, by wholesale terrorism. They actually hoped to succeed by Christmas, as shown in a secret order intercepted by us. In the South, the guerilla offensive has been carried out for so long, and so vigorously, that any attempt by the RIC to regain control of areas is out of the question and the enemy can only rely on a big military concentration. There is a certain amount of method in the enemy's madness. The terrorism resorted to seems to be employed with concentrated malice on parts of Connacht. This is explained by the fact that the parts in question have not been playing much part in the guerilla warfare until recently, and the enemy believes that he will be able to cow the people in these districts rapidly and "reassume control", so that he will be able to concentrate his energy on the parts where the Republican forces are best organised and most active. He counts on having this done at an early date.

In the latter half of 1920, the RIC received a pay rise which had been promised to them earlier following the recommendations of the Ross Commission, which had enquired into the pay and allowances of the RIC and DMP in 1919. Pay scales for county inspectors varied between £700 and £900 per annum, and the salary of district inspectors ranged from £400 to £650 per annum. Head constables received between £310 and £355 pounds per annum. Sergeants' pay was between £5 and £5 12s. 6d. per week, and constables' pay ranged from £3 10s. per week to £4 15s. per week. There was an increase in the cost-of-living allowance for all members, with constables receiving 12s., sergeants 13s. 6d. and head constables 15s., weekly. In keeping with the times and the nature of the duties being performed, drivers of official police transport vehicles received an allowance of 2s. 6d. a day, while mechanics engaged on transport maintenance received a daily allowance of 5s.

The list of counties "Proclaimed to be in a State of Disturbance", (in accordance with the provisions of 6 Wm. 4) on 31 December 1920 was as follows: Clare, Galway, Cork East Riding, Cork West Riding, Kerry, Limerick, Roscommon, Tipperary North Riding, Tipperary South Riding, Dublin, Longford, Louth, Sligo, Waterford, Westmeath and Wicklow. The proclamation of these counties authorised an additional establishment in RIC strengths. The total number of protection huts had dwindled to five: Moorpark, Corgary and Castlegrove in County Galway and Geashill and Ballinahoulart in King's County (Offaly). The increase and spread of ordinary criminal activities during 1920 was one of the off-shoots of that troubled period. With the closing down of RIC barracks, large tracts of the country were cut off from a police service and criminal elements took advantage of this. Many robberies were carried out, and long-standing disputes were settled through the murder or serious wounding of some party involved. There was a plentiful supply of guns available to those who wanted to kill. The deaths of ordinary people through violence or in furtherance of the commission of a crime were not recorded by the authorities in the same way as if they had been the murders of RIC members or Black and Tans. No professional investigation could be carried out on killings without any apparent political motive. Poteen-making spread to parts of the country where it had never been carried out before. Illegal fishing of rivers and lakes went on unhindered. There was a general breakdown in the enforcement of the laws of the land. On the other hand, there was stricter enforcement of the issuing of permits for use of motor vehicles over this period to try to limit their availability for use by the IRA Volunteers. In some areas where ambushes were frequent, restrictions applied to the use of bicycles.

There was little pleasure and many problems for motorists, as outlined by Richard Bennett in *The Black and Tans*:

> With or without a permit, the hard-pressed Irish motorist was liable to have his car commandeered by the military on Monday, by the Royal Irish Constabulary on Tuesday, the Auxiliaries on Wednesday, the IRA on Thursday and a band of armed bank robbers on Friday, leaving him the weekend in which to trace it and with luck, recover it, and have it ditched on the way home in a trench dug in the road by the Volunteers, or blocked by felled trees or loose stone walls. These obstacles frequently provided the occasion for an ambush and were designed to combat the growing mobility of the Crown forces and reduce the effectiveness of the Peerless and Rolls Royce armoured cars.

On 5 December 1920, when Sir T.J. Smith, the inspector general, retired after only nine months in office, Major General Tudor assumed control of the RIC until its disbandment. From a management perspective, the RIC underwent major internal structuring and personnel changes during 1920. Apart from the almost total sweep of all officers at the top and the big numbers of resignations, retirements and deaths in the force during the year, there was an unprecedented number of transfers and promotions in all ranks within the force. One hundred and thirty-six district inspectors – more than 60 per cent of the total – moved on transfer during the year. Seventy-six cadets were promoted to third class district inspectors and nine county inspectors were transferred. Considering the previous stability of the force and the slow but steady turnover of officers and personnel in key positions, the numerous personnel changes made during the year could not but have had a traumatic effect insofar as the administration of the force was concerned. It is also evident from the many changes made that the force as a whole was being subjected to extreme pressures and that its overall stability and structures were being undermined.

As the force moved towards 1921, its members knew that the new year was unlikely to be any better than 1920. They knew that they were again going to be the prime target for the IRA as they tried to perform some duties, in uniform in small numbers. There was no safe refuge for them, even when attending their religious duties on Sundays. During the second half of 1920, the press appeared to get more hostile in its attitude towards the force, possibly because of the large number of reprisals carried out by the Crown forces and the resultant counter-reprisals. The newspapers had become far more sympathetic to the IRA and Sinn Féin. Many press reports devoted only one or two lines to a member of the RIC being murdered, but went to great lengths to describe in detail some act of reprisal carried out by Crown forces following the murder of a policeman. Before 1920 came to a close, the IRA and Sinn Féin had succeeded in establishing a very efficient propaganda machine which ensured the maximum publicity for all matters beneficial to its own cause.

With all the problems facing the Royal Irish Constabulary at this time, it would be natural to expect the force to have been totally demoralised, but the members who served through the period always remained adamant that morale amongst the members was high and that they had at that time taken a decision to stick it out. They knew in their hearts that the situation could not go on for ever, and all they could do was to hope for the best. At the end of 1920 it was evident that the Anglo-Irish War was costing the British Exchequer a lot of money to maintain and supply all the extra troops and Auxiliary forces in the country. There was the added problem of claims for damage arising from the troubles. In the eighteen months prior to the end of December 1920, the amount paid out on foot of claims for malicious damage to property came to £2,250,695. This did not include the massive claims arising from the burning of Cork city, which had not yet been processed.

The Ulster Special Constabulary

At the end of October 1920, Dublin Castle announced the formation of a "Special Constabulary" for Ulster. New legislation was not necessary, as the Special Constables (Ireland) Acts, 1832 and 1914, were still in force. There were three categories: the A Specials who would be full-time employed, the B Specials who would be employed part time and the C Specials who would be available in the event of an emergency. The A Specials were enrolled for a period of six months, were equipped with firearms and uniform, and received the same salary as members of the RIC. The Special Constabulary was under the control of Lieutenant Colonel C.G. Wickham, who was divisional commissioner of the RIC in Ulster. Under his command a county commandant was appointed for each of the six counties. Each county was divided up into districts and sub-districts under the command of district and sub-district commandants. The county commandant liaised closely with the county inspector of the RIC. The Special Constabulary members took the same oath as the RIC. In a short time they had assumed the same powers as the RIC. In January 1921 a set of rules defining the relationship of the Special Constabulary with the RIC were published.

As a result of Catholics' being discouraged by their Church and nationalist organisations from joining the Special Constabulary, almost the entire force were Protestants. The number of A Specials sworn in before the end of December 1920 was 1,500. There was a mixed reaction by the RIC to the A Specials, and there was frequent friction and a number of confrontations between the forces. On one occasion, members of the Special Constabulary were arrested by RIC members for involvement in a riot.

Within twelve months a total of 33,000 members had been enrolled in the Special Constabularies. While they provided a useful service in curtailing IRA activities in the six north-eastern counties, the Special Constabularies complicated the overall situation still further and in time became a law unto themselves.

January 1921

Martial law was extended to Counties Clare, Waterford, Kilkenny and Wexford, with effect from 4 January 1921. At Ballingarry, County Limerick, on 3 January, two young men were shot dead by Auxiliaries, the official excuse given being that "they were shot while trying to escape from custody". General Sean McEoin, the IRA leader from Ballinalee, County Longford, while staying at a friend's house on 7 January, was surrounded by a party of RIC under District Inspector Thomas McGrath. As he ran from the house, he threw a grenade at the district inspector and killed him. McEoin was arrested a few months later, court-martialled for the crime and sentenced to death. He was reprieved when the Truce came later in the year.

An ambush on RIC members and Black and Tans took place in Tramore, County Waterford, on 8 January and three of the ambushers were killed. An RIC sergeant and a constable were shot dead in an ambush on them at Cratloe, County Clare, adjacent to Limerick city. There were ambushes on police and Black and Tans at Borrisoleigh, County Tipperary; Mountjoy Square in Dublin; and at Charleville, County Cork on the 19th, but there were no fatalities. On the following day, two prisoners who were natives of County Westmeath were shot dead at Ballykinlar Internment Camp.

On 20 January, District Inspector Tobias O'Sullivan was shot dead by the IRA on the public street while walking hand in hand with his six-year old child, about fifty yards from his barracks at Listowel. He had only been in Listowel for a few months and had distinguished himself in the defence of Kilmallock barracks of which he was in charge when it came under a night-long sustained bomb and gunfire attack by the IRA on 28 May 1920. On 21 January, the RIC had one of its blackest days of the troubled period when six members of the force were shot dead near Sixmilebridge in County Clare. Later that night, Black and Tans went on a rampage of destruction as a reprisal for the killings.

Nine RIC barracks were attacked in County Tipperary on the 22nd but with limited success. In the early hours of the 27th, two RIC constables were shot dead in their beds in a Belfast hotel. Near Tuam, County Galway, three men were shot dead while in custody of the Crown forces; the official excuse again given was that they were shot while attempting to escape from custody. In an IRA ambush at Tureengarriffe, north Cork, on 28 January, a divisional commissioner, Major General Philip Holmes, was shot dead and six soldiers were wounded.

Other events during the month included the murder of William McGrath, King's Counsel, on the 14th, by armed men at his home in Dublin. Neither the reason for his murder nor the identity of his killers was apparent. One hundred prisoners were deported to England from Dublin at the end of the month and claims to the amount of £160,000 were lodged for damage to property, arising from the sacking of Balbriggan by Black and Tans in September 1920. There were a number of attacks on Crown forces in Dublin city and a number of people were shot dead in other unrelated incidents.

February 1921

The RIC sustained many casualties during February, which was a particularly violent month. The situation deteriorated so badly that on 15 February, King George V publicly stated that Ireland with its problems caused him much distress. On 1 February, the wife of RIC County Inspector William King was shot dead while she was waiting for a train at Mallow railway station, in what could only be described as an attack of the most cowardly nature. Following her killing, a party of Auxiliaries from the local barracks entered the railway station and sprayed it with bullets, killing three railway workers and wounding five others.

On the 2nd, the first execution under martial law took place, that of Con Murphy from Ballydaly, near Millstreet, County Cork, for possession of arms. On that same day an RIC constable was shot dead in County Cork and a resident magistrate was shot dead in County Wicklow. Three Black and Tans were killed in an ambush carried out by a flying column of the IRA under General Sean McEoin at Ballinalee, County Longford. This was followed by another black day for the RIC when on the 4th a serious ambush took place at Dromkeen, near Pallasgreen, County Limerick, when Sergeant Samuel Adams and nine constables (including a number of Black and Tans) were killed. Another ambush on the Crown forces took place on the same day at Ballinhassig, County Cork. Fifteen RIC members were killed in those two ambushes. A young boy was shot dead by Crown forces while playing football at Ballinagree, County Cork, on the 7th and an alderman and another man were shot dead in Drogheda. A train was ambushed at Rathcoole, near Millstreet, County Cork, on the 12th and a sergeant was killed.

During the weekend ending the 14th, a total of eight people were killed in different parts of the country. On 15 January a major ambush set up at Upton railway station for a train travelling from Cork to Bandon went badly wrong. Military forces were on the train in strength, and nine of the IRA ambushers and civilians were killed.

On the 19th, a man was found shot dead in Cork city with a label attached to his neck with a warning "Spies Beware". There were sixteen deaths in County Cork alone during the weekend ending on the 21st, and there were eleven other deaths through shootings elsewhere in the country. Three RIC members and three British soldiers were killed in different incidents on the 23rd, and on the following day an RIC constable and two British soldiers were shot dead in Bandon, County Cork. Four Black and Tans and one RIC constable were ambushed and killed near Macroom, County Cork on the 25th. At Victoria Barracks (now Collins Barracks) in Cork, six men were executed in pairs under the provisions of martial law, for possession of a revolver and for levying war against the state. There were a number of other incidents in Dublin and throughout the country resulting in loss of life.

Early in the month James Craig was elected Unionist leader in Belfast. The Irish hierarchy in their Lenten pastorals issued in mid-February condemned the reprisals and the general repression of the Crown forces, and they appealed to people not to commit acts of violence. Dr Gilmartin, Bishop of Galway, had some weeks previously appealed to his flock to hand up any firearms in their possession and said that the shooting dead of three Black and Tans near Headford, County Galway, was murder.

On 9 February, a group of Auxiliaries raided a grocery and public house belonging to a family named Chandler, close to Trim, County Meath. They helped themselves to large quantities of food and provisions, money, drink and personal jewellery. The incident was raised in both houses of the British parliament and investigated personally by General Crozier. After a preliminary hearing, he dismissed twenty-one Auxiliaries and arranged to put five forward for criminal trial for the looting. He was also displeased about the lenient manner in which a number of other Auxiliaries had been dealt with in Dublin for shooting two apparently innocent men – one fatally – at Drumcondra. When General Tudor, who was in command of the police forces in Ireland, reinstated the twenty-six Auxiliaries involved in the Trim incident, General Crozier sensationally resigned on 25 February. He vented his feelings in the British press about General Tudor and the difficulties which he (General Crozier) had encountered while trying to control the Auxiliaries since their arrival in Ireland. He was extremely critical of the Auxiliaries and their behaviour. His outspoken remarks caused embarrassment to the British government and provided further material for the Opposition in its criticism of the handling of the Irish problem by the British authorities.

March 1921

Six British soldiers were killed by snipers in Cork city on the 1st, presumably in retaliation for the six men executed at Victoria Barracks a few days previously. The curfew in Cork city was then extended to 6pm to 3am. Also on 1 March, a signalman at Cork railway station was pulled from his signal box by a number of masked men and shot dead. On the 2nd, two men were shot dead in County Tipperary, allegedly while they were attempting to escape from custody. Brigadier General Cummings, who was the officer in charge of the military in County Kerry, and two other officers and soldiers were shot dead in an ambush at Clonbanin, County Cork, on the Mallow/Killarney road, on 4 March. On 5 March a former soldier was shot dead by the IRA in County Roscommon, and again his body bore a tag "Spies Beware". On the night of 7 March, masked men entered the home of George Clancy, mayor of Limerick, shot him dead and seriously wounded his wife. A former mayor, Alderman Michael O'Callaghan, was also murdered on the same night. The Crown forces were believed to be responsible for the killings which caused much horror and indignation in Limerick and throughout Ireland. The murders were widely publicised. On the same day, there were ambushes in Cork and Dublin which resulted in eleven deaths.

Three men were shot dead in Thurles by armed men on 10 March. Six attackers were killed in an ambush in County Leitrim on the 12th. On the 14th, there were six executions by hanging in Mountjoy "for levying war against the Crown". A large crowd of up to 40,000 people gathered outside the prison and maintained a vigil there on that date. Constable John Grant was shot dead at Abbeydorney, County Kerry, and a chemist was shot dead in County Carlow on the 16th. Two major ambushes in counties Waterford and Cork on the 19th claimed eleven lives.

At Crossbarry, County Cork, one of the biggest ambushes ever undertaken by the IRA took place under the command of General Tom Barry on 21 March. An all-out effort was made by the British forces to wipe out Barry's flying column, which consisted of 104 officers and men, as the military were aware of its location. In a pincer movement, the military approached the column's location from different directions but their times of arrival did not coincide. Barry's flying column took up position near Crossbury village and attacked twelve lorryloads of British troops which arrived in the ambush position. Following heavy gunfire from both sides, the British sustained casualties, abandoned their lorries and left the scene. After the initial ambush there were three further engagements when separate sections of the flying column attacked further detachments of British troops who were approaching Crossbury from three other directions. Eight members of the military were killed and several were wounded. Three members of the IRA were killed and several were wounded.

The IRA in County Kerry made a daring attack on a train at Headford Junction outside Killarney on the 22nd, which resulted in six British soldiers, the commanding officer of the IRA and one innocent civilian being killed. On the 24th, four young men who ambushed an RIC patrol near Cork city were shot dead. On the last day of the month, the IRA in west Cork launched an attack on Rosscarbery RIC barracks in the centre of the town. The substantial building was well fortified. The IRA kept up the attack for several hours with gunfire, bombs and grenades. After a long struggle, the barracks was captured and destroyed by fire. Five members of the RIC who were involved in the defence of the barracks were killed.

There were numerous other incidents throughout the country during the month, with many incidents taking place in Dublin. The curfew hours for Cork and Dublin cities and Bandon town were again extended. Mrs Margaret Pearse, mother of the Pearse brothers executed in 1916, made the headlines with a claim for £3,600 for damage caused to her home – Cullenswood House – by the Auxiliaries in January 1921.

The census of population which was taken once every ten years in the month of April was again due in 1921, and on 11 March, Dáil Éireann passed a resolution prohibiting the taking of the census during the following month. This was a duty always carried out by the RIC and earlier by the Irish Constabulary, but considering the chaotic state of so much of the country, it would not have been feasible during 1921.

April 1921

The month of April commenced with the sensational and unexpected news that Lord French was being recalled as lord lieutenant of Ireland, by the British government, with effect from 1 April. His replacement was to be Lord Edmond Talbot. As events transpired, the newly appointed viceroy made little contribution to Irish affairs following his appointment. On 2 April, there were attacks on Crown forces at Londonderry, Newry, Ballyhaunis and Kells, and there was an outbreak of shooting and bombing in Derry city. On the 3rd, the IRA burned a number of business premises in the Manchester area. Two members of the RIC were shot dead in County Cork on the 11th.

In what must rank as one of the most brutal crimes of the period, an elderly gentleman, Sir Arthur Vicars, was taken by the IRA from his bed in his home at Kilmorna Castle, Listowel, County Kerry, shot dead while still in his dressing gown, and his castle burned down. A label was tied around his neck which read "Spies and Informers beware. The IRA never forgets." He formerly held the position as "Ulster King at Arms" and was the man with overall responsibility for the safety of the Irish crown jewels, which were mysteriously stolen from Dublin Castle in 1907 and which were never recovered. His murder provoked much anger in the British press and amongst the many people of all denominations and different shades of political opinion who had a very high regard for the elderly gentleman. Sir Arthur was married but had no family. A military court of inquiry held at Tralee into his death returned a verdict that he had been wilfully murdered by persons unknown.

The next day, 15 April, four IRA members shot dead Major McKinnion, the officer in charge of the Auxiliaries in County Kerry, as he played golf on Tralee golf course. The Black and Tans and Auxiliaries in Tralee carried out reprisals in Tralee following his death and burned down a number of premises. The next day, the IRA in Tralee took a woman named Kitty Carroll, who was the sole support of her aged parents and invalid brother, from her home and shot her as a spy. Her murder created much embarrassment for the IRA hierarchy. A few nights later, a Black and Tan was shot dead in a Tralee public house. There were attacks on Bray and Cabinteely RIC barracks on the 19th, and on the 20th, two RIC men were dragged from a train in County Sligo and shot dead. A goods train was seized by the IRA in County Monaghan and destroyed by fire.

On the 25th, Thomas Trainor, a forty-year-old father of ten children was executed at Mountjoy Gaol for his part in an ambush in Dublin city some weeks previously. Many pleas for clemency were made on his behalf due to his family circumstances, but to no avail. In mid-April, District Inspector Gilbert Potter of Cahir RIC barracks was kidnapped and detained by the IRA in south Tipperary. The IRA informed the authorities that the district inspector would be released safely by them in return for the safe release of Thomas Trainor who was then awaiting execution. General Macready would not consent to any exchange, and when it was announced that Trainor had been executed, the IRA decided to execute the district inspector. In *My Fight For Irish Freedom*, Dan Breen described what transpired: "I was very distressed at having to carry out such an unpleasant duty. We had considered the matter most carefully and concluded that we had no other alternative. Potter was a kind and cultured gentleman, and a brave officer. Before he was executed on 27th April, he handed over a diary, a signet ring and a gold watch with the request that we should convey them to his wife. We fulfilled this request." A report in *The Irish Times* of 10 May 1921 confirmed that District Inspector Potter's widow had received a parcel by post bearing a Cahir, County Tipperary, postmark, containing the late district inspector's signet ring, watch and diary. Also enclosed was a farewell letter which he had written on the morning of his death. In the letter he very affectionately bade farewell to his wife and four little children and also expressed a wish to be remembered by his friends.

Professor O'Rahilly of UCC, an outspoken critic of British policy in Ireland, was arrested by Crown forces on 26 April. On the 28th, Black and Tan reprisals carried out in Listowel town resulted in the destruction of a number of business premises. On the same date, three men were executed in Cork "for levying war against the Crown". In the latter part of April, the Cork No. 1 Brigade of the IRA captured Major Compton-Smith, who was attached to the Royal Welsh Fusiliers based in Limerick, and detained him as a hostage. The IRA made approaches to the British authorities, promising to free the major if three men who had been captured in the Clonmult, County Cork, ambush and who had been condemned to death were freed unharmed. The British authorities again refused to exchange prisoners. On the execution of the IRA members, the Cork No. I Brigade executed Major Compton-Smith.

There was universal condemnation of his death, as he was regarded as an inoffensive, harmless man who had never acted improperly. Representations for his release were even made by high-ranking IRA officers from adjoining counties, and pleas to spare his life were also sent to Michael Collins, but arrived too late to prevent his execution. It is believed that Michael Collins would have stopped it. The major and District Inspector Potter, who was executed on the previous day in Tipperary, both went to their deaths with a cheery fortitude. They wrote letters to their wives which were later published, and Piaras Béaslaí later observed: "they breathed a spirit of charity and resignation, which was in striking contrast to the bitter passions of those dreadful times". A problem was encountered by the relatives in retrieving the body of Major Compton-Smith, and it was left to the intervention of Michael Collins to have it recovered and handed over to the relatives.

Around this time also, another remarkable "execution" was carried out by the IRA Mrs Lindsay, a lady aged over seventy years, resided at Leemount, Coachford, County Cork. She apparently became aware of an ambush prepared for Crown forces by the IRA and went to Ballincollig RIC barracks with the information. In a follow-up operation, six IRA members were arrested in possession of arms, court-martialled and five were sentenced to death in Cork. The Cork No. 1 Brigade of the IRA arrested Mrs Lindsay, held her as a hostage, and bargained with the British authorities in Cork for the release of the six IRA men in military custody in return for the safe release of Mrs Lindsay. The British authorities would not agree to the exchange of prisoners. On learning that the five men had been executed in Cork, the IRA then executed Mrs Lindsay and her elderly male servant, without receiving sanction to do so from their headquarters. Michael Collins and the IRA headquarters staff were very displeased over the action taken, as it gained exceptionally bad publicity for the IRA cause.

During this period the IRA appeared to be obsessed about spies. They tortured and shot dead a total of seventy-three persons whom they regarded as spies or informers between 1 January and 1 May 1921. In the majority of these cases, the flimsiest reasons were given to justify the assassinations of the unfortunate victims. Many were totally innocent and were sentenced to death on the whim of some IRA officer who wanted to establish his authority. In many cases, the victims were tortured in an effort to extract information or confessions from them before they were shot. The evidence given at the military inquiries which investigated these deaths followed a very similar pattern. At one such inquiry into the "execution" of sixty-three-year-old Martin Daly of Inchincummer, Farranfore, County Kerry, the following evidence was given by an RIC member from Castleisland:

I knew the deceased Martin Daly. He had been unpopular in the locality for some time. As much police protection as possible was afforded to
him. The reason for his unpopularity was his having given information
to the military about being summoned to a Sinn Féin Court. At a townland called Ranaleen, I found lying by the roadway, the dead body of
Martin Daly. His hands were tied behind his back with a handkerchief.
Another handkerchief was tied across his eyes. He was fully clothed. He
had a bullet wound in the left breast and one in the right eye. I found a
notice [now produced] pinned to the breast of his coat which read
"Informers Beware. Convicted Informer". The body was found about
four miles from Daly's home.

A doctor gave evidence of having examined the body of Martin Daly on 21
March at the mortuary in Tralee military barracks:

His hands were tied behind his back and his eyes were blindfolded. On
turning over the body and removing some of the clothes, I found five
wounds of a terrible nature. The face and head were peppered with
small shot and the upper jaw was fractured. The hands of the deceased
man were filled with mud and tightly clenched which probably indicated
a struggle before unconsciousness supervened.

Evidence was given by a sister of the deceased who was with him herding cattle
when he was kidnapped and taken away. When her dog attacked the kidnappers they
shot it and they prevented her from following the men who took her brother away.
The inquiry returned "a verdict of murder by some person or persons unknown".

On 17 April, one of the most extraordinary events of the period took place at the
Shannon Arms Hotel, Castleconnell, County Limerick. The incident was played
down very much in the House of Commons by the British authorities, as it was most
embarrassing to them. It was, however, raised in the House of Lords, as the brother
of one of the lords had been on holidays in Ireland and was a guest in the hotel at
the time the incident took place. The circumstances appear to be as follows: three
members of the RIC who were off duty were drinking together in the lounge bar,
when the hotel was surrounded by a large party of Black and Tans and Auxiliaries,
who started firing on it from a machine-gun and rifles. Even when the RIC men
identified themselves to the attackers, the Black and Tans and Auxiliaries paid no
attention to them and kept on shooting. Finally, the RIC men drew their revolvers
to defend themselves and returned the fire. One of the RIC men was fatally
wounded and one of the Auxiliaries was killed. The RIC men were overpowered
when their ammunition ran out. One of the RIC men and the hotel proprietor,
Denis O'Donovan, were taken out to the rear yard of the hotel, where they were

both riddled with bullets by the Black and Tans and Auxiliaries. Guests in the hotel were terrorised and the bar was wrecked with grenades. The Black and Tans and Auxiliaries accused the owner's wife, Mrs O'Donovan, of harbouring Sinn Féiners. It would appear that some mischief-maker had passed word to them that members of the IRA were then drinking in the hotel. Two of the those killed were Sergeant William Hughes and Auxiliary Cadet Donald Pringle. A military inquiry was held into the circumstances of the affair.

During the months of March and April 1921, eight military officers were killed, seven were wounded and one was listed as missing. In the lower ranks of the military, twenty-two were killed, four died of wounds and sixty-three were injured.

May 1921

While some tentative moves were being made to bring about peace during May 1921, there was no let-up in the killings on both sides, and there were several serious incidents during the month. On 2 May, three RIC men were killed in incidents in Counties Cork and Longford. Six members of the IRA were killed in an ambush set up by them at Knocklong, County Limerick, on the 3rd. On the same day, Eamon de Valera had a meeting with James Craig, leader of the Unionist Party, in Dublin. Also on the 3rd, Sergeant John O'Regan and two RIC constables were killed and three RIC men were injured in an IRA ambush at Tourmakeady, County Mayo. In a follow-up operation by the military in the nearby mountainous area, a number of IRA Volunteers were killed. A bomb was thrown into a shop at Clonakilty, County Cork, and two RIC members were badly injured. On the following Sunday, prayers were offered by the clergy at all masses in Clonakilty for the recovery of the injured men. During the same week an attempt was made to sink six navy vessels at Queenstown (now Cobh), County Cork.

On the morning of 4 May 1921, an eighty-year-old man named Thomas O'Sullivan was taken by an IRA unit from his home a short distance from the village of Rathmore, County Kerry. He was shot dead and a label stating that he was a "Spy and Informer" was tied around his neck. His body was left on the road known locally as the Bog Road. A report was made at the RIC barracks in Rathmore to the effect that the body of a man was lying on the Bog Road less than one mile southeast of the village. Such were the fears of attack by the RIC at the time, that Sergeant Thomas McCormick took eight constables with him to the scene to investigate and recover the body. As they arrived, they were caught in a very well-prepared ambush by a large unit of the IRA, who opened up with rifle and machine-gun fire on Sergeant McCormick and his men. The sergeant and seven of his constables (Constables Phelan, Woodcock, Dyne, Hillyer, Walker, Browne and Fleck) were riddled with bullets and all died instantly. Constable Hickey escaped the slaughter and ran back to the village to summon assistance. Three of the dead constables were Black and Tans who supplemented the local RIC party.

It was generally accepted in the locality that there was no justification whatsoever for the "execution" by the IRA of the elderly Thomas O'Sullivan, who was regarded as a harmless pensioner. He appeared to have been killed solely as part of the plan to lure the local RIC station party into a trap. O'Sullivan's body and those of the eight RIC men lay on the road for several hours before the military recovered them and took them to Killarney. The tragedy was denounced by *The Irish Times* of 5 May 1921, which described the trap laid for the constabulary by the IRA as a "callous ruse". It was one of the biggest mass killings of RIC personnel.

On 6 May, two IRA Volunteers were killed in a gunfight with Crown forces in County Mayo; two soldiers were shot dead in Nenagh, County Tipperary; and Crown forces fired on a group of armed men who were found robbing a mail van in County Tipperary. The Half-Way House public house at Crumlin in Dublin was also burned to the ground by armed men on the same date. Bray RIC barracks came under attack on the night of the 6th. Six houses were burned down in County Cork. A small party of RIC were ambushed at Newtown, County Tipperary, on 6 May and Sergeant James Kingston and one of the IRA attackers were killed. In Ballivor, County Meath, an RIC constable was fired on and seriously injured. Mrs Conway, a young married woman, was shot dead at the door of her home at Caherina, Tralee, shortly after curfew on 6 May, evidently by a member of the Crown forces. On 7 May, an RIC constable was killed and a sergeant injured when ambushed at Inch, County Wexford. Several RIC barracks were attacked all over Ireland, and those at Cabinteely, County Dublin, and Bray, County Wicklow, were both attacked for the third time. In an ambush on Crown forces in County Cavan, one of the attackers was killed, two were injured and nine were arrested. A retired soldier was shot dead at Youghal, County Cork.

On Sunday 8 May, a constable was shot dead as he cycled to mass at Greenore, County Louth. On the same day, RIC Head Constable William Storey, was shot dead after leaving mass at the Catholic church in Castleisland, County Kerry. He was accompanied at the time by Sergeant Butler, who was also shot and seriously wounded. The sergeant's wife who was with them had a narrow escape from injury. A little boy was killed in Dublin when he handled a discarded grenade. District Inspector Ferris was shot and wounded in Belfast city. On 9 May, two elderly pensioners – one a constabulary pensioner and the other a retired postmaster – were dragged from their beds and shot dead by armed and masked men in County Roscommon. Another old-age pensioner was shot dead in his home in County Fermanagh. Two farmers were shot dead in County Cork, and Thomas Hopkins, an RIC constable, was shot while visiting his parents at Dromore, County Tyrone. Reprisals were carried out by Crown forces at Castleisland, County Kerry, where a number of houses were burned. Two RIC men and four civilians were shot dead on the 11th. Two days later, three members of the IRA were shot dead by Crown forces at Gortagleanna, near Listowel, County Kerry. An unsuccessful attempt was made by the IRA to rescue Sean McEoin and other IRA prisoners from Mountjoy Gaol on 14 May.

The days following were the Whit Weekend, and this turned out to be the worst weekend of deaths and violence since the Easter Rising of 1916. A total of thirty-six people were killed, including twenty members of the RIC and British soldiers. The remainder were innocent civilians, IRA members and people killed by persons unknown. All had met their deaths in ambushes, reprisals and general violence during that weekend. Fifteen RIC men and soldiers were killed on the Saturday, which was described in an *Irish Times* headline as "A Saturday of Horror". On the same day, District Inspector Henry Biggs, who was in charge of Newport barracks in County Tipperary, left Glenstal Castle, County Limerick, with his fiancée, Miss Barrington (only daughter of Sir Charles Barrington of Glenstal Castle), a military officer and two other ladies, and travelled towards Newport. Their car was ambushed at Coolboreen by about twenty men. Miss Barrington and District Inspector Biggs were killed and the remaining passengers wounded. At the subsequent military inquiry into the affair, evidence was given that twelve shots were fired into District Inspector Biggs' body as it lay on the road near his car.

A further casualty on that day was Head Constable Frank Benson, who was in charge of Tralee RIC barracks and who was shot dead at Pembroke Street, Tralee. As he left his home at 3pm after lunch, three men were waiting near by. One of them shot him through the forehead, and when he fell on the ground the other two men went forward and fired a number of bullets into his body. He was an exceptionally well-respected man. A little more than a year before, he had prevented a catastrophe in another town in Kerry, when he stood at the door of a Catholic church and prevented angry Black and Tans from throwing grenades into the congregation while mass was in progress.

On Whit Sunday, District Inspector Cecil Blake of Gort, County Galway, was returning from a tennis match at Ballyturin House, Gort, the home of John Baggot. He was driving his car and was accompanied by his wife; a Mrs Gregory, who was a daughter-in-law of Lady Gregory; and two army officers, Captain Cornwallis and Lieutenant McCreery. At the entrance gate to Ballyturin House, Captain Cornwallis got out to open the gate. There was a burst of gunfire from the nearby shrubbery and from the gatekeeper's residence directly opposite the gateway, which had been taken over by the ambush party. Captain Cornwallis was shot dead in the first volley and District Inspector Blake was badly wounded and lay on the roadway. When Mrs Blake went to his assistance, she was shot dead as she lay over his body. Several rounds were fired into both bodies. Lieutenant McCreery was also riddled with bullets. Miraculously, Mrs Gregory was not injured. After holding her for some time, the IRA column, which numbered about twenty, let her go. District Inspector Blake, who was twenty-eight, and his wife were buried side by side at Galway cemetery, and the bodies of both army officers were taken back to England for burial.

At Ballaghaderreen, County Roscommon, the IRA seized a train and as it passed close to the local RIC barracks, forced the driver to stop, and they launched an attack with firearms and grenades on the barracks from the steam engine of the train. The RIC returned the fire and one train passenger was injured.

A Cork city curate, Fr J. O'Callaghan, CC, was shot dead in the early hours of Sunday in the home of Alderman Liam de Roiste, TD, in Cork city. In Dromcollogher, County Limerick, three RIC constables went to a local shop to purchase some groceries. As they left the shop they were ambushed by an IRA unit, Constable Thomas Bridges was shot dead and the other two constables were seriously wounded. In an ambush on a small group of RIC members near Athy, County Kildare, two members of the attacking party were shot dead. At Bansha, County Tipperary, Sergeant O'Sullivan and two constables were leaving Bansha Catholic church after mass when they were ambushed by an IRA unit. Constable Nutley was shot dead and the other constable was wounded. Sergeant O'Sullivan received very serious injuries, but made a miraculous recovery. (Many years later his son – Bishop Diarmuid Ó Súilleabháin – became bishop of the Kerry Diocese.) Raids were also made on the same weekend by the IRA at the homes of members of the Black and Tans in the London area. A further eight people were killed on the 18th. On the 20th, two Dublin banks were raided by armed men, and the bodies of three ex-British soldiers were found in a quarry near Cork city. Eight members of the Crown forces were killed on the 23rd, including members of the RIC. Four members of the RIC and five civilians were shot dead on 30 May.

The biggest single event of destruction carried out by the IRA during the War of Independence was the burning down of the Dublin Custom House on 25 May. Much thought and planning was given to its destruction and over 120 IRA members took part in the operation. Having entered the building, they methodically poured petrol over the contents and furniture in each room and set it alight. Very shortly after commencing the operation, they were surrounded by police and military and there was an exchange of gunfire. Five of the attackers lost their lives, eighty were taken prisoner and several were badly wounded. Effectively it caused the loss of almost all active members of the Dublin IRA. Through the burning of the Custom House, all records connected with the Departments of Local Government, Estate Duties, Inland Customs and Revenue, Company Registration, the Stamp Duty Office, the Stationery Office and the Assay Office were destroyed. The building was reduced to ruins, and it burned and smouldered for several days afterwards.

An tÓglach commented: "The burning Custom House symbolised the final collapse of English civil administration in this country." Despite the loss of so many valuable records, the resilience of the civil servants who ran the different departments was remarkable, and within a few days they were all back working for their various departments at different locations throughout Dublin city.

Under the Government of Ireland Act, 1920, general elections were fixed for the north and south of Ireland during May 1921, to be held under the proportional representation system. In fact no election took place in the southern twenty-six counties as all elected members of Dáil Éireann were returned unopposed. Apart from four Unionist members representing Trinity College, the second Dáil was comprised of unopposed Republican deputies. While some members of Dáil Éireann did win a few seats in the nationalist areas in the northern Ireland election, James Craig and his Unionist party won forty of the fifty-two seats. There was much violence during the northern Ireland election campaign by the Orangemen and IRA, which kept the RIC in the counties involved very busy. On 23 May Pope Benedict XV made an appeal for peace in Ireland and suggested the setting up of an all-Irish conference to discuss proposals for peace.

June 1921

Six British soldiers were killed and twenty-one were injured by a landmine at Youghal, County Cork, on 1 June. On the same day a cycling party of RIC and Black and Tans under District Inspector Michael McCaughey, were returning from Tralee to their base at Killorglin when they were ambushed by a party of IRA just outside Castlemaine. The district inspector, Sergeant J. Calleary and Constables J. Cooney, J. McCormick and John Quirke were killed. On 2 June, District Inspector Stevenson, Sergeant Francis Cregan, Constables John Doherty and Thomas Dowling, along with three Black and Tans named French, Brown and Bright, were ambushed and killed at Leenane Road, Carrowkennedy, County Mayo. On the 4th, a man was executed in Limerick for possessing firearms, and on the 7th two men were executed in Mountjoy Gaol for their part in the Knocklong ambush in 1919. The trials arising from the Knocklong ambush had dragged on over a considerable period of time. At one stage when they were ready to proceed, the IRA kidnapped an RIC sergeant to prevent his attendance. He was later released unharmed but the trial again had to be adjourned. The courthouse in Skibbereen was burned down on the 10th, and there were twenty violent deaths over the weekend, along with serious rioting in Belfast.

During the weekend of the 18th to 20th, there were more violent deaths of constabulary, soldiers, members of the IRA and civilians, and six coastguard stations were captured and set on fire by the IRA in County Dublin. On 21 June, Lord

Bandon, one of the most influential loyalist figures in the south of Ireland, was kidnapped near Bandon and his castle was burned down. Armed and masked men took over Knocknagroghery, County Roscommon, on the same day and burned a number of houses to the ground. Two magistrates were kidnapped in County Cork on the next day. Two members of the RIC were shot dead in Grafton Street on 25 June, and two more were shot dead in Dolphin's Barn, Dublin, on the 29th. A number of prisoners were rescued from Sligo Gaol, also on the 29th.

King George and Queen Mary came to Belfast on 22 June where the king officially opened the Northern Ireland parliament. The king made a plea for reconciliation and peace in the country, in the course of his address to the parliament:

> I speak from a full heart when I pray that my coming to Ireland today may prove to be the first steps towards the end of strife amongst her people, whatever their race or creed. In that hope I appeal to all Irishmen to pause, to stretch out the hand of forbearance and conciliation, to forgive and to forget, and to join in making for the land which they love a new era of peace, contentment and goodwill. It is my most earnest desire that in Southern Ireland too, there may ere long take place a parallel to what is now passing in this hall; that a similar occasion may present itself and a similar ceremony be performed.

Documents and telegrams were exchanged between de Valera and Lloyd George during the month with a view to arranging a truce, but the ambushes and killings continued, with the Royal Irish Constabulary suffering very severe loses during these months. On 24 June, the IRA bombed and derailed a train travelling from Belfast to Dublin containing the horses and military who had been on escort duty for the king in Belfast two days previously. Four soldiers of the 10th Royal Hussars were killed and twenty wounded. Eighty horses were either killed or had to be put down due to serious injuries.

July 1921

Shootings in Cork, Offaly, Armagh and Newry on the first day of the month resulted in seven deaths. Arthur Griffith and a number of other Sinn Féin leaders were released from prison on the same day. On 2 July, two RIC constables were shot dead in an ambush at Ballina, County Mayo. Two days later, on the 4th, there were fifteen violent deaths, including eight policemen and seven civilians. A young girl was shot dead in Newry, County Down, while helping her brother to escape from armed men. On the 8th a train carrying British military was bombed near Clondalkin, County Dublin. Two brothers were shot dead by armed men in County Roscommon on the 9th.

On 9 July, a Truce was agreed between Eamon de Valera and General Macready. Hostilities in Ireland were to officially cease at 12 noon on the 11th. Even though the Truce was signed on 9 July there was a last-minute flurry of activity by the IRA. They shot dead the daughter of a retired RIC man whose house they raided in Tipperary on the 9th, and on the same day wounded a soldier and a member of the RIC. in Wexford. On the following day they fired at and injured one soldier and an RIC. man. Early on 11 July, they kidnapped five British soldiers in Cork city, shot four of them dead and wounded the other. The IRA in Kerry killed three British soldiers on the day the Truce became effective. Serious rioting took place in Belfast during most of the month and several people were killed, including fourteen people on the 11th alone. Military and RIC reinforcements were despatched by special trains from Dublin in an effort to get the Belfast riots under control.

The other event which dominated the news stories during the month was an exceptional heatwave with very high temperatures being recorded in Dublin, including a temperature of 99 degrees Fahrenheit on the 11th, the day when the Truce officially came into force. There were a number of incidents in Dublin city early in the month, but the middle of the month was taken up with bonfires celebrating the Truce. Amongst the main headlines for 14 July was "Rain at Last".

Apart from some deaths in Belfast as a result of rioting, there was little violence over the next few months, and practically all of the headlines were good news stories. In the policing of the twenty-six counties, the Republican police became more active and assertive and the Republican courts continued to operate. They were very well established in some parts of the country while non-existent in others. The Republican police got much publicity for arresting an armed bank robbery gang in Dublin in September. The punishment inflicted was that three members of the gang were deported from the country for a period of twenty years. In September, 100 internees escaped from the Curragh military camp and thirty prisoners escaped by digging a tunnel out of Kilworth Camp in County Cork. Two hundred prisoners who went on hunger strike at Mountjoy Gaol in November had their demands acceded to by the government after a few days.

The news up to the end of the year was dominated by the day-to-day negotiations between officials in London and Dublin and by the Dáil debates relating to the Treaty proposals. Following the Truce, the situation relating to the RIC amounted to an anti-climax. Much of the terrible stress and pressure which had dominated their lives over the previous three years was removed and they endeavoured to settle down to some kind of normal living. In parts of the country where the IRA had not been previously active, the RIC carried on with their duties as before, but this was to change as time went on. They were still careful, as serious threats had previously been made against many of them and the possibility remained that these threats would be carried out. They were also aware of divisions within the IRA and

Sinn Féin. Well before the Treaty was signed, they were certain that a civil war was going to take place in Ireland following their disbandment.

From October onwards, the Black and Tans were leaving. While the RIC had accepted their support, with some misgivings, the majority were glad to see the last of the Black and Tans and Auxiliaries. At the same time, the RIC, left with very few men in many barracks, felt very isolated and exposed. It was only at that point that the huge toll taken of the "old RIC" force became obvious. The Black and Tans had filled the gaps created by the numerous retirements, resignations and deaths of members in the last few years and had created an artificially high numerical strength for the force.

The Black and Tans were officially disbanded, with effect from 18 February 1922. General Tudor was generous in his praise for them and the work which they had performed in Ireland. He said that he was proud to have them under his command and that they all deserved well of their country. The Black and Tans were eligible for pensions to be paid by the British Exchequer for their duties in Ireland, the amounts varying from 20s. to 25s. per week. In his book *The Black and Tans*, Richard Bennett summed up the part played by them:

> The Treaty was, thus, both an end and a beginning. The major credit for such settlement as it provided was accorded to Lloyd George, but some at least should attach to the Black and Tans. They had played a decisive part in the long sad history of Anglo-Irish relations. They had, indeed, made Ireland "a hell for rebels to live in", and had carried out the Government's policy so successfully that the Prime Minister was forced to abandon it and come to the conference table. "The IRA never beat the Tans," an old Volunteer commander has said; "It was the British who did it." The men who achieved this remarkable military and political result returned home to join the growing army of the unemployed. Some of them later enlisted in the Palestine Police, and one became its commanding officer. At least two ended their lives at the end of a hangman's rope and another ex-Black and Tan murderer committed suicide before the police could arrest him. Most of them were no better and no worse than the rest of us. Black and Tans are made, not born. Nearly all of them enjoyed the spectacle of Irishmen cutting one another's throats in the Civil War of 1922–23 with sardonic satisfaction, and without being aware that they had helped to brutalise the young men of Ireland and were at least partly responsible for it. None of them could know that he had been an actor in the first scenes of a post war drama that was to continue in Egypt, India, Burma, Indonesia, Indo-China, Malaya, Kenya, the Gold Coast, Cyprus and Algeria and is still far from finished.

They had all left Ireland by February 1922.

Policing of the 1921 "Soviets" by the RIC

The RIC continued with its policing role, but only to a limited degree and in a low-key manner. The War of Independence resulted in huge unemployment. Following the Truce, many employers became very overbearing, some going so far as to cut wages. As a result, "mini-Soviets" were established in a small number of locations. Arising from a trade dispute at Charleville, County Cork, in August, workers took over the large creamery there and hoisted the Red Flag. Shortly afterwards, the mills and bakery at Bruree, owned by the Cleeve family of Limerick, were taken over and occupied by workers, the Red Flag was again flown and a large sign displayed: "Bruree Workers Soviet Mills. We Make Bread Not Profits." Dáil Éireann warned the workers to vacate the mills or the IRA would be sent in to remove them. This did not happen, and a suitable agreement was reached a week later.

A number of industries in the Cork Harbour area were also affected and Red Flags were flown. The RIC were able to prevent the situation getting out of hand in the areas where the problems were cropping up. On 14 September 1921, workers took over a foundry premises at Drogheda, County Louth. The management asked for RIC help and on 15 September a lorryload of RIC men arrived at the premises, armed only with ordinary police batons, entered the foundry premises and in a very short time cleared all the workers from it. Thereby ended the "Drogheda Soviet".

Chapter Ten

THE DISBANDMENT OF
THE ROYAL IRISH CONSTABULARY

From the commencement of the Truce on 11 July 1921, the disbandment of the Royal Irish Constabulary was inevitable, and it was the subject of discussion during the following months between Michael Collins and Sir Hamar Greenwood. A definite decision was taken to retain the Dublin Metropolitan Police force as it was then constituted. Michael Collins had some discussions with well-disposed officers within the RIC and DMP about the disbandment of the RIC and proposals for a suitable police force to replace it.

The Truce

The Truce and its provisions did not result in a cessation of attacks against the RIC. As rumours spread of a split within Sinn Féin ranks, the outbreaks of violence got worse from August 1921 onwards. In late August there were a number of armed bank raids. On 4 September, a discharged Dublin Fusilier was taken from his home by a number of masked and armed men and shot dead. On 9 September, two RIC constables were kidnapped and disappeared near Bandon, County Cork. Robbery, arson and violent crime continued unabated, and in October, attacks on RIC barracks recommenced.

The British authorities took the Truce seriously and kept their side of the bargain. There was an apparent cessation of violence by the Crown forces following the Truce and the serious attacks made on the RIC were not followed by reprisals as had been the practice prior to the Truce. This is all the more surprising when the English military authorities were not happy when the Truce was called in July. They felt that they had the IRA on the run and blamed the politicians for interfering. A secret report on the situation made in September 1922, intercepted by General Michael Collins, presented the military's point of view:

> Three months ago the rebel organisation throughout the country was in a precarious condition, and the future, from the Sinn Féin point of view, may be said to be well nigh desperate. The Flying Columns and Active Service Units, into which the rebels had been forced, by the search for prominent individuals, to form themselves, were being constantly defeated and broken up by the Crown forces; the internment camps were rapidly filling up; the Headquarters of the IRA was functioning under the greatest difficulty, many of its officers having been captured. De Valera himself had been captured and released for political reasons; a number of rebels found in possession of arms, or actually engaged in warlike operations against His Majesty's forces, had been condemned to death and execution was only delayed pending an appeal of a certain case to the House of Lords; the coal strike in Great Britain was over, the reinforcements were pouring into Ireland; martial law was about to be proclaimed throughout the 26 counties, and three months of good weather was still ahead of us. The total casualties, which had been inflicted on the troops, were little, if any, more (in 18 months) than many a battalion suffered in a single morning in the War in France. The police had suffered more severely than the troops. Such were the conditions on the 11th July, and it is small wonder that the rebel leaders grasped at the straw that was offered, and agreed to negotiations, accompanied by cessation of activities on both sides.

The sincerity and commitment of the British authorities to maintaining the truce is reflected in an internal document sent by the commander in chief of the British forces to General Strickland, which came into the hands of the First Southern Division of the IRA:

> There is a lot of trouble up here about the man who is charged with the hold-up in Bandon. The County Inspector has made a damn fool of himself, and seems to be doing his utmost to break the Truce. Two policemen were kidnapped as a set off, but the Shinners have sent down someone in authority today to have them released. We will let the matter lie quiet, as we do not want to cause any trouble. Tell the District Inspectors in your area and the County Inspector not to be making damned idiots of themselves. You had better acquit that man of the charge. We are trying to maintain that all cars in possession of the Shinners, or in our possession, before the Truce should be left so. You know the Shinners have sent their reply through to the Government today,

and I hear it is very hot, so we must take things easy, and let the Government understand plainly that we do not want another such scrap as we had before, especially at this time of year. See to this matter as soon as possible.

While the British performed well in maintaining the Truce, the same cannot be said of the IRA. The divisions within Sinn Féin were certainly a factor, but there were other reasons also. The best assessment of the situation from the IRA aspect is probably that given by Piaras Beaslaí in *Michael Collins and the Making of a New Ireland*:

A great many eleventh-hour warriors, in comparatively peaceful parts of the country, hastened to make up arrears by firing shots at the last moment, and there were attacks on the English forces up to within a few minutes of the Truce. These belated exhibitions of prowess, with no military objective, when the danger seemed past, reflected no credit on Irishmen, but they were only the beginning of a period which patriotic Irishmen felt little pride in recording. The prolonged Truce, the relaxation of the strain which had kept the brave men of the IRA and the people generally up to the mark, and the chaotic conditions which prevailed in the country for many months, proved the seeds of a subtle demoralisation.

Piaras Béaslaí also made the following observations about the situation:

The Truce was a very doubtful problem to the IRA. The men who had been on permanent active service, while remaining Volunteers and not regular troops, had now to be kept on hand during the prolonged Truce whose issue was uncertain. Men from the "columns" returned to their homes, but owing to the circumstances, found it hard to settle down to work. They were feted, subjected to hero-worship, spoiled for the dull routine work on the farms. Men who had been fine fellows when there was danger became spoiled when the danger was over. They learned to swagger about in trench coats and leggings, with a revolver in their pocket, to "commandeer" motor cars to any place to which they wished to go, on the plea of "IRA" business. Men who had been the models of sobriety, took to hard drinking. Restrained neither by the strict discipline which war conditions rendered necessary, nor by the discipline of regular troops living in camps or barracks, the six months truce caused a general deterioration. Another factor in the situation was the inrush of new recruits to the IRA. Those who had been most timid suddenly became most aggressive and warlike.

The decision to accept recruits during the Truce was of doubtful expediency. The English "secret report" refers to the influx of new recruits, and expresses a doubt "whether the quality of the new recruit is up to the standard of the Irish Volunteer of the past". Training camps for Volunteers were established, but these proved not an unmixed blessing. In fact while de Valera was busy exchanging dialectics with Mr Lloyd George, the country was steadily drifting into a state of anarchy, and any attempt to get back to pre-Truce conditions became daily more impossible. The prolonged haggling and arguing only increased the general unsettlement and uncertainty. There was no established law or order as there was no authority supreme anywhere. Men, forgetting the days of terror grew truculent; and the magic of the name "IRA" was abused daily. The man with a gun in his hand learned to be a law unto himself. Local Captains and Commandants, perhaps only lads of 19 or 20 years, arrogated to themselves the right to be arbiters of their neighbour's affairs, and intervened in local disputes and quarrels over land. At this time all the seeds of the later disorder and bloodshed were sown. The longer the Truce lasted the more impossible the return to war status, and at the same time, the more inevitable became disorder and revolt, in case of any settlement or attempt to re-establish regular government.

Until its disbandment, the RIC took the brunt of this breakdown of discipline amongst the IRA factions, and during the last months of the force's existence it paid a heavy penalty for the anarchy which ensued from August 1921 onwards. The Treaty was signed on 6 December 1921, and this confirmed the agreement already reached between Michael Collins and Sir Hamar Greenwood for the disbandment of the RIC

Further Attacks on the RIC

Between December 1921 and February 1922, when the withdrawal of the Black and Tans was completed, there were eighty-two attacks recorded on the RIC resulting in twelve deaths and twenty-seven people being seriously injured. On 13 December 1922, Sergeant John Maher was shot dead while walking the street unarmed in Ballybunion, County Kerry. On 14 December, Sergeant Thomas Enright was killed and Constable M. Timoney was seriously injured while they attended a race meeting, unarmed and in plain clothes, at Kilmallock, County Limerick. On 15 December, Constable J. Mooney was shot dead while waiting for a train at Carlow railway station. On 3 February 1922, two off-duty constables, unarmed and in civilian clothes, were shot dead as they left a public house at Lisdoonvarna, County Clare.

On 11 February 1922, District Inspector Michael Keany, who was stationed in Cork city, was brutally shot dead as he left a hotel at Clonakilty, County Cork. His teenage son, who was with him at the time, was also shot and died from his wounds a short time later.

What was one of the most cowardly attacks ever made on the RIC took place on 15 March 1922, when armed gunmen entered Galway Hospital where two members of the RIC. Sergeants John Gilmartin and Tobias Gibbons, were recovering from injuries – and shot them dead as they lay in their hospital beds. A male civilian patient in the hospital at the time was also shot dead, obviously mistaken for a member of the RIC. A state of general lawlessness continued into April and May 1922 with the shooting of a number of Protestants in west Cork – allegedly as reprisals for the shooting of Catholics in Belfast. Three RIC constables were shot dead in County Clare on 6 April, and two days later Sergeant McManus of the RIC was shot dead in Templemore, County Tipperary.

To settle old scores with retired RIC members, the IRA killed several of them during April. The country was in a state of anarchy, and the situation looked so bad during April that the disbandment of the RIC was temporarily suspended on the 7th, although recruiting for the RIC had ceased on 11 July 1921. On 24 January 1922 at a meeting held in the Colonial Office between Michael Collins and Sir Hamar Greenwood, 20 February 1922 was fixed as the official date for the disbandment of the RIC. The provisional government agreed that recruiting for a new police force (the Civic Guard) would commence immediately after the RIC ceased to be operational. The actual disbandment proved to be a huge logistical operation and it was August 1922 when the last members of the RIC evacuated Dublin Castle.

Evacuation of Barracks and Dublin Castle by the RIC

As the attacks on the RIC barracks and shooting of RIC men continued during February and March 1922, the smaller barracks were evacuated and the personnel transferred to the larger centres pending their disbandment. In some cases they took up occupation in military barracks for their own safety. In Republican areas of the country they were virtually under siege despite the Treaty and the arrangements made for their disbandment.

The British authorities had to arrange the orderly evacuation of about 800 barracks all over the twenty-six counties and the transportation of the RIC members from those barracks to central locations like Gormanstown and Collinstown Camps, Mullingar and Dublin Castle. Group photographs exist of 500 to 600 members of the force assembled for disbandment at these centres. Special groups were organised at the RIC depot from amongst the Reserve to implement the evacuation procedures and to ensure that the members got safely to the disbandment centres.

This proved extremely difficult. Some of the main roads and the railway lines were still out of commission, where bridges blown up during the previous two years had not been repaired. This was particularly the situation in the southern Munster counties. In Munster, in nearly all cases, the RIC members travelled on lorries, and were accompanied by armoured vehicles to the principal ports. From there they were conveyed by boat or destroyers to Dublin and Drogheda, and then by lorries and armoured vehicles to the disbandment centres. Here they stayed for some days or weeks before being paid off. At Gormanstown Camp they were being discharged from the force, with their final payments and travel tickets to prearranged locations, at the rate of 100 men per day.

On evacuating their barracks throughout the country, the RIC parties had strict instructions to destroy all official records, old files and correspondence. In most instances they left barrack furniture behind, including bedding, cooking utensils, notice boards and garden implements etc. In all cases, without exception, emphasis was placed on the collection of all firearms, ammunition, flares and the heavy metal RIC badges which had been displayed over the main front door for the previous half a century. These items were meticulously accounted for and taken away for security to the RIC depot, Gormanstown Camp or Dublin Castle. Each member of the RIC left his barracks with his personal issue of firearms, his regulation box and whatever items of civilian attire and personal property he possessed.

The gun racks fitted to the day room walls and the steel shutters fitted to the windows and doors were left behind. For the next 50 years or more, these remained in situ in Garda Síochána stations and RUC barracks as grim reminders of what life in the RIC had been like during the final years before the disbandment of that force.

In many instances, the takeover of the barracks by the new Free State forces came as a great relief to the RIC members, who felt that they had endured as much as they could of attacks and violence in the preceding years. Until the very last barracks was evacuated, even in previously relatively peaceful areas, there were numerous "eleventh-hour" IRA gunmen, as Béaslaí called them, around to have a last shot at the departing policemen and hoping to get their names into the history books by attacking or shooting soft targets.

The RIC evacuated Dublin Castle at 8am on 17 August 1922. They left the Castle in charge of a detachment of the King's Shropshire Light Infantry. In the afternoon of the same day, a detachment of 380 members of the new Civic Guards, under the command of Commissioner Michael Staines and Chief Superintendent Matthias McCarthy, marched into Dublin Castle and took it over. Dublin Castle had been the administrative headquarters of all the constabularies in Ireland, as well as being the centre of British government in Ireland for several centuries.

Stand Down Parades at the Depot and Collinstown

On 4 April, 1922, members of the RIC – now commonly referred to as the "old RIC" – assembled at the depot for their "farewell" or "stand-down" parade. For various reasons, many members were unable to attend and just over 300 were present. Some described it as a joyous occasion, as the terrible ordeals suffered by them over the previous four years were over. Others felt that they had given the force their best endeavours during their service and now felt sad and very isolated. Major General Sir Henry Hugh Tudor inspected the parade and addressed the assembled members. The RIC Band, under the command of District Inspector Rafter, played a fine selection of music during the ceremonies. Major General Tudor said that he could not leave for Palestine without bidding a formal farewell to their splendid force. He knew what hard times they had been through and the difficulties which they had encountered. He was sorry to see such a magnificent body of men being dispersed, for they had always loyally and consistently supported him. He was glad to say, that about 300 members of the force had joined the Palestine Police and he looked forward to meeting them again. From the bottom of his heart he wished them all a sad farewell and the best of luck in the future.

The depot commandant, Mr Heard, replying to General Tudor, said that the officers and men desired him to convey their deep appreciation of his words. They much regretted their own impending disbandment, for in the past they had endeavoured loyally and faithfully to do their duty. No matter where General Tudor went he had the goodwill of the RIC and they now wished him luck and prosperity. The officers and men cheered for the general who shook hands with each member before leaving. The RIC officers present on the occasion were Mr Heard, county inspector and depot commandant; Mr McClelland, barrack master; County Inspector Peacock, the surgeon; District Inspectors Mordant, Baynham, Long, Nelligan, Byrne, Connolly, Breally, Stagg and Dunn-Cook.

Later on 4 April, Major General Tudor went to Collinstown Camp, where he inspected over 500 members of the force who had assembled there for disbandment. The members, who represented all ranks, came from different counties and were under the command of County Inspector Neylon of Sligo. General Tudor was accompanied by W.T Rigg, divisional commissioner, and he was received at the camp by County Inspector H. M. Loundes of Howth. The general said that he had come to thank the force for the splendid assistance which was at all times at his disposal. He hoped that success would follow them back to civilian life and that they would always cherish the high standard of discipline, courage and loyalty of the magnificent force, which would in the future, as in the past, command the admiration of their countrymen and indeed the whole civilised world. County Inspector

Lowndes said that they were very glad to meet General Tudor again and he was sure that they all wished him every success in his new appointment.

It was ironic that on the same day, 4 April 1922, Commandant General Rory O'Connor, who was in charge of the anti-Treaty Republican forces, publicly exposed the major differences and bitterness which then existed between his forces and the Provisional government and army of the Irish Free State. This split led on to the Irish Civil War and another tragic chapter in Irish history.

Disbandment of the Cork RIC

The RIC personnel travelled in uniform from their barracks to the disbandment centres and maintained the strict discipline instilled into them from the time they had joined the force until their very last day in the service. Former Sergeant Michael Sullivan in an eyewitness account vividly recalled the arrival of the Cork city contingent of the RIC at Gormanstown Camp. There were at least 200 of them, all very well turned out in full uniform. They marched in fours, in absolutely perfect military formation, carrying their rifles. None of them was under six feet in height, and all were well built, handsome in appearance and all extremely fit. A finer body of men would be difficult to find anywhere in the world. The comradeship and camaraderie that existed between every one of them was apparent to everybody in the camp at the time. They had come by boat from the port of Cork, with the final leg of their journey by lorries and armoured vehicles. The tragedy was that within a few days, this outstanding body of men would be scattered towards the four corners of the globe, and very few of them were ever likely to meet again.

Takeover of Barracks from the RIC

Even after evacuating their barracks and while making their way to Gormanstown Camp and other centres, the RIC members were not immune to attack, particularly in the southern part of the country. After being evacuated by the RIC, the barracks were, in most cases, handed over to representatives of the new Free State government, and the larger ones were immediately manned by the new Free State army. In several instances in the south of Ireland, however, the barracks were taken over by the Republican (or anti-Treaty) forces. A number of barracks were entered, burgled and set on fire by anti-Treaty forces to prevent their takeover by the Free State army or the newly awaited Civic Guard force. Where the barracks remained unscathed, the new Civic Guards very much appreciated them, as the accommodation was superior to anything else available.

The eagerness to acquire these buildings, which for so long had been seen as the symbol of British rule in Ireland, was unbelievable. In some instances the new occupants had the tricolour flying from the rooftop before the evacuating RIC men had their regulation boxes and accoutrements taken outside the door. The official handovers took place without rancour or bitterness, and both sides fully appreciated each others' role and feelings. In a few instances, drinks were shared and presents exchanged at the handover stage.

Pension Arrangements

Prior to disbandment, practically all of the RIC who were eligible for pension had retired from the force. They did not see a future in it and left while it was safe to do so. Many others, through personal fear or fear for their families, following threats from the IRA during the previous two years, had resigned before they became eligible for full pension. Others who had been seriously injured were discharged on compassionate grounds with a pension. When disbandment came, therefore, there was quite a young force, with the average service being fifteen years, and some members were left in a very unenviable situation, In the ordinary course of events, their entitlements would be meagre, but under the Constabulary Act of 1920, members of the RIC were entitled to add ten years to their actual service for the purpose of pension eligibility. In certain cases, the ten-year extension could be increased upwards to twelve years. They were also entitled to one-fiftieth or one-sixtieth of their highest salary for each year of their service. Members who had completed fifteen years service in the force were, therefore, eligible to almost a full pension, and those with short service got better pension than usual.

There were a number of exceptional cases which would have resulted in very low pensions, but following representations and protests to Dublin Castle on their behalf, suitable arrangements were made for the payment of decent pensions. In accordance with the provisions of article 10 of the Treaty agreement, the Irish Free State government undertook to pay the pensions of all former members of the RIC, as well as judges and other public officials who became unemployed. The maximum pensions payable to members of the RIC amounted to approximately £20 per month, which was considered as being quite good.

The Free State government was not responsible for pensions or payments made to the Black and Tans or Auxiliaries, which, it was agreed, would be paid by the British Exchequer. The average service of the Black and Tans was less than two years' but they too benefited from the ten-year bonus extension which entitled them to a pension of approximately £5 per month.

Agitation continued for many years after disbandment to secure pensions for members of the constabulary who had resigned from the force prior to 1922, but with very limited success. The issue was raised in Dáil Éireann on many occasions during the following decade and well into the 1930s.

Options Open to Former RIC Men

The disbanded RIC men found themselves in an extreme quandary. For practically every one of them, there was no returning to their native place or any place close to it. Many of them had been threatened and death sentences had been passed on some of them by IRA elements. In many cases their families had been threatened, and some had been shot at while home on holidays or while paying visits to elderly parents. The prospects were bleak for many.

One option open to them was to join the Palestinian Police force, where recruits were badly needed. The situation there was in as disturbed a state as it had been in Ireland over the previous three years, however, and there was a question about the permanency of any appointments to that force. As well, many of the disbanded Black and Tans had already gone to Palestine. For the majority of RIC men, who had a difficult time put behind them, it was not an attractive proposition and they did not take up the offer. Some who did join the Palestine Police served out their time there, while others found the heat oppressive and left it after a year or two.

A number of the English police forces were seeking recruits at the time and some joined them. Some went to Canada and joined the police forces there. A very small number joined the Ulster Special Constabulary which was set up in November 1920 and for which there was ongoing recruiting as several thousand men were required.

Formation of the RUC

The RIC in the six north-eastern counties (now called Northern Ireland) were disbanded in June 1922. Many members of the RIC hoped to join the Royal Ulster Constabulary which was established to replace the RIC Only 1,100 members of the RIC succeeded in getting into the new force, of whom 400 were Catholics. Very many were disappointed at their failure to gain entry to the new Royal Ulster Constabulary.

Evacuation of Phoenix Park Depot

On 14 May 1922, the RIC vacated the Phoenix Park depot, which had been the home of the Irish and Royal Irish Constabulary since 1842, and handed it over to the care of the Royal Horse Artillery, who stayed until it was taken over by the Civic Guards later in that year.

Shooting of Lieutenant Wogan-Browne and Field Marshal Sir Henry Wilson

Two very serious incidents occurred during the period of disbandment of the force, either of which could have resulted in the wrecking of the peace process. The first occurred at Kildare town on Friday morning, 10 February 1922, when Lieutenant Wogan-Browne, who was attached to the artillery barracks in Kildare, went to the Hibernian Bank in Kildare to collect the weekly pay for his regiment. As he was returning to the barracks, a short distance from the barracks gate, a motor car pulled up and three men jumped from the vehicle, robbed the money from him and shot him through the forehead. He died instantly. His death caused revulsion and angered the British authorities. He was the only son of Colonel Wogan-Browne, Keredern, Naas, County Kildare, and on the day of his funeral he was due to play a rugby match at Lansdowne Road, Dublin.

The second incident occurred in June 1922, when Longford-born Field Marshal Sir Henry Wilson was shot dead in Eaton Place in London. His death almost caused a British military revolt in Dublin, and would have done so but for the direct intervention of General Macready, who refused to carry out certain instructions issued to him. The totally unnecessary shooting of Sir Henry Wilson was carried out by two IRA members named Dunne and O'Sullivan, both of whom were arrested for the crime. Claims were subsequently made that they had instructions from Michael Collins on official government paper to carry out the shooting.

For the disbanded RIC men who did not want to join the other police forces, there was little alternative but to "take the boat". For those who were most hunted by the IRA, the further away from Ireland they went, the better. Some of them would later say that their greatest regret was that they had been unable to return to their homes to see their ageing parents before they emigrated, and many of them knew that they would never see their parents alive again. They were scattered to the four corners of the globe and paid a huge penalty for their loyalty to the Royal Irish Constabulary, of which they spoke with pride until the day they died.

RIC Brothers – Sergeant Michael and Constable Con Sullivan

The fate of two brothers – Con and Michael Sullivan – who were members of the RIC typifies the problems faced by many members of the force on disbandment. Both recounted their experiences to the author forty years later. They were natives of Maularaha, Kealkil, Bantry, County Cork, and came from a large farming family. Both were intelligent and ambitious, and with the exception of emigrating to America there were few career choices at that time for young men like them other than joining the RIC. They saw it as a life-long career and pensionable, and in the early 1900s the force was well respected and looked up to by all decent law-abiding people. The members of the force were perceived as being of the highest integrity and well disciplined. There certainly was no animosity from anybody towards them as a result of their joining. Many of their friends and neighbours also joined the force. Parents were proud that they had a son in the RIC, as it was an acknowledged that only the "cream of Irish manhood" succeeded in getting into it.

Con Sullivan joined the force on 16 March 1911. He served in County Wexford and at Myshall and Cloneygal, County Carlow. On appointment as district inspector's clerk, he transferred to Cashel, County Tipperary, in January 1919, which coincided with the shootings of two constables at Soloheadbeg, County Tipperary. He later transferred to the district inspector's office at Nenagh, County Tipperary, and finally moved to a clerical position in Dublin Castle, where he remained until disbandment on 14 July 1922 and the Castle's evacuation some weeks later.

Michael Sullivan joined the RIC on 10 September 1914, and on completing his training was assigned to Pallasgreen, County Limerick, and later served at Doon and other barracks in the same county. He was promoted to sergeant rank and served at Oola, County Limerick, during the 1919–1921 period. On the closure of Oola barracks, he completed his service in the military barracks in Tipperary town and was disbanded on 19 April 1922. He subsequently moved to Dublin Castle where he remained for a period.

Both brothers enjoyed their early years in the force. They had a passion for fishing, horse racing and game shooting. When they went home to their parents and family for their annual holidays, they enjoyed their vacations at home: meeting up with old friends and colleagues in the force, helping on the farm saving hay, reaping corn, helping out with threshings on their neighbours farms and attending parties and dances.

This was the pattern up to 1918, but after the shootings at Soloheadbeg in January 1919, things were never the same again. Through 1919 and 1920 they visited their home and parents twice a year, but the situation was entirely different. They took their holidays together, and both were armed with revolvers when they came home. It was no longer safe for them to attend parties or dances or even mass at their local church. They rarely moved out of their home while on leave, and then only in each other' s company. While one slept in the family home, the other sat on a chair inside an upstairs window overlooking the main entrance door, armed with two loaded revolvers. This caused apprehension among their parents and younger family members, and what should have been joyous homecomings for both brothers were looked forward to with reservation and trepidation. It was a relief when they returned safely to their barracks.

In 1921 and 1922 it was considered too dangerous for them to visit their home and parents. Both men were single. Con had been engaged to be married, but because of the circumstances in which he found himself in the latter years of his service, he considered it unwise to go ahead with his marriage plans. From 1919 onwards, he anticipated the end of British rule in Ireland and the disbandment of the RIC. As he was not in the operational field during the last three years of his service the risk to his life would not have been as great.

Michael Sullivan was an active operational policeman during his entire service. He had spent all his service in the Tipperary/Limerick area which happened to be one of the most consistently active Republican areas in Ireland from 1919 until disbandment. There were regular attacks on the police barracks where he served, and from time to time he was engaged in the escort of prominent Republicans to prison, as well as other routine duties relating to Republican activities. He was also involved in a number of IRA ambush situations. On 30 July 1920, he successfully led the constables under his control at Oola in breaking up an IRA flying column attack under Dan Breen and Sean Treacy on military vehicles travelling between Pallasgreen and Tipperary town. Sergeant Sullivan and his party's arrival on the scene caused the IRA column to abandon their attack on the military and disperse. While it did not become known until later, General Lucas, a military commander based in Fermoy, County Cork, who had been kidnapped by the IRA a month earlier, had succeeded in escaping from his captors that morning near Pallasgreen, County Limerick, and was a passenger in the military vehicle under attack by the IRA. Sergeant Sullivan was threatened on several occasions but ignored all threats and continued to do his duty. He was a marked man by the local IRA leaders and threatened with death on a number of occasions.

On disbandment of the force and while together at Dublin Castle, the brothers discussed their future. There certainly was no going back to their native home place or to any area where they had served. Neither saw any future or prospects for themselves in Ireland. The brothers did not consider the Palestine Police, as neither was anxious to renew acquaintance with the many former Black and Tans who had joined it. They very regretfully accepted the fact that they could not get home to see their parents again before they left Ireland.

On the evacuation of Dublin Castle by the RIC, they marched from the Castle to the boat taking them and hundreds of their comrades to England. Con got married in Leicester a week later, with Michael as best man. Con had little problem in getting a position with the local health service in Leicester city, in which he served until he qualified for a further pension. It was 1960 before he ventured to return to Ireland again, by which time his parents were long dead. He visited Ireland on a regular basis after that up to the time of his death.

A few days after Con Sullivan's wedding, Michael Sullivan left for Australia, where he lived until his death in 1980 at the age of ninety-three.

The brothers never met again, but kept in close contact through letters. Despite pleas from his family to make a visit to Ireland, Michael never did. He never saw his parents or other family members again. He identified 1918 as the year when he perceived a coldness of attitude by the people towards the Royal Irish Constabulary as a police force, and this grew progressively worse. Until his death, he was extremely conscious of the death threats made to him and could not be convinced but that the Troubles in Northern Ireland in the 1950s and '70s were a direct continuation of the IRA activities which he had experienced from 1919 to 1922.

He had no regrets and was very proud of his service in the Royal Irish Constabulary.

Disbandment of the RIC Officers

The majority of the RIC officers went to England following disbandment, although a small number went to other countries. They formed an organisation and kept in close touch with each other. Once every year they met in London for a dinner, where they told and retold stories of their experiences in Ireland. They maintained a very close bond of comradeship and friendship and continued to meet annually up to the late 1950s.

In the officers' mess at the RIC depot in Phoenix Park, the most cherished possession was the Regimental snuff box, which was made of silver and mounted on the hoof of a horse which had carried a soldier at the Battle of Waterloo in 1815. The horse was brought back to Ireland and served for thirty-three years with the Dublin Metropolitan Police. In 1849, the snuff box was presented by Lieutenant Colonel George Browne, one of the DMP commissioners (and a former Irish Constabulary officer) to the newly formed officers' mess at the depot. It was ceremoniously passed around the table on guest nights after dinner, and guests were expected to take a pinch of snuff with their hosts. Kings and viceroys had from time to time been guests, and the box was handled by every officer of the constabulary between 1849 and 1922 and by the hundreds of colonial officers who were trained at the depot. The silverware at the mess was dispersed amongst the officers on disbandment of the force. As a token of their loyalty to the king, the RIC officers presented him with the snuff box, and it now sits in Buckingham Palace in the study of His Royal Highness, Prince Philip, Duke of Edinburgh.

On their disbandment, the Royal Irish Constabulary officers also made a presentation to Timothy M. Healy, the new governor general of the Irish Free State, as a token of their goodwill towards the new Irish Free State. The presentation made was a very ornate silver cup, engraved with the crest worn by RIC officers on their pouch belt: the old Celtic cross design surmounted by an Irish harp in its centre. The cup was appropriately referred to as the "Cup of Peace". It was presented by family members of the late Timothy M. Healy to the commissioner of the Garda Síochána in 1963 and is now on display at the Garda Síochána Museum in Dublin Castle. Besides being a wonderful gesture to the new state, the officers' gift of a cup also signified the noble qualities and professionalism of the officers, who despite all their losses and tribulations in the preceding three years were then leaving the force and the country without rancour or bitterness and displaying their chivalry in the best military tradition.

Families of RIC Members

Members of the RIC reared families throughout Ireland in most trying and difficult circumstances, particularly between 1916 and 1922. The wives and children lived in fear in nationalist areas of the country. Very many lived in barrack accommodation, which increased their danger, as barracks were regularly subjected to armed attacks. Despite all the hardships and difficulties encountered, the members of the force and their wives raised families which were models for their community. They were deeply interested in the education and welfare of their children. Their sons and daughters distinguished themselves in the academic, business and commercial life of Ireland. An exceptionally big number of their sons and daughters entered religious life, some becoming bishops and superiors of their religious orders. They were always marked out as having some exceptional qualities which could only be attributable to their well-disciplined and well-organised upbringing.

They also became very active in politics, and it is believed that fourteen members of the first Dáil were in fact the sons of former members of the RIC. Eamon Ceannt, who was one of the signatories of the Proclamation of the Irish Republic in 1916, was the son of a head constable of the RIC from Ballymoe, County Roscommon. Michael Staines, the first commissioner of the Civic Guards, was the son of a former member of the force. Two of the Garda Síochána commissioners, Michael Wymes and Lawrence Wren, were also sons of RIC members. The sons of many former members of the force joined the Garda Síochána and the Royal Ulster Constabulary. It was an acknowledged fact that the sons and daughters of former members of the RIC excelled in whatever career or station in life they chose. They had a greater sense of values and sense of responsibility and commitment than the average civilian family.

The hardship endured by widows and children following the deaths of members was extreme. Invariably they resided in barrack accommodation which they had tovacate or in rented accommodation which they found impossible to pay for when the family breadwinner was killed. Many widows of RIC men had to return and live with their parents when they were forced to evacuate accommodation. There were long delays in getting pensions and long-drawn-out procedures in trying to get some compensation for the deaths of their loved ones. The untimely and violent deaths of their fathers had a traumatic effect on the children, many of whom were very young at the time. Widows and children found it very hard to survive, and many were forced to emigrate to places as far away as New Zealand or Australia in order to seek out a living. The wives and children of RIC members were innocent victims in a situation over which they had no control and were condemned for the fact that their husbands/fathers were Irishmen serving in the police force of their country.

The Contribution of the Royal Irish Constabulary to the Garda Síochána

Foundation of the Civic Guards

During the latter months of 1921 and early 1922, there was a marked deterioration in the maintenance of law and order in the Irish Free State with which the new Irish government was unable to cope. Criminals were taking full advantage of the absence of any regular police force in the state. The Provisional government, and particularly Michael Collins, were coming under much pressure from their supporters to provide a police force to replace the Royal Irish Constabulary. A meeting was arranged to take place at the Gresham Hotel, Dublin, on the night of 9 February 1922. The government representatives who attended were General Michael Collins; General Richard Mulcahy, who was minister for defence; Eamon Duggan, TD; Michael Staines, TD; and Colonel Patrick Brennan, TD. There were two IRA Volunteer officers present: Commandant Martin Lynch who was in charge of the Republican police in County Laois, and General Michael Ring from County Mayo.

General Collins and other members of the government, realising full well that the experience of former members of the RIC was essential in setting up any new police force, invited a number of former members of the force who had assisted Michael Collins and who were trusted by him to attend. The most prominent of these members were District Inspector Patrick Walsh, who had been attached to the RIC at Letterkenny, County Donegal; District Inspector John A. Kearney, Boyle, County Roscommon; Sergeant Matthias McCarthy, Musgrave Street barracks, Belfast; and former Sergeant Jeremiah Maher of Naas RIC barracks, who had kept Michael Collins up-to-date over a number of years on the secret codes used by the RIC in correspondence. Michael Collins proposed Richard Mulcahy as chairman of the meeting. It was agreed to set up a police force along the same lines as the RIC, which would be lightly armed. (This was understood to mean that members would carry revolvers only.) It was agreed that the new force should have a different colour uniform from that of the RIC as well as new badges and insignia. While being organised on a similar basis to the RIC, it should have different rank titles.

Michael Collins may have expected Richard Mulcahy to take charge of the new force, but Mulcahy felt that he was already deeply involved with his own department. He proposed that Michael Staines should act as chairman of the new organising committee. The son of a member of the RIC who served as a constable and sergeant at many locations in the west of Ireland, Michael Staines, in effect, became the first commissioner of the new force. For some years previously he had been in overall charge of the Republican police force throughout the country. He had been active in the organisation of the Irish Volunteers and was elected to the supreme council of the IRB in 1917. He was an alderman on Dublin City Council and a member of Dáil Éireann since 1918. He had fought in the Easter Rising at the GPO in Dublin in 1916 and been one of the stretcher bearers for the injured James Connolly on evacuation of the GPO. He was interned for a period at Frongoch in Wales following the Easter Rising.

Michael Staines selected as his deputy District Inspector Patrick Walsh, who was later appointed assistant commissioner of the new "Civic Guard" force. He also appointed General Michael Ring as depot commandant. The appointments of Michael Staines and Michael Ring to such prominent posts in the new force must have come as a disappointment to the former members of the RIC who were present, many of them with long experience, who probably considered themselves as being very suitable for the positions.

The committee sat for several hours, and a number of sub-committees were appointed to organise, train and recruit the new Civic Guard force. Included in these sub-committees were the following members and former members of the RIC: Head Constable J. Foley and Acting Sergeant Matthias McCarthy, Musgrave Street, Belfast; District Inspector John A. Kearney, Boyle, and Sergeant Patrick Harte, Roscommon; District Inspector Patrick Riordan, Cork city; District Inspector T. McGettrick, Howth; Head Constable J. Brennan, RIC depot; Sergeant Michael McCormack, Letterkenny; Sergeant Edward Prendiville, Clonmel; and former Sergeants Thomas J. McElligott (who had been active in establishing the Police Union) and Jeremiah Maher. Also appointed to the sub-committees were Inspector Michael Kelly and Constable Thomas Neary of the DMP and former DMP Sergeant Edward Broy. With a few exceptions, all members of the RIC appointed to the sub-committees worked hard at the tasks allocated to them and made a substantial contribution to the establishment of the Civic Guards.

General Michael Ring became disillusioned with the force as a result of the Kildare Mutiny and resigned. He rejoined the Free State army and some months later met his death in County Mayo during an engagement with the anti-Treaty forces. All the members and former members of the Royal Irish Constabulary and Dublin Metropolitan Police appointed to the sub-committees were well known to the ministers of the Provisional government and were trusted by them. The majority of them – if not all – had supplied high quality Intelligence information to Michael Collins and his intelligence officers during the Anglo Irish War.

District Inspector Patrick Walsh of the RIC and Later Deputy Commissioner of the Civic Guards

In the early years of the Civic Guard – which later became the "Garda Síochána" – none of the headquarters officers contributed as much to the organisation of the new force as did former District Inspector Patrick Walsh of the RIC. He had progressed through the ranks of the RIC and was a most efficient administrator. Under the provisions of the Garda Síochána (Temporary Provisions) Act, 1923N, he was officially appointed assistant commissioner of the force, a rank in which he was to serve for a number of years before becoming deputy commissioner, despite initial teething troubles and changes of commissioners at the head of the new police force. The following tribute was paid to Deputy Commissioner Walsh on his death in the editorial of *Iris an Gharda*, October 1957:

> Yet another of our Headquarters officers, in the person of ex-Assistant Commissioner P. Walsh, who ruled the destinies of the Garda Síochána during the first ten years following the establishment of the force, has "passed beyond the bourne from whence no traveller returns". Of those five Headquarters officers of the first years, there was probably no other whose influence on the new force was so much felt as that of the late Mr Walsh. Indeed, the whole pattern of Garda establishment, from the smallest station unit up to the Headquarters departments, can be well described as his. In addition to his Commissionership, it will be remembered that he was also a member of the original Committee appointed to advise the Government on the setting up of a national police force, to succeed the disbanded Royal Irish Constabulary. Because of his experience it is more than likely that his viewpoints dominated the findings of the Committee, since it must be remembered that the late Mr Walsh was a man of no mean ability. The fact that he graduated through all the ranks of the RIC from that of constable to reach the rank of County Inspector carries its own testimony of this ability. At the same time, we have often wondered if the result might not have been different had the original advisory committee been composed of police experts from other countries who had the correct conception of a national police service and its relationship with the people. As it was, the Garda Síochána was modelled to a major extent on the RIC pattern and the fact that its principal adviser was destined to hold senior administrative rank in the new force ensured that the pattern was to be a lasting one. To this we owe so many of the irritating restrictions in the way of regulations which even yet are hamstringing the Garda Síochána.

In the forty intervening years since that editorial was written, the Garda Síochána has – with a few hiccups and adjustments – survived and has given an excellent service as a national civil police force despite the niggling regulations which it inherited.

District Inspector John A. Kearney of the RIC Who Later Joined the Civic Guards
District Inspector John A. Kearney, who had served with the RIC at Boyle, County

Roscommon, had potential for high office and the prospects of a bright career in the new force. He was invited by Michael Collins to attend the first meeting at the Gresham Hotel. Placed in charge of the sub-committee relating to the organisation of the Civic Guards, he worked very hard at the task allocated to him. On 5 April 1922 he was disbanded from his post as district inspector of the RIC at Boyle and on the following day joined the new Civic Guards with the rank of superintendent. He settled down to his administrative position in the force and gave of his best, but he was identified by recruits to the force from County Kerry as the officer in charge of the RIC barracks at Tralee, County Kerry, when Roger Casement was detained there during Easter Weekend 1916. They alleged that he had betrayed Casement and ill-treated him. In an outburst in Dáil Éireann in February 1922, the Republican TD for north Kerry, Mr Austin Stack, also made false accusations against John Kearney. Nothing could have been further from the truth, because as the then head constable at Tralee barracks, he had treated Casement most humanely when he became aware of his identity and the fact that Roger Casement was a very sick man. Regrettably, life was made so difficult for John Kearney in his early months in the Civic Guards that he was virtually a prisoner in his office, and he resigned from the force and went to England.

He worked for a short while at Westminster, tidying up records arising from the disbandment of the RIC. He was offered high-ranking positions in the Royal Canadian Mounted Police and in the Seychelles police, but he turned down both offers. He was extremely disillusioned as a result of his experience in the Civic Guards, where he most certainly got a very raw deal. Two of his sons were killed in World War II and he died in England in 1946. He had been a close friend of Michael Collins.

Sergeant Matthias McCarthy of the RIC and Later Chief Superintendent of the Civic Guards

Acting Sergeant Matthias McCarthy was stationed in the RIC barracks at Musgrave Street in Belfast and during his service there he regularly came to Dublin to secretly pass information from there to Michael Collins. He was the first chief superintendent appointed in the new Civic Guards. With Commissioner Michael Staines, he led the party of 380 Civic Guards which they marched into Dublin Castle in the afternoon of 17 August 1922 and took over Dublin Castle from its temporary custodians, the King's Shropshire Light Infantry, who had taken over the Castle some hours earlier on the departure of the RIC

Sergeant Eamon Broy of the DMP and Later Commissioner of Garda Síochána

Ex-Sergeant Eamon Broy had been a sergeant clerk in the DMP, College Street Station, and was one of the most important suppliers of vital intelligence to Michael

Collins over a number of years. He was also credited with having saved Michael Collins from certain arrest at one time by actually concealing him in his barracks. During the early years of the Garda Síochána, Eamon Broy briefly held a military appointment and was a secretary in the office of the DMP commissioner. On the amalgamation of the DMP and Garda Síochána in 1925, he was transferred to Garda headquarters with responsibility for crime and was promoted to the rank of chief superintendent. On the dismissal of General Eoin O'Duffy by the de Valera government in 1933, Eamon Broy was appointed Garda commissioner in February 1933, a position which he held with some controversy until June 1938. He had the unique distinction of having served in the RIC, the DMP and the Garda Síochána.

Sergeant David Nelligan of DMP and Later Chief Superintendent of Garda Síochána
David Nelligan, author of *The Spy in the Castle*, was a constable employed as a filing clerk in the confidential section in the DMP commissioner's office in Dublin Castle. He also provided a steady flow of intelligence to Michael Collins in the period leading up to 1922. Nelligan was appointed chief superintendent in charge of the Detective Branch in the DMP, and remained as chief superintendent after its amalgamation with the Garda Síochána in 1925.

Other Former RIC Members Who Joined the Civic Guards
In all, a total of five district inspectors and approximately 170 other ranks of the RIC joined the new Civic Guard and the Garda Síochána during the early years of the force. Of an immense asset to the force in the early days, their background and experience in policing was very much appreciated by the young members of the new force, who looked to them for guidance and advice on policing problems or simply when they needed to know the correct way to keep records. The vast majority of the former RIC members who joined the Civic Guards or the Garda Síochána were given the rank of sergeant. Many were promoted to the rank of inspector shortly afterwards and a number progressed to higher ranks in the force. It is possible that almost every former member of the RIC who joined the new Civic Guard would have automatically been given a high rank in the new force, were it not for the Kildare Mutiny and the fact that new recruits to the Civic Guard (most of whom had been active with Sinn Féin and the IRA) would not accept the authority of former RIC members.

One former RIC member who joined the Garda Síochána was John Henry Reynolds, who lived in Kilkenny and died there in 1968. He was a native of County Leitrim, and as a young man he joined the RIC and served in County Galway, but resigned in 1921. On joining the Garda Síochána he was appointed an inspector and after serving for a period at Ennistymon, County Clare, he was promoted to superintendent. He served as a superintendent at Cahirciveen, Dundrum, Cahir, Baltinglass and Kilkenny before retiring in 1954. As a former RIC member, he had one of the longest periods of service in the Garda Síochána. A number of other former members of the RIC also attained the rank of superintendent, and a small number the rank of chief superintendent.

The first three members to be attested to the Civic Guards were former members of the RIC. The member who was "Registered No. 1" was P.J. Kerrigan. He had served in the RIC some years previously, but his stay in the new force lasted only about six months. Number 2 was Patrick McAvinia, who had served in the RIC for a number of years and had resigned in 1917. On joining the Civic Guard he was allocated the job of providing bedding, food and other provisions for the new recruits at the RDS at Ballsbridge and later at Kildare and Newbridge training barracks. His role was akin to that of barrack master for the new force. After spending a period in Dublin involved with the training of the new Garda recruits, he was promoted sergeant and transferred to Julianstown, County Louth, and later to Drogheda, where he retired in 1947. The third man to join the Civic Guard, James C. Clarke, had also spent a number of years in the RIC. Former members of the RIC played a very important role as instructors in the training of the new Civic Guard. Regrettably, a good number of former RIC members who joined the Civic Guards retired early from the force, some within a few years of joining it.

Other Benefits Left by the RIC to the New Civic Guard Force
Apart from providing key personnel, the RIC left other legacies to the new police force. The fine RIC depot at the Phoenix Park, Dublin, which served the constabulary from 1840 to 1922, has been used as the headquarters of the Garda Síochána since the inception of the force. The RIC left several hundred well-constructed, substantial and comfortable barracks, fitted out with cells and other essential policing needs, spread all over the country in the most central locations in towns, villages and rural areas. Where some of the barracks had been burned down by the anti-Treaty forces (otherwise known as "the Irregulars"), before they could be taken over by the new Civic Guard, the new police force was obliged to occupy accommodation which in most cases was far inferior to the barracks which had been occupied by their predecessors. The RIC left behind furniture, bedding and equipment for the use of the new force. Their iron bedsteads, trestle tables, large wooden filing presses, forms (bare wooden seats on iron frames measuring either four feet or six feet in length), fire-irons, fenders, fire buckets, and Windsor style chairs were in common use in Garda Síochána stations for over forty years after the disbandment of the RIC. The only training material available for training the new force were the police manuals which had been on issue to the RIC. Even though most of the official record books used by the RIC were destroyed by direction of the inspector general on disbandment of the force, some survived and were used as official Garda Síochána records for some time after the foundation of the force.

A new "Code" was prepared for the Garda Síochána by Assistant Commissioner Patrick J. Walsh, and it incorporated many of the provisions which had been contained in the RIC Code and which, through experience over very many years, were found to be essential to maintain order, set down procedures and generally control a well-disciplined police force. Likewise, the RIC barrack regulations were adapted for use by the Garda Síochána. The RIC had also left behind an established pattern of policing, which was on a par with the policing of any civil police force anywhere and which had been built up by the force for about twenty-five years, from the early 1890s. The people of Ireland were very happy with the service given by the RIC during that period. They had every confidence in the force, which provided a very efficient social type of service to the community as well as a police service. They were at the beck and call of their local communities for seven days a week and twenty-four hours per day. After 1917, the War of Independence intervened and the role of the RIC changed dramatically.

Takeover of Policing by the Civic Guards

The new Civic Guards, who were, of course, all Irishmen too, did not meet with overnight success or ready acceptance when they took up duty in many parts of Ireland in the latter part of 1922 and early 1923. They too were called "spies" and "peelers". They were not welcomed with open arms in the Republican parts of Ireland, and it took this new unarmed police force at least ten years and the sacrifice of the lives of some of its members, and much hardship, to establish itself as the lawful police force of the country and to gain the confidence of the people. Despite the troubled period of 1917 to 1922 for the RIC, it had established a sound pattern of policing prior to that which had not been totally eroded by the events of that period. There was an element of normality in the policing of about six counties of the new Free State by the RIC up to the Truce.

All the duties of a non-policing nature carried out by the Royal Irish Constabulary were assigned to the new Civic Guards by the new Free State government. These duties included: the annual collection of agricultural and livestock statistics; the collection of census of population returns once every five years; the inspection of foods and drugs; the enforcement of the weights and measures legislation; the verification and distribution of old age pension books; the checking of voters and jurors lists and the licensing of dogs. The Civic Guards – later the Garda Síochána – performed these non-police duties for over fifty years before they were transferred to the government departments to which they rightly belonged. The enforcement of the weights and measures acts is still carried out on behalf of the relevant department by an "ex-officio inspector" who is a sergeant of the Garda Síochána.

Like their predecessors in the RIC, the new Civic Guards were also denied voting rights at elections under the Electoral Act, 1923. This situation was only reversed under the Electoral Act, 1960. Provision was made under article 73 of the Irish Free State Constitution for the carryover of all legislation and acts of parliament in force at the time of the Treaty to the new Irish Free State, most of which fell to the new police force for enforcement. Article 50 of the Irish Constitution of 1937 again reaffirmed the transfer of this legislation for enforcement in the Irish Free State. Under section 19 of the Garda Síochána Act, 1924, the powers which had been vested in the Royal Irish Constabulary in relation to the enforcement of existing legislation were transferred to the Garda Síochána as follows:

> Every member of or reference to the Royal Irish Constabulary or any inspector, sergeant, constable, or other officer or man of the Royal Irish Constabulary contained in any statute or statutory rule, order or regulation in force in Saorstat Éireann immediately after the passing of this Act shall be construed and take effect as a mention of or reference to the Garda Síochána, or a superintendent, inspector, sergeant, guard, or other officer or man (as the case may require) of equivalent rank in the Garda Síochána, and if any question shall arise whether generally or in any particular case as to what is the equivalent rank, such question shall be determined by the Minister whose decision shall be final.

While the Civic Guard, later to become known as the Garda Síochána, has operated since its inception as an unarmed civil police force, it owes much for the success of its foundation to the Royal Irish Constabulary, even though the latter was a semi-military police force. The new force was established amidst the political turmoil and chaos of a civil war and the general lawless situation of 1922 and 1923. Of necessity, personnel had to be hastily recruited and trained in large numbers and a suitable administrative structure had to be put in place. This could not have been accomplished without the guidance, assistance, experience and commitment of the key personnel involved in the administration of the Civic Guard and their training in huge numbers. These key personnel – such as Assistant Commissioner Walsh – were former members of the RIC. Had the ready-made barracks not been available at so many locations throughout Ireland, it is difficult to envisage how the new state could have afforded them. Very many of the practices, procedures and policing precedents established by the Royal Irish Constabulary and its predecessors over a span of one hundred years, and which were adopted by the Civic Guards, have stood the test of time and have been very instrumental in making the Garda Síochána the very successful and acceptable police force which it is today. Several sons of former RIC members became members of An Garda Síochána and gave outstanding service to the new force. In addition to Michael Staines, two other garda commissioners, Michael Wymes and Lawrence Wren, were also sons of former members of the Royal Irish

Constabulary. Eamon Broy, who had been a member of the RIC and DMP, became the third commissioner of the Garda Síochána.

The Legacy of The RIC to the Royal Ulster Constabulary

In the six counties of Northern Ireland, a committee was appointed to look into a replacement police force for the Royal Irish Constabulary in that part of Ireland. On 31 March 1922, the committee submitted its report and recommended that a new police force should be established, to be known as the "Ulster Constabulary" and that, like the RIC, it should be armed. A recommendation was made that the new force should be allowed to retain the "Royal" prefix granted to the Royal Irish Constabulary by Queen Victoria in 1867. It also recommended, that pay and conditions should remain the same as that of the RIC, that the strength of the force would be 3,000 members, of whom one third should be Catholics, and that preference for membership of the force should be given to suitable former members of the RIC and members of the Special Constabularies – especially the A Specials – who were already in existence. The new force known as the "Royal Ulster Constabulary" was established under the Constabulary Act (Northern Ireland), 1922. The fixed established strength of the RIC in 1921 for the six counties of Northern Ireland, including Belfast, was 2,817 members. The force was at that time augmented by the Special Constabularies.

The allocation along religious lines was the subject of much debate in the Northern Ireland parliament at the time, but it was accepted that the committee in making its recommendation was only being fair to the community in ensuring that all, no matter what their religious persuasion was, would be treated fairly so long as they remained loyal to the Crown. The parliament also accepted the other principal recommendations of the committee in relation to pay and conditions of service and rank structure of the new force. There was unanimous agreement that the name of the new force should be the Royal Ulster Constabulary.

The changeover from the Royal Irish Constabulary to the Royal Ulster Constabulary on 9 June 1922 was far less traumatic for all concerned than what it had been in the Irish Free State. The RIC rifle-green uniform was retained by the RUC and, with the exception of "Ulster" replacing the word "Irish", badges and insignia remained almost identical. All RIC barracks and buildings, stores, vehicles, training facilities, firearms, accoutrements and equipment automatically transferred to the control of the RUC, creating no logistical or administrative problems for the new force on its takeover. The rank structure and different titles of the force remained the same. The only real problem encountered was in the adjustment of barrack strengths and reallocation of personnel. The enlistment of 1,100 former RIC members in the Royal Ulster Constabulary gave the new force a high degree of stability and a wealth of experience. They formed the backbone of the new force and were evenly distributed throughout the province. The former members of the Special Constabulary who joined the new force had also received some training and had an elementary practical knowledge of police work.

Concern amongst members of Dáil Éireann and other southern nationalists about the fate of Catholics under the new Northern Ireland administration led to provisions governing the setting up of the new police force to replace the RIC in the north being incorporated in writing into the Irish Free State Agreement which was signed by all parties in London on 31 March 1922. The conditions which were to apply specifically to police in Belfast included provisions that an advisory committee of Protestants and Catholics in equal numbers would be set up to assist in selecting Catholic candidates for the Special Constabulary; that all police on duty, except those engaged in secret service, would wear uniform and be identifiable; that any searches for arms should be carried out by police, half of whom would be Catholics and half of whom would be Protestants; and that the police working in mixed districts should be composed of equal numbers of Protestants and Catholics. While the intentions were good at the time, undertakings were subsequently not adhered to. For several reasons, the RUC did not prove attractive to potential Roman Catholic recruits, and by the late 1960s the number of Catholics in the force accounted for only 12 per cent of the total force.

While the new RUC did not encounter such serious hostility as experienced by the new Civic Guards and Garda Síochána during the first decade of their existence, they did, however, inherit other problems which were to erupt and cause huge difficulties for the force decades later. Since the very early eighteenth century, Orangeism had been a dominant force in Ulster, and through regular parades and demonstrations it asserted the dominance of the majority Protestant population of the province. Successive Unionist-dominated Northern Ireland governments after 1922 maintained the status quo, blindly pursuing a policy of maintaining and enforcing the dominant position of the majority Protestant population with little regard to the civil rights of the minority. This was very much to the detriment of the Catholic minority, who perceived the Royal Ulster Constabulary as being the arm and agent of the government and closely aligned with the Protestant majority. The sons of many former RIC members joined the Royal Ulster Constabulary and one of them – Sir Jamie Flanagan – reached the highest rank of chief constable in the force.

The RUC dealt effectively with many serious riot situations and with an IRA campaign of violence during the 1950s when six members of the force were killed and eighteen were injured. Organised civil rights marches in 1969 brought the RUC into violent confrontations with the protesters, thereby sparking off a cycle of unprecedented violence which lasted for twenty-six years. During this most difficult period for the RUC, it became very dependent on British army regiments in an effort to maintain law and order. The social deprivation of the Catholic minority in Northern Ireland yielded a rich harvest of recruits for the Irish Republican Army. The IRA latched on to the Civil Rights Movement and mounted a long, intensive campaign of violence against the RUC and the Northern Ireland and British governments.

The activities of the IRA resulted in para-military forces also being formed by the Protestants, leaving the RUC in a most unenviable situation. Ironically, many of the difficulties experienced by the RUC over this period bore a similarity to the problems experienced by their predecessors, the Royal Irish Constabulary, from 1919 to 1922. The force got caught up in a no-win situation, which again was not of its making. Never was a police force anywhere in the world subjected to such a protracted, vicious and murderous campaign of death and injury as the RUC was between 1969 and 1995. Three hundred of its members were killed and several hundred more were injured. It had the sympathy and support of every police force in the world during these difficult years. It survived the ordeal, and out of sheer necessity and a commitment to survive and fulfil its role, it has developed into one of the most efficient and unquestionably the most technologically advanced police force in the world. High-ranking police officers from all over the world now visit the headquarters of the RUC to study its advanced police and information technology systems.

The Royal Ulster Constabulary inherited the rank structures, procedures, uniform, "harp and shamrock" insignia, traditions and character of its predecessor and can rightly lay claim to be externally more "Irish" in its appearance than the Garda Síochána. The Royal Ulster Constabulary, which with justification claims to be the true successor of the Royal Irish Constabulary, has always been extremely proud of its RIC roots and origins, and pride of place is given in its official Police Museum to its excellent collection of RIC uniforms, records and other RIC memorabilia.

EPILOGUE

In March 1922, the committee set up by the Northern Ireland parliament under the chairmanship of Lloyd Campbell, MP, to make recommendations for a police force to replace the RIC, submitted its report, proposing that:

1. the new force should be permitted to retain the "Royal" prefix;
2. pay and conditions should remain the same as those for the RIC;
3. the strength of the force should be 3,000, one third of whom should be Catholic;
4. preference for membership of the new force should be given to suitable former members of the RIC and the Special Constabularies, especially the A Specials.

The Northern Ireland parliament, after much debate, accepted that the committee was trying to ensure that all would be treated fairly, irrespective of their religion, so long as they remained loyal to the Crown, and accepted all the recommendations.

With widespread sectarian attacks, murders and arson, concern grew amongst southern nationalists about the fate of northern Catholics, who pleaded with Michael Collins for support and protection. The British government was also worried about the increasing spiral of violence in Northern Ireland, and when Michael Collins expressed his fears to Winston Churchill, then the colonial secretary, he arranged a meeting between Collins and James Craig. On 22 March 1922, they reached an agreement which proposed, among other items, that:

1. an advisory committee of Protestants and Catholics in equal numbers would be set up to assist in selecting Catholics for the new constabulary;
2. all police on duty, except those in the secret service, would wear uniform and be identifiable;
3. any searches for arms would be carried out by police, half of whom would be Catholics;
4. the police working in mixed districts would be equally composed of Protestants and Catholics.

The Royal Ulster Constabulary was finally established under the Constabulary Act (Northern Ireland) 1922, and the force officially came into existence on 1 June 1922.

When the advisory committee met on 16 May 1922, only seven of the twelve members attended, and when it met on 7 June for the third and last time, only three members turned up. Had this committee been effective it might well have changed the subsequent course of history in Northern Ireland. James Craig, however, had little commitment to implementing the provisions of the agreement, and after the untimely death of Michael Collins on 22 August 1922, Craig filled the remaining vacancies in the new RUC – which had been rightfully reserved for Catholics – from the ranks of the Special Constabularies. The RUC proved unattractive to potential Catholic recruits, and by 1925 when the strength of the force was 2,990 it had only 541 Catholic members. In the same year nine of the thirty-eight district inspectors and two of the eight county inspectors were Catholics. Although the officer corps has consistently included about 25 per cent Catholic membership, by the late 1960s the number of Catholics in the force accounted for only 12 per cent of the total number.

The change-over from the Royal Irish Constabulary was far less drastic than in the Irish Free State. The RIC rifle green uniform was retained by the RUC, and with the exception of "Ulster" replacing the word "Irish" badges and insignia remained identical. All RIC barracks and buildings, stores, vehicles, training facilities, firearms, accoutrements and equipment automatically transferred to the control of the RUC, thereby creating no logistical or administration problems for the new force on its takeover. A total of 896 Protestant and 434 Catholic members of the RIC, trained and experienced, joined the RUC and by contributing a high degree of stability formed the backbone of the new force. They were evenly distributed to stations throughout the province to provide an immediately available police force. The balance of the force was recruited from the Special Constabularies who had an elementary practical knowledge of police work. Members of the RUC were given permission to become members of Orange Lodges provided that they did not wear uniform while attending meetings and that their attendances did not interfere with their duties, but the force became engaged in police work in a short period and was luckier than its Civic Guards counterpart in the Irish Free State which was endeavouring to police in a civil war situation at the time. A pattern of policing along Royal Irish Constabulary lines was established, and this continued with little change until 1969. The force dealt with many strike and riot situations from time to time and in the early 1940s and 1950s it faced two campaigns of violence by the IRA, the second of which ended in 1962.

From the foundation of the force in 1922, it was always perceived by the Catholic minority in the Six Counties as being the firm bastion of Protestant control. The 33 per cent quota for Catholic membership was never filled, and no serious effort was made to encourage Catholics to join. It carried on with its duties in a society where discrimination against Catholics was rampant, through housing allocations, job allocations and in the political system. The Unionist-dominated Stormont parliament continued with the discrimination for more than forty years, and the United Kingdom parliament took little cognisance of the state of affairs in Northern Ireland during this period. The discrimination against the minority was considered the norm. The vast majority of the force members shared the culture, religion and prejudices of the Protestant community from which they were drawn, and the RUC policed the province as an arm of the Unionist government.

Arising from concern expressed by a number of members of parliament in Great Britain, the National Council for Civil Liberties arranged for an investigation of affairs in Northern Ireland. The report submitted by the investigating members accused the RUC of partisanship and of abusing its powers of search and interrogation, noting that the force was under the direct control of the Northern Ireland Home Office, unlike the regular police forces in England. No apparent action was taken following this report.

The civil rights demonstrations of the late 1960s jolted the force. Its first reaction was to meet the challenge with force, in accordance with the wishes and views of its taskmasters in Stormont. The first incident in a long saga of policing problems for the RUC occurred during the general election campaign in September 1964, when a Republican candidate – Liam McMillan – displayed a tricolour flag at his election office in Divis Street, Belfast. Revd Ian Paisley, who had set up his own Free Presbyterian Church, threatened to remove it himself if the authorities failed to do so. The RUC was ordered in to remove the flag, and this resulted in rioting by Catholic groups in the area. When members of the RUC, wearing helmets and carrying pick-axe handles, removed a replacement flag some days later, violence again erupted. The Catholic community was enraged by the actions of the force in complying with the wishes of Paisley and his followers.

Marches in 1966 by the nationalists to commemorate the 1916 Rising caused further tensions when Paisley organised rival demonstrations. During marches by Paisleyites later in the year, the RUC baton-charged Catholics to facilitate the marchers.

In 1967 the Northern Ireland Civil Rights Association was formed. Its leaders were reputable individuals, and its main objective was to challenge the entrenched Unionist government's discriminatory policies. In this it had the support of the Catholic population. In June 1968, Austin Currie, a young university graduate, took possession of a house at Caledon, County Tyrone, which had been allocated to a teenage Protestant girl while several Catholic families remained on the housing list. The RUC evicted him some days later but the matter received considerable publicity. A civil rights march from Coalisland to Dungannon on 24 August was restricted by the police, while the Revd Paisley was permitted to organise a counter-march on the same occasion.

A further civil rights march was organised for Derry city on 5 October. When the marchers entered Duke Street, they were confronted by an RUC cordon, a police loud hailer announced that the march was illegal and the police then baton-charged the marchers, many of whom were injured, including Gerry Fitt, the West Belfast MP. When the marchers tried to retreat, they found that their line of retreat was blocked by another RUC cordon and they were again attacked by the police with batons and water canons. Riots arising from this confrontation lasted for several days, and the violence was the subject of the official inquiry conducted by Lord Cameron. In his report he stated that while an extremist section of the crowd wished to provoke violence with the police, the baton charge was premature, uncontrolled and unnecessary and that the handling of the situation was ill co-ordinated and ill conducted. The confrontation between the civil rights marchers and the RUC at Derry on 5 October marked the start of a violent period in Northern Ireland.

During the remainder of 1968, further marches organised by the Civil Rights Association and counter-marches organised by Revd Ian Paisley kept the police at full stretch.

On 1 January 1969, a civil rights group led by the People's Democracy, which had been formed amongst students of different religious denominations in Queen's University Belfast, set out to march the seventy-two miles from Belfast to Derry city. The march met with demonstrations and counter-marches by Protestant groups en route. As the march approached Burntollet Bridge, about ten miles from Derry, a large group of Protestants assembled near the bridge and collected stones and missiles in readiness to attack the marchers. The RUC who witnessed this failed to take any action. When the marchers approached they were violently attacked with stones, missiles, cudgels, iron bars and pick-axe handles by the Protestant mob. The marchers later regrouped and continued into Derry where further attacks were made on them and rioting took place. A total of 300 people were injured in the clashes. Lord Cameron again condemned the actions of the police and stated that their conduct was an immediate and contributory cause of the disorders and condemned the breakdown of discipline which had taken place.

Further serious riots took place in Derry city on 19/20 April, resulting in more than 200 members of the force being injured. Eight RUC men, while giving chase to a group of youths, burst their way into the home of Samuel Devenney and his family at William Street in the Bogside area. Samuel Devenney, who received serious eye, skull and internal injuries, was hospitalised for several days and died following a heart attack on 17 July of the same year. This event had reverberations for several years, and two inquiries set up to investigate the assault failed to identify any of the eight policemen who carried out the attack on Devenney.

Derry was again the scene of serious rioting for several days the following August on the occasion of the Apprentice Boys Parade. During the "the Battle of the Bogside" tear gas was used by the RUC for the first time. The RUC failed to contain the situation, and on 14 August army detachments were drafted in and took over control of the city. Riots were simultaneously taking place in Belfast, Dungannon, Newry and Armagh. In Belfast four Catholics were killed by the RUC and one Protestant was shot by a rioter. Death and destruction continued, and within a week 6,000 troops were deployed in an effort to contain the situation. On 19 August, Lieutenant General Sir Ian Freeland was appointed director of operations and given supreme responsibility for maintaining law and order.

A committee under Lord Hunt was appointed to advise on the policing problems, and amongst the recommendations made by it were that the B Specials should be abolished; that an RUC Reserve should be set up; that the strength of the force should be increased and that the rank structure should be changed; that the force should be disarmed and that military-style duties by the RUC should end. It was also recommended that the colour of the uniform should be changed to blue. Inspector General Peacock was asked to resign and was replaced by Sir Arthur Young, commissioner of the City of London Police, who became the first RUC chief constable.

Towards the end of 1969 the Irish Republican Army split into the Official IRA and the Provisional IRA. The latter included the hardliners within the organisation and by early 1970 was organised and involved in the disturbances. It perfected the booby-trap car bomb which it used with devastating effect. The organisation shot and killed members of the RUC and other security forces – whether on or off duty – and has caused billions of pounds worth of damage in Northern Ireland and in Great Britain. The social deprivation of the Catholic minorities in the ghettos and deprived areas of Northern Ireland yielded a rich harvest of recruits for the Provisional IRA. Loyalist paramilitary forces set up to "defend" loyalists grew in strength, and deaths and violence caused by the paramilitary groups continued to spiral in spite of political activity which sought to defuse and control the overall situation.

Internment, introduced in August 1971, proved to be a disaster. It was selective in nature, targeting only nationalists and Republicans, and as many of those interned had no subversive involvement, it was obvious that there was a lack of good intelligence on the part of the police. Serious rioting and bombing followed, and reports persisted of serious beatings and ill-treatment of suspects by the police.

Attacks on the RUC continued unabated during 1972, and thirteen of its members were killed by terrorists. Sectarian killings became commonplace and there were 106 such deaths in 1972. The strength of the force had been increased to 4,300 members, with 2,000 Reserve members, and backed up by 17,500 troops.

Jamie Flanagan, who was the first Catholic chief constable, took up duty on 1 November 1973, and during his term of office the strength of the force was increased to 6,500 and the Reserve brought up to 4,000. The number of troops was reduced by 1,000. There was a reduction in murder and crime levels, but attacks on members of the force continued. In 1974 Chief Constable Flanagan met Patrick Malone, commissioner of the Garda Síochána, to discuss arrangements relating to cross-border security issues.

Kenneth Newman, a London Metropolitan Police commander, replaced Jamie Flanagan as chief constable in May 1975. He reorganised the structure of the force and introduced some innovative features. His primary objective was to restore the "primacy of policing" in Northern Ireland, with the army being available to support the police where necessary. The RUC had considerable success under his leadership, but its reputation was marred by serious allegations about the ill-treatment of prisoners and the interrogation methods used at Castlereagh holding centre. Concern was voiced by prominent churchmen, doctors, lawyers and politicians, and a number of television documentaries highlighted the abuses taking place. An Amnesty International team accused the RUC of ill-treating prisoners with sufficient frequency to justify a public inquiry. A committee of inquiry under Judge Harry Bennett, QC, concluded that a small number of RUC members had resorted to brutality in order to obtain confessions, and recommended, *inter alia*, a suggested code of conduct for investigating officers and that closed circuit television should be installed in interrogation rooms. The claims of brutality to the prisoners, which received international publicity, did much harm to the reputation of the RUC and provided valuable propaganda material for the paramilitaries engaged in the conflict.

The biggest criminal investigation challenge faced by the RUC during the 1970s was the investigation of several murders of Catholic men in the Belfast area by an extreme loyalist group who became known as "the Shankill Butchers". The victims were first tortured at length and then stabbed before their bodies were dumped at different locations. Through very detailed and professional police work, eleven of the murderers were sentenced to forty-two life sentences at a Belfast court in 1979.

The chief constables who have headed the RUC since 1970 came from different backgrounds and each brought his own style of leadership to the force, but the top priority of each was to improve police/community relations. They were all conscious that the poor relations between the Catholic community and the RUC lay at the roots of the violent situation in Northern Ireland. The hard line maintained by Chief Constable Jack Hermon against the Revd Ian Paisley and the activities of his followers was indicative of the policy of keeping policing matters independent of politics. While each had some measure of success, each left office with much work still to do.

Jack Hermon, who had been deputy chief constable of the force for a short period, took command of the RUC on 1 January 1980 and remained in office as chief constable until May 1989. On taking up his post he sent a clear message to the force that he expected the highest professional standards from its members and warned that disreputable conduct would not be tolerated. He insisted that the force should be totally impartial in its dealings with both political traditions in Northern Ireland. He was his own man, maintaining a very independent line in policing. His term of office was a most difficult and testing time for the force and he was subjected to many pressures, but he kept his head.

The deaths of ten prisoners on hunger strikes during 1981 resulted in riots, violence and tension throughout the province and fully stretched the resources of the force in dealing with the situation. The early 1980s was the era of the "supergrass" trials, where former terrorists agreed to give evidence against their former comrades. The supergrasses provided a major breakthrough to the force in its investigations of very serious crimes and outrages and created consternation amongst the terrorist groups. Many active terrorists were convicted and taken out of circulation. Following later decisions of the appeal court, the practise of using supergrasses ceased.

In November 1982 three men were shot dead in their car at a police checkpoint; no firearms or explosives were found in the vehicle. Two weeks later another man was shot dead in a haybarn near Lurgan and another was seriously injured. In December two men were shot dead in their car at Armagh. The six deaths caused much concern amongst people of all shades of opinion and created a belief that the RUC was operating a "shoot to kill" policy. John Stalker, deputy chief constable of Greater Manchester, was appointed in May 1984 to investigate the deaths. Met with obstruction from amongst the RUC, he submitted an interim report in September 1985. Sir Barry Shaw, director of public prosecutions, insisted on the investigations being completed. In the meantime, John Stalker had been suspended from his post in Manchester under mysterious circumstances, resulting in his removal from the Northern Ireland investigation. On the insistence of the attorney-general and director of public prosecutions, the investigation was reopened by Colin Sampson, chief constable of west Yorkshire, and disciplinary action was taken against a number of members of the force as a result of his findings. Attempts to hold inquests on the victims dragged on until 1994. The long drawn-out "Stalker Affair" was most controversial and highly publicised, and also resulted in strained relationships between the RUC and the senior law officers.

Following the signing of the Anglo-Irish agreement between the English and Irish governments at Hillsborough in November 1985, there was a serious backlash by the Unionist and loyalist organisations. Over a two-year period the loyalist mobs directed their anger at the RUC, perceiving the force as being the enforcers of the terms of the agreement. The homes of a number of RUC members were petrol-bombed or otherwise damaged, and several members who lived in mainly Protestant areas had to move out of their homes due to loyalist intimidation and threats made to them and to their families. The force found it very difficult to come to terms with the viciousness of the attacks made on it by that section of the community from which it had drawn its support and to which it had provided a police service for more than sixty years.

Evidence came to light late in 1989 following the fatal shooting of Loughlin Maginn at Rathfriland, County Down, that classified, confidential RUC documents relating to terrorist suspects had fallen into the hands of loyalist paramilitary groups. John Steevens, deputy chief constable of Cambridgeshire, was appointed to investigate the matter. With a highly qualified and experienced team of investigators, he carried out an exhaustive investigation over several months. Members of the RUC were found to be blameless, and several members of the Ulster Defence Regiment were charged with various offences arising from the investigation, which also disclosed close links between the Ulster Defence Regiment and extreme loyalist groups.

Mr Steevens and an investigation team returned to Northern Ireland in 1999 to investigate the circumstances surrounding the death of Pat Finucane, a Belfast solicitor, and the more recent death of another solicitor, Rosemary Nelson, who was killed when a bomb exploded underneath her car. Both solicitors in their professional capacities represented Republicans, and threats were made on their lives. Allegations persist that the victims did not receive the protection which they should have from the security forces, and that members of the security forces may have had some complicity in the killings.

Controversy also surrounds the death in 1997 of Robert Hamill, who was beaten to death by a loyalist mob while members of the RUC allegedly witnessed the occurrence and took no action.

The Provisional IRA called a ceasefire with effect from 31 August 1994. This lasted until February 1996 when the Provisionals detonated a massive lorry bomb in the Docklands area of London, killing two people and causing millions of pounds worth of damage. During the ceasefire, intensive political negotiations took place involving the political parties of Northern Ireland and the Dublin, London and USA governments.

The annual Orange parades to and from Drumcree church at Dungannon, County Tyrone, became the flash-points for serious confrontations in 1995 and 1996. In 1995 there was a three-day stand-off while negotiations took place with the residents of Catholic area through which the parade was to march after leaving the church. The parade was eventually permitted to pass through the area, which the Orange marchers regarded as a victory. In 1996 a decision was taken not to allow the parade along the disputed route and police and army reinforcements were brought in to enforce the ban. Violent confrontations took place over a number of days, and loyalist groups throughout the province hijacked vehicles, blocked roads and created huge disruption. Eventually, Chief Constable Hugh Annesley (a Dublin-born Protestant) decided to allow the march to proceed and provided security for the marchers as they passed through the Catholic area. His reasons for doing so were that the police and army could not hold out indefinitely against the violence of the Orangemen. The result was a serious set-back for the confidence of Catholics in the RUC.

In November 1996 Ronnie Flanagan, who had served in several branches of the RUC, replaced Hugh Annesley as chief constable. On taking up duty he gave an undertaking that he would commit himself and the force to a process of internal reform and to police/community reconciliation.

Never was a police force anywhere in the world subjected to such a protracted, vicious and murderous campaign of death and injury as the Royal Ulster Constabulary was from 1969 to 1999. It had the support and sympathy of every police force in the world during these difficult years. Three hundred members of the force were killed and over 8,000 members were injured. Hundreds of those injured have lost limbs, eyesight, hearing or have sustained other crippling injuries. Many of its members have justifiably received awards for bravery and the number of lives which members of the force have saved through their commitment and dedication to duty can never be assessed. Interpol Statistics published in *The International Criminal Police Review* of 1983 indicated that the Royal Ulster Constabulary was the most dangerous police force in which to serve, more than twice as dangerous as the next on the list: the El Salvador police.

In his book *The RUC 1922–1997: A Force Under Fire,* Chris Ryder observes:

> In writing this book I have been motivated by a limitless admiration for the valiant men and women of the modern RUC. They represent all that is best about the good people of Northern Ireland and they are truly the cement that holds the divided community together. In saying that, however, I believe that no mature society should give its police a blank cheque, and that proper accountability and safeguards are essential for both the police and the community. In the particular circumstances of Ulster this is crucially important.

> The RUC was established as an armed force and has remained armed to date. It inherited the rank structures, procedures, uniform, traditions, culture and character of its predecessor the Royal Irish Constabulary. With its green uniform and the harp and shamrock incorporated in its insignia, the RUC can claim to be more Irish in appearance than its

neighbour the Garda Síochána. The force has always been proud of its RIC roots and origins, and pride of place is given in its museum to RIC uniforms, records and memorabilia.

In a democracy, a police force should represent the needs of the society which it serves and it should meet the changing demands of that society. The RUC has never succeeded in meeting these goals. It could never claim to be a community-based police force, and it remains the only armed police force in the British Isles. Whenever there was a prospect for an improvement in relations with the minority, some action of the RUC or favouritism shown to the majority cancelled out the goodwill. The politicians in Northern Ireland, however, must also shoulder blame for their inactivity in creating a climate suitable for community style policing by the RUC. As the violence of the last twenty-five years progressed, it became more obvious that a radical overhaul of the force is inevitable if it is to become acceptable to the minority Catholic/nationalist population.

In ongoing peace negotiations over a number of years the question of future policing and the future of the RUC was always high on the agenda. In the agreement signed on Good Friday 1998 between the London and Dublin governments and the elected representatives of Northern Ireland, the reform of the RUC was one of the principal issues.

Following the Good Friday Agreement, a commission was appointed to look into the future of policing in Northern Ireland under the chairmanship of Chris Patten, a former British government minister and governor of Hong Kong. The commission published its report on 9 September 1999. Commenting on the report on its publication, Dr Mo Mowlam, the Northern Ireland secretary, said,"This is the chance for a new beginning to set the standards for policing in the new millennium. I urge everyone involved to read the report, reflect on it and seize the opportunity it offers for the whole community." The comprehensive and wide ranging report has a total of 175 recommendations, the principal of which are that:

1. the RUC should be renamed the Northern Ireland Police Service;
2. the force should have a new badge and symbols free of British or Irish association;
3. the force should have a new form of oath expressing commitment to human rights;
4. the strength of the force should be cut to 7,500 members, with 2,500 part-timers;.
5. a major effort should be made to recruit more Catholics;
6. the Police Authority should be replaced with a new board;
7. generous financial terms should be arranged for officers to leave the RUC;
8. the Crime Branch and Special Branch should be brought together;

9. local councils in Northern Ireland should establish policing partnership boards;
10. holding centres, including Castlereagh, should be closed;
11. there should be greater co-operation with the Garda Síochána; and
12. policing should be devolved to the executive as soon as possible.

The report is currently being examined and digested by all interested parties – including the RUC – and it is to be hoped that its recommendations will be implemented.

The RIC members from 1919 onwards were used and abused by their masters, the British government and authorities at Dublin Castle, who dithered on serious issues and adopted policies which were totally unsuitable to the shaky political situation. They were maligned and reviled, and this denigration of the force continued for many years after its disbandment to the point that in the nationalist areas of Ireland, a social stigma attached to families who had had members in the RIC. For more than sixty years after disbandment, decent, law-abiding people were reluctant to admit that they had had brothers, fathers, grandfathers or uncles in the Royal Irish Constabulary.

The Royal Irish Constabulary at all times saw themselves as Irishmen and were proud of that fact. At least eighty per cent of the membership were Roman Catholics. All members of the lower ranks were Irishmen, with Irish parents, brothers, sisters and relatives. Subject to their meeting the required educational and medical standards, they were very glad to avail of the job opportunity presented by the force. Their loyalty was to their oath of office and the Crown, but they never saw that as taking away their Irish identity. They paid a very high price for their loyalty during the War of Independence, when 425 of them were killed – most in cold blood – and 725 were wounded. Sixteen members committed suicide during the period and about thirty were accidentally shot dead. Rarely has a police force anywhere suffered such a high percentage of casualties from amongst its personnel. Elaborate monuments abound all over Ireland marking the locations where members of the force were shot down, or where they or members of the Crown forces were ambushed during the War of Independence. These monuments perpetuate and glorify the memory of the IRA Volunteers who participated in these events. In some instances the monuments commemorate the deaths of Volunteers who lost their lives in engagements with the Crown forces.

There are no monuments commemorating the members of the Royal Irish Constabulary who were shot down and ambushed throughout the country, while performing the policing duties to which they were committed and who like their opponents were also Irishmen. There is no cenotaph or national memorial in Ireland to their memory. Apart from memorials at Westminster Abbey and at St Paul's Cathedral in London, and tablets in a few Church of Ireland churches in Ireland, there are no memorials to the Royal Irish Constabulary and sadly there is no Roll of Honour.

The constabularies played an extremely important social, administrative and peace-keeping role in Ireland for the century from 1822 to 1922. Their existence and the duties performed by them were very closely entwined with the historical events of the most momentous century in Ireland's history. They have not received due credit from historians for the positive contributions made by them during that period. It was said of the Royal Irish Constabulary "that nowhere in the world was the British Commonwealth served so well as it was by the Royal Irish Constabulary in Ireland". This was very true of the Royal Irish Constabulary as well as of the Irish and County Constabularies. Not alone did the constabularies serve the British Commonwealth well, but they also served the people of Ireland well over a period of one hundred years. They had nothing to be ashamed of.

BIBLIOGRAPHY

Allen, Gregory. "The Dublin Police and Their Times", *Friendship*, vol. 5, 1978, p. 5.

— "Cup of Peace", *Garda Review*, February 1978, pp. 16–8.

— "Introduction to *A History of Police in Ireland*, by Patrick J. Carroll", *Garda Review*, January 1985, pp. 16–7.

— "Fading out the Barony Constable", *Garda Review*, November 1985, pp. 19, 21, 28. From *A History in Ireland* by Patrick J. Carroll.

— "Genesis of the Code, Rules and Regulations" and "The Munster Constabulary Barrack Regulations", *Garda Review*, October 1986, pp. 31–3.

— "Oldest Irish Police Society Celebrates Diamond Jubilee", *Garda Review*, October 1986, pp. 26–7.

Barry, Tom. *Guerilla Days in Ireland*, 2nd ed. Cork: Mercier Press, 1955.

Beckett, J.C. *The Making of a Modern Ireland 1603–1923* revd ed. London: Faber and Faber, 1973.

Béaslaí, Piaras. *Michael Collins and the Making of a New Ireland*, 2 vol. Dublin: Phoenix Publishing Co., 1926.

Bennet, Richard. *The Black and Tans*. New York: Barnes and Noble, 1975.

Bonsell, Penny. *The Irish R.Ms*. Dublin: Four Courts Press, 1997.

Boyd, Andrew. *The Rise of Irish Trade Unions 1729–1970*. Tralee, Co. Kerry: Anvil Books, 1972.

Boylan, Henry. *Wolfe Tone*. Dublin: Gill and MacMillan, 1981.

Brady, Conor. *Guardians of the Peace*. Dublin: Gill and MacMillan, 1974.

Breathnach, Seamus. *The Irish Police – from the Earliest Times to the Present Day*. Dublin: Anvil Books, 1972.

Breen, Dan. *My Fight For Irish Freedom*. Tralee, Co. Kerry: Anvil Books, 1964.

Brennan, William. The Growth of Licensing Legislation, *Garda Review*, March 1950, p. 301.

Brewer, John D. *The Royal Irish Constabulary – an Oral History*. Belfast: Queens University, 1990.

Broeker, Galen. *Rural Disorder and Police Reform in Ireland 1812–1836*. London: University of Toronto Press, 1970.

Buckland, Patrick. *Ulster Unionism and the Origins of Northern Ireland – 1886 to 1922*. Dublin: Gill and MacMillan, 1973.

Callwell, C.E. *Field Marshal Sir Henry Wilson, His Life and Diaries*, 2 vol. London: Cassel and Company, 1927.

Carroll, Patrick J. "Notes for a History of Police in Ireland – Watch and Ward", *Garda Review*, January 1961, pp. 137–43.

— "Notes for a History of Police in Ireland – Plurabis Unum", *Garda Review*, February 1961, pp. 217–9.

— "Notes for a History of Police in Ireland – Recruiting and Traffic", *Garda Review*, March 1961, pp. 297–301.

— "Notes for a History of Police in Ireland – Publish and Be Damned", *Garda Review*, April 1961, pp. 401–7.

— "Notes for a History of Police in Ireland – Dublin's new Police of 1808", *Garda Review*, May 1961, pp. 457–9.

— "Notes for a History of Police in Ireland – Major Sirr and Others", *Garda Review*, June 1961, pp. 537–47.

— "Notes for a History of Police in Ireland – Reshuffle of 1824", *Garda Review*, August 1961, pp. 689–713.

— "Notes for a History of Police in Ireland – County Dublin Constabulary", *Garda Review*, October 1961, pp. 833–7.

— "Notes for a History of Police in Ireland – Crime", *Garda Review*, November 1961, pp. 905–9.

— "Notes for a History of Police in Ireland – Crime, continued", *Garda Review*, December 1961, pp. 37–41.

— "Notes for a History of Police in Ireland – Crime, continued", *Garda Review*, January 1962, pp. 137–41.

Comerford, Maire. *The First Dáil*. Dublin: Joe Clarke, 1969.

Coogan, Tim Pat. *Michael Collins: A Biography*. London: Hutchinson, 1990.

Conroy, John C. *Report of the Conroy Commission on the Garda Siochana*. Dublin: 1970.

Crane, C.P. *Memories of a Resident Magistrate 1880–1920*. Edinburgh: T. and A. Constable, 1938.

Crowley, Flor. *In West Cork Long Ago*, 2nd ed. Cork: Mercier Press, 1980.

Curtis, Robert. *The History of the Royal Irish Constabulary*. London: 1869.

Cusack, Jim and McDonald, Henry. *The U.V.F.* Dublin: Poolbeg Press, 1997.

Dagg, D.E. *The Road and Route Guide of the Royal Irish Constabulary*. Dublin: Hodges, Figgis & Co., 1893.

D'Alton, E.A. *History of Ireland from Earliest Times to the Present Day*, *1782 to 1879*, *vol. 5*. London: Gresham Publ. Co.

Desmond, Liam. *With the Constabulary in Roscommon*. Midleton, Co. Cork: Litho Press, 1993.

De Vere White, Terence. *Kevin O'Higgins*, 2nd ed. Tralee, Co. Kerry: Anvil Books, 1966.

Duff, David. *Victoria Travels*. London: Frederick Muller, 1970.

Dungan, Myles. *Distant Drums*. Dublin: Appletree Press, 1993.

Dwyer, T. Ryle. *De Valera, The Man and The Myths*. Dublin: Poolbeg Press, 1995.

Edwards, R. Dudley and Williams, T. Desmond. *The Great Famine*. Dublin: Browne and Nolan, 1956.

Flood, J.M. *In Five Provinces*: *A Journal of Wanderings in Ireland*. Dublin: 1918.

Gaughan, J. Anthony, ed. *Memoirs of Constable Jeremiah Mee R.I.C.* Dublin: Leinster Leader, 1975.

— *Austin Stack: Portrait of a Separatist*. Dublin: 1977.

Glynn, J.F. *The New Zealand Policeman*. Wellington: 1975.

Greaves, C. Desmond. *The Life and Times of James Connolly*. London: Lawrence and Wishart, 1972.

Green, George Garrow. *In the Royal Irish Constabulary*. Dublin: 1905.

Hall, J. *A Tour Through Ireland in 1807*. London: 1807.

Hall, Mr and Mrs Samuel Carter. *Hall's Ireland*, condensed ed. London: Sphere books Ltd., 1984.

Harrington, Niall C. *The Kerry Landing*. Dublin: Anvil Books, 1992.

Head, Francis B. *A Fortnight in Ireland*. London: John Murray, 1852.

Herhily, Jim. *The Royal Irish Constabulary – A Short History and Genealogical Guide*. Dublin: Four Courts Press, 1997.

Hexlett, Arthur. *The B Specials: A History of the Ulster Special Constabulary*. Belfast: Mourne River Press, 1977.

Humphreys, Henry. *The Justice of the Peace for Ireland*, 9th ed. Dublin: Hodges, Figgis & Co., 1897.

Hussey, Samuel. *Reminiscences of an Irish Land Agent*. London: 1904.

Kelly, Denis. *Salute to the Gardaí*. Dublin: Parkside Press, 1958.

Kelly, Seamus. *The Glorious Seven*. Dublin: Irish News Service and Publicity, n.d.

Kelly, William, and Kelly, Nora. *Policing in Canada*. Toronto: MacMillan, 1976.

Kohl, Johann Georg. *Ireland*. London: 1844.

Labour Party. *Report of The Labour Commission to Ireland*. London: The Labour Party, 33 Eccleston Square, 1921.

Lieberson, Goddard. *The Irish Uprising*. Dublin: MacMillan.

Litton, Helen. *The Irish Civil War*. Dublin: Wolfhound Press, 1995.

Longford, Earl of, and O'Neill, Thomas P. *Eamon de Valera*. London: Arrow Books, 1970.

Lyons, F.S.L. *Ireland Since the Famine*, 6th ed. Kent: Fontana Books, 1979.

Macardle, Dorothy. *The Irish Republic*. London: Corgi, 1968.

MacColl, Rena. *Roger Casement, a New Judgement*. London: Hamish & Hamilton, 1956.

McLoughlin, Majella. "A Police Force Which Was Too Successful", *Garda Review*, March 1991, p. 29.

MacMauns, M.J. *Thomas Davis and Young Ireland 1845–1945*. Dublin: Stationery Office, 1945.

McCann, John. *War by the Irish*. Tralee, Co. Kerry: 1946.

McCarthy, Michael J.F. *Five Years in Ireland 1895–1900*. Dublin: Hodges & Figgis, 1901.

Moody, T.W. *The Fenian Movement*. Cork: Mercier Press, 1968.

Murphy, John A. *Ireland in the Twentieth Century*. Dublin: Gill and MacMillan, 1975.

Neligan, David. *The Spy in the Castle*. London: 1968.

O'Brien, G.M. *The Australian Police Forces*. London: Oxford University Press, 1961.

O'Connor, Seamus. *Tomorrow Was Another Day*. Dublin: R.O'C. Publications, 1987.

O'Donnell, Patrick. *The Irish Faction Fighters of the Nineteenth Century*. Dublin: Anvil Books, 1975.

O'Farrell, Fergus. *Daniel O'Connell*. Dublin: Gill and Macmillan, 1981.

O'Hanlon, Redmond. "Memories of the R.I.C.", *Garda Review*, May 1978, pp. 21–5.

O'Malley, Ernie. *The Singing Flame*. Dublin: Anvil Books, 1978.

O'Neill, Cormac. "Law and Police Tradition in Irish History", *Garda Review*, June 1956, pp. 573–5.

O'Suilleabhain, Michael. *Where Mountainy Men Have Sown*. Tralee, Co. Kerry: Anvil Books, 1965.

Philips, W. Alison. *The Revolution in Ireland 1906–1923*. London: Longmans, Green & Co., 1923.

Pollard, H.B.C. *The Secret Societies of Ireland, Their Rise and Progress*. Kilkenny: Irish Historical Press, 1998.

Portéir, Cathal. *The Great Irish Famine*. Cork: Mercier Press, Radio Telefís Éireann, 1995.

Reith, Charles. *The Blind Eye of History*. London, 1952.

Robinson, Christopher Lynch. *The Last of the Irish R.M.s*. London: Cassell and Co. Ltd, 1950.

Ryan, Desmond. *Sean Treacy and the Third Tipperary Brigade I.R.A.* Tralee, Co. Kerry: Anvil Books, 1945.

Ryder, Chris. *The R.U.C. 1922–1997: A Force Under Fire*, Rev ed. London: Mandarin Paperbacks, 1997.

Shea, Patrick. *Voices and the Sound of Drums – An Irish Autobiography*. Belfast: Blackstaff Press, 1981.

Sinclair, R.J.K., and Kelly, F.J.M. *Arresting Memories – Captured Moments in Constabulary Life.* Belfast: R.U.C. Diamond Jubilee Commitee, 1982.

Supple, Kerry Leyne. *The Irish Justice of the Peace, for Justices, Members of the R.I.C. and P.S. Clerks.* Dublin: William McGee, 1899.

Tierney, Mark. *Modern Ireland Since 1850*, rev. ed. Dublin: Gill and MacMillan, 1978.

Tobias, J.J. *Crime and Police in England, 1700–1900.* London: Gill and MacMillan,

Vaughan, W.E. *Sin, Sheep and Scotsmen, John George Adair and the Derryveagh Evictions, 1861.* Belfast: Appletree Press and Ulster Society of Historical Studies, 1983.

Waldron, Jarlath. *Maamtrasn: The Murders and The Mystery.* Dublin: Edmund Burke, 1992.

Woodham-Smith, Cecil. *The Great Hunger*, new ed. Dublin: Anvil Books, 1975.

Whyte, Louis. *The Wild Heather Glen: The Kilmichael Story of Grief and Glory.* Cork: Kilmichael/Crossbarry Committee, 1995.

Young, Sherwood. *With Confidence and Pride.* Wellington: New Zealand, Police Trust, 1994.

Younger, Carlton. *Arthur Griffith.* Dublin: Gill and MacMillan, 1981.

The Black Book of England. London: C. Mitchell, 1847.

Dublin's Fighting Story. Tralee, Co. Kerry: The Kerryman, 1949.

The Ghosts of Kilmainham. Dublin: Kilmainham Jail Restoration Committee, 1966.

Kerry's Fighting Story 1916–1921. Tralee, Co. Kerry: The Kerryman, 1947.

1916 Rebellion Handbook. Dublin: Weekly Irish Times, 1916.

Oidhreacht 1916–1966. Dublin: Government Publications Office, 1966.

Rebel Cork's Fighting Story. Tralee, Co. Kerry. The Kerryman, 1946.

Report of Committee of Inquiry into R.I.C. 1901 with Evidence Taken. London: HMSO, 1902.

Rossa – The Hawk O' The Hilltop. Skibbereen, Co. Cork: O'Donovan Rossa Memorial Committee, 1948.

Tales of the R.I.C. London: William Blackwood & Sons, 1922.

With the I.R.A. in the Fight for Freedom, 1919 to the Truce. Tralee, Co. Kerry: The Kerryman, 1946.

Newspapers

Belfast Newsletter.

Citizen, 5 March 1870.

Clonmel Herald.

Cork Evening Echo, 19 October 1904.

Cork Examiner, 26 November 1981; 15 April 1982; 5 August 1982; 10 July 1985; 14 August 1985; 20 January 1990; 15 October 1990; 12 February 1991; 29 April 1994; 20 June 1994; 13 December 1920. Anniversary Supplement of 1 September 1991.

Evening Herald, 12 July 1971.

Evening Telegraph, 27 June 1903.

Freeman's Journal, 13 March 1896; 2 December 1919.

Illustrated London News, 1860–1900.

Illustrated Penny Paper, 16 August 1873.

Irish Catholic, 10 September 1996.

Irish Independent, Special Supplement of 21 January 1969; Special Insurrection Anniversary Supplement 11 April 1966; Special Supplement of 1 and 2 January 1980.

Irish Press. 16 April 1979; 16 October 1979; 18 September 1980; 20 January 1981; 14 October 1982; 18 February 1983; 10 January 1984; 20 January 1990.

— 50th Anniversary Special Supplement of 5 September 1981.

— 70th Anniversary of the Rising Special Supplement of 24 April 1986.

The Irish Times, January 1916 to July 1922 and 28 April 1981.

Irish Weekly Independent, 25 January 1919.

John Bull, 27 September 1829.

The Kerryman, 1916 to 1997.

Kerry Evening Post, 20 February 1867.

Kerry's Eye, 8 May 1985; 21 August 1997.

Kilkenny Moderator, December 1831.

Leinster Leader, 18 July 1989.

The Nation.

Nenagh Guardian, 17 September 1865.

Skibbereen Eagle and Munster Advertiser.

Southern Star, Centenary Supplement 1889–1989. Publ. 1989.

Sunday Independent, 4 January 1981.

Sunday Press, 10 April 1966; 8 January 1984.

Tipperary Star, 9 January 1965; 14 August 1982; 12 March 1983; 5 August 1989. Special GAA Centenary Supplement of 5 August 1984.

Tipperary Vindicator, October 1845.

Weekly News, 17 March 1866; 13 March 1869; 10 April 1869; 12 February 1870; 5
    March 1870; 4 June 1870; 11 June 1870; 18 June 1870; 28 January 1871; 29 April
    1871.
Weekly Times.
West Cork Eagle, 1 July 1882.

The Internet

The Royal Ulster Constabulary has established a world wide web site, which can be
accessed via the RUC home page at www.ruc.police.uk. It is possible through this
virtual museum to scan the exhibits on view at the actual museum located at RUC
headquarters in Belfast and to obtain brief details of the RIC and RUC.

Journals/Periodicals/Manuals

An Cosantoir. Journal of the Irish Army.
The Bulletin. Newsletter of the New Zealand Police Force, Wellington, NZ.
Constabulary Gazette, the Journal of the Royal Irish Constabulary. 1898–1916.
Defence of the Realm Manual. London: 1916 and 1917.
Friendship Magazine. Magazine of the International Police Association – Irish Sec-
    tion.
Garda Gazette. Newsletter of the Garda Siochana Historical Society, 1995 –
Garda Journal. Journal of the International Police Association, Irish Section.
Garda News. Magazine of Association of Garda Sergeants and Inspectors.
Garda Review/Iris an Gharda. Magazine of Garda Representative Association. 1923
    to date.
Hue and Cry. Issued every Tuesday and Friday to the RIC and DMP.
International Criminal Police Review. London: 1983.
Irish Constable's Guide, 2nd ed. Dublin: Alex Thom & Co., 1888.
Irish Constable's Guide, 4th ed. Dublin: Alex Thom & Co., 1901.
Irish Constable's Guide, 6th ed. Dublin: Alex Thom & Co., 1913.
Irish Police Guide, 8th ed. Dublin: Alex Thom & Co., 1923.
The Motor. July 1903.
Newsletter of The Irish Veteran and Vintage Car Club. Summer 1993.
Patrol. Magazine of the Garda Federation, 1995 to date.
Police Journal. Quarterly Journal of the British and other police forces.
Policeman's Manual, 2nd ed. Dublin: Alex Thom & Co., 1883.
Policeman's Manual, 7th ed. Dublin: Alex Thom & Co., 1908.
Proceedings. Newsletter of the Royal Ulster Constabulary.
Royal Irish Constabulary List Directories, 1912–1921.

Royal Irish Constabulary, 6th ed. Dublin: H.M.S.O. 1909.

Rules and Regulations for the Control and Management of the Finance Department of the Constabulary of Ireland. 5th ed. Dublin: 1913.

Siochain. Magazine of the Garda Pensioner's Association, 1962 to date.

Vincent's Police Code and General Mannual of the Criminal Law. 16th ed. London. Butterworth & Co., 1914.

Booklets/Pamphlets

History. University of Limerick, Department of Government and Society.

Official Correspondence re Peace Negotiations, June–September, 1921.

R.I.C. Handbook on Illicit Distillation Acts. HMS Stationery Office, 1896.

Rolla Onora 75th Anniversary Issue 1922–1997. Garda Síochána Museum, 1997.

Sinn Féin Constitution. Dublin: Fodhla Printing, 1925.

Who Were the Fenians. Kilmainham Jail Restoration Committee, 1966.

Acknowledgements

I wish to record my appreciation for the assistance which I have received from the following persons while researching and compiling this book.

The director and staff of the National Archives, Bishop Street, Dublin. Inspector John Duffy, archivist, Donal Kivlehan and Pauline Duffy of the Garda Síochána Museum, Dublin Castle. The curator and staff of the Royal Ulster Constabulary Museum, Belfast. The staff at the Public Records Office at Kew, Surrey. Denis Lucey, National Transport Museum, Killarney.

The librarians and staff members of the County Libraries at Tralee, Co. Kerry; County Hall, Cork; Thurles, Co. Tipperary; Ennis, Co. Clare and at the Cork City Library, Grand Parade, Cork.

Seamus McConville, editor (retired), *The Kerryman*, Tralee. Gregory Allen, archivist (retired), Garda Síochána Museum. Dr T. Ryle Dwyer, Tralee, Co. Kerry. Breandán Feirtéar, An Cheathrú Rua, Co. na Gaillimhe. Ruaidhrí Ó Tuairisg, Indreabhán, Co. na Gaillimhe. Séamus Ó Saothraí, Na Clocha Liatha, Co. Chill Mantáin. Tadhg Ó Coileáin, Daingean Uí Chúise, Co. Chiarraí.

Michael Sullivan, former RIC sergeant and Con Sullivan, former RIC constable (both deceased). Patrick J. O'Sullivan and Christy Larkin, Upton, Co. Cork. The O'Regan family and Ted Healy, Ballyheigue, Co. Kerry. Patrick Houlihan, Historic Photos, Killorglin, Co. Kerry. Sean Clery, Thornhill, Cardiff. Ms Rosaleen Stevens, Maidstone, Kent. Ms Lorna Lincks and Ms Dympna Burkhart, Florida, USA. Stephen Clements, Hyattsville, Maryland, USA. Ms Sheila Torr, Ardfert, Co. Kerry. Tom Marnell, Castlecomer. Patrick Purcell, Carlow. Éamon de Búrca, Blackrock, Co. Dublin. P. and F. Whelan, Booksellers, Tonbridge, Kent. Steve Baker and staff at Copywrite, Tralee. Spectra Photo Laboratories, Listowel. Staff at *Kerry's Eye*, Tralee.

Chief Superintendent Liam Harris, Garda Síochána, Thurles. Superintendent. Pat Killalea, Garda Headquarters, Dublin. Superintendent Michael Neill, Killarney, Inspector Martin Cummins, Garda Síochána, Dún Laoghaire. Inspectors Barry O'Rourke and Martin McCarthy, Tralee. Garda James Groarke, Anglesea Street, Cork. Garda Joe Fanning, Garda College, Templemore. Garda P.J. McGlinchy, Castledermot, Sergeant Eugene O'Sullivan, Sneem. Sergeant David Allen, Police Headquarters, Nelson, New Zealand. Chief Inspector Sherwood Young, New Zealand Police Headquarters, Wellington, New Zealand. Carmel Payne, Altona, Victoria, Australia.

Mr Eddie O'Sullivan, State Solicitor, Tralee. Mr Robert Pierse, solicitor, Listowel. Mr Gay Berkery, District Court Clerk, Dundalk, Co. Louth. Richard Maguire and Donal McCarthy, District Court Office, Tralee. Kieran Corridan and staff, District Court Office, Listowel. Aidan McGaley and staff, District Court Office, Killarney.

Sean Ginty, Letterkenny, Co. Donegal. Peter McGing, Clane, Co. Kildare. James Wall, Skibbereen. John Leen, Martin Muldoon, Patrick McMonagle and Michael Burke, Killarney. Patrick Moss, Roscrea. Liam Wall, Templemore. John Fitzpatrick, Limerick. Con O'Donohue, Farranfore. The O'Donoghue family and Dick Keane, Kenmare. The O'Shea family, Ladies View Stores, Killarney.

Mícheál Ó Ruairc (deceased), Donie Kelly, Jerry Kennelly, Patrick Kennedy, Edmund Moriarty, John Petit, Dick Coady, Pat Murphy, James Ledwith, Pat Long, Tom Gleasure, Seamus Breathnach, Sean Kenny, Maurice Murphy, Martin Moore, Brian Kenny and Billy Nolan of Tralee.

The officers and members of the Kerry Archaeological and Historical Society.

To my publisher Steve MacDonogh for his courtesy, patience, tolerance and professionalism in the publication of this book.

To my family, Ursula, Caroline, Colm, Jacinta, Clodagh, Donal, Olivia and Dearbhla for their support and assistance. Finally to my wife Olive for tolerating my research and obsession with the subject for more than twenty-five years.